MW00617832

THE *Psychomachia* OF Prudentius

OKLAHOMA SERIES IN CLASSICAL CULTURE

OKLAHOMA SERIES IN CLASSICAL CULTURE

SERIES EDITOR
Ellen Greene, *University of Oklahoma*

ADVISORY BOARD
Ronnie Ancona, *Hunter College and CUNY Graduate Center*
Carolyn J. Dewald, *Bard College*
Nancy Felson, *University of Georgia*
Helene P. Foley, *Barnard College*
Thomas R. Martin, *College of the Holy Cross*
John F. Miller, *University of Virginia*
Richard F. Thomas, *Harvard University*

THE *Psychomachia* OF Prudentius

TEXT, COMMENTARY, AND GLOSSARY

Aaron Pelttari

UNIVERSITY OF OKLAHOMA PRESS : NORMAN

Library of Congress Cataloging-in-Publication Data

Names: Prudentius, 348– author. | Pelttari, Aaron, 1982– editor.

Title: The Psychomachia of Prudentius : text, commentary, and glossary / edited by
    Aaron Pelttari.

Other titles: Psychomachia | Oklahoma series in classical culture.

Description: Norman : University of Oklahoma Press, 2019. | Series: Oklahoma series in
    classical culture

Identifiers: LCCN 2018058219 | ISBN 978-0-8061-6402-1 (pbk. : alk. paper)

Subjects: LCSH: Prudentius, 348– Psychomachia.

Classification: LCC PA6648.P6 P73 2019 | DDC 871/.01—dc23

LC record available at https://lccn.loc.gov/2018058219

The Psychomachia of Prudentius: Text, Commentary, and Glossary is Volume 58 in the
Oklahoma Series in Classical Culture.

The paper in this book meets the guidelines for permanence and durability of the
Committee on Production Guidelines for Book Longevity of the Council on Library
Resources, Inc. ∞

Copyright © 2019 by the University of Oklahoma Press, Norman, Publishing Division of
the University. Manufactured in the U.S.A.

All rights reserved. No part of this publication may be reproduced, stored in a retrieval
system, or transmitted, in any form or by any means, electronic, mechanical, photo-
copying, recording, or otherwise—except as permitted under Section 107 or 108 of the
United States Copyright Act—without the prior written permission of the University of
Oklahoma Press. To request permission to reproduce selections from this book, write to
Permissions, University of Oklahoma Press, 2800 Venture Drive, Norman, OK 73069, or
email rights.oupress@ou.edu.

For David and Lucas

CONTENTS

ILLUSTRATIONS

FIGURES

MAP

ABBREVIATIONS

For commonly known ancient authors and texts, I follow the abbreviations of the *Oxford Classical Dictionary* (4th ed.). For books of the Bible, I used the short abbreviations from the *Chicago Manual of Style* (17th ed.). Authors and texts that are less commonly known have not been abbreviated. Other abbreviations are as follows:

A&G	Allen and Greenough's *New Latin Grammar for Schools and Colleges* (Boston: Ginn & Co., 1903)
CC	Corpus Christianorum, Series Latina
CIL	*Corpus Inscriptionum Latinarum*
CSEL	Corpus Scriptorum Ecclesiasticorum Latinorum
DGE	*Diccionario griego-español*
FGrH	F. Jacoby, *Fragmente der griechischen Historiker* (1923–)
Kühner-Stegmann	R. Kühner and C. Stegmann, *Ausfürhliche Grammatik der lateinischen Sprache,* zweiter Teil (Leverkusen: Gottschalk, 1955)
LIMC	*Lexicon Iconographicum Mythologiae Classicae*

MS(S)	manuscript(s)
New Pauly	Hubert Cancik and Helmuth Schneider, ed. *Brill's New Pauly* (Leiden: Brill, 2002–2010)
OLD	*Oxford Latin Dictionary*
RSV	Revised Standard Version
SC	Sources chrétiennes
TLL	*Thesaurus Linguae Latinae* (Boston: De Gruyter, 1900–)

PREFACE

This edition is meant to make the *Psychomachia* accessible for students. The commentary is structured so that almost every note begins with what is most essential for understanding the poem. Where the Latin is difficult or noteworthy, I include a translation or a comment on the grammatical construction (usually with reference to Allen and Greenough's *New Latin Grammar,* which is now available in an elegant online edition at http://dcc .dickinson.edu/allen-greenough/). But some students will want to know more about the background of the *Psychomachia,* about the decisions I made in editing the text, and about the poem's historical and literary context, not to mention its reception. They are encouraged to read to the end of each note. Beyond students, I hope that what I have learned from teaching the *Psychomachia* will be useful in some way for more advanced readers and researchers working on Prudentius. I think there is need for a new full-scale commentary on the poem, and I expect that the *Psychomachia* commentary in progress for the Cambridge Greek and Latin Classics will fill at least most of these gaps. As for previous commentaries, I have made thorough use of them. In the notes, I acknowledge a commentator by name when his or her contribution was original or when it seemed at risk of being overlooked in the future; but throughout I benefited from the work of those who have gone before me.

The commentary includes citations and sometimes quotations of parallels and intertexts, mainly from earlier Latin poetry but also from prose and from some texts later than Prudentius. No two readers will agree in every case (or even most cases) on which are the important comparisons to make. Although I have had to depend on my own competence as a reader of later Latin poetry, I sought to enable rather than forestall interpretation. When I say that Prudentius borrowed from and emulated Claudian (see the commentary on line 23), I mean that a reasonable reader might recall Claudian's poetry at this point and conclude from the resemblance that Prudentius meant to surpass his contemporary. The text of the *Psychomachia* cannot guarantee any such interpretation, and we might discover tomorrow a new manuscript or papyrus that reveals a more convincing intertext. Despite these precautions, we talk about the author as a convenient shorthand for the entire complex of systems that determine how texts are interpreted. The beauty of human communication is that you (often enough) know what I mean. And, every now and then, we might even agree about what Prudentius meant, even though there is ambiguity all the way down. In the same way, tables and chairs seem to be solid and permanent objects even though their particles are in constant and random motion.

I have tried to strike a good balance between offering parallels and providing interpretation for passages cited. Non-referential allusions (see the note on line 31) are those that include a precise verbal repetition without any apparent similarity between the contexts of the two passages concerned. With most intertexts that I cite, it is easy to make connections. Therefore, whenever a little information would allow the reader to make up his or her own mind, I have sought not to belabor an interpretation. For example, on line 678, I cite the intertext "tenui . . . puncto" from Ausonius, and I explain that the line refers in the *Cupido cruciatus* to the stylus used by outraged women to torment Cupid. This is enough information to demonstrate that there might be a meaningful allusion, and I have no interest in removing any likely interpretation.

Parallel texts are those less obviously relevant to the *Psychomachia*. Sometimes they are cited to illustrate a common philosophical or theological background, sometimes for what they reveal about the regular context in which a word or phrase was used. I have been selective with parallels that are cited and even more selective with those that are quoted. I assume that readers can use a website such as the currently available *Musisque deoque* (http://mizar.unive.it/mqdq/public/) to access intertexts in verse. For example, if you want to know which Latin poets use *tonans* in reference to Jupiter (see the note on line 640), you can use the search function on *Musisque deoque* to search for *tonans* and *tonant** across essentially all extant Latin poetry. Being selective in this way allowed me to keep the notes to a sensible length. When I cite multiple parallels with little or no interpretation, this means that I could not find any very plausible reason to interpret one of them as a meaningful intertext. Most often, when I cite such parallels, it is to demonstrate the tone or ordinary context of a given word or phrase—for example, if it occurs primarily in prose, poetry, Christian writings, or in some other linguistic register. Thus, in the note on line 279, I suggest that the phrase *ultor gladius* sounds legal or religious and cite the parallel texts that lead me to such a conclusion. Of course, I might be wrong about this or many other points; but in such cases the evidence cited should be enough to suggest the kind of argument that could be drawn out. For reasons of economy, I do not cite imprecise intertexts or other parallels that seemed irrelevant for understanding the poem. Surely I have missed some highly interpretable intertexts in this way, although I think that most readers will be thankful that the commentary is not cluttered with the detritus of earlier indices of imitations.

In citations of ancient texts, I name a particular edition only when the passage in question is more difficult to locate or modern editors use different systems of reference (for example, Paulinus of Nola). Citations of the Bible are complicated. All English translations are from the Revised Standard Version. For the Latin, I have consulted the editions of the *Vetus latina* (Beuron) where possible or the *Vetus latina* database produced by Brepols where those editions are not yet available. Wherever there is a good reason to think that one of the pre-Vulgate translations is closest to that used by Prudentius, I cite it using the sigla of the Beuron editions. Where there is no relevant difference in extant Latin translations, I quote from the Vulgate version, on the grounds that it is more readily accessible. In the commentary, when I quote an intertext or a passage for comparison, sometimes I provide my own literal English translation and sometimes only the Latin; hopefully, some students will be adventurous enough to read snippets of Servius and company in Latin. Words printed in SMALL CAPS in the Commentary are explained in appendix B, the glossary of literary terms.

I expended a considerable amount of time and energy on the Latin-to-English glossary because I expect that students will find it to be even more helpful than the simple electronic parsing tools or the shorter lexica now openly accessible to them. Each entry was carefully written so as to provide only the information that is essential for understanding the *Psychomachia*.

My last task is the most pleasant: to express my gratitude to the many people who have helped make this book a reality. I am thankful to the friends and colleagues who provided assistance at many points, including Judy Barringer, Glenys Davies, Andreas Gavrielatos, Ben Harriman, Gavin Kelly, Erik Kenyon, Calum Maciver, Keith Rutter, and Justin Stover. I am also thankful to the two reviewers for the University of Oklahoma Press; I only wish that I could have followed all of their suggestions. For images and the permission to use them, I am thankful especially to Hans Goette, to Federico Gallo, and to the several librarians and archivists who responded to my requests with unfailing professionalism. The library staff at the University of Edinburgh deserve credit because they managed my interlibrary loan requests without fail. The map was made quickly and with expertise by Erin Greb. Everyone working for the University of Oklahoma Press met my requests with constant diligence, including Brian Bowles, Stephanie Evans, Amy Hernandez, and Alessandra Tamulevich. The School of History, Classics and Archaeology at the University of Edinburgh provided several small grants to cover some research and publication costs; in particular, they made it possible to hire Anna-Sofia Alitalo to help with proofreading and formatting the bibliography. I am happiest to say that students in several classes at the University of Edinburgh challenged me to improve my understanding and explanation of the *Psychomachia*, and I am most thankful to them. On an even more personal note, I am grateful for the support and good humor of my family, which is why I dedicate this book to David and Lucas.

THE *Psychomachia* OF Prudentius

INTRODUCTION

1. PRUDENTIUS: LIFE AND POETRY

The manuscripts cite our author as Aurelius Prudentius Clemens. Because no surviving contemporary sources mention him by name, the best available evidence for his life comes from what Prudentius wrote, in particular a certain *Praefatio* that can be dated to the year 404 on the basis of two statements: he says that his fifty-seventh year is close approaching and that he was born during the consulship of Salia (*Praef.* 1–3, 24), which occurred in 348 c.e.[1] We can infer that he was from Calahorra in Spain from several references in the *Peristefanon* poems (1.116, 2.537–40, and 4.31–32). He also mentions connections to Zaragoza (*Perist.* 4.1–4) and Tarragona (*Perist.* 6.143). Gennadius, who around the year 480 wrote a continuation of Jerome's encyclopedia of Christian authors, said that Prudentius was a man educated in secular literature (*De uiris illustribus* 13; "uir saecularis litteraturae eruditus"). The latter point would have been inferred from his poetry anyway, but the lack

---

1. We arrive at the year 404 by counting inclusively and by assuming that the phrase "annum cardo rotat" (*Praef.* 2–3) means that he is writing before his fifty-seventh birthday, which will come before the end of the consular year in question. On the life of Prudentius, see Coşkun 2008; and O'Daly 2012, 1–5. Introductions to the study of Prudentius include Bastiaensen 1993a (in English) and Rivero García 1996 (in Spanish).

of any reference to religious training probably implies that Prudentius did not join a monastic community after the end of his political career.

The career that Prudentius describes for himself in his *Praefatio* is thoroughly conventional. He passed the first part of his life sadly under the rod of a grammarian, and then from a rhetor he learned how to tell lies (*Praef.* 7–9). After a degenerate youth and some time spent as a lawyer, he oversaw cities twice, probably during two terms as a provincial governor in Spain (*Praef.* 10–18). Finally, Prudentius was elevated to a position in the first rank of imperial service (*Praef.* 19–21); the precise language suggests that he was *Comes primi ordinis*.[2] The latter post would have been in the western capital of Milan and either for the Spaniard Theodosius, who was emperor from 379 to 395, or for his young son Honorius, who was nominally western emperor from 395 until his death in 423. Relevant perhaps is Prudentius's praise for Theodosius in *Symm.* 1.408–642, although Coşkun is convinced that Prudentius was promoted only under Honorius and between 395–400 (2008: 303–7). Imperial service in the 390s would have left Prudentius enough time in retirement to write or finish most of his poetry by 404.

Prudentius mentions traveling in Italy in several of the *Peristefanon* poems. In *Perist.* 9, he says that while he was on his way to visit Rome he stopped to appeal for help from the martyr Cassian, at his shrine in modern Imola, the ancient Forum Cornelii. Then, *Perist.* 11 and 12 describe a visit to Rome and devotion to Hippolytus and to the apostles Peter and Paul on their feast day (29 June). Related perhaps is *Perist.* 2, which celebrates the Roman martyr Lawrence and describes the inhabitants of Rome as fortunate because they can visit his shrine at any time (2.529–36); he probably wrote *Perist.* 2 in Spain before visiting Rome (Palmer 1989, 259). Because Prudentius portrays himself as a pilgrim in Italy and because he looks forward to his return journey home, we infer that he traveled to Rome after his retirement from imperial service, and a visit during 401 or 402 would very nicely fit all of the known facts.

In addition to the religious benefits of his visit to Rome, Prudentius quite possibly saw in Rome two of the outstanding Latin poets of his day. In *Symm.*

---

2. On this interpretation of the phrase, see Coşkun 2008, 305. Prudentius says that he was ordered to stand in the first rank (*Praef.* 21; "proprius stare iubens ordine proximo").

2.696–768, Prudentius describes the battle of Pollentia (6 April 402), in which Stilicho turned away Alaric and the Visigoths; several allusions from that passage point to Claudian's celebratory *De bello Getico* (Dorfbauer 2012, 54–58), a poem that he performed in the Senate house in Rome not long after Stilicho declared victory. Since Prudentius must have been a member of the Senate because of his imperial service, he would have been entitled to attend the gathering, and he could have heard Claudian's first reading of the poem. To be sure, Prudentius could also have met Claudian in Milan while he was working there in the imperial administration. After coming from Egypt to the West in 395, Claudian spent much of his time in Milan; and from the year 396 on, he worked as a panegyrical poet for Honorius's regent Stilicho. Whether or not Prudentius knew Claudian personally, his visit to Rome provides context for three apparent reminiscences of *De bello Getico* in *Psychomachia* (see the commentary on lines 275, 771, and 816). During the same visit to Rome, Prudentius also could have met the Christian ascetic and poet Paulinus of Nola, who regularly visited Rome each year between 400 and about 405 to celebrate the same Feast of the Apostles described by Prudentius.[3] Whether or not he met these specific individuals, he certainly traveled; and we have every reason to think that he was involved in the political, religious, and literary revolutions that took place during his lifetime.[4]

Prudentius continues in his *Praefatio* by describing a kind of conversion after the end of his political career. He admits that worldly advancement is of no benefit beyond the grave, and he says that he will seek a higher kind of utility. For the end of his life, Prudentius dedicates his sinful soul to celebrating God with his voice:

> Atqui fine sub ultimo
> peccatrix anima stultitiam exuat;
> saltem uoce deum concelebret, si meritis nequit. (*Praef.* 34–36)

---

3. See Paulinus of Nola, *Epist.* 20.2, along with his *Epist.* 17.2 and Guttilla 2005; Trout 1999, 115; and Costanza 1983. In *Symm.* 1.558–59, Prudentius refers either to this Paulinus or to his family: "Non Paulinorum, non Bassorum dubitauit / prompta fides dare se Christo." Even more, Guttilla made a plausible case for thinking that the "Nolanus" in *Perist.* 11.208 is a specific reference to Paulinus of Nola.

4. On the author's more local context as a Spanish poet, see Hershkowitz 2017.

> And so with the ultimate end in view
> let my sinful soul strip off its foolishness;
> at least may it celebrate God with my voice if not with merits.

A turn away from sinful foolishness has sometimes been read as a kind of conversion to Christianity or as Prudentius devoting himself to an informal monastic existence. But Prudentius was more likely born into a Christian family, and there is not enough evidence to conclude that Prudentius ever retreated from the world, in the way that Paulinus of Nola and Augustine of Hippo spent some time after their conversions in a kind of intellectual and spiritual retreat. Although his extant writings suggests that Prudentius took his Christian devotion perfectly seriously, the *Praefatio* is not good evidence for anything other than a poetic conversion. His denial of merit in line 36 is even a kind of humble acknowledgment of Horace's crowning achievement as a lyric poet (*Carm.* 3.30.15; *meritis*).[5] Rather than a literal fact, conversion is a useful metaphor for understanding the poetry of Prudentius through the author's devotion to his new creative work; indeed, Prudentius also describes his poetry as a service to God and as a means to salvation in *De opusculis suis* and in *Perist.* 10.1136–40. Therefore, even if his self-portrait in this *Praefatio* is not prosaically accurate or fully informative, it provides an important structure and lens through which to read his poetry.

In the following stanzas, Prudentius lists the kinds of poetry to which he is now dedicating himself. By convention, the list cites poems that have already been written:

> Hymnis continuet dies
> nec nox ulla uacet quin dominum canat;
> pugnet contra hereses, catholicam discutiat fidem,
>   Conculcet sacra gentium,
> labem, Roma, tuis inferat idolis,
> carmen martyribus deuoueat, laudent apostolos. (*Praef.* 37–42)

---

5. For other influences of Horace on the *Praefatio*, see Witke 1968, 509–16; Pucci 1991, 679–85; Lühken 2002, 260–61; and O'Daly 2016, 222–26.

> May [my soul] fill the days with hymns
> and may no night miss singing my Lord;
> let it fight against heresies, discuss the universal faith,
>> May it crush the rituals of the nations,
> bring destruction, Rome, to your idols,
> devote a song to the martyrs, praise the apostles.

The first two lines refer to the *Liber Cathemerinon*, a collection of lyric hymns centered on the daily and annual calendars of Christian devotion; they are in a variety of meters and indebted most of all, for their poetry, to Horace and to Ambrose, bishop of Milan (340–97 C.E.). Next, the didactic poems *Apotheosis* and *Amartigenia* treat the divinity of Christ and the origin of sin, respectively, as well as a variety of related heresies. Then, Prudentius's two hexameter books of *Contra Symmachum* offer a triumphalist vision of Christian Rome and attack the arguments of that noteworthy pagan senator. Lastly, the *Liber Peristefanon* is a collection of poems in various meters honoring Christian martyrs; *Perist.* 12 is for the apostles Peter and Paul; the poem known as *Perist.* 10 in modern editions is for the martyr Romanus and includes a long section criticizing traditional Roman religion. This is the corpus of poetry that must have been presented in one large codex in the year 404. Only a few of Prudentius's poems are not cited in his preface: *Tituli historiarum* (a collection of forty-eight quatrains on Biblical scenes); maybe *Psychomachia* (for the possible reference to it in line 39, see below on page 26); the short poem *De opusculis suis*, which responds to the *Praefatio* and is presented in the manuscripts as an epilogue to his collection; and the *Exameron* on the creation of the world that is attested only in Gennadius (*De uiris illustribus* 13).

In the final stanza of the preface, the poet longs for release in his writing. He prays for salvation, and he equates himself with his book of poetry:

> Haec dum scribo uel eloquor,
> uinclis o utinam corporis emicem
> liber, quo tulerit lingua sono mobilis ultimo. (*Praef.* 43–45)

> While I am writing or pronouncing this,
> O that I would spring from the chains of my body
> free, to where my tongue in motion will head at its last sound.

FIGURE 1. The poet in his study. MS *U*, p. 67. *Photograph courtesy Codices Electronici AG, http://www.e-codices.ch.*

Prudentius imagines freedom from the chains of his body as coming in the act of writing or speaking. The pun on the word *liber* equates the finality of the poet with the completion of his book (see Malamud 1989, 77). In this way, the poet describes his final release from the body as an act of communication with his reader and with God. The reader who encounters Prudentius as a book and who follows his narrative all the way to this final vision of communication covers the same ground, and reaches—through a shared belief in the persona's poetic future—his or her own hermeneutic release. The final sound (*ultimo sono*) is also *our* sounding of the poem. Therefore, the author and his body (*corpus*) are fully involved in a literary system that depends on active readers who participate in creating a fictional world through the bound language (*oratio uincta*) of poetry. In this way, the life and career described by Prudentius offer his view of what it means to be a Christian poet.

2. THE LITERARY WORLD IN LATE ANTIQUITY

If you stop to think about it, the point of poetry is not entirely clear. In late antiquity, people stopped to think about it. Ausonius, the grammarian and consul from Bordeaux, turned his pen to catalogues of fishes and delightful lists of monosyllables. Claudian decided to serve the young emperor Honorius and his regent Stilicho by writing epic panegyrics. Prudentius, for his part, made the classical tradition into a vehicle for a new Christian poetry. He is outstanding both for the breadth of his poetic vision and for how he combined the classical and Christian traditions. Like many of their contemporaries from the fourth century, these individuals felt the need to question and justify their verbal artistry in ways that had not seemed necessary in many previous centuries.

Renewed Platonic attacks on the lies of poets provide a context for the self-justifications of literary authors, as do new Christian criticisms along the same lines. Thus, in the preface to his philosophical commentary on the Dream of Scipio, Macrobius presented fictional writing as an inferior form, insufficient for describing the highest truths (*In somnium Scipionis* 1.2.14–16). Augustine of Hippo famously avoided poetry and wrote in a lowly style (Auerbach 1965). As for rhetoric more broadly, Jerome was convicted in a dream of being a Ciceronian rather than a Christian (*Epist.* 22.30). Part of this story can been seen as a decline in the prestige of poetry in the fourth century (Mastrangelo 2009); part of it has to do with late-antique criticisms of classical mythology (Cullhed 2015); and some of it is related to how poetry came to serve as a vehicle for deeper truths (Mastrangelo 2017). But for the most part, changes in the form and function of poetry cannot be divorced from the intermittent breakup and gradual renewal of the entire ancient literary system. Despite every pressure, poets never stopped writing; books continued to circulate; and audiences continued to delight in the verbal dexterity of their performers. Like carbon under intense pressure, this literary climate produced a few bright gems.

Ever since the Renaissance, the transformation of the ancient world has fascinated modern readers. In the last half-century, an entire academic field has grown up in the tracks of Peter Brown's pathbreaking book *The World of Late Antiquity* (1971). In the meantime, of course, Western civilization continues to find its way through intermittent crises occasioned by cultural, political, and technological changes too large for any of us to grasp. We struggle when new ways of thought clash with the old, and sometimes such crises boil over into conflict. In the fourth and fifth centuries, many of the changes that brought conflict were related either to religion, politics, or culture.

Although in its first centuries Christianity as a religion had grown slowly from its Jewish roots, after Constantine's reputed conversion in 312, Christians found themselves with real access to political power. Already in 329 (or very close to that date), we can see the literary repercussions of this change: Juvencus, author of an epic poem on the theme of the Gospels, addressed Constantine as the world's ruler and spoke of his justice and the eternal reign of Christ in one and the same breath (*Euangeliorum libri quattuor* 4.806–12; McGill 2016, 3–5). From that point on, the rise of Christianity was not met with any sustained or effective resistance (Cameron 2011), which is not to say that religious transformation was ever uncomplicated. While orthodox theology developed gradually and through controversies,[6] individual Christians experienced their new identity as one among many

---

6. For a readable if somewhat dated introduction to the first six centuries of the church, see Chadwick 2001.

that they lived out on a daily basis (Rebillard 2012). Although Prudentius surely counted pagans and the nonreligious among his friends and audience, the ideal reader for most of his poetry is a faithful Christian; that is, he imagined himself as writing within a likeminded community of religious believers. In order to fully understand how and why Prudentius wrote, we must take into account contemporary religious developments.

Political changes involved the administration of the empire, urban redevelopment, and the so-called barbarian invasions. Over the course of the third century, the imperial bureaucracy had tripled in size, and this created a whole new class of social elites. The reforms of Diocletian offered the empire a degree of stability, which also contributed to the social mobility that changed life for many talented provincials like Prudentius. Differences in city life were simple only at the top. We know how some of the largest cities gained or lost as the empire changed: from the end of the third century, Milan was preferred ahead of Rome as an imperial residence; Constantinople, from its foundation in 324, played an outsized role in the political imagination; after the death of Theodosius in 395, the empire was split between western and eastern emperors; Ravenna came to serve as the site of the western court because it provided more protection from Alaric and the Goths; and as for Rome, it was eventually sacked by Alaric in 410. The sack of Rome was psychologically important, but it was just one step in the continuing struggle between the traditional powers and the other peoples who were now claiming a place for themselves within the territories of the Roman Empire. It was only in stages and over the course of the fifth century that the western empire came apart under all this pressure.

Cultural changes are hardest to measure. Knowledge of classical literature and grammatical education came to play a surprisingly important role in elite society, even in the imperial bureaucracy (Kaster 1988; Brown 1992). Poetry took a new turn with an increasing delight in verbal brilliance and fragmentation (Roberts 1989), and readers and interpretation came to play a more significant role within the entire literary system (Pelttari 2014). In terms of philosophy, Neoplatonists of all kinds were drawn away from the here and now by the allure of an otherworldly essence; in particular,

Augustine, seeking to understand what he believed, looked within himself to find the image of God (Rist 1994). As individuals began to relate to their bodies in new ways, asceticism and the rise of Christian monasticism were only the two most obvious results (Brown 2008). In one or another of the works of Prudentius, politics, religion, classical learning, and asceticism are all equally at home. His poems contain all of the turbulence and diversity and new brilliance of the times in which he lived because in his hands poetry was a way to work through, to understand, and to improve every aspect of life. The *Psychomachia*, in particular, negotiates all of these tensions within a profound allegorical framework.

3. *PSYCHOMACHIA*

A preface of 68 iambic trimeters introduces the 914 hexameters of the *Psychomachia* (an extra line was interpolated in 728–29). The preface does not directly address the central theme of the conflict between virtue and vice; instead, it offers a retelling and an allegorical interpretation of two linked events from the life of the Hebrew patriarch Abraham. The poem itself is divided into seven battles between personified virtues and vices, with a separate proem and a generous conclusion in three parts. As the following breakdown shows, the number of lines given over to each battle scene grows progressively:

Proem	1–20	(20)
1. Fides vs. Veterum cultura deorum	21–39	(19)
2. Pudicitia vs. Libido	40–108	(69)
3. Patientia vs. Ira	109–77	(69)
4. Mens humilis (and Spes) vs. Superbia	178–309	(132)
5. Sobrietas vs. Luxuria	310–453	(144)
6. Ratio (and Operatio) vs. Auaritia (and Fraus)	454–628	(175)
7. Concordia vs. Discordia	629–725	(97)
The speeches of Concordia and Fides	726–822	(96)
The construction of a temple for Pax	823–87	(65)
Epilogue	888–915	(28)

Although the length of each episode is one obvious way in which Prudentius structured his poem, the simplicity of the poem's structure conceals its underlying complexity.[7] The battle of Fides is given less space than any of the other duels, but she is the only Virtue who reappears later in the poem. Discordia, the last of the Vices to appear, is the only one who manages to wound her opponent. The longest battle scene is that between Ratio and Auaritia (with the assistance of Operatio on the one side and Fraus on the other); as you would expect, its length is not accidental: Auaritia was identified as the root of all evils (see below, page 158), and the character of Fraus allows Prudentius to confront the tension in his work between theological positivism and allegorical disguise (see Nugent 1985, 50–55). Although each of the individual battle scenes is a miniature poem unto itself, they also progress from beginning to end and partake in a grander allegorical design.

The structure of the *Psychomachia* was influenced by the apostle Paul's naming of faith, hope, and love as key virtues. I do not think that anyone has noticed this before, but it seems unavoidable that Prudentius must have planned the poem with 1 Cor. 13:13 in mind: "So now faith, hope, and love abide, these three; but the greatest of these is love." These three qualities appear at the beginning, middle, and end of the poem: Fides is the first to do battle; Spes appears exactly in the middle; and the praise of Pax (Peace) at the end clearly alludes to Paul's encomium of love (*agapē*) from 1 Cor. 13.[8] Prudentius retains the order of the three virtues but replaces love as the most important one with peace, which is praised in similar lofty terms ("Pax plenum uirtutis opus, pax summa laborum," 769). The three theological virtues had not been defined as such yet, but contemporaries of Prudentius did understand 1 Cor. 13:13 as having special significance (see, for example, Ambrose, *De uirginitate* 9.53 and *Epist.* 9.66.6; and Augustine, *De doctrina Christiana* 1.37.90). Maybe Prudentius replaced love with peace because many philosophers regarded an imperturbable mind (*ataraxia*) as the

---

7. The best study of the poem's structure and narrative is still Nugent 1985.
8. For the parallels between peace and charity, see the commentary on lines 775–78 and 779–81.

height of virtue.[9] In any case, this is just one of the ways in which a careful reading of the poem reveals its structure.

3.a. Models and Intertexts

Prudentius was influenced by a wide range of sources, including contemporary poetry, philosophical discussions, and theological teaching. But two intertexts play a greater part than all the rest: the Christian scriptures and Vergil's *Aeneid*. They provide the precise language and the models of thought that undergird the entire *Psychomachia*.

The preface of the *Psychomachia* recounts two episodes from the life of Abraham, the father of the Hebrew people and the first believer; his story was told in Genesis, the first book of the Christian Bible. The *Psychomachia* ends with the description of a temple that corresponds to the heavenly Jerusalem that appears at the end of Revelation, the last book in the Bible (see the introductory note on lines 823–87). In a sense, the poem covers all of history within the framework of the Christian scriptures, from the beginnings of their faithful ancestors all the way to the end of the world. This grand narrative from the scriptures underlies the *Psychomachia*. On a smaller scale, individual stories and figures are often in the background or directly referenced in the text. On the level of individual words, Prudentius sometimes repeats the very vocabulary of the Latin scriptures; likewise, Greek loan words from the scriptures stand out (*eremus, heresis, idolum*), as do a number of Hebrew names.

The vocabulary of the scriptures adds a certain dynamic energy to the *Psychomachia*, because the Hebrew and Greek scriptures were translated into Latin by unknown scribes and in a remarkably low style. Although there is a great deal that we do not know about the scriptures read by Prudentius, he did use pre-Vulgate translations similar to those known to have circulated in Africa and Spain (Charlet 1983, 8–40). Scholars used to speak of an African version of the *Vetus latina*, but there was more than one translation

---

9. For Lucretius's influence on Prudentius, see Rapisarda 1950; Rapisarda 1951; Fabian 1988, 219–70; and Dykes 2011, especially 234–41. For a prehistory of Epicurean *ataraxia*, see Warren 2002.

used in Africa, and we do not know where any of them were produced.[10] When the scriptures influence the poetry of Prudentius, this often comes across in a low style and unpoetic diction; and this creates tension with the poet's regular style, which is usually high and predominantly Vergilian.[11]

Vergil's influence on the *Psychomachia* includes obvious references and the constant gravitational pull of his vocabulary.[12] The first line of the proem is a light adaptation of the opening of Aeneas's prayer to Apollo from book six of the *Aeneid*:

> Christe, graues hominum semper miserate labores. (*Psych.* 1)
>
> Phoebe, grauis Troiae semper miserate labores. (*Aen.* 6.56)

By making the repetition obvious and changing only two key words, Prudentius both identifies Vergil as his source and demonstrates the difference of his epic. As for the pervasive influence of Vergil, the beginning of line 122 nicely demonstrates the extent to which his vocabulary can determine Prudentius's language, even when every resemblance is casual; that line begins "per teneros crispata notos" (brandished on the light breeze): the verb *crispare* was used by Vergil in *Aen.* 1.313 and 12.165; *noti* refers to breezes in *Aen.* 3.268, 5.512, and 11.798; and *tenerum* modified *aera* in *Aen.* 9.699. None of these intertexts are particularly significant on their own; together they demonstrate that the epic language of the *Psychomachia* is largely the language of the *Aeneid*. Beyond individual references and elements of vocabulary, Vergil influenced the epic vision of the *Psychomachia*. His national epic and the sufferings of Aeneas undergird the master narrative of the *Psychomachia*, the idea that history and scripture foretell the Christian reader's final victory over sin. In the same way that Vergil reworked Homeric

---

10. The *Vetus latina* translations predate Jerome's so-called Vulgate revision of the Gospels and of some of the other books of the Bible (it is not clear how many or which). On the Latin New Testament and for a good introduction to all of the difficulties of the Latin scriptures, see Houghton 2016.

11. On such blending of styles, see Fontaine 1977, a groundbreaking study on unity and diversity in late antique Latin poetry.

12. The best full study of Prudentius's use of Vergil is Lühken 2002; even students who do not read German can benefit from her extensive index of parallel passages. On Prudentius as a successor to Vergil, see Mastrangelo 2008, 14–40.

epic to suit the needs of imperial Rome, Prudentius reworks Roman epic within the context of Christian salvation history.[13] Indeed, the historical allegory of the *Psychomachia* offers a vision of the Christian faith in triumph (Smolak 2001). Prudentius reworks Vergil on multiple levels, and he uses each of his models to create an entirely new kind of epic about human reality.

3.b. The Theme of an Inner Conflict

Although the *Psychomachia* has cosmic implications, the struggle between good and evil that takes place within the individual human being will also continue until the end of time. Prudentius develops this point throughout his epic, but he highlights it at the end of the poem:

> Spiritibus pugnant uariis lux atque tenebrae
> distantesque animat duplex substantia uires. (908–9)

> Darkness and light fight with their different spirits,
> and our divided nature inspires opposed forces.

The story of a battle between good and evil is much older even than Hesiod, but this inner conflict has certain recognizable roots for Prudentius. His likely models include the apostle Paul, the Stoic Seneca, Christian authors, and Latin poets.[14]

Paul described a struggle between the flesh and the spirit in Gal. 5:17: "For the desires of the flesh are against the Spirit, and the desires of the Spirit are against the flesh; for these are opposed to each other." Paul's understanding of this conflict between sinful desires and godly impulses was influential and widely quoted. The Spanish bishop Priscillian of Avila collected nine different passages in which Paul described this spiritual struggle; he cited them in his topical index for the Letters of Paul, under the following heading: "Quia iustorum militia et arma et hostes et lucta uel pugna spiritalia sint, quorum conuersatio est in caelis, unde et Christum

---

13. For Vergil's use of Homer as a kind of typological interpretation, see Hardie 2017 and Knauer 1964.
14. For a full study of the sources of Prudentius's allegory, see Beatrice 1971, although his subtle distinctions do not always hold, especially when he treats Prudentius's virtues and vices as spiritual forces. On Prudentius's allegory and his readers, see Pelttari 2014, 84–96.

dominum exspectant" (*Canones* 38; That the warfare of the just and their weapons and enemy and struggle and fight are spiritual; and that their life is in heaven, from which place they also await Christ the lord).[15] Prudentius was definitely influenced by Paul, even though he does not list the same virtues and vices as Paul, and even though many earlier moralists and teachers had made similar statements about this inner battle.

One of the popular philosophers who developed the idea of this inner conflict was Seneca the Younger, the wealthy Stoic forced by Nero to commit suicide in 65 C.E. He described the moral life as a kind of military campaign: "Nobis quoque militandum est, et quidem genere militiae quo numquam quies, numquam otium datur: debellandae sunt in primis uoluptates" (*Epist.* 51.6; We also are at war, and indeed in a kind of warfare in which there is never peace, never is there a break. First of all, we must war against pleasure). Seneca goes on to cite grief, labor, poverty, ambition, and anger as further opponents (*Epist.* 51.8). Although the list of vices depended on the school and outlook of the teacher, such ideas were certainly widespread.

The Christian Tertullian (c. 160–c. 240) described this inner conflict as a kind of entertainment that could replace the spectacles of the gladiators; he says that those who desire real pleasures and a real show should look to the victories of the virtues:

> Vis et pugilatus et luctatus? Praesto sunt, non parua et multa. Aspice impudicitiam deiectam a castitate, perfidiam caesam a fide, saeuitiam a misericordia contusam, petulantiam a modestia adumbratam, et tales sunt apud nos agones, in quibus ipsi coronamur. (*De spectaculis* 29)

> Do you want fighting and wrestling? They are here, and plenty of them. Look at immodesty thrown down by chastity, dishonesty cut down by faithfulness, savagery struck by compassion, wantonness overshadowed by modesty; such are our contests; in these are we victorious.

We know that Prudentius read Tertullian, and he may well have had this passage in mind (Lavarenne 2002, 23). For different reasons as well, one scholar has described our poem as a Christian spectacle for Roman viewers

---

15. Not all of the passages cited by Priscillian have been identified; on this topic in Paul, see also the commentary on line 908.

(James 1999). As for other important parallel passages, Cyprian, who was a slightly younger contemporary of Tertullian, referred to a series of evils with which the human mind is in conflict (*De mortalitate* 4); and Ambrose described this daily battle in his *De Abraham* 2.62.

Commodian, who may have been active around the beginning of the fourth century, devoted his *Carm.* 2.18 (22) to the daily battle against vice ("Bellum cottidianum"). He says that the struggle continues from our first day to our last; he names Libido and Luxuria as enemies; and he offers a range of advice to counteract the forces of evil. Unfortunately, we do not know where or when he wrote. Definitely closer to Prudentius is a passage from the beginning of the second book of Claudian's poem on the consulship of Stilicho. Claudian praised Stilicho as being himself a temple for personified Virtues; he names Clementia as the first of these Virtues:

> Haec dea pro templis et ture calentibus aris
> Te fruitur posuitque suas hoc pectore sedes. (12–13)

> Instead of temples and altars warm with incense, this goddess enjoys you, and in this heart made her abode.

Claudian goes on to describe Fides in similar terms (30–32; "corde tuo delubra tenens") and then Iustitia, Patientia, Temperies, Prudentia, and Constantia (100–109); ranged against them are Auaritia, Ambitio, Luxuries, and Superbia (109–72). His poem was apparently recited in Milan in January 400, and it is easy to think that Prudentius was influenced by his personifications and by his description of a temple for internal virtues (see Shanzer 1989, 361).

Prudentius himself had written a catalogue of semi-personified vices in *Am.* 389–405; it reads like a first attempt at the theme that would become the *Psychomachia*. He says that Satan, a powerful thief, afflicts souls with destruction and sows his ministers throughout their entire body; and he includes a long list of evils who fight under their master's lead. Three of these evils reappear in the same guise in *Psychomachia*, namely Ira, Discordia, and Fraus. The others are different or appear under different names, which is unsurprising since writers created lists of vices to match their precise rhetorical and situational needs. Prudentius himself offered a different list of vices in *Cath.* 7.11–14, and he was clearly not following any single or canonical list.

The list of vices closest to those in the *Psychomachia* is in John Cassian, who described the vices against which monks had to struggle; Cassian had followed Evagrius of Pontus in coming up with this list of eight vices (Beatrice 1971, 48–51): *gastrimargia* or *uentris ingluuies* (≈ Luxuria), *fornicatio* (≈ Libido), *filargyria* or *auaritia, ira, tristitia, acedia* or *anxietas, cenodoxia* (vanity), *superbia* (Cassian *Collationes* 5.2). Of course, *tristitia, acedia,* and *cenodoxia* are not featured in the *Psychomachia*; and Veterum cultura deorum and Discordia are not on Cassian's list. More important than whether Prudentius had read Cassian is the fact that Prudentius's Virtues and Vices take part in a struggle that is public and historical rather than monastic or merely personal.

The conflict in *Psychomachia* is violent, and often extravagantly bloody. This violence can be explained in part from a common delight in spectacle and as a result of the development of the personifications as epic characters. Even more relevant is that the violence of the scenes neatly corresponds to the character of each Vice. The Roman idea that the penalty should match the crime, the so-called *Lex talionis*, explains the exaggerated violence of the poem (Gnilka 1963, 51–81). This is the case throughout the poem; but it is most obvious in the dismemberment of Discordia, a gruesome scene that is pictured without any apparent disquiet in MS *Br* (fig. 2). Although this aspect of the poem is troubling to many modern readers, Georgia Nugent concludes that the violence of the Virtues is "motivated not by bad taste but by logical necessity," because Prudentius is writing an allegory in which his characters are mutually opposed universals, rather than particulars (1985, 20). In other words, Prudentius took the idea of an inner conflict between Virtues and Vices and set their fighting within a complex and profound allegorical framework.

3.c. Allegory and Interpretation

The *Psychomachia* was the first full-scale personification allegory in the Western literary tradition.[16] Any claim to originality as broad as this naturally meets with skepticism, and every ingredient used by Prudentius can be found in earlier works.[17] Nevertheless, Prudentius combines them all

---

16. See Pelttari 2014, 84–85 for some explanation and defense of this large claim.
17. Philip Hardie (2017) evinces some disquiet and reads several passages from the *Aeneid* through the *Psychomachia*.

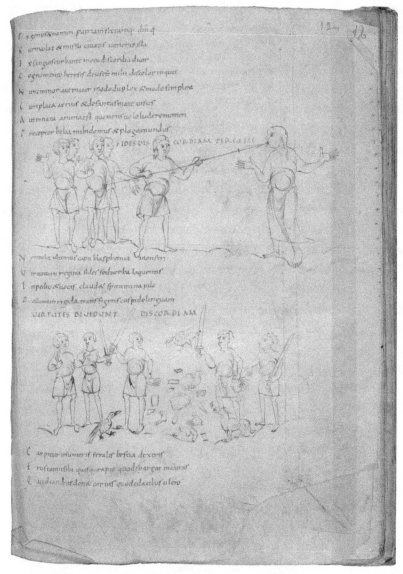

FIGURE 2. Lines 707–21, with illustrations of Discordia being pierced and her scattered parts. MS *Br*, fol. 124r. *Courtesy Bibliothèque Royale de Belgique.*

to create something that deserves to be called original, as much as any text ever could be. Unhelpfully, the term "allegory" is used in more than one way. Several varieties are important for understanding Prudentius: allegory as a figure of speech, allegoresis, typological interpretation, and personification. Prudentius combines each of these elements to create an introspective epic in which the reader is fully engaged.

Quintilian, the famous Roman rhetorician, defined allegory as a figure of speech in which the surface meaning is different from the intended meaning (*Inst.* 8.6.44–59; "aliud uerbis, aliud sensu ostendit"); allegory is produced, he goes on to say, when a series of metaphors are linked together. Of course, this definition is extremely broad. It can be made to cover many different kinds of figured speech (on the ancient division of its rhetorical uses, see the entry for ALLEGORY in my appendix of literary and rhetorical terms). The intended secondary meanings of the *Psychomachia* are allegorical in this rhetorical sense.

Allegoresis is the technical term for allegorical interpretation, and this was a common way of reading canonical texts. In ancient Greece, learned philosophers interpreted Homer allegorically, and the practice was borrowed in Alexandria by Jewish interpreters and then eventually by Christians.[18] Stoic philosophers developed a complex theoretical model for allegorical interpretation; they understood allegoresis as a method for investigating the remnants of divine logic within human language (Long 1992). The *De Abraham* of Ambrose definitely influenced Prudentius, and it will provide a good example of ancient allegoresis. After a first book in which Ambrose interpreted the story of Abraham as offering lessons in morality, the second book understood the patriarch allegorically as a figure for the mind:

> Abraham mentis loco inducitur. Denique Abraham transitus dicitur. Ergo ut mens quae in Adam totam se delectationi et illecebris corporalibus desiderat, in formam uirtutis speciemque transiret, uir sapiens nobis ad imitandum propositus est." (*De Abraham* 2.1.1)

---

18. On the allegorical interpretation of Homer, see Lamberton 1986; Struck 2004; and Ramelli and Lucchetta 2004. On Jewish and Christian allegoresis, see Niehoff 2011 and Young 1997.

Abraham is introduced in place of the mind. Moreover, Abraham is said
to have crossed over. In Adam, the mind fell completely to delight and
to the pleasures of the body. Therefore, in order that it may cross over
into a virtuous form and class, we were offered a wise man to imitate.

Abraham stands for the mind, and while the story of his life says one thing it
means another. Thus, allegoresis works by finding a connection between the
surface meaning of a text and some other deeper meaning. Just as Prudentius
read the scriptures allegorically, he expected his readers to find allegorical
meaning in the *Psychomachia*.

Typological interpretation was often applied by Christians to their scriptures in late antiquity.[19] A type (Gk. *typos*) is a mold or model. Abraham
was interpreted typologically as a figure for Christ and for the individual
Christian. Rather than offering a free-floating conceptual map, typological
allegoresis works within the framework of history: whereas mind is something ahistorical, Abraham and Christ and individual readers exist within
the same historical continuum. Therefore, King David's victory over the
giant Goliath can be read as a type for Christ's victory over sin; likewise, in
Psychomachia 646–64, the Israelites singing after crossing the Red Sea are
a type for the praises offered by the victorious Virtues. Obviously, when a
figure is read as a type for a modern reader or actor, this is a kind of ethical
interpretation and hardly to be distinguished from Roman exemplarity.[20]

A personification is an invented character made to represent an abstract
idea as a human person.[21] This category of thought underlies the invention
of gods such as the Graces and Memory, and it was used widely in Greek
and Latin poetry and rhetoric. We have already mentioned Claudian's
poem on the consulship of Stilicho; in addition to describing personified
virtues in Stilicho's heart, Claudian also describes the cave of Time and the

---

19. On typology or figural interpretation, see Auerbach 1944 and Dawson 2002.
20. On Roman exempla, see Roller 2018; for typology as providing a link between theol-
    ogy and moral allegory in the *Psychomachia*, see Mastrangelo 2008, 82–120.
21. Quintilian glosses the Greek term *prosopopoeia* (which is broader than the English
    word "personification" in that it includes dramatization of all kinds) as "fictiones
    personarum" (*Inst.* 9.2.29).

appearance of Nature (*Stil.* 2.424–76). These are personifications that make abstract ideas visible. As for rhetoric, a series of characters were brought to life by Pacatus Drepanius in a panegyric presented in 389 for the emperor Theodosius; he gave a very short speech to each of these five virtues: Constantia, Patientia, Prudentia, Fortitudo, and Fortuna (*Panegyrici latini* 2 [12] 40). Despite the widespread use of personification, it is apparently true that no one until Prudentius devoted an entire long poem to personified actors. In no small way, it was the shared influence of the *Psychomachia* and Martianus Capella's slightly later *De nuptiis Philologiae et Mercurii* that caused personification allegory to enjoy a long period of flourishing throughout the Middle Ages.

The allegory of the *Psychomachia* is something more than the sum of its parts, and a number of scholars have tried to understand the poem as a whole. Nugent describes the poem as a speculative model designed to enable readers to think through the complexities of the inner life (1985, 95–100). Marc Mastrangelo concludes that the *Psychomachia*'s reader is "compelled to make a choice between good and evil, faith and godlessness, immortal life and death" (2008, 38). Barbara Machosky analyzes the *Psychomachia* as a struggle "to make the *imago Dei* in man appear, an image of the human soul" (2013, 68). Within the context of Stoic language theory, Jeffrey Bardzell describes the poem as formative of the reader's sensible perception of the world: "The poem trains the reader how to assent to impressions, and these impressions are not things by themselves, but rather things disposed in the world" (2009, 43). Such observations reveal the underlying complexity of the poem, and they suggest that Prudentius meant to address serious human and philosophical problems. Indeed, the allegory of the *Psychomachia* invites the reader's participation; and, therefore, even the variety of these interpretations is a sign of its effectiveness. I would emphasize that Prudentius combines epic figures and allegoresis to create an image of historical and spiritual reality and that he places the reader at the center of this drama. To summarize in a single statement, the end in view (*skopos*) of Prudentius in the *Psychomachia* is the creation of a Roman and Christian reader pleased to ken the depths of the world within and without through language.

3.d. Date of Composition and Contemporary Editions

We do not know when the *Psychomachia* was written or how it was published. Slight but intriguing evidence suggests the following: that the poem was written in 408 or 409, that Prudentius wrote it with illustrations in mind, and that he presented the poem as a trilogy with *Apotheosis* and *Amartigenia*.

The *Praefatio* of Prudentius does not include any apparent reference to the *Psychomachia*, and this strongly implies that the poem was not finished when the *Praefatio* was written in 404.[22] A persuasive though circumstantial case for dating *Psychomachia* to within 408 or 409 was put forward by Danuta Shanzer (1989, 356–62). The key evidence comes from three references within the poem to barbarians, which seem to fit a reasonably anxious climate during Gothic incursions into Italy during those two years (see the commentary on pr. 21). A later date is unlikely because the triumphalist tone of the poem suggests that Prudentius was writing before Alaric's sack of Rome in 410. Support for this dating comes from (admittedly very weak) intertextual evidence, namely, an apparent echo in line 567 of a poem that Paulinus of Nola presented in January 407 (on which see the commentary).

Illustrations for the *Psychomachia* survive in twenty different manuscripts made between the ninth and the thirteenth century. Art historians suggest that they descend from a common archetype produced in the fifth century, and no one has refuted the idea.[23] The primary evidence for the dating of the original illustrations has to do with their iconography (Woodruff 1929, 36–46), for example, angels without wings and Isaac in the nude on the altar prepared by Abraham (fig. 3). An illustrated *Psychomachia* would fit everything we know about contemporary illustrated copies of the scriptures, of Vergil, and of Homer. Prudentius's ecphrastic *Tituli historiarum* also offer a kind of parallel, whether or not the paintings they envision are real (Lubian 2014, 184–90). In addition to this external evidence, there is one possible reference in the *Psychomachia* to suggest that

---

22. Shanzer 1989, 347–50. For a full accounting of previous scholarship on line 39 of the *Praefatio*, see Coşkun 2003, 222n21.
23. Woodruff 1929; Beer 1980, 51n147; Gnilka 2000–2003, 1:136–37.

FIGURE 3. The sacrifice of Isaac, with the capture of Lot and Abraham's rescue of him. MS *F*, fol. 55v. *Courtesy Bibliothèque nationale de France.*

Prudentius had illustrations in mind; in the proem, he says that his poem will make it possible to recognize the very appearances of the virtues ("ipsas / uirtutum facies"). Such a phrase can be nothing more than suggestive, but see my note on lines 18–20 for further discussion. Although Richard Stettiner (1895–1905) published a full study of the illustrations along with reproductions of them, further research is desirable both because of their intrinsic interest and because of the possibility of uncovering something more definite about their sources.

The manuscripts reveal that *Apotheosis, Amartigenia,* and *Psychomachia* were grouped together as a trilogy at some early date (Cunningham 1966, xxv). They present the three poems as books 1, 2, and 3 of some unidentified work. For example, manuscript *B* introduces the poem with "Incipit lib· tertius Psychomachia" (fig. 4; "secundus" was lightly erased to yield "explicit lib· primus Amartigenia"). Likewise, MS *A* has running headings on the top of each page, *Psychomachia* on the right-hand side of the opening and "Prudentii lib· iii" on the left (see fig. 5 on page 28). This grouping of the poems must have been very early because it appears in each branch of the manuscript tradition. Besides this evidence from the manuscripts, the so-called *Hymnus de trinitate* (the first preface to *Apotheosis*) could actually have been a preface to the three poems together, although that idea is controversial.[24] Some internal thematic links between the poems were noted by Maurice Cunningham, but this is the weakest evidence, and no one so far as I know has ever claimed that the three poems were written from the beginning as a trilogy. Nevertheless, we have a parallel for Prudentius grouping together already written poems: long sections of *Contra Symmachum* were written years before the whole was put together in 402–403.[25] As far as this idea of a trilogy is concerned, line 39 of the *Praefatio* would make sense if it referred to these three poems together; however, the arguments for a late dating of the *Psychomachia* carry more weight.

---

24. Cunningham thought that it introduced the three poems (1966, 73), but there is no scholarly consensus. Bastiaensen, for example, thought that it was a self-standing poem (1993b), whereas Gnilka judged it to be an interpolation (2000–2003, 1:461–88).
25. For a recent discussion of the composition of *Contra Symmachum*, see Cameron 2011, 337–49.

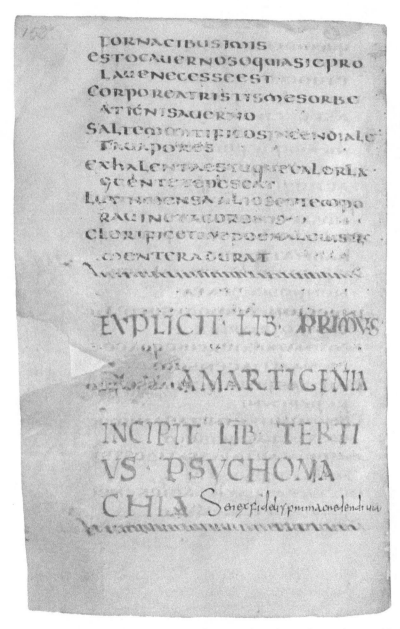

Figure 4. The explicit of *Amartigenia* and incipit of *Psychomachia*, with pr. 1 added in the margin. MS *B*, fol. 152v. *Courtesy Biblioteca Ambrosiana.*

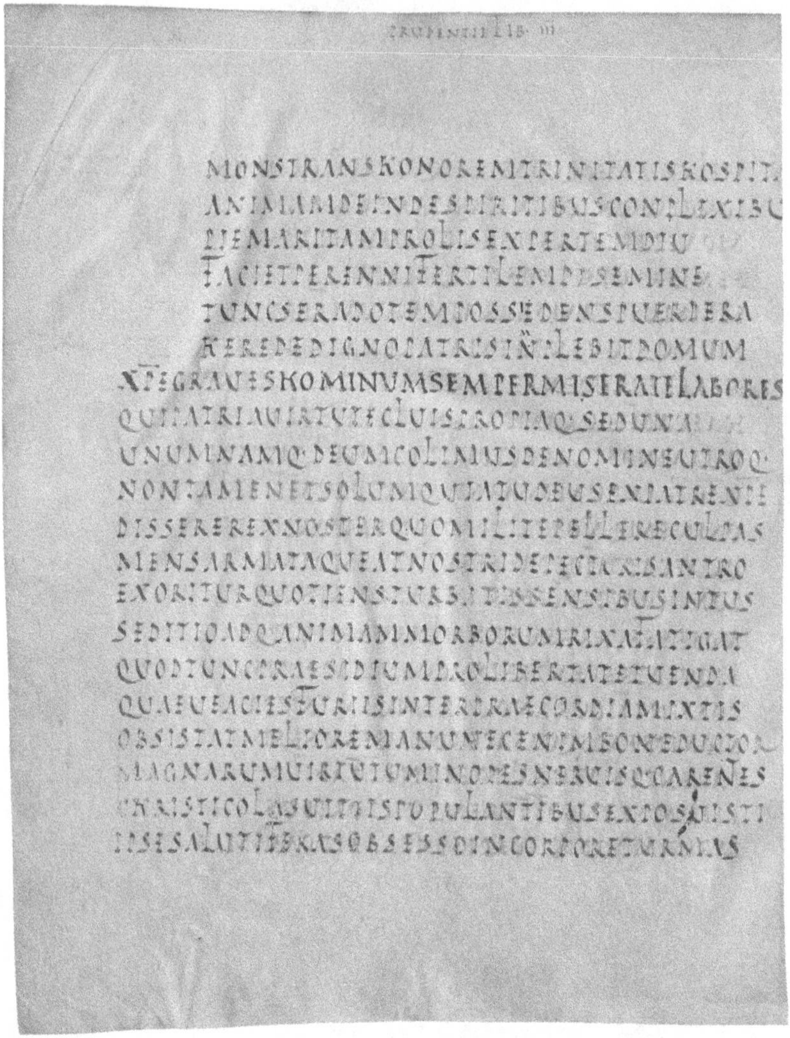

FIGURE 5. From pr. 62 to line 14, with the running head along the top of the page. MS *A*, fol. 101v. *Courtesy Bibliothèque nationale de France.*

There is no solid proof, but it is plausible that Prudentius himself grouped together the three poems at some point after completing *Psychomachia*.

The poems of Prudentius circulated separately in late antiquity (Cunningham 1958), and so it is no great surprise that we can identify some variations in how the *Psychomachia* was published. To be sure, publication was an informal process. As often happens on the Internet today, publication in antiquity meant distribution by an author or editor to one or more friends or associates, who were expected to pass it on via their own literary network. Whether or not Prudentius oversaw the illustrated edition and whether or not he grouped the poem with *Apotheosis* and *Amartigenia*, there has been no disagreement that these editions were produced very early. Is there any evidence for revisions (authorial or not) in these early editions? Lines 261 and 787 are intriguing in this regard. However, as I conclude in the note on line 787, the evidence currently available is not enough to support identifying any variants with specific editions, partly because the manuscript tradition is heavily contaminated between its different branches. Along with a high degree of contamination, the manuscript tradition is also incredibly uniform. We would expect both of these to be the case if Prudentius oversaw more than one edition and if he made no major changes to the text.

3.e. Manuscripts and Transmission

More than three hundred manuscripts of Prudentius survive, and two of these were produced as early as the sixth century. In his edition from 1926, Johannes Bergman attempted to map out a basic *stemma codicum*, a graph of the relations between all of the most important manuscripts. Some flaws in his *stemma* and his messy apparatus criticus led Cunningham to produce a new edition in 1966; because Cunningham had concluded that the manuscripts were too contaminated to improve very much on Bergmann's stemmatic analysis, he based his edition on the two earliest manuscripts and three groups of closely related manuscripts, which were represented by individual examples. Some critics insensibly criticized him for not taking into account inconsistencies in Bergman's understanding of the tradition[26]; in

---

26. See Bastiaensen 1993a, 101–3.

fact, Cunningham had taken them into account and explained the rationale for his edition in a lengthy article published in 1962. Because it has not yet been possible to work out all of the contamination in the tradition, I follow Cunningham's essentially eclectic approach and cite throughout the following five manuscripts (where a digital facsimile of a manuscript is currently available, I indicate the website at which it can be found):

A   Parisinus latinus 8084 (gallica.bnf.fr), written in rustic capitals dated to the first half of the sixth century. The name Vettius Agorius Basilius written on fol. 45r suggests that the manuscript was owned by the consul of 527.

B   Ambrosianus D 36 sup, from the sixth century and from Italy, written in uncials; the original copy of lines 668–892 is missing. Independent mistakes on both sides show that MSS *A* and *B* are not very closely related.

T   Parisinus latinus 8087 (gallica.bnf.fr), ninth century and written in Carolingian minuscule. Agrees with *B*, *E*, and *S* more often than with *A*.

E   Leidensis, Bibl. Vniu., Burmannus Q 3 (disc.leidenuniv.nl), written in the beginning or the middle of the ninth century in Carolingian minuscule and illustrated. Shares many distinctive readings with *A* but often agrees with *B*, *T*, and *S*, which shows most clearly that there was contamination between the two main branches of the tradition. In several places, this manuscript (and its group) offers attempts to improve the text by conjecture (see the note on lines 105–6).

S   Sangallensis 136 (e-codices.unifr.ch), from the middle of the ninth century and written in Carolingian minuscule. Agrees with *B*, *T*, and *E* more often than with *A*.

As implied above, none of these manuscripts consistently agree with each other in error, which is why it has not yet been possible to reduce any further the number of necessary witnesses. The assertion that they provide some independent testimony depends partly on evidence from the other poems of Prudentius, not necessarily for good reason, since we have already seen evidence that his poems circulated independently of each other in antiquity. The following apparently correct (although trivial) readings are transmitted in only one manuscript or branch of the tradition: *prospicit* in line 275 (*A*); *haud* in 396 (*B*); *horrificos* and *asperet* in 431 (*E*); and *discincta* in 822 (*S*). Only in four places do I doubt the transmitted text, in lines 396, 431, 558, and 726–29. Even in these passages, the errors are insubstantial or perhaps nonexistent: in lines 396 and 558, the question is only orthographical; in line 431, I suspect that MS *E* is correct but by conjecture; and in lines 726–29, I think that there is a plausible interpretation of the transmitted text. In every other line, at least one branch of the tradition preserves the correct reading. That there is so little corruption implies that our text descends from one or more very, very accurate sources. As a result, my text of *Psychomachia* is very conservative (only in that insubstantial spelling in line 558 do I depart from the manuscripts). At least as far as this poem is concerned, I find no evidence to support Christian Gnilka's assertion that Prudentius was subject to widespread interpolation before the sixth century.[27]

A few manuscripts are cited in my apparatus selectively, either for scribal conjectures or to verify that a particular reading belongs to one of the groups of manuscripts represented by *T* or *S*:

C   Cantabrigensis, Corp. Christi 223 (corpus.cam.ac.uk), from around the middle of the ninth century and written by a scribe who had access to the tradition(s) represented by *A* and E (Cunningham 1966, xix–xx).

J   Montepessulanus sch. med. H220, from the ninth century and belonging to the same family as *T*.

Y   Neapolitanus IV G 68, second half of the ninth century and from the same family as *S*.

In addition to MS *E*, important illustrated manuscripts include the following:

F   Parisinus latinus 8085 (gallica.bnf.fr), ninth century with colored illustrations and from the same family as *E*.

U   Bernensis, Bongarsianus 264 (e-codices.unifr.ch), end of the ninth or first half of the tenth century, with colored illustrations.

Br   Bruxellensis, Bibliothèque Royale. Ms. No. 9987–91 (kbr.be), tenth century with illustrations.

---

27. See especially Gnilka 1986 and my notes on lines pr. 41–42, 309, 456–58, 708, and 726–28.

My critical apparatus is usually negative, which is to say that I cite only the manuscripts that depart from the printed text. But I occasionally cite all my witnesses where there might be some doubt or for the sake of clarity. The apparatus is also selective, except that I include some readings that are definitely incorrect but show how medieval scribes worked; for similar reasons, I provide a complete collation of MS *A*, namely, to demonstrate what could be found in a luxury copy of Prudentius from the first half of the sixth century; likewise, I report a number of trivial errors from MS *B*. Because I report every reading from *A*, the apparatus includes a large number of orthographical variants. In order to save space, I mention only here three variants: MS *A* has *ad* in place of *at* in lines 66, 267, 393, and 868; *adque* instead of *atque* in 8, 74, 263, 318, 472, 594, 597, 628, 645, 748, 764, 780, 822, 908, and 912; and *inquid* for *inquit* in 155 and 710.[28] Likewise, I do not report the *nomina sacra* (abbreviated forms) XPS and IHS, which were regularly used for the Greek name Christus Iesus.

I note these orthographical variants, and sometimes discuss others in the commentary, because the precise written form affects the way that the poem looks and the way that it is read. Of course, we can only infer the spellings that he preferred, just as we must infer how Prudentius pronounced his Latin. Nevertheless, when the best and oldest manuscripts agree on a spelling that differs from the Classical norm, this is noteworthy. As for the process by which the text of Prudentius was gradually altered so as to conform to the grammatical standards, we can track these changes, in minute detail, from the time of the Carolingian Renaissance through the nineteenth century. Among modern editors, Bergman was the first to make a systematic attempt to reject these supposed corrections and return instead to the orthography of Prudentius; Cunningham continued and refined Bergman's study of this aspect of the poetry of Prudentius. Most notably, all of the evidence suggests that Prudentius used forms like *Amartigenia* and *Peristefanon*[29]; although they may look strange, they should be retained because they are a visual reminder

---

28. Full information on these is provided in Cunningham's index orthographicus (1966, xxix–xxxiii).
29. On the specific question of the writing of Greek in contemporary Latin texts, see Pelttari 2011.

of everything that is different about his poetry. Writing such unusual forms is a small but important way to demonstrate the considerable gap, a full four hundred years, between his poems and those of a Horace or a Vergil.

Several manuscripts are cited only for their glosses or commentary on the *Psychomachia*. These glosses belong to several groups. One set of them was published from MSS *U* and *L* by Iohannes Weitzius (1613) and attributed, without explanation, to Iso, a teacher in the Abbey of Saint Gall (Weitzius 1613, 2: 771; O'Sullivan 2004, 26). Sinéad O'Sullivan (2004) has edited the glosses in this so-called Weitz tradition; rather than attempt to reconstruct a single archetype from heterogeneous exemplars, she edited versions represented by these three manuscripts:

L   London British Library, Add. 34248, eleventh century.
Clm 14395   Munich, Bayerische Staatsbibliothek Clm 14395 (digitale-sammlungen.de), tenth century.
Cologne 81   Cologne, Dombibliothek 81 (ceec.uni-koeln.de), end of tenth or beginning of eleventh century.

Two other sets of glosses were published by John Burnam. The first set, which is known as B I, was published in 1905 and was plausibly attributed by Herbert Silvestre (1957, 55–56) to the Irish intellectual John Scotus Eriugena, a leading figure at the court of Charles the Bald in Aachen during the ninth century. The expanded B II glosses published by Burnam in 1910 were tentatively attributed by Silvestre (1957, 62) to Heiricus of Auxerre, a younger contemporary of Eriugena. The latter commentary was edited from a single manuscript:

Valenciennes 413   Valenciennes Bibliothèque municipale Ms. 413 (gallica.bnf.fr), ninth century.

It is surprising, when reading these medieval commentaries, how much continuity there is between their notes and modern commentaries, especially in the passages on which there has been disagreement or misunderstanding (for example, with interpretations of "umbonis equini" [255], "toreumata" [370], and the four ages [843]).

A critical edition and its textual apparatus are often opaque, but interested students will now find a wonderful introduction to the challenges of textual criticism in Richard Tarrant's *Texts, Editors, and Readers* (2016). In my apparatus, I have used the following shorthand and abbreviations:

ac	*ante correctionem*, the reading before a correction.
c	a correction, possibly made by the original scribe.
pc	*post correctionem*, after the correction.
v	a variant reading added usually in the margin.
*	indicates an erasure the space of one letter.
1	i.e., A^1, the scribe correcting himself or herself.
2	a second hand in the manuscript.
add.	*addidit*, usually when a scribe adds a word or a line.
coni.	*coniecit*, of a conjectural emendation in the text.
def.	*deficit*, "is lacking," when a manuscript breaks off.
fort.	*fortasse*, used to denote some uncertainty.
om.	*omisit*, when a scribe left out a word or a line.
ut uid.	*ut uidetur*, "as it seems," of a reading that is not clear.

3. f. Reception

The reception of Prudentius can be traced essentially from his first readers to the present day; it is an enormous topic that has been studied only in parts.[30] Although none of his contemporaries cite him by name, his influence has been detected in Augustine (see note on lines 769–71), Claudian (Dorfbauer 2012), and maybe Paulinus of Nola (Costanza 1983). Among the next generation of poets, Sedulius definitely took Prudentius as a model; likewise, Prosper of Aquitaine responds to the *Psychomachia* and to Prudentius in general, especially in *Liber epigrammatum* 95, 86, and 67. In the second half of the fifth century, Sidonius Apollinaris juxtaposed Horace and Prudentius (*Epist.* 2.9.4), and Claudianus Mamertus cited a line from the *Cathemerinon*

---

30. See the overviews in Lavarenne 1943, xvi–xxi and 2002, 25–45; Bastiaensen 1993a, 131–34; Rivero García 1996, 203–17; Richardson 2016, 26–28; and Putter 2016, 367–70. It is remarkable to what an extent these and other very good surveys each cover different ground.

in *De statu animae* 3. Claudianus referred to Prudentius, not by name, as a *poeta notissimus* (in the same work, he also cited Terence, Vergil, and Statius, but without any comparable praise). Shortly thereafter, Gennadius wrote the entry on Prudentius for his *De uiris illustribus* cited above; this became the basis for introductions to Prudentius written throughout the Middle Ages. In the sixth and seventh centuries, Prudentius was cited by name in the poetry of Alcimus Avitus (*De uirginitate* 372), Venantius Fortunatus (*Vita Martini* 1.19), and Isidore (*Epigrammata* 10.3). These are only the most important of the many allusions and references to Prudentius that survive from the fifth to the seventh centuries. During the Middle Ages, the *Psychomachia* was widely influential. For example, Alan of Lille imitated Prudentius in his cosmological poem *Anticlaudianus* written around 1182, in which he includes in the ninth book a grand battle between Virtues and Vices. The *Psychomachia* is also reflected in medieval art and sculpture (Lavarenne 2002, 41–45). However much it may surprise some modern readers, this allegorical poem was anything but a dry and sterile abstraction.

From the sixth century if not earlier, Prudentius was studied by scholars, and his poems were read in schools during the Middle Ages. Revealing in this context is the author portrait on page 8 (fig. 1), in which Prudentius has one hand raised in prayer (as in the original version of the portrait, on which see the note on lines 888–915); he is writing with the other hand and is seated with his bookrolls beside him like a classical poet. Three early grammatical works cite Prudentius: the anonymous treatise *De dubiis nominibus. Cuius generis sint* (On uncertain nouns: What gender they are), which is probably from the end of the sixth century and from around Bordeaux; the *Ars grammatica* attributed to Julian of Toledo; and Bede's *De arte metrica*. Likewise, glosses on the vocabulary of Prudentius are attested in the pre-Carolingian *Arma* glossary (Austin 1926). From the Carolingian period on, the role that Prudentius played in education can be reconstructed from a number of introductions, glosses, and marginal annotations. In addition to the glosses and commentaries mentioned above in the section on the transmission of Prudentius, scholars have analyzed some manuscripts from the tenth and eleventh centuries for what they show about how Prudentius was studied (Babcock 2017; Wieland 1983); these manuscripts include glosses written in the vernacular (for those in Old High German, see the references at O'Sullivan 2004, 33–34). Medieval commentaries were incorporated into some of the first printed editions, and the *Psychomachia* was translated into vernacular languages, with one of the earliest being Francisco Palomino's prose translation into Spanish, which was entitled *Batalla o pelea del anima* (1529). During this period, Prudentius continued to receive the notice of prominent intellectuals, including Erasmus, the famous Dutch scholar and theologian, who wrote notes on *Cath.* 11 and 12 and imitated in his own verse the *Psychomachia* and several other poems of Prudentius.[31] The first printed editions were improved by the editorial labors of a number of scholars, including the brilliant Nicolaas Heinsius (1667); and scholarship was advanced by several omnibus editions unencumbered by restrictive copyrights. These culminated in the fine two-volume edition and commentary of Faustinus Arevalo (1788–89). Then, Albert Dressel (1860) produced the most important edition of Prudentius in the nineteenth century. Although Dressel relied too much on Italian manuscripts, his study led to Johannes Bergman's groundbreaking edition published in the series Corpus Scriptorum Ecclesiasticorum Latinorum in 1926. Remarkably, in preparing to edit the text, Bergmann took into account the majority of the extant manuscripts (over three hundred of them). As we have already noted, Cunningham's edition (1966) was an imperfect but incremental improvement on Bergmann's. In order to advance our understanding of the text any further, it will be necessary to work out the contamination in the tradition and to determine whether it is possible to reconstruct any of the earliest versions, whether or not Prudentius was responsible for them. For this task, a full electronic edition would seem to be the only practical solution.

Just as the *Psychomachia* continues until God comes ("donec praesidio Christus deus adsit"), its reception is ongoing. Almost one hundred years ago, Maurice Lavarenne observed with melancholy that "once again the educated are interested in Prudentius, just as they are in his entire tormented period (toute son époque tourmentée), which is comparable perhaps to our own" (Lavarenne 1933a, 26). The name most often used now for this

---

31. On Erasmus and Prudentius, see Green 2000.

period, late antiquity, was still hardly known in the 1930s; and more than one cultural crisis has come and gone since then. But interest in Prudentius has not shown any signs of decreasing. Indeed, many readers continue to find something of worth in the *Psychomachia* and its convoluted struggles to capture, within words bound by meter, the realities of individual human experience. For my part, I remain fascinated by how this author represents the critical and volitional faculties within himself and within myself.

The western Mediterranean around 400 C.E. *Map by Erin Greb Cartography.*

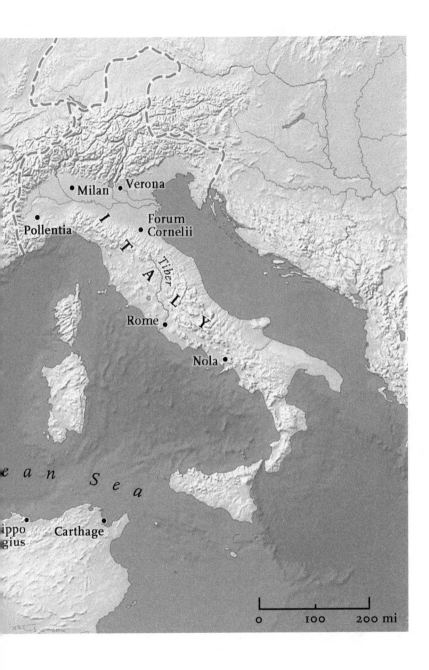

Milan • • Verona

Pollentia • I T A L Y

Forum
• Cornelii

Tiber

Rome •

Nola •

e a n S *e a*

ippo
gius • Carthage •

0   100   200 mi

39

THE TEXT OF *PSYCHOMACHIA*

PRUDENTII LIBER TERTIUS
PSYCHOMACHIA

Senex fidelis prima credendi uia
Abram, beati seminis serus pater,
adiecta cuius nomen auxit syllaba,
Abram parenti dictus Abraham deo,
senile pignus qui dicauit uictimae   5
docens ad aram cum litare quis uelit
quod dulce cordi quod pium quod unicum
deo libenter offerendum credito,
pugnare nosmet cum profanis gentibus
suasit suumque suasor exemplum dedit   10
nec ante prolem coniugalem gignere

Inscriptio: incipit lib. tertius psychomachia *B*, incipit psychomachia liber tertius *T*,
explicit liber secundus prudentii amartigenia incipit psychomachia *E*, incipit psychomachia lib. iii. *S*
Tituli: prudentii lib. iii psychomachia *A summa in pagina per folia totius operis*
Inscriptio ad praefationem: praefatio *T*, incipit brefatio *S*

1 *om. B, add. B*²

deo placentem, matre uirtute editam,
quam strage multa bellicosus spiritus
portenta cordis seruientis uicerit.

    Victum feroces forte reges ceperant   15
Loth inmorantem criminosis urbibus
Sodomae et Gomorrae, quas fouebat aduena
pollens honore patruelis gloriae.
Abram sinistris excitatus nuntiis
audit propinquum sorte captum bellica   20
seruire duris barbarorum uinculis.
armat trecentos terque senos uernulas,
pergant ut hostis terga euntis caedere,
quem gaza diues ac triumfus nobilis
captis tenebant inpeditum copiis.   25
quin ipse ferrum stringit et plenus deo
reges superbos mole praedarum graues
pellit fugatos, sauciatos proterit;
frangit catenas et rapinam liberat:
aurum puellas paruulos monilia   30
greges equarum uasa uestem buculas.
Loth ipse ruptis expeditus nexibus
adtrita bacis colla liber erigit.
Abram triumfi dissipator hostici
redit recepta prole fratris inclytus   35
ne quam fidelis sanguinis prosapiam
uis pessimorum possideret principum.
adhuc recentem caede de tanta uirum
donat sacerdos ferculis caelestibus,
dei sacerdos rex et idem praepotens   40

---

14 saeuientis *U*   15 coeperant *A*ᵃᶜ   24 triumfus *ABT*, triumphos *ES*
31 greges *TES*, graeges *B*, oues *A*   buculas] bucula *A*   32 nexibus] uinculis *TS*
35 inclytus] inclytis *A*, inclitus *B*   37 possideret] possederet *A*, possidere *B*

origo cuius fonte inenarrabili
secreta nullum prodit auctorem sui
Melchisedec, qua stirpe quis maioribus
ignotus uni cognitus tantum deo.
mox et triformis angelorum trinitas   45
senis reuisit hospitis mapalia,
et iam uietam Sarra in aluum fertilis
munus iuuentae mater exsanguis stupet
herede gaudens et cachinni paenitens.

   Haec ad figuram praenotata est linea   50
quam nostra recto uita resculpat pede:
uigilandum in armis pectorum fidelium
omnemque nostri portionem corporis
quae capta foedae seruiat libidini
domi coactis liberandam uiribus,   55
nos esse large uernularum diuites,
si quid trecenti bis nouenis additis
possint figura nouerimus mystica.
mox ipse Christus, qui sacerdos uerus est,
parente natus alto et ineffabili   60
cibum beatis offerens uictoribus
paruam pudici cordis intrabit casam
monstrans honorem trinitatis hospitae.
animam deinde spiritus conplexibus
pie maritam, prolis expertem diu,   65
faciet perenni fertilem de semine,
tunc sera dotem possidens puerpera
herede digno patris inplebit domum.

41–42 *BTES, om. A*   **42** prodit] *B²*, prodet *B*   **43** melchisedec] *A*, melchisedech
BTES   **53** corporis] *AT*, pectoris *JES*ᵖᶜ   **60** *ABSY*, parente inenarrabili a(t)que uno
satus *TE atque eundum uersum add. S post 60 et ante correctionem*   **64** spiritus] *BTS*,
spiritibus *AE*   **67** possidens] *A²*, possedens *A*   **68** inplebit] implebit *A²*, inpleuit *B*,
impleuit *E*

Christe, graues hominum semper miserate labores,
qui patria uirtute cluis propriaque sed una
(unum namque deum colimus de nomine utroque,
non tamen et solum, quia tu deus ex patre, Christe),
dissere, rex noster, quo milite pellere culpas   5
mens armata queat nostri de pectoris antro,
exoritur quotiens turbatis sensibus intus
seditio atque animam morborum rixa fatigat,
quod tunc praesidium pro libertate tuenda
quaeue acies furiis inter praecordia mixtis   10
obsistat meliore manu. nec enim, bone ductor,
magnarum uirtutum inopes neruisque carentes
Christicolas uitiis populantibus exposuisti.
ipse salutiferas obsesso in corpore turmas
depugnare iubes, ipse excellentibus armas   15
artibus ingenium quibus ad ludibria cordis
obpugnanda potens tibi dimicet et tibi uincat.
uincendi praesens ratio est, si comminus ipsas
uirtutum facies et conluctantia contra
uiribus infestis liceat portenta notare.   20
    Prima petit campum dubia sub sorte duelli
pugnatura Fides agresti turbida cultu
nuda umeros intonsa comas exerta lacertos.
namque repentinus laudis calor ad noua feruens
proelia nec telis meminit nec tegmine cingi;   25
pectore sed fidens ualido membrisque retectis
prouocat insani frangenda pericula belli.
ecce lacessentem conlatis uiribus audet
prima ferire Fidem Veterum cultura deorum.
illa hostile caput falerataque tempora uittis   30
altior insurgens labefactat et ora cruore

---

3 utroque] *ABT*ˡᵛ*JES*, trino *TY*   10 *om. T, add. T*ˡ   16 ludebria *A*
24 calor] labor *A*   29 fide *A*

de pecudum satiata solo adplicat et pede calcat
elisos in morte oculos; animamque malignam
fracta intercepti commercia gutturis artant
difficilemque obitum suspiria longa fatigant.   35
exultat uictrix legio, quam mille coactam
martyribus regina Fides animarat in hostem.
nunc fortes socios parta pro laude coronat
floribus ardentique iubet uestirier ostro.

    Exim gramineo in campo concurrere prompta   40
uirgo Pudicitia speciosis fulget in armis,
quam patrias succincta faces Sodomita Libido
adgreditur piceamque ardenti sulpure pinum
ingerit in faciem pudibundaque lumina flammis
adpetit et taetro temptat subfundere fumo.   45
sed dextram furiae flagrantis et ignea dirae
tela lupae saxo ferit inperterrita uirgo
excussasque sacro taedas depellit ab ore.
tunc exarmatae iugulum meretricis adacto
transfigit gladio. calidos uomit illa uapores   50
sanguine concretos caenoso, spiritus inde
sordidus exhalans uicinas polluit auras.

    "Hoc habet" exclamat uictrix regina. "supremus
hic tibi finis erit, semper prostrata iacebis.
nec iam mortiferas audebis spargere flammas   55
in famulos famulasue dei, quibus intima casti
uena animi sola feruet de lampade Christi.
tene, o uexatrix hominum, potuisse resumptis
uiribus extincti capitis recalescere flatu,
Assyrium postquam thalamum ceruix Olofernis   60
caesa cupidineo madefactum sanguine lauit
gemmantemque torum moechi ducis aspera Iudith

---

32 adplicat] applicat *B*   **34** intercoepti *A*   guttoris *A*   **36** exultat] *B*ᵖᶜ,
exultant *B*ᵃᶜ   uictrex*A*   **51** caenoso] sanioso *coni. Heinsius*   **53** uictris *AS*¹,
uictrit *S*

spreuit et incestos conpescuit ense furores,
famosum mulier referens ex hoste tropaeum
non trepidante manu, uindex mea caelitus audax!   65
at fortasse parum fortis matrona sub umbra
legis adhuc pugnans, dum tempora nostra figurat,
uera quibus uirtus terrena in corpora fluxit,
grande per infirmos caput excisura ministros?
numquid et intactae post partum uirginis ullum   70
fas tibi iam superest? post partum uirginis, ex quo
corporis humani naturam pristina origo
deseruit carnemque nouam uis ardua seuit
atque innupta deum concepit femina Christum,
mortali de matre hominem sed cum patre numen.   75
inde omnis iam diua caro est, quae concipit illum
naturamque dei consortis foedere sumit.
uerbum quippe caro factum non destitit esse
quod fuerat uerbum, dum carnis glutinat usum,
maiestate quidem non degenerante per usum   80
carnis sed miseros ad nobiliora trahente.
ille manet quod semper erat, quod non erat esse
incipiens; nos quod fuimus iam non sumus, aucti
nascendo in melius. mihi contulit et sibi mansit.
nec deus ex nostris minuit sua, sed sua nostris   85
dum tribuit nosmet dona ad caelestia uexit.
dona haec sunt quod uicta iaces, lutulenta Libido,
nec mea post Mariam potis es perfringere iura.
tu princeps ad mortis iter, tu ianua leti;
corpora conmaculans animas in Tartara mergis.   90
abde caput tristi iam frigida pestis abysso;
occide, prostibulum, manes pete, claudere Auerno,

---

66 sub] sum *A*   68 *om. T, add. T*²   74 innubta *AB*   75 mortali] mortalem *C*ᵃᶜ
80 *om. S, add. S*²   87 iaces] iacis *AB*ᵃᶜ*E*   88 mea] meam *A*ᵃᶜ*E*ᵃᶜ
90 conmaculans] commaculans *B*

inque tenebrosum noctis detrudere fundum!
te uoluant subter uada flammea, te uada nigra
sulpureusque rotet per stagna sonantia uertex.   95
nec iam Christicolas, furiarum maxima, temptes,
ut purgata suo seruentur corpora regi."
    Dixerat haec et laeta Libidinis interfectae
morte Pudicitia gladium Iordanis in undis
abluit infectum, sanies cui rore rubenti   100
haeserat et nitidum macularat uulnere ferrum.
expiat ergo aciem fluuiali docta lauacro
uictricem uictrix abolens baptismate labem
hostilis iuguli. nec iam contenta piatum
condere uaginae gladium, ne tecta rubigo   105
occupet ablutum scabrosa sorde nitorem,
catholico in templo diuini fontis ad aram
consecrat aeterna splendens ubi luce coruscet.
    Ecce modesta graui stabat Patientia uultu
per medias inmota acies uariosque tumultus   110
uulneraque et rigidis uitalia peruia pilis
spectabat defixa oculos et lenta manebat.
hanc procul Ira tumens, spumanti feruida rictu,
sanguinea intorquens subfuso lumina felle,
ut belli exsortem teloque et uoce lacessit   115
inpatiensque morae conto petit, increpat ore
hirsutas quatiens galeato in uertice cristas.
"en tibi, Martis" ait "spectatrix libera nostri,
excipe mortiferum securo pectore ferrum;
nec doleas quia turpe tibi gemuisse dolorem."   120
sic ait, et stridens sequitur conuicia pinus
per teneros crispata notos et certa sub ipsum

---

98 leta *A*   105 ne tecta] *S in rasura*   105–6 ne sorde latenti / occupet ablatum
rubigo scabra nitorem *E*   114 subfusa *A*   115 expertem *C*   116 petit] petit et *A*
117 hyrsutas *A*

defertur stomachum rectoque inliditur ictu;
sed resilit duro loricae excussa repulsu.
prouida nam uirtus conserto adamante trilicem   125
induerat thoraca umeris squamosaque ferri
texta per intortos conmiserat undique neruos.
inde quieta manet Patientia, fortis ad omnes
telorum nimbos et non penetrabile durans,
nec mota est iaculo monstri sine more furentis   130
opperiens propriis peritura uiribus Iram.
scilicet indomitos postquam stomachando lacertos
barbara bellatrix inpenderat et iaculorum
nube superuacuam lassauerat inrita dextram,
cum uentosa leui cecidissent tela uolatu   135
iactibus et uacuis hastilia fracta iacerent,
uertitur ad capulum manus inproba et ense corusco
conisa in plagam dextra sublimis ab aure
erigitur mediumque ferit librata cerebrum.
aerea sed cocto cassis formata metallo   140
tinnitum percussa refert aciemque retundit
dura resultantem, frangit quoque uena rebellis
inlisum chalybem, dum cedere nescia cassos
excipit adsultus ferienti et tuta resistit.
Ira ubi truncati mucronis fragmina uidit   145
et procul in partes ensem crepuisse minutas,
iam capulum retinente manu sine pondere ferri
mentis inops ebur infelix decorisque pudendi
perfida signa abicit monumentaque tristia longe
spernit et ad proprium succenditur effera letum.   150
missile de multis quae frustra sparserat unum
puluere de campi peruersos sumit in usus.

---

123 sthomacum *A*   **127** conmiserat] commiserat *B*   **131** perituris *A*
132 sthomacando *A*   **137** et ense] et inse *A*, et se *B*, ense *B*² **140** sed] set *A*
formata] informata *A*   **146** ense *A*   **148** inobs *AB*   **150** succendetur *A*

rasile figit humi lignum ac se cuspide uersa
perfodit et calido pulmonem uulnere transit.

Quam super adsistens Patientia "uicimus" inquit   155
"exultans uitium solita uirtute sine ullo
sanguinis ac uitae discrimine. lex habet istud
nostra genus belli furias omnemque malorum
militiam et rabidas tolerando extinguere uires.
ipsa sibi est hostis uaesania seque furendo   160
interimit moriturque suis Ira ignea telis."

Haec effata secat medias inpune cohortes
egregio comitata uiro; nam proximus Iob
haeserat inuictae dura inter bella magistrae
fronte seuerus adhuc et multo funere anhelus   165
sed iam clausa truci subridens ulcera uultu
perque cicatricum numerum sudata recensens
milia pugnarum, sua praemia, dedecus hostis.
illum diua iubet tandem requiescere ab omni
armorum strepitu captis et perdita quaeque   170
multiplicare opibus nec iam peritura referre.
ipsa globos legionum et concurrentia rumpit
agmina uulniferos gradiens intacta per imbres.
omnibus una comes uirtutibus adsociatur
auxiliumque suum fortis Patientia miscet.   175
nulla anceps luctamen init uirtute sine ista
uirtus; nam uidua est quam non Patientia firmat.

Forte per effusas inflata Superbia turmas
effreni uolitabat equo, quem pelle leonis
texerat et ualidos uillis onerauerat armos,   180
quo se fulta iubis iactantius illa ferinis
inferret tumido despectans agmina fastu.

---

164 magistrae] magistras *A*, magisterae *B*ᵃᶜ, magnistrae *T*ᵃᶜ   **165** funere] uulnere *Y*²ᵛ*C*
166 truci] trucid *A*ᵃᶜ, truci* *S*ᵖᶜ   **177** nam] *B*²*ES*¹*T*ᵛ, et *ABTS*ᵃᶜ   **182** despectans] *BTS*,
dispectans *AE*   agmina] omnia *S*

turritum tortis caput adcumularat in altum
crinibus, exstructos augeret ut addita cirros
congeries celsumque apicem frons ardua ferret.   185
carbasea ex umeris summo collecta coibat
palla sinu teretem nectens a pectore nodum;
a ceruice fluens tenui uelamine limbus
concipit infestas textis turgentibus auras.
nec minus instabili sonipes feritate superbit   190
inpatiens madidis frenarier ora lupatis,
huc illuc frendens obuertit terga negata
libertate fugae pressisque tumescit habenis.

   Hoc sese ostentans habitu uentosa uirago
inter utramque aciem supereminet et faleratum   195
circumflectit equum uultuque et uoce minatur
aduersum spectans cuneum, quem milite raro
et paupertinis ad bella coegerat armis
Mens humilis, regina quidem sed egens alieni
auxilii proprio nec sat confisa paratu.   200
Spem sibi collegam coniunxerat, edita cuius
et suspensa ab humo est opulentia diuite regno.
ergo Humilem postquam male sana Superbia mentem
uilibus instructam nullo ostentamine telis
aspicit, in uocem dictis se effundit amaris: 205
"non pudet, o miseri, plebeio milite claros
adtemptare duces ferroque lacessere gentem
insignem titulis, ueteres cui bellica uirtus
diuitias peperit laetos et gramine colles
imperio calcare dedit? nunc aduena nudus   210
nititur antiquos, si fas est, pellere reges!
en qui nostra suis in praedam cedere dextris
sceptra uolunt! en qui nostras sulcare nouales

---

189 ingestas *S*^pc*Y*^c*U*   **190** instabili] stabili *AT*   **192** obuertit tega *A*, obuertiterga *B*
210 nudos *A*   **212** predam *A*

aruaque capta manu popularier hospite aratro
contendunt duros et pellere Marte colonos!   215
nempe, o ridiculum uulgus, natalibus horis
totum hominem et calidos a matre amplectimur artus
uimque potestatum per membra recentis alumni
spargimus et rudibus dominamur in ossibus omnes.
quis locus in nostra tunc uobis sede dabatur,   220
congenitis cum regna simul dicionibus aequo
robore crescebant? nati nam luce sub una
et domus et domini paribus adoleuimus annis,
ex quo plasma nouum de consaepto paradisi
limite progrediens amplum transfugit in orbem   225
pellitosque habitus sumpsit uenerabilis Adam,
nudus adhuc, ni nostra foret praecepta secutus.
quisnam iste ignotis hostis nunc surgit ab oris
inportunus iners infelix degener amens,
qui sibi tam serum ius uindicat, hactenus exul?   230
nimirum uacuae credentur friuola famae,
quae miseros optare iubet quandoque futuri
Spem fortasse boni, lenta ut solacia mollem
desidiam pigro rerum meditamine palpent.
quid ni illos Spes palpet iners quos puluere in isto   235
tirones Bellona truci non excitat aere
inbellesque animos uirtus tepefacta resoluit?
anne Pudicitiae gelidum iecur utile bello est,
an tenerum Pietatis opus sudatur in armis?
quam pudet, o Mauors et Virtus conscia, talem   240
contra stare aciem ferroque lacessere nugas
et cum uirgineis dextram conferre choraeis,
Iustitia est ubi semper egens et pauper Honestas
arida Sobrietas albo Ieiunia uultu

---

216 nempe, o] nempe *S* hoc *supra lineam add.*, nempe hoc *YCU*   220 uobis] nobis
*B*ac   222 robure *AB*   223 adolebimus *E*ac   224 paradissi *A*

sanguine uix tenui Pudor interfusus aperta   245
Simplicitas et ad omne patens sine tegmine uulnus
et prostrata in humum nec libera iudice sese
Mens humilis, quam degenerem trepidatio prodit!
faxo ego sub pedibus stipularum more teratur
inualida ista manus; neque enim perfringere duris   250
dignamur gladiis algenti et sanguine ferrum
inbuere fragilique uiros foedare triumfo."
   Talia uociferans rapidum calcaribus urget
cornipedem laxisque uolat temeraria frenis
hostem humilem cupiens inpulsu umbonis equini   255
sternere deiectamque supercalcare ruinam.
sed cadit in foueam praeceps, quam callida forte
Fraus interciso subfoderat aequore furtim
Fraus detestandis uitiorum e pestibus una
fallendi uersuta opifex, quae praescia belli   260
planitiem scrobibus uiolauerat insidiosis
hostili de parte latens, ut fossa ruentes
exciperet cuneos atque agmina mersa uoraret,
ac, ne fallacem puteum deprendere posset
cauta acies, uirgis adopertas texerat oras   265
et superinposito simularat caespite campum.
at regina humilis, quamuis ignara, manebat
ulteriore loco nec adhuc ad fraudis opertum
uenerat aut foueae calcarat furta malignae.
hunc eques illa dolum, dum fertur praepete cursu,   270
incidit et caecum subito patefecit hiatum.
prona ruentis equi ceruice inuoluitur ac sub
pectoris inpressu fracta inter crura rotatur.

---

252 foedare] foedera *B*, foederare *TS*   triumfo] *A*, triumpho *B*pc, triumphos *B*ac
258 interciso] interfuso *A*, inter**so *T*ac   261 uiolauerat] *BTES*, uitiauerat *AC*v
264 posset] possit *A*   272 -c sub *B*2 in rasura   273 om. *B*, add. *B*2   inpressu]
inpraessu *A*ac

At uirtus placidi moderaminis, ut leuitatem
prospicit obtritam monstri sub morte iacentis,   275
intendit gressum mediocriter, os quoque parce
erigit et comi moderatur gaudia uultu.
cunctanti Spes fida comes succurrit et offert
ultorem gladium laudisque inspirat amorem.
illa cruentatam correptis crinibus hostem   280
protrahit et faciem laeua reuocante supinat.
tunc caput orantis flexa ceruice resectum
eripit ac madido suspendit colla capillo.
extinctum uitium sancto Spes increpat ore:
"desine grande loqui, frangit deus omne superbum.   285
magna cadunt, inflata crepant, tumefacta premuntur.
disce supercilium deponere, disce cauere
ante pedes foueam quisquis sublime minaris.
peruulgata uiget nostri sententia Christi
scandere celsa humiles et ad ima redire feroces.   290
uidimus horrendum membris animisque Golian
inualida cecidisse manu; puerilis in illum
dextera funali torsit stridore lapillum
traiectamque cauo penetrauit uulnere frontem.
ille minax rigidus iactans truculentus amarus   295
dum tumet indomitum, dum formidabile feruet,
dum sese ostentat, clipeo dum territat auras
expertus pueri quid possint ludicra parui
subcubuit teneris bellator turbidus annis.
me tunc ille puer uirtutis pube secutus   300
florentes animos sursum in mea regna tetendit,
seruatur quia certa mihi domus omnipotentis
sub pedibus domini meque ad sublime uocantem

275 prospicit] A, perspicit BTES   277 comi] com A   280 cruentatam] BTS,
cruentatum AE   291 golian] A, goliam B   298 possint] E, possit A, possent BTS
ludicra] BS, ludrica ATE

uictores caesa culparum labe capessunt."
dixit et auratis praestringens aëra pinnis   305
in caelum se uirgo rapit. mirantur euntem
uirtutes tolluntque animos in uota uolentes
ire simul, ni bella duces terrena retardent.
confligunt uitiis seque ad sua praemia seruant.

   Venerat occiduis mundi de finibus hostis   310
Luxuria extinctae iam dudum prodiga famae,
delibuta comas, oculis uaga, languida uoce,
perdita deliciis, uitae cui causa uoluptas,
elumbem mollire animum petulanter amoenas
haurire inlecebras et fractos soluere sensus.   315
ac tunc peruigilem ructabat marcida cenam,
sub lucem quia forte iacens ad fercula raucos
audierat lituos atque inde tepentia linquens
pocula lapsanti per uina et balsama gressu
ebria calcatis ad bellum floribus ibat.   320
non tamen illa pedes, sed curru inuecta uenusto
saucia mirantum capiebat corda uirorum.
o noua pugnandi species! non ales harundo
neruum pulsa fugit nec stridula lancea torto
emicat amento frameam nec dextra minatur,   325
sed uiolas lasciua iacit foliisque rosarum
dimicat et calathos inimica per agmina fundit.
inde eblanditis uirtutibus halitus inlex
inspirat tenerum labefacta per ossa uenenum
et male dulcis odor domat ora et pectora et arma   330
ferratosque toros obliso robore mulcet.
deiciunt animos ceu uicti et spicula ponunt
turpiter heu dextris languentibus obstupefacti,
dum currum uaria gemmarum luce micantem

---

305 praestringens] peraestringens *A*ᵃᶜ   312 delibata *A*   319 labsanti *A*   323 ales]
alis *BE*   324 neruo *B*ᵖᶜ*E*², stridola *AB*   331 obliso] ubliso *AE*ᵃᶜ   331 robure *A*

mirantur, dum bratteolis crepitantia lora   335
et solido ex auro pretiosi ponderis axem
defixis inhiant obtutibus et radiorum
argento albentem seriem quam summa rotarum
flexura electri pallentis continet orbe.
et iam cuncta acies in deditionis amorem   340
sponte sua uersis transibat perfida signis
Luxuriae seruire uolens dominaeque fluentis
iura pati et laxa ganearum lege teneri.
    Ingemuit tam triste nefas fortissima uirtus
Sobrietas dextro socios decedere cornu   345
inuictamque manum quondam sine caede perire.
uexillum sublime crucis, quod in agmine primo
dux bona praetulerat, defixa cuspide sistit
instauratque leuem dictis mordacibus alam
exstimulans animos nunc probris, nunc prece mixta.   350
"quis furor insanas agitat caligine mentes?
quo ruitis? cui colla datis? quae uincula tandem
(pro pudor!) armigeris amor est perferre lacertis,
lilia luteolis interlucentia sertis
et ferrugineo uernantes flore coronas?   355
his placet adsuetas bello iam tradere palmas
nexibus, his rigidas nodis innectier ulnas,
ut mitra caesariem cohibens aurata uirilem
conbibat infusum croceo relegamine nardum
post inscripta oleo frontis signacula per quae   360
unguentum regale datum est et chrisma perenne,
ut tener incessus uestigia syrmate uerrat,
sericaque infractis fluitent ut pallia membris
post inmortalem tunicam quam pollice docto
texuit alma Fides dans inpenetrabile tegmen   365

---

338 quam] quem *B*   351 insanus *E*   357 -dis innectier ulnas *om. S ante correctionem*
359 relegamine] *AB*ac, religamine *B*pc   360 inscribta *AB*   361 chresma *A*

pectoribus lotis, dederat quibus ipsa renasci,
inde ad nocturnas epulas ubi cantharus ingens
despuit effusi spumantia damna Falerni
in mensam cyathis stillantibus, uda ubi multo
fulcra mero ueterique toreumata rore rigantur?   370
excidit ergo animis eremi sitis, excidit ille
fons patribus de rupe datus quem mystica uirga
elicuit scissi salientem uertice saxi?
angelicusne cibus prima in tentoria uestris
fluxit auis, quem nunc sero felicior aeuo   375
uespertinus edit populus de corpore Christi?
his uos inbutos dapibus iam crapula turpis
Luxuriae ad madidum rapit inportuna lupanar,
quosque uiros non Ira fremens non idola bello
cedere conpulerant saltatrix ebria flexit!   380
state, precor, uestri memores, memores quoque Christi.
quae sit uestra tribus, quae gloria, quis deus et rex
quis dominus meminisse decet. uos nobile Iudae
germen ad usque dei genetricem qua deus ipse
esset homo, procerum uenistis sanguine longo.   385
excitet egregias mentes celeberrima Dauid
gloria continuis bellorum exercita curis;
excitet et Samuel, spolium qui diuite ab hoste
adtrectare uetat nec uictum uiuere regem
incircumcisum patitur, ne praeda superstes   390
uictorem placidum recidiua in proelia poscat.
parcere iam capto crimen putat ille tyranno,
at uobis contra uinci et subcumbere uotum est.
paeniteat per si qua mouet reuerentia summi
numinis hoc tam dulce malum uoluisse nefanda   395
proditione sequi; si paenitet, haud nocet error.

---

368 dispuit *B*   371 erimi *A*   378 inportuna] inporna *A*   381 memores, memores]
memores *B*   383 meminisset *BJ*   388 samuel] *ABS*, samuhel *TE*   390 ne] nec *BJ*
396 haud] *B*, haut *TS*ᵖᶜ, aut *AES*

paenituit Ionatham ieiunia sobria dulci
conuiolasse fauo sceptri mellisque sapore
heu male gustato, regni dum blanda uoluptas
oblectat iuuenem iurataque sacra resoluit.   400
sed quia paenituit nec sors lacrimabilis illa est
nec tinguit patrias sententia saeua secures.
en ego Sobrietas, si conspirare paratis,
pando uiam cunctis uirtutibus, ut malesuada
Luxuries multo stipata satellite poenas   405
cum legione sua Christo sub iudice pendat."
  Sic effata crucem domini feruentibus offert
obuia quadriiugis lignum uenerabile in ipsos
intentans frenos. quod ut expauere feroces
cornibus obpansis et summa fronte coruscum   410
uertunt praecipitem caeca formidine fusi
per praerupta fugam. fertur resupina reductis
nequiquam loris auriga comamque madentem
puluere foedatur, tunc et uertigo rotarum
inplicat excussam dominam; nam prona sub axem   415
labitur et lacero tardat sufflamine currum.
addit Sobrietas uulnus letale iacenti
coniciens silicem rupis de parte molarem,
hunc uexilliferae quoniam fors obtulit ictum
spicula nulla manu sed belli insigne gerenti.   420
casus agit saxum, medii spiramen ut oris
frangeret et recauo misceret labra palato.
dentibus introrsum resolutis lingua resectam
dilaniata gulam frustis cum sanguinis inplet.
insolitis dapibus crudescit guttur et ossa   425
conliquefacta uorans reuomit quas hauserat offas.
"ebibe iam proprium post pocula multa cruorem"

---

401 nec sors] ne sors *A*   **410** oppansis *A*, obpansis *B*   **414** foedatur] foedat humi
*T*ᵖᶜ*S*ᵖᶜ*Y*   **421** agit] *B*ᶜ*J*ᶜ, ait *BJ*   ut oris] odoris *A ut uid. E*   **424** frustis] frustris *B*ᵃᶜ*E*

uirgo ait increpitans. "sint haec tibi fercula tandem
tristia praeteriti nimiis pro dulcibus aeui.
lasciuas uitae inlecebras gustatus amarae   430
mortis et horrificos sapor ultimus asperet haustus!"
    Caede ducis dispersa fugit trepidante pauore
nugatrix acies. Iocus et Petulantia primi
cymbala proiciunt; bellum nam talibus armis
ludebant resono meditantes uulnera sistro.   435
dat tergum fugitiuus Amor, lita tela ueneno
et lapsum ex umeris arcum faretramque cadentem
pallidus ipse metu sua post uestigia linquit.
Pompa ostentatrix uani splendoris inani
exuitur nudata peplo, discissa trahuntur   440
serta Venustatis collique ac uerticis aurum
soluitur et gemmas Discordia dissona turbat.
non piget adtritis pedibus per acuta frutecta
ire Voluptatem, quoniam uis maior acerbam
conpellit tolerare fugam; formido pericli   445
praedurat teneras iter ad cruciabile plantas.
qua se cumque fugax trepidis fert cursibus agmen,
damna iacent: crinalis acus redimicula uittae
fibula flammeolum strofium diadema monile.
his se Sobrietas et totus Sobrietatis   450
abstinet exuuiis miles damnataque castis
scandala proculcat pedibus nec fronte seueros
coniuente oculos praedarum ad gaudia flectit.
    Fertur Auaritia gremio praecincta capaci
quidquid Luxus edax pretiosum liquerat unca   455

---

428 ait] *om. S ante correctionem*   429 tristia] tristitia *T*ᵃᶜ*S*   dulcibus] *ABES*ᵖᶜ,
luxibus *B²Y²*, ducibus *T*   431 horrificos] *E*, horrifico *ABTS*ᵖᶜ   asperet] *E*, asperat
*ABT*ᵃᶜ*S*   haustus] *AE*, haustu *BTS*   433 nugatrix] nugatrex *B*ᵃᶜ   437 lapsum ex
umeris] labsumeris *A*, labsum ex umeris *B*   438 linquid *A*   447 agmen] agmendam
*B*ᵃᶜ   448 iacent] iaceat *B*ᵃᶜ   451 castis] costis *B*ᵃᶜ   453 coniuente] *ABE*, conibente
T, coni*bente *S*

corripuisse manu pulchra in ludibria uasto
ore inhians aurique legens fragmenta caduci
inter harenarum cumulos. nec sufficit amplos
inpleuisse sinus; iuuat infercire cruminis
turpe lucrum et grauidos furtis distendere fiscos,   460
quos laeua celante tegit laterisque sinistri
uelat opermento. uelox nam dextra rapinas
abradit spoliisque ungues exercet aënos.
Cura Famis Metus Anxietas Periuria Pallor
Corruptela Dolus Commenta Insomnia Sordes,   465
Eumenides uariae, monstri comitatus aguntur.
nec minus interea rabidorum more luporum
crimina persultant toto grassantia campo
matris Auaritiae nigro de lacte creata.
si fratris galeam fuluis radiare ceraunis   470
germanus uidit conmilito, non timet ensem
exerere atque caput socio mucrone ferire
de consanguineo rapturus uertice gemmas.
filius extinctum belli sub sorte cadauer
aspexit si forte patris, fulgentia bullis   475
cingula et exuuias gaudet rapuisse cruentas.
cognatam ciuilis agit Discordia praedam
nec parcit propriis Amor insatiatus habendi
pigneribus spoliatque suos Famis inpia natos.
   Talia per populos edebat funera uictrix   480
orbis Auaritia sternens centena uirorum
milia uulneribus uariis. hunc lumine adempto
effossisque oculis uelut in caligine noctis
caecum errare sinit perque offensacula multa
ire nec oppositum baculo temptare periclum.   485

---

460 destendere *B*   463 exercet aenos] *S*, exercet*aenos *T*, exercit aenos *E*,
exercetaaenos *AB*   464 cura] cu *A*   479 inpia] improba *E*
484 offendicula *A*   485 nec oppositum] neconpositum *A*

porro alium capit intuitu fallitque uidentem
insigne ostentans aliquid, quod dum petit ille
excipitur telo incautus cordisque sub ipso
saucius occulto ferrum suspirat adactum.
multos praecipitans in aperta incendia cogit,   490
nec patitur uitare focos quibus aestuat aurum
quod petit arsurus pariter peculator auarus.
omne hominum rapit illa genus. mortalia cuncta
occupat interitu neque est uiolentius ullum
terrarum uitium, quod tantis cladibus aeuum   495
mundani inuoluat populi damnetque gehennae.
quin ipsos temptare manu, si credere dignum est,
ausa sacerdotes domini, qui proelia forte
ductores primam ante aciem pro laude gerebant
uirtutum, magnoque inplebant classica flatu.   500
et fors innocuo tinxisset sanguine ferrum,
ni Ratio armipotens, gentis Leuuitidis una
semper fida comes, clipeum obiectasset et atrae
hostis ab incursu claros texisset alumnos.
stant tuti Rationis ope, stant turbine ab omni   505
inmunes fortesque animi; uix in cute summa
praestringens paucos tenui de uulnere laedit
cuspis Auaritiae. stupuit luis inproba castis
heroum iugulis longe sua tela repelli.
ingemit et dictis ardens furialibus infit: 510
"uincimur heu segnes nec nostra potentia perfert
uim solitam. languet uiolentia saeua nocendi,
sueuerat inuictis quae uiribus omnia ubique
rumpere corda hominum; nec enim tam ferrea quemquam

---

487 insigne] insignae *B*ᵃᶜ   490 praecipitans] praecepitans *B*ᵃᶜ   492 peculator]
*AB*ᵖᶜ*T*, peculatur *B*ᵃᶜ*S*, speculator *B²JEY*   498 sacerdotes domini] *B²*,
sacerdotealumini *B*   501 fors] for *A*   504 alumnus *S*   508 luis] *AT*,
lues *B*ᵖᶜ*ES*   510 ingemuit] *B*   514 tam] *om. S, add. S*ᶜ

formauit natura uirum, cuius rigor aera   515
sperneret aut nostro foret inpenetrabilis auro.
ingenium omne neci dedimus. tenera aspera dura
docta indocta simul bruta et sapientia nec non
casta incesta meae patuerunt pectora dextrae.
sola igitur rapui quidquid Styx abdit auaris   520
gurgitibus. nobis ditissima Tartara debent
quos retinent populos. quod uoluunt saecula nostrum est;
quod miscet mundus, uaesana negotia, nostrum.
qui fit praeualidas quod pollens gloria uires
deserit et cassos ludit fortuna lacertos?   525
sordet Christicolis rutilantis fulua monetae
effigies, sordent argenti emblemata et omnis
thensaurus nigrante oculis uilescit honore.
quid sibi docta uolunt fastidia? nonne triumfum
egimus ex Scarioth, magnus qui discipulorum   530
et conuiua dei, dum fallit foedere mensae
haudquaquam ignarum dextramque parabside iungit?
incidit in nostrum flammante cupidine telum
infamem mercatus agrum de sanguine amici
numinis, obliso luiturus iugera collo.   535
uiderat et Iericho propria inter funera quantum
posset nostra manus, cum uictor concidit Achar.
caedibus insignis murali et strage superbus
subcubuit capto uictis ex hostibus auro,
dum uetitis insigne legens anathema fauillis   540
maesta ruinarum spolia insatiabilis haurit.
non illum generosa tribus, non plebis auitae
iuuit Iuda parens, Christo quandoque propinquo

---

515 formauit] *ABTESC*ᵛ, durauit *B²S²C*   rigor] uigor *E*ᵖᶜ*S²*ᵛ*C*   **520** rapuit *A*
524 qui fit] quid fit *BC*ᵛ, quid sit *CU*   **527** omnis] omnes *AB*, omn*s *E*ᵃᶜ
529 triumfum *AB*   **532** dextramque] dextraque *ABE*   **538** murali] morali *AB*ᵃᶜ
540 anathema fauillis] anathematauillis *A*

nobilis et tali felix patriarcha nepote.
quis placet exemplum generis, placeat quoque forma   545
exitii; sit poena eadem quibus et genus unum est.
quid moror aut Iudae populares aut populares
sacricolae summi (summus nam fertur Aäron)
fallere fraude aliqua Martis congressibus inpar?
nil refert armis contingat palma dolisue."   550
dixerat et toruam faciem furialiaque arma
exuit inque habitum sese transformat honestum.
fit uirtus specie uultuque et ueste seuera
quam memorant Frugi, parce cui uiuere cordi est
et seruare suum. tamquam nil raptet auare,   555
artis adumbratae meruit ceu sedula laudem.
huius se specie mendax Bellona coaptat,
non ut auara luis sed uirtus parca putetur;
nec non et tenero Pietatis tegmine crines
obtegit anguinos, ut candida palla latentem   560
dissimulet rabiem, diroque obtenta furori,
quod rapere et clepere est auideque abscondere parta,
natorum curam dulci sub nomine iactet.
talibus inludens male credula corda uirorum
fallit imaginibus. monstrum ferale sequuntur   565
dum credunt uirtutis opus. capit inpia Erinys
consensu faciles manicisque tenacibus artat.
    Attonitis ducibus perturbatisque maniplis
nutabat uirtutum acies errore biformis
portenti ignorans quid amicum credat in illo   570
quidue hostile notet. letum uersatile et anceps
lubricat incertos dubia sub imagine uisus,

545 generis] ueneris *A*   546 genus] uenus *A*   548 aaron] aaroo *B*   549 inpar]
inpo *B*, inpar *B*²   553 ueste] uoce *Berol. Ham.* 542 (s. x–xi)   555 tamquam] tamqua
*A*ᵃᶜ   556 sedula] *B*, sedola *A*   558 luis] *Cunningham*, lues *codices*   564 uirorum]
uiuorum *A*   566 erinys] rinys *A*   572 incertus *BTEU*

cum subito in medium frendens Operatio campum
prosilit auxilio sociis pugnamque capessit,
militiae postrema gradu sed sola duello   575
inpositura manum ne quid iam triste supersit.
omne onus ex umeris reiecerat, omnibus ibat
nudata induuiis multo et se fasce leuarat,
olim diuitiis grauibusque obpressa talentis
libera nunc miserando inopum quos larga benigne   580
fouerat effundens patrium bene prodiga censum.
iam loculos ditata fidem spectabat inanes
aeternam numerans redituro faenore summam.
horruit inuictae Virtutis fulmen et inpos
mentis Auaritia stupefactis sensibus haesit   585
certa mori. nam quae fraudis uia restet, ut ipsa
calcatrix mundi mundanis uicta fatiscat
inlecebris spretoque iterum sese inplicet auro?
inuadit trepidam Virtus fortissima duris
ulnarum nodis obliso et gutture frangit   590
exsanguem siccamque gulam; conpressa ligantur
uincla lacertorum sub mentum et faucibus artis
extorquent animam, nullo quae uulnere rapta
palpitat atque aditu spiraminis intercepto
inclusam patitur uenarum carcere mortem.   595
illa reluctanti genibusque et calcibus instans
perfodit et costas atque ilia rumpit anhela.
mox spolia extincto de corpore diripit auri
sordida frusta rudis nec adhuc fornace recoctam
materiam, tiniis etiam marsuppia crebris   600
exesa et uirides obducta aerugine nummos

---

575 postrema] posttrema *A*   578 se] *om. B*   582 fidem] *ABT*^ac *ut uid.*, fide *E*^pc*S*^pc*T*^pc
585 stupefactus *A*   587 calcatrix] galeatrix *B*   590 gutture] guttore *A*, gutturae *B*^ac
595 inclusam] *A*¹, inlusam *A*   598 exuncto *A*, exuto *Heinsius*   599 recoctam]
recocta *BE*   601 uirides] uerides *AB*^ac

dispergit seruata diu uictrix et egenis
dissipat ac tenues captiuo munere donat.
   Tunc circumfusam uultu exultante coronam
respiciens alacris media inter milia clamat: 605
"soluite procinctum, iusti, et discedite ab armis!
causa mali tanti iacet interfecta. lucrandi
ingluuie pereunte licet requiescere sanctis.
summa quies nil uelle super quam postulet usus
debitus, ut simplex alimonia, uestis et una   610
infirmos tegat ac recreet mediocriter artus
expletumque modum naturae non trahat extra.
ingressurus iter peram ne tollito neue
de tunicae alterius gestamine prouidus ito
nec te sollicitet res crastina ne cibus aluo   615
defuerit; redeunt escae cum sole diurnae.
nonne uides ut nulla auium cras cogitet ac se
pascendam praestante deo non anxia credat?
confidunt uolucres uictum non defore uiles,
passeribusque subest modico uenalibus asse   620
indubitata fides dominum curare potentem
ne pereant. tu, cura dei, facies quoque Christi,
addubitas ne te tuus umquam deserat auctor?
ne trepidate, homines; uitae dator et dator escae est.
quaerite luciferum caelesti dogmate pastum   625
qui spem multiplicans alat inuitiabilis aeui
corporis inmemores. memor est qui condidit illud
subpeditare cibos atque indiga membra fouere."
   His dictis curae emotae. Metus et Labor et Vis
et Scelus et placitae fidei Fraus infitiatrix   630
depulsae uertere solum. Pax inde fugatis

---

606 iusti] iussi *coni. Bentley*   **613** ne] *om. B, add. B*[2]   **624** trepidate] trepidante *AB,*
trepida*te *S*   dator est dator escae *U*   **625** docmate *A*   **630** scelus et placitae] *B*[2],
scaelasemblacstae *B*

hostibus alma abigit bellum. discingitur omnis
terror et auulsis exfibulat ilia zonis.
uestis ad usque pedes descendens defluit imos
temperat et rapidum priuata modestia gressum.   635
cornicinum curua aera silent; placabilis inplet
uaginam gladius; sedato et puluere campi
suda redit facies liquidae sine nube diei;
purpuream uideas caeli clarescere lucem.
agmina casta super uultum sensere tonantis   640
adridere hilares pulso certamine turmae
et Christum gaudere suis uictoribus arce
aetheris ac patrium famulis aperire profundum.
dat signum felix Concordia reddere castris
uictrices aquilas atque in tentoria cogi.   645
numquam tanta fuit species nec par decus ulli
militiae, cum dispositis bifida agmina longe
duceret ordinibus peditum psallente caterua,
ast alia de parte equitum resonantibus hymnis.
non aliter cecinit respectans uictor hiantem   650
Istrahel rabiem ponti post terga minacis,
cum iam progrediens calcaret litora sicco
ulteriora pede stridensque per extima calcis
mons rueret pendentis aquae nigrosque relapso
gurgite Nilicolas fundo deprenderet imo   655
ac refluente sinu iam redderet unda natatum
piscibus et nudas praeceps operiret harenas.
pulsauit resono modulantia tympana plectro
turba dei celebrans mirum ac memorabile saeclis
omnipotentis opus liquidas inter freta ripas   660
fluctibus incisis et subsistente procella

---

632 discinditur *U*^pc   633 ilia zonis] elazonis *A*   640 super] simul *E*
641 adride *A*   646 spescies *A*^ac   651 posterga] *BES*   minacis] minaces *A*
652 cum iam] cumia *A*   654 relapso] *SE*, relabso *BT*, relaxo *A*

crescere suspensosque globos potuisse teneri.
sic expugnata uitiorum gente resultant
mystica dulcimodis uirtutum carmina psalmis.

Ventum erat ad fauces portae castrensis, ubi artum   665
liminis introitum bifori dant cardine claustra.
nascitur hic inopina mali lacrimabilis astu
tempestas, placidae turbatrix inuida Pacis,
quae tantum subita uexaret clade triumfum.
inter confertos cuneos Concordia forte,   670
dum stipata pedem iam tutis moenibus infert,
excipit occultum uitii latitantis ab ictu
mucronem laeuo in latere. squalentia quamuis
texta catenato ferri subtegmine corpus
ambirent sutis et acumen uulneris hamis   675
respuerent rigidis nec fila tenacia nodis
inpactum sinerent penetrare in uiscera telum,
rara tamen chalybem tenui transmittere puncto
commissura dedit qua sese extrema politae
squama ligat tunicae sinus et sibi conserit oras.   680
intulit hoc uulnus pugnatrix subdola uictae
partis et incautis uictoribus insidiata est.
nam pulsa culparum acie Discordia nostros
intrarat cuneos sociam mentita figuram.
scissa procul palla structum et serpente flagellum   685
multiplici media camporum in strage iacebant.
ipsa redimitos olea frondente capillos
ostentans festis respondet laeta choraeis;
sed sicam sub ueste tegit, te, maxima Virtus,
te solam tanto e numero, Concordia, tristi   690
fraude petens. sed non uitalia rumpere sacri
corporis est licitum, summo tenus extima tactu

---

664 pialmis *B*   667 *post 667 def. B usque ad 893*   668 placida *A*   674 subtegmine]
AS, subtemine *TE*   681 subdola] sordida *C*ᵛ   690 te solam] et solam *SY*

laesa cutis tenuem signauit sanguine riuum.
exclamat Virtus subito turbata: "quid hoc est?
quae manus hic inimica latet, quae prospera nostra   695
uulnerat et ferrum tanta inter gaudia uibrat?
quid iuuat indomitos bello sedasse furores
et sanctum uitiis pereuntibus omne receptum,
si uirtus sub pace cadit?" trepida agmina maestos
conuertere oculos. stillabat uulneris index   700
ferrata de ueste cruor. mox et pauor hostem
comminus adstantem prodit; nam pallor in ore
conscius audacis facti dat signa reatus
et deprensa tremunt languens manus et color albens.
circumstat propere strictis mucronibus omnis   705
uirtutum legio exquirens feruente tumultu
et genus et nomen, patriam sectamque, deumque
quem colat et missu cuiatis uenerit. illa
exsanguis turbante metu: "Discordia dicor,
cognomento Heresis; deus est mihi discolor" inquit,   710
"nunc minor aut maior, modo duplex et modo simplex;
cum placet, aërius et de fantasmate uisus;
aut innata anima est, quotiens uolo ludere numen.
praeceptor Belia mihi, domus et plaga mundus."
non tulit ulterius capti blasfemia monstri   715
uirtutum regina Fides, sed uerba loquentis
inpedit et uocis claudit spiramina pilo
pollutam rigida transfigens cuspide linguam.
carpitur innumeris feralis bestia dextris.
frustatim sibi quisque rapit, quod spargat in auras,   720
quod canibus donet, coruis quod edacibus ultro
offerat, inmundis caeno exhalante cloacis
quod trudat, monstris quod mandet habere marinis.

---

720 spargit *A*

discissum foedis animalibus omne cadauer
diuiditur, ruptis Heresis perit horrida membris.   725
    Conpositis igitur rerum morumque secundis
in commune bonis tranquillae plebis ad unum
sensibus in tuta ualli statione locatis,   728
exstruitur media castrorum sede tribunal   730
editiore loco, tumulus quem uertice acuto
excitat in speculam, subiecta unde omnia late
liber inoffenso circum inspicit aëre uisus.
hunc sincera Fides simul et Concordia sacro
foedere iuratae Christi sub amore sorores   735
conscendunt apicem. mox et sublime tribunal
par sanctum carumque sibi supereminet aequo
iure potestatis; consistunt aggere summo
conspicuae populosque iubent adstare frequentes.
concurrunt alacres castris ex omnibus omnes.   740
nulla latet pars mentis iners quae corporis ullo
intercepta sinu per conceptacula sese
degeneri languore tegat. tentoria apertis
cuncta patent uelis; reserantur carbasa ne quis
marceat obscuro stertens habitator operto.   745
auribus intentis expectant contio quidnam
uictores post bella uocet Concordia princeps
quam uelit atque Fides uirtutibus addere legem.
    Erumpit prima in uocem Concordia tali
adloquio: "cumulata quidem iam gloria uobis,   750
o patris, o domini fidissima pignera Christi,
contigit. extincta est multo certamine saeua
barbaries, sanctae quae circumsaepserat urbis

727–29] in commune bonis postquam intra tuta morari / contigit ac statione frui
ualloque fouere / pacificos fusos (sensus E^4F) et in otia soluere curas *EF*
733 circum inspicit] *A*, circumspicit *TES*   734 hunc] *TS*, huc *AE*   736 sublime]
suble *A*   740 ex] *om. S*   742 intercoepta *A*   746 expectant] *AT*, expectat *JES*
751 patris] patres *AE*^{ac} 752 contigit] hoc habet *S*^{ac}*Y*

indigenas ferroque uiros flammaque premebat.
publica sed requies priuatis rure foroque   755
constat amicitiis. scissura domestica turbat
rem populi titubatque foris quod dissidet intus.
ergo cauete, uiri, ne sit sententia discors
sensibus in nostris, ne secta exotica tectis
nascatur conflata odiis, quia fissa uoluntas   760
confundit uariis arcana biformia fibris.
quod sapimus coniungat amor, quod uiuimus uno
conspiret studio. nil dissociabile firmum est.
utque homini atque deo medius interuenit Iesus,
qui sociat mortale patri ne carnea distent   765
spiritui aeterno sitque ut deus unus utrumque,
sic quidquid gerimus mentisque et corporis actu
spiritus unimodis texat conpagibus unus.
pax plenum uirtutis opus, pax summa laborum,
pax belli exacti pretium est pretiumque pericli,   770
sidera pace uigent, consistunt terrea pace.
nil placitum sine pace deo. non munus ad aram
cum cupias offerre probat, si turbida fratrem
mens inpacati sub pectoris oderit antro;
nec, si flammicomis Christi pro nomine martyr   775
ignibus insilias seruans inamabile uotum
bile sub obliqua, pretiosam proderit Iesu
inpendisse animam, meriti quia clausula pax est.
non inflata tumet, non inuidet aemula fratri,
omnia perpetitur patiens atque omnia credit,   780
numquam laesa dolet, cuncta offensacula donat,
occasum lucis uenia praecurrere gestit
anxia ne stabilem linquat sol conscius iram.
quisque litare deo mactatis uult holocaustis,
offerat in primis pacem. nulla hostia Christo   785

---

781 cuncta] contra *E*   783 conscius] concius *A*

dulcior, hoc solo sancta ad donaria uultum
munere conuertens puro oblectatur odore.
sed tamen et niueis tradit deus ipse columbis
pinnatum tenera plumarum ueste colubrum
rimante ingenio docte internoscere mixtum   790
innocuis auibus; latet et lupus ore cruento
lacteolam mentitus ouem sub uellere molli
cruda per agninos exercens funera rictus.
hac sese occultat Fotinus et Arrius arte
inmanes feritate lupi. discrimina produnt   795
nostra recensque cruor, quamuis de corpore summo,
quid possit furtiua manus." gemitum dedit omnis
uirtutum populus casu concussus acerbo.
    Tum generosa Fides haec subdidit: "immo secundis
in rebus cesset gemitus. Concordia laesa est,   800
sed defensa Fides; quin et Concordia sospes
germanam comitata Fidem sua uulnera ridet.
haec mea sola salus, nihil hac mihi triste recepta.
unum opus egregio restat post bella labori,
o proceres, regni quod tandem pacifer heres   805
belligeri armatae successor inermus et aulae
instituit Solomon, quoniam genitoris anheli
fumarat calido regum de sanguine dextra.
sanguine nam terso templum fundatur et ara
ponitur, auratis Christi domus ardua tectis.   810
tunc Hierusales templo inlustrata quietum
suscepit iam diua deum, circumuaga postquam
sedit marmoreis fundata altaribus arca.
surgat et in nostris templum uenerabile castris,
omnipotens cuius sanctorum sancta reuisat!   815
nam quid terrigenas ferro pepulisse falangas

---

787 puro] *A*, liquido *TES*   791 auibus] ouibus *T*ᵃᶜ*E*   802 comitata] comita *A*
807 salomon *TES*

culparum prodest, hominis si filius arce
aetheris inlapsus purgati corporis urbem
intret inornatam templi splendentis egenus?
hactenus alternis sudatum est comminus armis;   820
munia nunc agitet tacitae toga candida pacis
atque sacris sedem properet discincta iuuentus!"
    Haec ubi dicta dedit, gradibus regina superbis
desiluit tantique operis Concordia consors
metatura nouum iacto fundamine templum.   825
aurea planitiem spatiis percurrit harundo
dimensis, quadrent ut quattuor undique frontes,
ne commissuris distantibus angulus inpar
argutam mutilet per dissona semetra normam.
aurorae de parte tribus plaga lucida portis   830
inlustrata patet, triplex aperitur ad austrum
portarum numerus, tris occidualibus offert
ianua trina fores, totiens aquilonis ad axem
panditur alta domus. nullum illic structile saxum,
sed caua per solidum multoque forata dolatu   835
gemma relucenti limen conplectitur arcu
uestibulumque lapis penetrabile concipit unus.
portarum summis inscripta in postibus auro
nomina apostolici fulgent bis sena senatus.
spiritus his titulis arcana recondita mentis   840
ambit et electos uocat in praecordia sensus;
quaque hominis natura uiget, quam corpore toto
quadrua uis animat, trinis ingressibus aram
cordis adit castisque colit sacraria uotis.
seu pueros sol primus agat, seu feruor ephebos   845
incendat nimius, seu consummabilis aeui
perficiat lux plena uiros, siue algida borrae

---

818 inlabsus *A*   822 discincta] *SY*, distincta *ATE*   836 reculenti] *A*   arcu] actu *A*
838 inscribta *A*   845 sol primus] supremus *A*   ephebos] efybos *A*

aetas decrepitam uocet ad pia sacra senectam,
occurrit trinum quadrina ad conpeta nomen,
quod bene discipulis disponit rex duodenis.   850
quin etiam totidem gemmarum insignia textis
parietibus distincta micant animasque colorum
uiuentes liquido lux euomit alta profundo.
ingens chrysolitus natiuo interlitus auro
hinc sibi sappirum sociauerat inde beryllum,   855
distantesque nitor medius uariabat honores.
hic calchedon hebes perfunditur ex yacinthi
lumine uicino; nam forte cyanea propter
stagna lapis cohibens ostro fulgebat aquoso.
sardonicem pingunt ametystina; pingit iaspis   860
sardium iuxta adpositum pulcherque topazon.
has inter species smaragdina gramine uerno
prata uirent uoluitque uagos lux herbida fluctus.
te quoque conspicuum structura interserit, ardens
chrysoprase, et sidus saxis stellantibus addit.   865
stridebat grauidis funalis machina uinclis
inmensas rapiens alta ad fastigia gemmas.
   At domus interior septem subnixa columnis
crystalli algentis uitrea de rupe recisis
construitur, quarum tegit edita calculus albens   870
in conum caesus capita et sinuamine subter
subductus conchae in speciem, quod mille talentis
margaritum ingens opibusque et censibus hastae
addictis animosa Fides mercata pararat.
hoc residet solio pollens Sapientia et omne   875
consilium regni celsa disponit ab aula
tutandique hominis leges sub corde retractat.
in manibus dominae sceptrum non arte politum

862 smragdina *A*ᵃᶜ   865 stillantibus *AE*   870 quarum] *ATS*, quadrum *JE*
873 censibus] *AE*ᵛ, uiribus *TES*   878 dominae] *A²*, domine *A*

sed ligno uiuum uiridi est, quod stirpe reciso
quamuis nullus alat terreni caespitis umor   880
fronde tamen uiret incolumi, tum sanguine tinctis
intertexta rosis candentia lilia miscet
nescia marcenti florem submittere collo.
huius forma fuit sceptri gestamen Aäron
floriferum, sicco quod germina cortice trudens   885
explicuit tenerum spe pubescente decorem
inque nouos subito tumuit uirga arida fetus.
 Reddimus aeternas, indulgentissime doctor,
grates, Christe, tibi meritosque sacramus honores
ore pio; nam cor uitiorum stercore sordet.   890
tu nos corporei latebrosa pericula operti
luctantisque animae uoluisti agnoscere casus.
nouimus ancipites nebuloso in pectore sensus
sudare alternis conflictibus et uariato
pugnarum euentu nunc indole crescere dextra,   895
nunc inclinatis uirtutibus ad iuga uitae
deteriora trahi seseque addicere noxis
turpibus et propriae iacturam ferre salutis.
o quotiens animam uitiorum peste repulsa
sensimus incaluisse deo, quotiens tepefactum   900
caeleste ingenium post gaudia candida taetro
cessisse stomacho! feruent bella horrida, feruent
ossibus inclusa. fremit et discordibus armis
non simplex natura hominis; nam uiscera limo
effigiata premunt animum, contra ille sereno   905
editus adflatu nigrantis carcere cordis
aestuat et sordes arta inter uincla recusat.

---

879 uiridi est quod] *A²*, uiridquod *A* reciso] *AᵖᶜTES*, recisos *Aᵃᶜ*, recisum *E²Y*
891 latebrosa] *A¹*, latebrasa *A* 893 *denuo accedit B* 894 et] ac *B*
895 dextra] dextram *BᵖᶜS* 896 uirtutibus *ABE*, ceruicibus *T*, ceruitibus *S*
902 sthomaco *A* 905 animum] animam *A* 906 *om. B, add. B²*

spiritibus pugnant uariis lux atque tenebrae
distantesque animat duplex substantia uires,
donec praesidio Christus deus adsit et omnes   910
uirtutum gemmas conponat sede piata
atque, ubi peccatum regnauerat, aurea templi
atria constituens texat spectamine morum
ornamenta animae, quibus oblectata decoro
aeternum solio diues Sapientia regnet.   915

Subscriptio: exp. pyschomacia liber III feliciter *B*, finit liber III psychomachia *T*, explicit psychomachia *E*, finit lib. III Bsycomacia *S*

COMMENTARY

TITLE

Most of the manuscripts have an inscription or title along the lines of "Prudentii liber tertius Psychomachia." The same manuscripts cite Prudentius's *Apotheosis* as *Liber unus* and his *Amartigenia* as *Liber secundus*. Scholars have not yet found a wholly satisfying explanation for this arrangement, but the obvious inference is that the three poems were presented as a kind of trilogy. Nevertheless, because paratexts (headings and other materials surrounding a text) are notoriously unstable, there is no guarantee that Prudentius himself ever called the *Psychomachia* a "third book." Even in modern printed books such paratextual material can vary widely from one edition to the next. On the grouping of *Apotheosis*, *Amartigenia*, and *Psychomachia* as a trilogy, see the introduction, pages 24–29.

Other Latin poems with Greek titles include such canonical works as the *Aeneis* and *Metamorphoses*. *Psychomachia* (ψυχομαχία) means "battle in the soul," "battle of the soul," or "battle for the soul." The Greek noun and its cognate verb appear very infrequently in extant literature, and elsewhere the term means "fighting for your life" or "fighting desperately." In his short biographical entry on Prudentius, the fifth-century author Gennadius glosses the title ambiguously as *"De conpugnantia animi"* (*De uiris illustribus* 13), where *animi* could be analyzed as locative or as a subjective or objective genitive.

PRAEFATIO

Prudentius begins his epic with a separate preface presenting Abraham as a figure for the faithful reader. In contrast to earlier Latin poets, Prudentius introduces each of his long hexameter works with a separate preface in a different meter. Vergil, for example, began immediately with "Arma uirumque cano"; Ovid likewise began *Metamorphoses* without a preface: "In noua fert animus mutatas dicere formas / corpora." Rather than jumping straight into the poem, Prudentius includes a preface to show the reader how to approach his allegory of interior conflict. The first paragraph (1–14) introduces Abraham as a model; the second paragraph (15–49) recounts Abraham's rescue of Lot, his meeting of Melchizedek, and the birth of Isaac; the third paragraph (50–68) links the scriptural story with the reader's inner life. Earlier rhetorical prefaces were only loosely linked to what followed, but this preface is a miniature masterpiece that displays a remarkable degree of thematic and verbal coherence.

Abraham was the patriarch, or founder, of the Jewish nation, and Christians frequently interpreted the events of his life as foreshadowing Christ and as significant for their own interactions with God. Prudentius's understanding of Abraham was almost certainly influenced by Ambrose of Milan's treatise *De Abraham*, which was written in the 380s. In particular, the fact that Ambrose had described the patriarch as an allegory for the mind (*mens*) makes him an ideal figure for introducing the *Psychomachia* (*De Abraham* 2.1.1). On Prudentius's use of Ambrose's treatise, see Macklin Smith 1976, 222–33. On Prudentius's use of allegory and the inner conflict between virtue and vice, see the introduction, pages 16–23.

In later manuscripts, the heading "*praefatio*" was added before the first sixty-eight lines. It is not surprising for the preface to appear without a separate heading, since texts were often produced without such an apparatus in antiquity. Indeed, finished texts did not even include punctuation, which readers were expected to add for themselves after acquiring a copy. Even without the heading, the preface is clearly separated from the main text by its meter. The extra space between the margin and the edge of the text in our edition is modeled on the indentation in some manuscripts, including MS *A*, from the sixth century (see fig. 5).

On this preface and the role of the reader in late antique Latin poetry, see Pelttari 2014, 60–61. On Prudentius's reconfiguration of the epic hero, see Amiott 2010. For Claudian's influence on Prudentius's prefaces and their roots in rhetorical practice, see Dorfbauer 2010. On the preface and the faithful reader, see Mastrangelo 2008, 84–93. On the verbal links between the preface and the rest of the poem, see Charlet 2003. On the allegory in general, see Macklin Smith 1976, 206–12. On suspected INTERPOLATION in pr. 41–44 and in pr. 60, see Gnilka 1985.

Meter: iambic trimeter. Prudentius uses the same meter for the preface to *Amartigenia* and for *Perist.* 10. Contemporary Greek panegyrical poets used iambic trimeters for their prefaces, often with a more colloquial tone and with language drawn from comedy. Prudentius's preface is not particularly colloquial, but iambic trimeters do allow a bit more flexibility than dactylic hexameters.

pr. 1–14. Introduction of Abraham and of virtue's struggle in the soul against its enemies. The section is one long sentence in which the main verbs (*suasit*, *dedit*) are delayed until line 10. The first part of the sentence describes the *senex fidelis* with an extended series of modifiers: *uia*, *Abram*, *pater*, *cuius*, *dictus*, and *qui*. In the second part of the sentence, Prudentius layers together successive phrases and subordinate clauses.

pr. 1. Senex fidelis prima credendi uia: with the second word Prudentius indirectly introduces belief, which will be one of the main themes of the poem; then he focuses on the source or pathway for belief. The gerund (*credendi*) presents belief as an activity or way of being, whereas a finite verb might have treated it as a single action.

Ancient poets often claimed that they or their subjects were the first in some field, as for example Verg. *G.* 3.10–11 "Primus ego . . . Aonio rediens deducam uertice Musas" and *Aen.* 1.1–2 "Troiae qui primus ab oris / Italiam . . . uenit," and Claud., *Rapt.* 1, praef. 1 "Inuenta primus secuit qui naue profundum." By beginning with this old patriarch who was first, Prudentius subtly implies that his chosen material is preeminent. On the other hand, *uia* (in apposition to *senex*) presents Abraham as only a means, because Christ will be introduced as the proper object of belief. Because the second phrase echoes *Aen.* 6.97–98 "uia prima salutis / (quod minime reris) Graia pandetur ab urbe," Prudentius links a life of faith to Aeneas's Roman project, as he also does in the first line of the poem itself. We should also note that Abraham was called *senex* in Gen. 24:1, and that Jerome says Abraham was the first person in Genesis called *senex* for two reasons, because this adjective marked his wisdom (*In Esaiam* 2.3.2) and because it was a sign of his blessing (*Tractatus siue homiliae in psalmos* 91.225–27).

pr. 2. Abram: the name follows closely on the previous line; the ENJAMB-MENT creates a pause after the name and avoids a repetitive sequence of end-stopped lines. To be sure, both *Abram* and *pater* are in apposition to *senex*. **beati seminis serus pater:** Abraham fathered Isaac when he was one-hundred years old. Genesis says that the Israelites were descended from Isaac and that he was Abraham's only legitimate son (the Qur'an of course says that Isaac's half-brother Ishmael was Abraham's spiritual heir). For Prudentius, Abraham was the distant ("late") ancestor of Jesus Christ, and he would also have known that Paul referred to all Christians as the offspring of Abraham (Gal. 3:29). Thus, *beati* refers to the abundance of Abraham's offspring promised in Gen. 15:5, although its literal meaning is "blessed."

pr. 3. adiecta cuius nomen auxit syllaba: "whose name an extra syllable lengthened." The line offers a good example of HYPERBATON, i.e., poetic displacement.

pr. 3–4. Abraham's original name was Abram, but it was changed by God in Gen. 17:5, when God promised to make him the father of many nations ("pater multarum gentium"). Indeed, the name Abram means "exalted father," whereas Abraham means "father of many," with "nations" under-stood, as explained by Jerome, *Hebraicae quaestiones in libro geneseos* ad 17:3–5, ed. Paul de Lagarde (CC 72), p. 21. Since Prudentius is writing an allegorical poem deeply concerned with names and language, it makes sense that he pays careful attention to the name of his patriarch.

pr. 4. parenti . . . Deo: "by his father . . . by God." The perfect passive participle frequently takes a dative of agent (A&G §375).

pr. 5. Gen. 22 says that God tested Abraham and asked him to sacrifice his son Isaac; after Abraham obeys, God intervenes at the last minute and provides a ram instead for the offering. **senile pignus:** the child was born late in Abraham's life. The word *pignus* was extended to children "as the guarantee of the reality of a marriage" (*OLD* s.v. 4); in this passage, the original use of *pignus* as a "pledge" or "assurance" is also relevant, because Isaac was a sign of God's covenant with the patriarch (Franchi 2013, 19). **dicauit:** the vocabulary of traditional Roman religion was often used to translate the Jewish scriptures. **uictimae:** dative of purpose, "as a victim."

pr. 6–8. docens . . . quod dulce cordi . . . offerendum: "teaching that what is dear to your heart should be offered." Understand *esse* with the gerundive and *est* with the relative pronoun *quod*.

pr. 6. ad aram: probably should be taken with *offerendum*, despite the separation, because *litare* does not take *ad* + acc. whereas *offero* is frequently construed with *ad*, as in *Apoth.* 610. **quis:** indefinite pronoun = "anyone." Teachers have long been noting this use of *quis*; it is even glossed in MS *F* as *aliquis*. **uelit:** subjunctive from *uolo*.

pr. 7. This line's three parallel phrases offer a basic example of VARIATIO, a frequent figure in Prudentius. **unicum:** Prudentius borrows the adjective directly from Gen. 22:2, where God commands Abraham to take Isaac and sacrifice him: "accipe filium tuum illum unicum quem dilexisti" (*Vetus latina K*). The figure Concordia explains in line 785 that peace should be offered first to God, as pointed out by Jean-Louis Charlet (2003, 246).

pr. 8. libenter: according to 2 Cor. 9:7, "God loves a cheerful giver." **offerendum:** this meaning of *offerre* ("offer as a sacrifice") seems to have been used in antiquity primarily in Christian circles. **credito:** dative with *deo*; Prudentius continues with the theme of belief.

pr. 9–14. Prudentius comes now to the moral battle that will be the main topic of his poem. On the inner conflict between virtue and vice, see the introduction, pages 16–19.

pr. 9. pugnare: the same verb is used in line 22 (*pugnatura*) of the main poem, when *Fides* comes out to begin the battle. **nosmet:** the suffix -*met* makes *nos* more emphatic. The poet includes himself and the reader in this story that began with Abram. This crucial move informs his typological interpretations and calls the reader to play an active part in response to the poem. **profanis gentibus:** the gentiles are read TROPOLOGICALLY as figures for the vices that individuals must confront.

pr. 10. Note the ALLITERATION and FIGURA ETYMOLOGICA. **suasit:** = *persuasit*. In poetry a simplex form of the verb can be used in place of a compound. **suasor:** Prudentius was fond of agent nouns ending in -*tor* (-*sor*); he uses 134 such words in his poems, as opposed to only 51 in Vergil (Lavarenne 1933b, §1136–42).

exemplum: on the importance of historical examples in Roman culture, see Roller 2018. On the related question of typological interpretation, see page 22 in the introduction and below on pr. 50–51.

pr. 11. ante: take with *quam* in line 13. **prolem coniugalem:** "legitimate offspring." Jews and Christians have said that Isaac was Abraham's legitimate heir, and not Ishmael. **gignere:** an infinitive of implied indirect speech to explain the content of *exemplum*.

pr. 12. matre uirtute: in the exegetical tradition that Prudentius alludes to here, Abraham's wife Sarah was read as an allegorical figure for virtue (Ambrose, *De Abraham* 2.10.73).

pr. 13. strage multa: on violence in *Psychomachia*, see below on lines 30–35.

pr. 14. portenta: Prudentius uses the same word below in line 20. **seruientis:** that sin enslaves was a common theme in Christian circles, as in Jesus's saying from John 8:34 "omnis qui facit peccatum seruus est peccati" (*Vetus latina*). **uicerit:** perfect subjunctive in primary sequence, because the lesson (*exemplum dedit*) is current and not outdated (A&G §485a).

pr. 15–49. The story of Abraham, Lot, and Melchizedek is combined with the story of Abraham being visited by three angels. Gen. 14 tells how Abraham's nephew Lot was captured by enemy kings and how Abraham rescued Lot with an army of 318 men; when he was returning from the battle, Abraham was met by a shadowy figure called Melchizedek, king of Salem and priest of God most high. Melchizedek blessed Abraham, and Abraham gave him a tenth of the spoils. Then, Gen. 18 tells that three mysterious visitors came to Abraham and foretold that his wife Sarah would bear a son in their old age. Although Sarah was ninety years old and laughed at their message, she miraculously gave birth to Isaac.

As Amiott 2010 explains, Prudentius crosses a Biblical story with the expectations of epic poetry: i.e., he writes of Abraham but tells a story of arms and a man, of a hero who conquers his enemies and founds a people. For a modern study of Sarah's laughter, see Conybeare 2013, along with the further comments in Conybeare 2018.

pr. 16. Loth: accusative. Like many Hebrew names it is indeclinable in Latin. **inmorantem**: the verb implies that Sodom was not Lot's real home, and it takes the dative case, as do many other compounds verbs (A&G §370). **criminosis urbibus**: as today Sodom and Gomorrah were bywords for sin and judgment.

pr. 17. aduena: note that Abraham was told that his descendants would also be foreigners (Gen. 15.13) and that Christians are addressed as strangers and foreigners in 1 Pet. 2:11, where the precise word *aduena* was used in *Vetus latina* translations (*C, T*) and in the Vulgate. **fouebat**: the verb is used of frequenting or inhabiting a particular place, as noted by Servius, *Ad Aen.* 4.193 ("ueteres *fouere* pro *diu incolere* et *inhabitare* dixerunt"). See further *TLL* s.v. *foueo* I.4 = 6.1.1220.10–28 (Vollmer).

pr. 19. sinistris excitatus nuntiis: dative of agent, "roused by inauspicious messengers." Like so many other heroes, Abraham had to wake from a world of sleep and dreams in order to confront and conquer harsh reality. On such awakenings in the context of heroic narratives, see Amiott 2010, 203–4.

pr. 20. audit: the historical present tense for vividness. **sorte . . . bellica**: "by the chance of war." The phrase is echoed by *sub sorte duelli* in line 21 of the main poem.

pr. 21. barbarorum: glossed as *gentilium* in MS *L*, either to suggest that Prudentius was not hostile to barbarians or to interpret the real opponents as non-Christians. But Prudentius insults contemporary barbarians elsewhere (*Apoth.* 216, *Symm.* 2.816–17, etc.); he also links the Vices and barbarians below in lines 133 and 753. Shanzer interprets these references to barbarians and to Abraham's rescue of Lot as echoes of the unrest caused by Alaric around the year 408. She concludes (1989, 357–62) that the poem was written sometime after the first siege of Rome in 408 but before Alaric's sack of the city in 410 (see the introduction, page 24).

pr. 22. armat: an echo and spiritual reconfiguration of the famous first word of the *Aeneid* (Amiott 2010, 196). The change from noun to verb is nicely emblematic of Prudentius's transformation of Latin epic. Catherine Ware (2015) finds a similar oblique reference to Vergil's *arma* in Claudian's panegyric on the fourth consulship of Honorius and cites other comparable allusions to the beginning of the *Aeneid*.

pr. 22. terque senos: thrice six = *duodeuiginti*. On the numerology, see pr. 56–58.

pr. 23. pergant ut: of ANASTROPHE Prudentius is fond. **hostis terga euntis caedere**: *caedere* is an infinitive of purpose and *hostis* is a collective singular ("the enemy"), both of which occur in classical authors (A&G §460c and *OLD* s.v. *hostis* 2b).

pr. 24. gaza: the word is apparently Persian in origin and refers to treasures of every kind, just as Prudentius's contemporary Servius explained in his commentary on *Aen.* 1.119.

pr. 24. triumfus: this is the normal spelling in MSS *A* and *B*. The post-Carolingian manuscripts changed such spellings to *triumphus*, etc. The unclassical spelling was not restored until Johannes Bergman's modern and scientific edition was published in 1926. Regarding the mistake in MSS *E* and *S*, note that the same two manuscripts together transmit *Apoth.* 160, which is absent from *A*, *B*, and *T*.

pr. 26. quin is here an emphatic adv. ("yes," "indeed"). Elsewhere, *quin* is often used as a conjunction to introduce negative subordinate clauses with the subjunctive (A&G §558–59).

pr. 26. plenus deo: this recalls Lucan's description of Cato the Younger as "deo plenus" (*Bellum ciuile* 9.564), so that Abraham can be linked to a Roman hero.

But the phrase has a backstory even for Lucan. The rhetorician Seneca the Elder (*Suasoriae* 3.5–7) reports that the phrase *plena deo* was popular among the in-crowd and that Ovid used it in open imitation of Vergil. However, since the phrase is not found in the transmitted text of Vergil, we can only hypothesize about its origin, on which see Horsfall 2013, 627–29.

pr. 27. graues: passive in meaning, "weighed down by" or "heavy with." Other Latin adjectives with both active and passive meanings include *facilis*, *gratus*, and *tristis*.

pr. 28–29. Abraham moves from striking to crushing and from breaking to freeing in two evenly balanced lines. A gloss in MS *L* notes that the lines are an example of HYPOZEUXIS, a figure in which a closely connected series of clauses each has its own verb. Each line is also a good example of CHIASMUS.

pr. 30–31. A list of the retrieved spoils in apposition to *rapina* and in ASYN-DETON. Prudentius had a flair for VARIATIO and ACCUMULATIO. Note the careful ordering of the list; its inclusion of humans, animals, and material objects; and the avoidance of similar word endings.

pr. 31. greges equarum uasa: while most of the tradition gives *greges*, MS *A* has *oues* here. The variant is easy to explain because Gen. 13:5 mentions Lot's *greges ouium*. The variant would have arisen as a correction of Prudentius's *greges equarum*, which almost certainly derives from an early mistranslation of the Hebrew word for *substantia* that is attested in early Latin translations of three verses in the closely related Gen. 14 (for the details, see Gnilka 1988a). As Gnilka also explains, *equarum* should not be taken with *uasa* because the latter was not used of a horse's equipment.

pr. 32. nexibus was displaced in several manuscripts by *uinculis*, which would originally have been an explanatory gloss written by a scribe above the line or in the margin.

pr. 33. adtrita bacis colla: "(his) neck worn down by the links (of chain)." Poets often used *colla* in the plural with singular meaning. This use of *baca* with a transferred meaning does not appear in earlier extant Latin literature.

pr. 34. dissipator: in extant Latin the word appears predominantly in Christian authors and only beginning in the fourth century. The illustration for this scene in MS *U* offers a remarkably complex, layered depiction of Abraham's defeat of the kings (the image is included on the cover).

pr. 35. recepta prole fratris inclytus: "renowned for taking back his brother's offspring." Lot was Abraham's nephew. The ablative is causal. Like the gerundive, the perfect passive participle is sometimes used in place of a verbal noun, in what is called the *ab urbe condita* construction (A&G §497); in this case, *recepta* indicates verbal aspect rather than time. *Inclytus*, from the same root as the Greek *kléos* ("fame," "glory") clearly portrays Abraham as an epic hero. Compare Servius's note on *Aen.* 6.781 "INCLITA graecum est: nam *clyton* gloriosum dicunt."

pr. 36. ne quam: equivalent to "ne aliquam." The indefinite pronoun *quis* is found after *si, nisi, num,* and *ne* (A&G §310). **fidelis sanguinis prosapiam**: recalls pr. 1–2. Cicero already cited *prosapia* ("offspring") as an archaic word (*Timaeus* 11.39).

pr. 36–37. prosapiam / uis pessimorum possideret principum: ALLITERATION.

pr. 38–44. Abraham meets the mysterious figure of Melchizedek during his return from rescuing Lot. The meeting is described in Gen. 14:17–24 and explained in Heb. 7:1–10.

pr. 38. recentem caede de tanta uirum: the wording recalls Heb. 7:1, which is translated in the *Vetus latina* versions and in the *Vulgate* as "Melchisedech ... qui obuiauit Abrahae regresso a caede regum." **uirum**: probably accusative, because Abraham is a manly hero, also because of the balanced phrasing with *recentem* and contrast with *sacerdos,* not to mention the avoidance of repetition with *principum* in the previous line. If not accusative, *uirum* is genitive like *regum* in Heb. 7:1.

pr. 39. ferculis caelestibus: "heavenly dishes," with the same METONYMIC use of "dish" for "food" as is common in English. This food is interpreted as a figure for the eucharist in pr. 61.

pr. 40. Gen. 14:18 says that Melchizedek was both a priest and a king. **rex et:** the conjunction is postponed (ANASTROPHE). **praepotens:** the prefix denotes precedence, "eminently powerful."

pr. 41–42. These two verses are not in MS *A,* and a number of scholars including Heinsius and Bergman have thought they were INTERPOLATED. But the scribe of *A* was careless and fourteen times skipped a line or lines, once every 440 verses (Cunningham 1966, xxi). In several of these cases there is very good reason to think that the mistake was only mechanical and that it was caused when the scribe's eye jumped from one line to another, what is known as *saut du même au même.* Apart from their absence from MS *A,* the main argument against these lines is that they are repetitive with pr. 43–44. Christian Gnilka solved that problem by deleting pr. 43–44 (1985, 191–203), and he concluded that this passage is solid evidence of large-scale INTERPOLATION in the text at a very early date. But Prudentius often varies a single idea in successive lines, and the echo with *ineffabili* in pr. 60 matches the poet's practice in the rest of the preface. On the doublets between the second and third paragraphs of the preface, see the notes below, and compare especially the number 318 in pr. 22 and pr. 57, the word *mox* in pr. 45 and pr. 59, *trinitas* in pr. 45 and pr. 63, and *herede* in pr. 49 and pr. 68. On the exuberance of PLEONASM in Prudentius, see Rivero García 1996, 219–20 and Lavarenne 1933b, §1547–59 and 1569–77.

pr. 41. fonte inenarrabili: ablative of source (A&G §403). Melchizedek's origin is presented as a mystery for interpretation. Heb. 7:3 said he was "without father or mother or genealogy, and has neither beginning of days nor end of life, but resembling the Son of God he continues a priest for ever."

In pr. 59–63, Prudentius expands on the resemblance to the mysterious origins of Christ. For the adjective, compare Vergil's description of Aeneas's shield as a "non enarrabile textum" (*Aen.* 8.625). Whereas Vergil uses an inexhaustibility topos to reflect the wonder of Aeneas's shield, Prudentius uses allegory to say something that cannot be said. On his engagement with apophatic theology in *Psychomachia*, see Mastrangelo 2008, 82–120.

pr. 42. secreta modifies *origo*.

pr. 43. Melchisedec: this is the spelling of MS *A*. **qua stirpe quis maioribus:** indirect questions dependent on *ignotus*. *Quis* is a poetic form for *quibus*, and *esset* must be understood.

pr. 44. tantum: "only." The use of *tantum* as an adverb with this meaning is not uncommon.

pr. 45–49. Abraham is visited by three angels, and his aged wife Sarah conceives Isaac. For the story see Gen. 18.

pr. 45. triformis angelorum trinitas: the Genesis account is ambiguous about the visitors. They are referred to both as the Lord and as three men. Tertullian taught that Christ himself had appeared with the angels (*De carne Christi* 6 and *Aduersus Marcion* 3.9.6). Ambrose understood the visitors as the trinity (*De Abraham* 1.5.33).

Triformis was commonly used of mythological figures like Diana and Geryon. Prudentius also used this adjective in reference to the trinity at *Perist.* 6.142, but it was more frequent among his Christian contemporaries in criticisms of unorthodox theology, for example in Filastrius Brixiensis, *Diuersarum hereseon liber* 93 and Augustine, *De haeresibus* 74.

pr. 46. mapalia: "huts," a Punic word (*TLL* s.v. 8.0.369.36–41 [J. B. Hofmann]) that refers properly to the tents of nomads; the word suits Abraham because he was a nomad and because Punic was a Semitic language.

pr. 48. exsanguis: probably because Sarah had passed menopause (Gen. 18:11), which made the birth miraculous. But the adjective does not seem to have been used in this way elsewhere, and she could just be pale from the shock.

pr. 49. cachinni: *paenitens* takes an objective genitive denoting what Sarah regrets (A&G §349). Note the balance and VARIATION in *herede . . . cachinni*.

pr. 50–68. Prudentius offers a figural interpretation of Abraham's story that applies to "us," and he calls "our" soul to vigilance and to liberate the body so that Christ will come and the soul will produce its proper offspring.

pr. 50–51. ad figuram praenotata est linea . . . resculpat: *figura* was a translation of the Greek *typos* and a technical term of allegorical interpretation. Typology or figural allegory reads a given story as communicating a secondary message but also as being true in itself. Whereas with other allegories the surface meaning has to be looked through, early Christian interpreters usually insisted that allegorical interpretations of Abraham's life, for example, did not discredit the narrative's historical value. Auerbach (1959) established the importance of figural interpretation in late antiquity; he traced the history of the word *figura* and the reception of Paul's influential allegorical interpretations from Gal. 4:21–31 and elsewhere. Also, the verb *praenotare* was used from the second century on in reference to prophecies, signs, and types. For Prudentius's figural interpretations, compare *Am.* praef. 32 (*figura*) and especially 25–26 "Ergo ex futuris prisca coepit fabula / factoque primo res notata est ultima." On Prudentius as a typological poet, see the helpful discussion in Macklin Smith 1976, 169–94, along with Mastrangelo 2008, 84–120 and Pelttari 2014, 94–95.

In addition to typology, Prudentius imagines life as a process of artistic creativity, or even poetic composition. Indeed, the word *figura* could suggest a painting or sculpture, as does *resculpat*; and *linea* can mean "outline" (*OLD* s.v. 3b). But *praenoto* usually refers to writing, and *linea* may suggest *uersus*. In fact, *linea* apparently does refer to lines of writing in Tertullian (although not elsewhere so far as I know): "in lineis desuper notabuntur" (*Adv. Valent.* 6.2; translated by Jean-Claude Fredouille in *SC* 280 as "il sera noté au-dessus, entre les lignes"). On "dynamic writing" in Prudentius, see Ross 1995. Whatever the precise meaning of *linea*, our life is made into an artistic process, and the reader is encouraged to complete the sketch first begun by Abraham and then continued by the poet.

pr. 51. pede: the word is glossed in MS *L* as *tramite* ("path") and in MS *U* as *sensu* ("sense" or "interpretation"), which refers to a right interpretation of the typological forerunner. Literally, *recto . . . pede* refers to the sure-footedness with which one should follow the path. Metapoetically, *pede* can be read of the iambic feet of the preface.

pr. 52–58. A compound indirect statement dependent on the verb of saying or showing implied in pr. 50–51. Abraham's battle is now explained as representing an inner conflict.

pr. 52. uigilandum in armis: supply *esse*; and compare line 41 where Pudicitia shines "*in armis*" and Eph. 6:11–17 where Paul describes the weapons of faith.

pr. 53. corporis: a number of the manuscripts have *pectoris*, a typical corruption: the mistake was influenced by *pectorum* in the preceding line.

pr. 54. quae capta . . . seruiat: the verb is subjunctive in a subordinate clause in indirect speech. Prudentius recalls *captum . . . seruire* from pr. 20–21. Although he says that the body is enslaved to desire, he does not say that it is inherently evil. On views of the body in late antiquity, see Brown 2008 and Miller 2009, along with the note below on line 906.

pr. 55. liberandam recalls *liberat* above in pr. 29.

pr. 55–56. domi . . . uernularum: *uernulae* are properly slaves born in the home, and Prudentius emphasizes that help is already available within.

pr. 56–58. the number 318 stands for Christ because in Greek the number is written TIH: the *tau* represents the cross, while *iota* and *eta* are the first two letters of the name Jesus ('Ιησοῦς). This numerical interpretation was widespread, beginning perhaps with Ps. Barnabas, *Epist.* 9.8; it is explained in Ambrose, *De Abraham* 1.3.15 and assumed in 2.7.42; for further references, see Charlet 2003, 242–43n28.

pr. 56. uernularum: genitive of specification (A&G §349d). The word recalls *uernulas* (pr. 22).

pr. 57–58. quid … possint: an indirect question dependent on *nouerimus*; *trecenti* is the subject. For *possum* with an internal accusative rather than an infinitive, see *OLD* s.v. *possum* 8.

pr. 58. figura … mystica: that Christ is the mystical meaning of the number is implicit in the next line.

pr. 59–63. The arrival of Christ as true priest and within the individual.

pr. 59. mox: the repetition of the adverb used at pr. 45 clearly signals the coherence of figure and interpretation. **sacerdos** recalls *sacerdos* (Melchizedek) in lines pr. 39 and pr. 40. **uerus:** Christ was often described as the fulfillment or true version of a type from the Hebrew scriptures.

pr. 60. parente natus alto et ineffabili: the variant line *parente inenarrabili a(t)que uno satus* was a scribe's unnecessary attempt to avoid irregularity in the fourth foot (see Charlet 2003, 243n30). The final syllable of *alto* is shortened in HIATUS, and the following long syllable is resolved into two shorts to make a tribrach (a foot consisting of three short syllables): *altŏ ĕt ĭneffabili*. Even if *Perist.* 10.925 is not exactly analogous, the HIATUS is defensible here because it is effective: the metrical hesitation in the line figures the ineffability of God. Indeed, the phrase was reused as the first line of the apparently composite hymn "Alto et ineffabili" that was included in two manuscripts at the end of the Life of Ciaran of Clonmacnoise (*Analecta hymnica medii aeui* [Leipzig: Reisland, 1886–1955], vol. 51, p. 325).

MS *S* provides a good example of how such mistakes creep in. First, the variant line was added directly into the text after pr. 60; then either the same scribe or a later reader saw that both lines could not stand and expunged the second; he or she could have erased the first line just as easily. The erasure is clearly visible in the open and online digital facsimile of the manuscript.

ineffabili: for this allegorical poem that will abound in doublets, Prudentius explains the story of Melchizedek by echoing *inenarrabili* from pr. 41. Note that *ineffabili* must be a playful allusion to the metrical irregularity of the HIATUS in the phrase *alto et*.

pr. 61. cibum: a clear reference to the eucharist as the spiritual food offered to Christians by Christ. **uictoribus:** echoed by *uictrix legio* in line 36 below.

pr. 62. paruam ... casam: according to Genesis Abraham was nomadic and lived in a tent; his alternative lifestyle was already suggested by the exotic *mapalia* in pr. 46. A *casa* was a small and poor dwelling, in contrast to a *domus* or *uilla*, which partially explains why *casa* became the normal word for "house" in both Spanish and Italian.

pr. 63. trinitatis recalls *trinitas* in pr. 45.

pr. 64–68. The Spirit and soul produce their offspring.

pr. 64. spiritus refers to the Holy Spirit as the second person of the trinity rather than to a part of the individual soul. The variant *spiritibus* in MSS *A* and *E* was a simple mistake influenced by *conplexibus*. Because errors in common are the only definite evidence of manuscript affiliation, this mistake is valuable as being demonstrative of the close relationship between *A* and *E*.

pr. 65. pie recalls *pium* in pr. 7.

pr. 67. sera puns on the name of Sarah and recalls *serus* from pr. 2. **dotem** recalls *pignus* in pr. 5 and Abraham's child as the seal of God's covenant. Whether the offspring is peace or eternal life or wisdom or virtue, it marks the salvation of the individual just as the dowry guaranteed a woman's security in her marriage.

pr. 68. herede digno patris: *herede* recalls the same word in pr. 49. The adjective *dignus* sometimes takes the genitive case. The father is God the Father, the first person of the trinity. The heir of the soul has been identified variously as peace or wisdom. Thus, Charlet links this passage to line 805 and concludes that peace is the reward after the battle, just as Solomon reigned in peace after his father's battles (2003, 247–48). Otherwise, the heir is Sapientia, who comes to reign at the end of the poem (see the note on line 915).

inplebit domum: the soul is to fill its home as the reader follows and lives out the allegory. The final word of the preface is thematic, and Marc Mastrangelo (2008, 16–17) connects it to Aeneas's journey to his new home in Italy: like Aeneas, the Christian reader is on an epic journey to find his true home.

Some manuscripts have *inpleuit*, but that is a simple error arising from pronunciation. *Inplebit* is clearly correct because the soul (of the reader) will attain virtue in the future (as the poem is being read).

PROEM (1-20)

Prudentius invokes Christ as God with the Father and as "our king" (1-4); he asks Christ to explain how the mind and virtue can win their internal battle against vice (5-11); and he says that victory is at hand if you recognize the appearances of virtue and vice (11-20). Epic poems in the ancient tradition typically begin with a proem that includes an invocation and an explanation of the theme of the poem. By including a proem even after his preface, Prudentius continues in that tradition.

1. Christe, graues hominum semper miserate labores: the poet rewrites Aeneas's prayer to Apollo in the Sibyl's cave: "Phoebe, grauis Troiae semper miserate labores" (*Aen.* 6.56). This direct invocation of the *Aeneid* indicates Prudentius's intention to imitate Vergil. The intertext is easily recognized and was already quoted in MS *F* (fol. 56v): "Virgilii est iste uersus, qui ait 'Phoebe graues [etc.] . . . .'" Beyond the verbal borrowing, the Vergilian scene is evoked by the word *antro* in line 6. The borrowing suggests a spiritual reading of book 6 of the *Aeneid*, with its description of the hero's journey into the underworld and his exploration of the fate of souls; it also opens an epic frame onto the following battles described. By invoking a different god and expanding the scope of the divinity's mercy from a single people (*Troiae*) to humans in general (*hominum*), Prudentius sets up a contrast with the *Aeneid*, but otherwise the prayer is thoroughly Vergilian. Macklin Smith reads the allusion as an attack on Vergil (1976, 271-76); for essentially inclusive interpretations, see Mastrangelo 2008, 15-20 and Pelttari 2014, 154-57.

Paulinus of Nola used the same verse in *Natalicia* 6.260 = Hartel *Carm.* 18: "Felix sancte, meos semper miserate labores" (the poem was presented in January 400). The rustic cowherd in that poem prays to the saint. An allusion in one direction or the other makes no sense here, but it seems possible enough that Paulinus's prayer could have suggested to Prudentius the potential of *Aen.* 6.56.

miserate: this perfect passive participle of a deponent verb takes a direct object. Whether by chance or not, there is an echo with the opening of Claudian's *Gigantomachia*: "Terra parens quondam . . . / . . . miserata dolores" (1–2). On the possibility of a dialogue between these two poems, see below on 323–39.

2. qui patria uirtute cluis propriaque sed una: "you who are renowned because of the father's virtue and because of your own, but [they are] one." The relative clause in this line and the parenthesis in lines 3–4 slow down the invocation; all three lines take up the complexity of the trinity, in which the Father, the Son, and the Spirit are three persons but one God. As Macklin Smith says, "These doctrinal verses are *meant* to retard the invocation, meant to intrude by their very importance" (1976, 73). The developing doctrine of the trinity was central to the Christian theological disputes of the fourth century, and Prudentius deals with the nature of God at length elsewhere and especially in *Apotheosis*.

Cluo is cognate with the Greek *kleos* and takes an ablative of cause (A&G §404); for the heroic importance of this root, see above on pr. 35.

Thomson translated *uirtute* as "power," because the word is ambiguous and covers strength just as much as moral excellence; the importance of this ambiguity in the *Psychomachia* is discussed by Nugent (1985, 88).

The adjective *proprius* was sometimes used like a possessive adjective, as it is here and in line 427.

3. namque was common in prayers to explain the choice of divinity, as shown by Austin on *Aen.* 1.65 (1971, 46). **de nomine utroque:** MSS *T* and *Y* have *trino*, an obvious attempt on the part of a scribe to clarify what Prudentius does not say here, that his God has three names and not just two.

4. quia tu deus ex patre: Christ was described as "born from God" in the Nicene Creed, a formal statement of faith ratified by an ecumenical council of churches in 325 and propagated with slight revisions by the First Council of Constantinople in 381 C.E. This phrase is a nice example of how Prudentius includes in his epic poem echoes of other genres and conversations. The extant Latin translations of the Nicene Creed (the relevant phrase appears as "ex patre" and "de patre") are now accessible in Kinzig 2017, 1:294–335 and 1:519–52.

5. Prudentius invokes Christ instead of the Muse and asks him to discuss the following questions. On Juvencus's comparable invocation of the Holy Spirit, see Pollmann 2013, 318; on invocations in Paulinus, see Witke 1971, 75–83. **dissere:** the verb signals a didactic intent because a *dissertatio* was a (spoken) presentation from a rhetor or a teacher, and the verb was hardly used in poetry until the fourth century. Because the proem is a highly charged poetic space, the choice of how to invoke the Muse is usually significant, and here the request recalls *De rerum natura* 1.54–55 "Nam tibi de summa caeli ratione deumque / *disserere* incipiam, et rerum primordia pandam." This link was made by Bergman (1897, 1), but no one has yet offered a full study of the poem in relation to Lucretius; on Prudentius's use of Lucretius in general, see the introduction, page 14, note 9.

noster: Prudentius imagines a Christian audience who shares his king; thus, he engages with his persona in a fictive performance (see below on lines 888–915). **quo milite:** the first of a series of indirect questions, a common device in epic proems. **culpas:** "faults." The noun can mean "blame" and "guilt" (subjective) or "wrongdoing" (objective), and sometimes "the plural of abstract nouns denotes *occasions* or *instances* of the quality" (A&G §99c). These *culpae* could be personified, as they definitely are in lines 304, 683, and 817.

6. mens armata: the Pauline Letter to the Ephesians uses the same image of spiritual armor: "Induite uos arma Dei ut possitis stare aduersus insidias diaboli" (6:11; Vulgate). Lucretius equated *mens* and *animus* (*De rerum natura* 3.94), as noted by Servius in his commentary on *Aen.* 6.11. Prudentius uses a variety of words to refer to the mind and the soul and to their parts and capacities; these include *anima, animus, cor, flatus, halitus, mens, pectus, sensus,* and *spiritus*; for references, see Gnilka 1963, 11.

queat: subjunctive in an indirect question. **nostri de pectoris antro:** the action of the poem will be internal, within the individual human being. The cave of the heart recalls the cave of the Sibyl in *Aen.* 6.77; Prudentius transcribes Aeneas's physical journey to the underworld onto a spiritual battlefield (Mastrangelo 2008, 18–19). See also the note on line 774.

7. turbatis sensibus: *sensus* could describe the faculty of sensation (hearing, for example) or the effect of the sensation (the sound heard) and so be interpreted "interpretation" or "meaning." For the uses of *sensus* in this poem, see below on lines 728, 759, 841, and 893. Just as meanings and faculties are joined in the mind, they can be confused in poetry to create the sensation of depth.

8. seditio: glossed in MS *L* as "discordia," which will be the last of the Vices defeated in the poem. *Seditio* may also allude to Vergil's famous simile of the crowd ruled by an orator: "ac ueluti magno in populo cum saepe coorta est / *seditio* saeuitque animis ignobile uulgus" (*Aen.* 1.148–49).

morborum rixa: "the quarreling of the vices." In his philosophy, Cicero used *morbus* of sicknesses of the mind, for example at *De finibus* 1.18.59 (*animi morbi*); but in *Tusculanae disputationes* 3.4, the suggestion is made that *perturbatio* is better than *morbus* as a translation for the Greek *pathos*. For the choice of the word *rixa*, compare James 4:1 in the old Latin translation of scripture that was common in Spain and likely used by Prudentius: "unde bella, unde *rixae* in uobis? nonne de uoluntantibus uestris quae militant in membris uestris et sunt uobis suauissima?" (*S*).

9. quod . . . praesidium: a second indirect question dependent on *dissere*.
pro libertate tuenda: the preposition introduces a purpose construction with the gerundive replacing a gerund (A&G §503).

10. furiis: for the description of Vices as Furies, compare Lactantius, *Epitome diuinarum institutionum* 61.1: "Three desires exist, or I could call them three Furies, that arouse such great disturbances within human minds and that force them to err so much that they do not allow any concern for reputation or for danger: anger (*ira*), which seeks vengeance; avarice (*auaritia*), which desires wealth; and sexual desire (*libido*), which wants pleasure." Prudentius seems to have been influenced by Lactantius's description of the Vices as Furies, as pointed out by Lühken (2002, 50–54). Lühken details the Vergilian language used by Prudentius to describe precisely Libido, Ira, and Auaritia as Furies. For the most relevant allusions, see below on lines 96, 130, and 551–63.

Rhyming the syllable before the CAESURA with the end of the hexameter (*furiis . . . mixtis*) creates what's called a Leonine verse, a feature that became more prominent in the Middle Ages. By Lavarenne's count, *Psychomachia* has 109 such verses, and another 6 with alternation only of long and short vowels, -$\bar{i}$ / -$\breve{i}$ and -$\bar{e}$ / -$\breve{e}$ (1933a, §283). For such rhymes in previous poetry, see Wilkinson 1963, 32–34.

11. obsistat: takes the dative case (*furiis*), as do many other compound verbs (A&G §367 and §370). **meliore manu:** this collocation appears elsewhere in extant Latin poetry only in Claudian's *Laus Serenae* (= *Carm. min.* 30) 205a, where it stands at the same position in the line; Claudian also wrote *meliora manu* at *Get.* 268.

11–17. Prudentius explains that he calls on Christ because he has provided help for his followers.

11. bone ductor: Christ is invoked as a general, as well as a teacher and a savior.

13. The four-word line is weighty and memorable; lines 256, 261, 354, 568, and 888 are also composed of only four words. **Christicolas:** the word was used by Christian poets beginning around the end of the fourth century; *Christĭānus* did not fit into dactylic hexameters.

15. depugnare: compare Aeneas's mission to spare the humble and overcome the proud ("Parcere subiectis et debellare superbos," *Aen.* 6.853), which finds another echo in line 287.

16–17. quibus . . . dimicet . . . uincat: a relative clause of purpose. Compare Paulinus of Nola's description of Felix in intense prayer: "intusque forisque / dimicat" (*Natalicia* 4.208–9 = Hartel *Carm.* 15). The verb is not common in poetry, and Prudentius may have been influenced by Paulinus's description of an interior struggle. More speculative evidence for a link between the two poems can be found in the note on line 715 with a half-line from Ovid in common between *Psychomachia* and line 232 of Paulinus's poem. **ad ludibria cordis obpugnanda**: "to fight against the reproaches of the heart."

17. tibi … tibi: the repetition emphasizes the personal connection with Christ.

18–20. A rational method of winning is available, and the appearances of the virtues are at hand.

In addition to the importance of these lines for understanding Prudentius's creation of allegory, the emphasis on being able to see and note the material has led some readers to think that Prudentius had an illustrated copy of the poem in mind. The suggestion can be found already in the glosses in the Weitz tradition (O'Sullivan 2004, 170–71), for example in the gloss on line 18 written neatly in the right-hand margin of MS *U* (fig. 6): "Contra inuicem posita sunt, et repugnantia uitia, et expugnantes uirtutes. unde conicitur, uelut pictis historiis omne carmen ab auctore fuisse distinctum." (They are set against each other, both the vices resisting and the conquering virtues. And so, it is suggested that the whole poem was set out by the author, like in painted stories.) To complicate matters, a couple of manuscripts in the Weitz tradition do not include the words *ab auctore* (O'Sullivan 2004, 170), maybe because the idea was too controversial. Whether or not Bergman remembered these glosses, he hypothesized that Prudentius might have commissioned illustrations for the poem: "Verisimile videtur Prudentium Psychomachiam suam figuris pictis illustrandam curavisse vel ad picturas quasdam, publice notas, spectavisse ut in Dittochaeo sine dubio fit. Facile tamen concedo nihil certi de hac re ex verbis antecedentibus colligi posse" (1897, 4). On the illustrated manuscripts of the *Psychomachia*, see the introduction, pages 24–26 and 30–31.

19. conluctantia contra: "fighting back."

20. uiribus infestis: "with hostile strength." **liceat**: present subjunctive in the protasis of a future less vivid condition (A&G §516). **portenta**: the word can mean "monsters" or "fictions"; its primary use here is as a synonym for *uitia*. Prudentius used the same word in reference to terrors in the heart at pr. 14, and of terrors in dreams at *Cath.* 6.138. **notare**: the *Psychomachia*

FIGURE 6. Lines 1–20, with capital *chi*, interlinear glosses, marginal annotations, and the confrontation between Fides and Veterum cultura deorum. The author portrait (fig. 1) has bled through from the other side of the page. MS *U*, p. 68.
Photograph courtesy Codices Electronici AG, http://www.e-codices.ch.

promises the ability to recognize and represent the realities that exist within the human soul. On Stoic ideas of language and for the allegory of the *Psychomachia* as an attempt to map reality, see Bardzell 2009, 32–52.

FIDES VS. VETERUM CULTURA DEORUM (21–39)

The story begins with the struggle between Fides and Veterum cultura deorum, partly because faith is essential and partly to dismiss old religious practices. Augustine, among other contemporary Christians, described a great conflict between Christianity and traditional religions; most notably, his *De ciuitate dei* was a thoroughgoing demolition of the traditional Roman worldview. On the recent political and cultural ascendancy of Christianity within the Roman Empire, see the introduction, pages 10–11.

Fides dispatches her opponent quickly and without drama. This short scene sets the stage for the longer battles to come, and the swift pace of the narrative marks the easy victory of Fides. Note that Fides reappears with Concordia at the end of the poem (715–887).

Fides was fundamental to Roman religion and practice long before Christians developed their own ideas of faith. A temple for Fides was established on the Palatine Hill in Rome by the granddaughter of Aeneas according to the Hellenistic Greek historian Agathokles of Kyzikos (*FGrH* 472). Livy says that worship of Fides was introduced to Rome by Numa (1.21.4). Evidence of her cult in Rome survives from the third century B.C.E. on, and we hear from Tertullian that she was still worshipped in Rome in his day (*Apol.* 24.5). On Fides in Prudentius and his sources, see Stabryła 2006. On Fides as a figure in Silius Italicus and in religion of the imperial period, see Liebeschuetz 1979, 176–79. For a review of the evidence on Fides in Roman and Christian sources, see Becker 1969.

The illustrations in MSS *U* (fig. 6) and *E* (fig. 7) pick up on several aspects of the old religion: sacred fire, statuary, and animal sacrifice. In contrast to the crowded page of MS *E*, note the clean look of MS *B* (fig. 8), which is broken only by punctuation before line 29.

21. Prima: the first word of the narrative makes it clear that Prudentius's heroes are women, a significant departure from classical epic. **petit:** the

Figure 7. Lines 2–22, with illustration of the conflict between Fides and Veterum cultura deorum. MS *E*, fol. 122v. *Leiden University Libraries.*

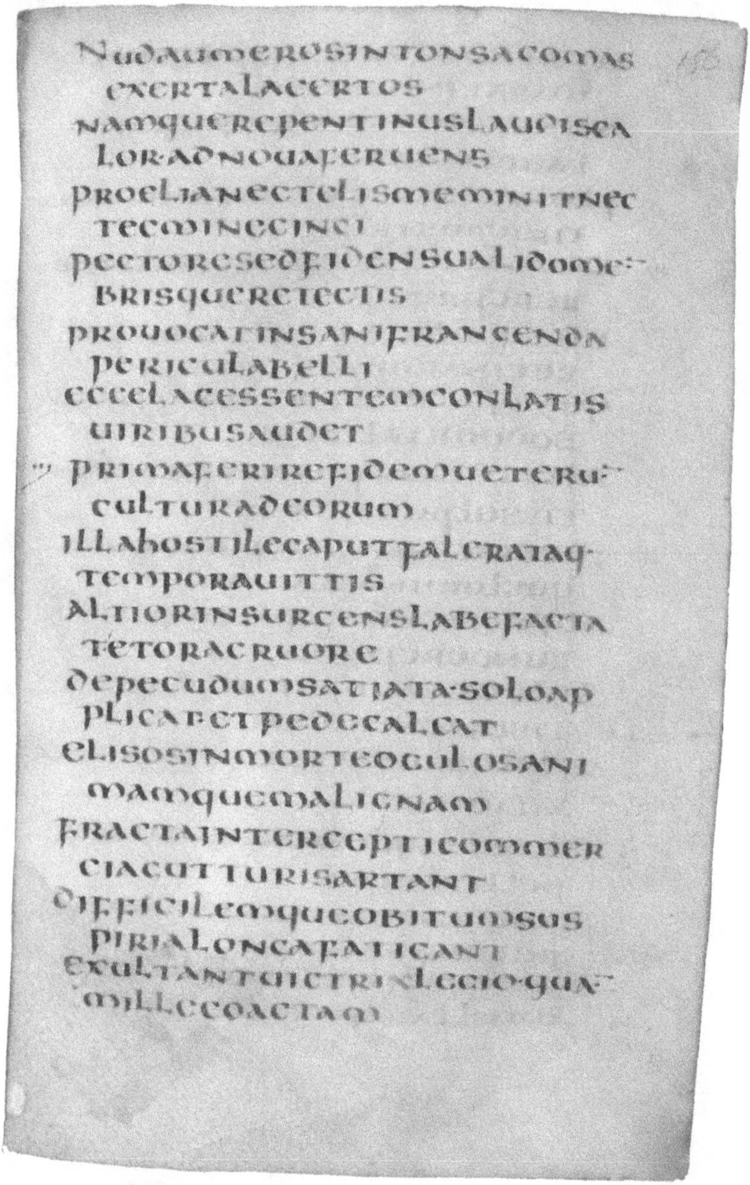

NUDAUMEROSINTONSACOMAS
EXERTALACERTOS
NAMQUEREPENTINUSLAUCISCA
LORADNOUAFERUENS
PROELIANECTELISMEMINITNEC
TECUINECINCI
PECTORESEDFIDENSUALIDOME
BRISQUERETECTIS
PROUOCATINSANIFRANGENDA
PERICULABELLI
ECCELACESSENTEMCONLATIS
UIRIBUSAUDET
PRIMAFERTREFIDEMUETERU
CULTURADEORUM
ILLAHOSTILECAPUTTALERATAQ
TEMPORAUITTIS
ALTIORINSURGENSLABEFACTA
FETORACRUORE
DEPECUDUMSATIATA·SOLOAD
PLICARETPEDECCALCAT
ELISOSINMORTEOCULOSANI
MAMQUEMALIGNAM
FRACTAINTERCEPTICOMMER
CIACUTTURISARTANT
OIFFICILEMQUEOBITUOSUS
PIRIALONCAFATICANT
EXULTANTOICTRINLCCIO·QUA
·MILLECOACTAM

FIGURE 8. Lines 23–36, with punctuation before line 29. MS *B*, fol. 156r. *Courtesy Biblioteca Ambrosiana.*

narration of this poem occurs overwhelmingly in the present tense because the allegorical action is not limited to any single place or time; on the tenses of the *Psychomachia*, see the notes on lines 98–108, 137, 505, 574, 809, and 820–21. **dubia sub sorte:** the same phrase appears in *Perist.* 9.103, which Prudentius wrote after his visit to Rome and return to Spain. **duelli:** an archaic equivalent of *bellum*. An incorrect etymology current in late antiquity explained the word as originally meaning "duel" (Ps-Acro, *Ad epistulas* 1.2.7, ed. Keller [Leipzig: Teubner, 1902–4], 2:217).

22. agresti turbida cultu: "disheveled with a wild appearance." *Cultus* refers to outer adornments or to the manner in which *Fides* cares for herself.

MS *L* explains *agresti* by saying that Christ chose fishermen rather than philosophers to do his preaching (O'Sullivan 2004, 172). The adjective could also suggest a contrast with the *pagani*, a word commonly related to *pagus*, a group or district from the countryside (see below on line 29). Prudentius's highly evocative poetic style invites such multiple interpretations.

23. umeros … comas … lacertos: an ASYNDETIC list featuring three Greek accusatives of respect (A&G §397b). Compare Claudian's description of the partially uncovered *Roma* from a poem performed in 395: "Dextrum nuda latus, niueos exserta lacertos" (*Prob.* 87). Also relevant is Claudian's description of Ceres at *Rapt.* 3.377: "Cincta sinus, exerta manus, armata bipenni." Prudentius seems to have borrowed wording from the first line and to have emulated the structure of the second. On the prehistory of Claudian's allusions in the prior passage (with intertexts in Vergil, Valerius Flaccus, and Silius Italicus), see Bernstein 2016.

24–25. Arming scenes are one of the most typical features of epics in the Homeric tradition. Prudentius gestures at such a scene here, but Fides has no time for weapons.

24. laudis: objective genitive with *calor*.

25. Fides forgets both offensive and defensive arms. **tegmine:** Prudentius is fond of nouns that end in *-men*. He uses 71 of them, whereas Vergil has only 38 (Lavarenne 1933b, §1151) and Lucretius 34.

26. fidens: Prudentius likes to pun, and this play on *fides* is a bit exaggerated. All the same, tautology, saying the same thing, is crucial to Prudentius's allegorical practice; this is the way that he tries to communicate some real substance through his words. On puns and wordplay in Prudentius, see Malamud 1989, 27–46.

27. insani frangenda pericula belli: "the trials to be crushed of raging war." Since *insanus* can mean "not whole," *frangenda* is redundant or overdetermined, as pointed out by Nugent (1985, 23). The phrase *pericula belli* appears at line end in *Aen.* 11.505 and Auson., *Mos.* 215; Ovid also has "adeunda pericula bellis" at *Met.* 14.119.

The word *pericula* also appeared in a syncopated form (*pericla*, etc.), usually with the same meaning. The only other case of the longer form in this poem is in the poet's closing prayer, at line 891. In his *Ars de orthographia*, the fifth-century grammarian Agroecius claimed that the two forms were used differently: "periculum ad discrimen pertinet, periclum ad experimentum" (ed. Mariarosaria Pugliarello [Milan: Marzorati, 1978], §128).

28. lacessentem: Fides challenges her opponent just like any traditional epic hero. **conlatis uiribus**: take as an ablative absolute and closely with *audet*, "in joining her strength," i.e., gathering herself together to confront Fides. Alternatively, *conlatis uiribus* could refer to the forces gathered for battle.

29. prima: Christians remembered imperial persecutions as beginning under Nero, long before the new religion had any power to strike back. **Veterum cultura deorum**: alludes to *Aen.* 8.185–87, where Evander says that they do not celebrate Hercules in vain: "non . . . uana superstitio ueterumque ignara deorum" ("Our religion is not in vain, nor is it ignorant of the ancient gods"). Prudentius appropriates Vergil's implicit criticism of empty religion, and his borrowing also gives the new personification a traditional sounding name. Furthermore, by using a PERIPHRASIS to name the opponent of Fides, Prudentius can distribute his opposition to Roman religion between its oldness (*ueterum*) and the multiplicity of its divinities (*deorum*). In opposition to this interpretation, Macklin Smith reads the allusion to Evander's religion as definitely ironic (1976, 283–84).

The abstract nouns *pāgānitās* and *pāgānismus* were new within Prudentius's lifetime and not used in poetry. On the development of the word *paganus*, which likewise was not widely used in our sense until the late fourth century, see O'Donnell 1977.

30–35. A detailed and vivid account of the Vice's death. The amount of blood, gore, and violence in *Psychomachia* has surprised many modern critics. Mastrangelo reviews their criticisms and attempted explanations before offering his own interpretation of the violent deaths of the Vices as material and Lucretian spirits (2008, 145–55). I do not think there is any single explanation for Prudentius's embrace of violent imagery. However, the image of crushing the devil underfoot is scriptural; Ambrose expands on the idea in *Expositio psalmi cxviii* 11.18, as observed by Franchi (2013, 29–30). Likewise, Prudentius presents the punishment of the Vices as just retribution for their crimes; in this case, Veterum cultura deorum is slaughtered as a final sacrifice on a bloody altar. On the question of violence and retribution in *Psychomachia*, see also the introduction, page 19.

30. hostile caput: "the enemy's head." **tempora uittis:** this phrase and *tempora uitta* are common in Latin epic at line end. When performing rituals, priests often wore headbands.

31. altior insurgens: this exact phrase was used by Vergil at *Aen.* 11.697 and, more importantly, at 12.902 in his description of Turnus's final, vain attempt to face Aeneas; the phrase also appears once in Sil. 5.294. Of course, a faithful reader would be hesitant to compare Fides and Turnus, and the context of the Vergilian source is probably not relevant. On such nonreferential intertexts, see Pelttari 2014, 131–37. **ora** was used in the plural in poetry with no difference in meaning.

31–32. cruore / de pecudum satiata: Christians often disparaged traditional Roman religion as barbaric and bloody, for example Ambrose in his letters arguing against the reinstatement of the altar of Victory (*Epist.* 72 and 73).

32. solo adplicat: for the phrase compare "terrae adplicat" from *Aen.* 12.303.

33. elisos . . . oculos: Vergil used this phrase to describe Hercules killing the monster Cacus in *Aen.* 8.261. For that scene as a prototype for Prudentius, see Hardie 2017, §11.

34. commercia gutturis: "the passageway of the throat." The word *commercium* in this sense was not uncommon in medical discussions; Ambrose uses it in reference to the respiratory system, in a passage on the symptoms of a kind of inflammation (*conclusio*): "concluditur unusquisque tumescentibus uisceribus internisue faucibus, cum intercluso spiritus commeatu spirandi ac respirandi commercia coartantur" (*Expositio psalmi cxviii* 19.1).

35. difficilemque obitum: Prudentius echoes Dido's "difficilisque obitus" from *Aen.* 4.694, but he changes Vergil's plural accusative to a singular for no obvious reason. **suspiria longa fatigant:** perhaps an allusion to the slow death of traditional Roman religion, as suggested by Shanzer (1989, 351) and Rohmann (2003). Alan Cameron's *The Last Pagans of Rome* (2011) describes the fading of paganism in the fourth and fifth centuries.

36–39. As Nugent notes, Prudentius hardly describes the space his characters inhabit, and these martyrs appear out of nowhere (1985, 20). Their appearance echoes the description from Heb. 12:1 of a "great cloud of witnesses" surrounding the Christian.

36. uictrix: the suffix *-trīx* produces feminine agent nouns (A&G §236). In addition to *uictrix* (53, 103, 480, and 602), parallel forms in the *Psychomachia* are *uexatrix* (58), *spectatrix* (118), *bellatrix* (133), *saltatrix* (380), *nugatrix* (433), *ostentatrix* (439), *calcatrix* (587), *infitiatrix* (630), *turbatrix* (668), and *pugnatrix* (681). Prudentius uses thirty-two such words in all; Vergil has eleven. Although the feminine characters of the *Psychomachia* are conspicuous, the ratio between the two poets is essentially the same as for masculine agent nouns (see Lavarenne 1933b, §1143–45 and above on pr. 10). **legio:** although they fight against traditional religion, the exultant martyrs are like a Roman legion.

36–37. mille coactam / martyribus: "gathered from a thousand martyrs" (ablative of source).

37. animarat: the syncopated form of the pluperfect *animauerat* (A&G §181).

39. uestirier ostro: Fides orders her allies to be clothed in the purple of a triumphant Roman general. *Vestirier* is the alternate and poetic form of the present passive infinitive (A&G §183.4); this *-ier* ending is also found in lines 191, 214, and 357.

PUDICITIA VS. LIBIDO (40–108)

The quick victory of Pudicitia (40–52) is followed by a long speech (53–97), after which she cleans her sword and dedicates it in a sacred temple (98–108). A gloss in MS *L* says that Pudicitia takes the field after Fides because the two foundations of virtue are purity of mind and chastity of body: "Iure post Fidem Pudicitia ponitur, quoniam sicut integritas fidei uirginitas est mentis, ita castitas carnis exordium est sanctae operationis. hac enim destructa, omnis uirtutum fabrica ruit" (O'Sullivan 2004, 177). We can also say that the second battle scene broadens the scope of the conflict since in her speech Pudicitia turns to theology; she says that Libido has lost her power now because a virgin has given birth to the Word of God. Her words on the incarnation of Christ are theologically significant, but also relevant to the poet's allegorical and figurative embodiment of metaphysics.

Worship of Pudicitia in Rome dates apparently to the fourth century B.C.E., and Augustus restored cult sites for her; in the third century, she was associated with the empresses Plotina and Crispina. On her cult, see *New Pauly* s.v. and *LIMC* 7.1:589–92.

40–52. Libido appears suddenly, and Pudicitia defeats her just as quickly. The scene borrows from descriptions of battle in epic poetry, and Prudentius emphasizes the hideousness of the Vice. The descriptions of both figures include allegorical details, for example, the respectful eyes of Pudicitia and the dark torches of Libido.

40. gramineo in campo: echoes Vergil's description of the grassy field that served as a ground for the funeral games of Anchises (*Aen.* 5.287; "gramineum in campum"). **concurrere prompta**: *promptus* takes the infinitive both in prose and in poetry.

41–47. Repetition of *uirgo*. Nugent (1985, 29–30) connects the repetitions in this passage to the incarnation, which is itself a kind of doubling.

41. uirgo: the noun is especially appropriate for a maidenly Virtue who goes on to boast of the victory of the Virgin Mary. **Pudicitiā:** the final syllable is lengthened before *speciosis*. Throughout his poetry, Prudentius consistently lengthens a short vowel before *st-* and *sp-*, on which see appendix A. **fulget in armis:** compare *Aen.* 6.826 ("fulgere . . . in armis") and 11.769 ("fulgebat in armis").

42. patrias . . . faces: "her homeland's flames." In the scriptures, Sodom was remembered as a place of excessive sexual desire, and Genesis recounts that it was destroyed by fire. In *Am.* 725–78, Prudentius recounts the story of Lot as an example of free will.

43. piceamque: pitch is the dark pine resin that was used for lamps and torches. **ardenti sulpure:** torches were also dipped in sulfur to make them more flammable. Prudentius uses the ablative ending *-ī* for the present participle here because he is using it as an attributive adjective; but neither he nor other Latin poets were consistent in this regard, especially when meter made the ending in *-e* more convenient.

44. Libido attacks the eyes because that is the way that desire gets in. C. S. Lewis (1936, 68) compared the attack on Pietas in Stat., *Theb.* 11.492–95. **ingerit:** *iniecit* ("she threw") is the gloss in the Weitz B tradition (O'Sullivan 2004, 178).

46. furiae: see above on line 10.

47. saxo ferit: rock throwing is common enough in epic warfare, and Vergil used the same words in *Aen.* 10.415. **inperterrita:** a poetic compound invented by Vergil according to Servius, *Ad Aen.* 10.770.

48. taedas depellit: Vergil has the phrase *depellit taedas* at *Aen.* 9.109.

49. adacto: from *adigo*.

50. calidos ... uapores: the hot, passionate breath of Libido. For *uapor* used of dangerous overheating in the body, see *OLD* s.v. 2b and Sen., *Phaedra* 640–41 "pectus insanum uapor / amorque torret."

51. sanguine concretos caenoso: "condensed of her dirty blood." The CATACHRESIS with *concretos* of a vapor is almost as violent as the Vice's gory bubbles of breath.

The conjecture of Nicolaas Heinsius (*sanioso*) is attractive, and the passage could easily have been corrupted under the influence of the following lines, which describe Libido as something dirty.

53–97. Pudicitia boasts in her victory; she introduces Judith as the poem's first typological exemplum; and she presents the Virgin Mary as the fulfillment of her earlier victory. The virgin birth leads to a discussion of the incarnation and the divinity of Christ. Her theological digressions push the boundaries of language and activate a reading of the story as being cosmologically significant.

53. hoc habet: this phrase was reportedly shouted when gladiators struck a fatal blow. It appears at *Aen.* 12.296 when the Italian Messapus kills Aulestes over an altar for the gods, and it was also used by Ter., *Andria* 83. In his commentary on Terence (ad loc.), the fourth-century grammarian Donatus explained the phrase as having been used of gladiators. Servius (*Ad Aen.* 12.296) cited the same passage from Terence, and Servius Danielis explained that in ancient authors "hoc habet" means "it's finished" ("peractum est"). Servius also describes the Vergilian passage as a case of SARCASM. From these commentaries, we can infer that the phrase was unfamiliar, archaic, and poetic in the fourth century.

54. hic: probably the adverb rather than the demonstrative adjective.

55. mortiferas: compound adjectives help set the tone in epic poetry, and in this poem Prudentius coined *Nilicola* (655) and *dulcimodus* (664). For a full account of compound words in Prudentius, see Lavarenne 1933b, §1214–60.

56. famulos famulasue: POLYPTOTON. Prudentius repeats this noun in line 643. Before Christ, Romans sometimes referred to the devotees of the gods as their servants or slaves; the usage is well known from Paul and later Christians who called themselves bondservants of God (see Rom. 1:1, for example, and *TLL* 6.1.267.61–68.25 [Jachmann]). **quibus**: dative of possession with *uena animi* (A&G §373); translate "whose" or "and their."

57. sola feruet de lampade Christi: "burns only from the light of Christ." *Sola* is ablative with *lampade*, and there is a contrast with the flames of *Libido*. Jesus called himself "the light of the world" in John 8:12. Prudentius echoes that phrase, but also "lampada mundi" (of the sun) from the same position in Lucretius 5.402, and "Veneris . . . lampade feruet" from Juv. 6.138 (I owe this point to Rosario Moreno Soldevila). Maybe the light is also an allusion to the parable of the bridesmaids, on which see below on lines 66–97.

58–65. The Book of Judith tells the story of a beautiful Jewish widow who tricked the Assyrian commander Holofernes, got him drunk, and then beheaded the enemy in his sleep. She bravely rescued her people from the foreign military leader who was besieging Jerusalem. Although the Book of Judith was widely known, it was not accepted as part of their scriptures by all Jews or Christians. Ambrose was apparently the first Latin author to interpret the heroine's actions as a victory for chastity; see *De uirginibus* 2.4.24, *De uiduis* 7.38–39, and *De officiis* 3.82, as well as Jerome, *Epist.* 79.11 (written around the year 399). On Ambrose's first use of the Judith story, see Doignon 1974. On Judith in the *Psychomachia*, see Mastrangelo 2013.

58. tene . . . potuisse: exclamatory infinitives (A&G §462) are often introduced by *-ne*, as pointed out by Austin 1971, 41. **uexatrix hominum**: echoes Lactantius's description of Fortuna as one harassing the human race (*Div. inst.* 3.29.10; "generi hominum uexatricem").

59. extincti capitis recalescere flatu: the ablative is instrumental. The METAPHOR derives from kindling a fire with one's breath, as is clear from a parallel use of the verb in Novatian, *De cibis Iudaicis* 3: ". . . ut iustitia in illis ignium more quasi adflatu quodam legis sopita recalesceret" (. . . so that justice among them, which had fallen asleep, might kindle anew, as happens with fires, from a breath of the Law as it were). Libido is described as a burning passion that can be rekindled rather than as a human figure who has expired. To put it less formally, the decapitated head of Holofernes should not be imagined as performing CPR on Libido.

61. sanguine lauit: echoes a phrase from Prop. 4.10.37–38 "desecta Tolumni / ceruix Romanos sanguine lauit equos."

62–63. torum . . . spreuit: instead of sleeping with Holofernes, Judith got him drunk and killed him.

65. caelitus: her courage is from heaven because she prayed for strength (Jth. 13:9).

66–97. Pudicitia explains that Mary's virgin birth fulfilled Judith's incomplete victory over sexual desire. The word and the flesh became one in Christ, and so his spiritual body made a way to purify the earthly bodies of his followers. Pudicitia finishes her speech angrily telling Libido to go to hell. Mastrangelo (2008, 93–96) links this speech to Jesus's parable of the coming of the kingdom of heaven, in which waiting for the kingdom is compared to bridesmaids waiting with torches to receive their huand (Matt. 25:1–13). There is not a clear link to that passage, but Prudentius is definitely presenting the Virtue's victory as a model for his readers to follow.

66. at fortasse introduces a possible objection. This combination was uncommon and prosaic; see, for example, Cic., *Nat. D.* 2.4.12 and Ambrose, *De uirginibus* 1.1.4. *Sed fortasse* appears in a similar usage just three times in Latin poetry, twice in Prudentius (*Apoth.* 183 and 820) and once in the verses of the grammarian Terentianus Maurus (*De metris* 1705), who flourished around the beginning of the third century C.E.

66–67. sub umbra / legis: "under the shadow of the Law." The Hebrew scriptures were called the Law, and Christians read them as offering shadowy prefigurations of Christianity. The precise wording here echoes Heb. 10:1, in which the law offers only "a shadow of the good things to come."

67. tempora nostra: a new era began with the arrival of Christ. **figurat:** see above on pr. 50–51.

68. quibus: ablative of time when. **uirtus** ("manliness") was one of the abstract deities worshipped in Republican Rome; she was often worshipped alongside *Honos*; and Augustus was honored in 27 B.C.E. for his *uirtus, clementia, iustitia,* and *pietas* (*Res gestae* 34.2). But perhaps Pudicitia does not count manly valor as true virtue.

terrena in corpora: just like Christ's true virtue came into earthly bodies, the spiritual and figural allegories of the poem fulfill the literal and bodily meaning of the words. The contrast between literal (bodily and earthly) and allegorical (figurative and spiritual) interpretations was common in Christian interpreters, for example in Augustine, *De doctrina Christiana* 3.9.13.

69. excisura: the future participle was used to express purpose (A&G §499).

70–71. The repetition is emphatic, and it draws attention to the words themselves and to the birth of Christ as a point of transition.

71. post partum uirginis: continues the syntax from the question above to make an extended parenthetical observation. **ex quo:** "from which point."

72. pristina origo: "the first beginning," in reference to the first man Adam, whom Christ replaced when he became the source of a new spiritual human nature, as described by the apostle Paul in Eph. 4:22–24 and 1 Cor. 15:45–49.

73. uis ardua: "a lofty power," which could be identified as the Holy Spirit. **seuit:** from *serere*, "to sow."

74–77. Mary became pregnant from the Holy Spirit without ever having sex, and her son was both a human and the one God (in three persons). Because he had both a divine nature and a human nature, all humans can now become divine in him.

74. innupta: the point is that Mary conceived as a virgin, not that she conceived before the wedding.

75. Gnilka thinks that this verse is inauthentic (2000–2003, 1:486n68). The line is parenthetical and perhaps unnecessary, but that does not mean it was added by anyone other than Prudentius. It does recall the theme of the *Apotheosis*.

76. quae concipit: figuratively, every Christian conceives like Mary.

77. dei consortis: Paul calls Christians coheirs with Christ (Rom. 8:17). **foedere sumit:** "assumes by treaty." This is the treaty or covenant that God made with humans, for *foedus* is a translation of the Greek *diathēkē* ("covenant"), as pointed out by Franchi (2013, 104).

78. See John 1:14, "and the Word was made flesh." Christ as the second person of the trinity is made human but remains God. **quippe** introduces a reason or confirmation.

79. glutinat: the word was prosaic and technical, and often used in discussions of medicine; in poetry, it was used of the process of creation, both by Prudentius at *Cath.*11.52 and by the poet of the so-called *Carmen Sibyllinum* (90), edited by Bernard Bischoff (1966–81, 1:164–68).

79–80. usum ... usum: verbal repetition offers a small figure for the metaphysical sameness of the Word of God; the word changes, and yet it is the same.

82–83. esse / incipiens: "beginning to be."

84. nascendo in melius: "by being born into something better." **mihi:** Prudentius continues including himself in what is, surprisingly perhaps, a deeply personal poem. **contulit ... mansit:** he offered a share in divinity to humans, but remained divine himself.

85. ex nostris minuit sua: he did not subtract anything from his account by sharing in ours. The financial METAPHOR is continued with *tribuit* and *dona* in the following lines.

87. dona haec sunt quod ... : "these are his gifts, that ..." For *quod* as "the fact that," see A&G §572. **lutulenta:** Libido was "filthy" because she makes humans do dirty things. On sexuality in late antiquity, see Brown 2008. On shame and sex in late antiquity, see Harper 2013.

88. nec: continues the *quod* clause of the previous line. **mea**: in contrast to *mihi* above, the first-person refers clearly to Pudicitia. **pŏtĭs ĕs**: synonymous with *pŏtĕs*, but the adjective draws attention to the quality of the subject.

89–97. Pudicitia boasts of her enemy's downfall. Prudentius's Vices are described as suffering the same punishments they inflict, as shown by Gnilka (1963, 51–81). This is why Libido is the only Vice described as burning in hell, because she makes her victims burn with lust.

89. tu princeps: as often the form of the verb "to be" (*es*) is understood from the context. **ad mortis iter**: the idea that life is like a journey is a commonplace, from Homer to modern pop music. More specifically, Jesus taught that there is a path that leads to destruction (Matt. 7:13), a phrase that Juvencus translated as "iter . . . mortis" (1.681). **ianua leti**: the phrase appears in Latin epic, including Lucr. 1.1112, Ov., *Met.* 1.662, and the poem *Laudes domini* 28.

90. corpora conmaculans: Paul described sexual sin as sin against one's own body (1 Cor. 6:18). **Tartara**: this Homeric word for the underworld was borrowed by Latin poets, and then taken up by Christian poets to refer to their own version of hell.

91. abde: the first of a series of imperatives addressed to Libido. **iam frigida**: she is already moribund (see *OLD* s.v. *frigida* 7). Vergil described Eurydice as already cold when she crossed the Styx for the second time: "illa quidem Stygia nabat iam frigida cumba" (*G.* 4.506).

92. prostibulum: an abusive description. **manes pete**: "go to hell." **claudere**: a passive imperative. **Auerno**: Lake Avernus, which is near Cumae, was said to be an entrance to the underworld.

93. detrūdĕre: another passive imperative.

94. The verse echoes Tiberianus 2.24 "te celent semper uada turbida, te luta nigra," which is a poem on the evils of gold; the intertext is discussed by Franchi (2013, 111–12 and 114). **uoluant:** the first of a series of jussive subjunctives after the imperatives of the previous lines. **subter:** adverb.

96. furiarum maxima: Vergil used the same phrase to describe an unidentified tormentor in his underworld (*Aen.* 6.605). Mastrangelo suggests that Prudentius's allusions to *Aen.* 6 portray the soul's battle as like Aeneas's journey through the underworld (2008, 14–40).

97. ut . . . seruentur: a result clause.

98–108. Pudicitia washes her sword in the Jordan River and then consecrates it. That is, she symbolically dedicates herself to a life of virginity. The topic was a current one. Contemporary texts on purity include Ambrose's *De uirginitate* from 378 and Augustine's *De sancta uirginitate* from 401. Both men lived most of their lives in determined chastity, and the renunciations of others including Melania the Elder and Eustochium were already famous. On Melania and her family, see Chin and Schroeder 2016.

The river Jordan is the first reference in the main poem to any external place. This passage suggests that the spiritual battle in the soul somehow exists in the same physical world that we know and that contemporary geographers imagined as surrounded by the river ocean. And yet, Prudentius continues to use present tense verbs that portray the action as happening outside of any particular moment.

In *Cath.* 7.72–80, Prudentius has a similar comparison of baptism to the cleansing of metal.

98. Dixerat haec: a common phrase in epic poetry. **interfectae:** the line ends heavily with a spondaic fifth foot, as does line 594.

99. morte: an ablative of cause (A&G §404). **Pudicitiā gladium:** on this lengthening of a short syllable before a mute and a liquid, see appendix A. **Iordanis in undis:** a sudden and surprising imposition of real space. The Jordan River is a symbol of spiritual cleansing in the scriptures because that is where John the Baptist baptized (Matt. 3:6 and Mark 1:5), but the river also has a real and physical substance; today, it divides Palestine and Israel from Jordan. The poem generates a current of energy from alternating between physical and spiritual realities.

100. sanies: in *De medicina*, the Roman encyclopedist Celsus helpfully explained the differences between the discharges that come from wounds, namely, *sanies, sanguis*, and *pus* (5.26.20.A), on which see also *OLD* s.v. *sanies* 1a.

101. macularat = maculauerat.

102. docta: for the holy learning of Pudicitia, compare the learned thumb of Fides in line 364 and the invocation to Christ as teacher in line 888. The word *docta* suggests continuity with the Roman, and previously Hellenistic, tradition of learned poetry.

103. uictricem uictrix: POLYPTOTON. baptismate: the Greek word means "dipping," but in Latin the word was used almost exclusively of ritual cleansing in a Christian context.

104–5. nec iam contenta . . . condere uaginae gladium: Pudicitia is not content for her chastity to remain private. The negative modifies *contenta*; the adjective takes an explanatory infinitive; and *uaginae* is dative.

The various Latin words for weapons were common euphemisms for the male anatomy (Adams, 1982, 19–22). Perhaps there is a pun here and below, when Pax announces an end to the battle and a peaceful sword ("placabilis . . . gladius") fills its sheath (636–37). In ancient Latin, *uagina* refers to private parts only in Plaut., *Pseud.* 1181, and there it refers to a man's anus: "conueniebatne in uaginam tuam machaera militis" (see Adams 1982, 20–21).

105–6. ne tecta rŭbigo / occupet ablutum scabrosa sorde nitorem: the first syllable of *rubigo* (*robigo*) is normally long (including in Prudent., *Cath.* 7.205 and *Symm.* 2.976), and MS *E* offers an alternate version of these lines. However, the same manuscript also offers a significantly different version of the text in 726–28, and the most likely explanation is that some scribe or reader was trying to improve the text in both cases. For other possible conjectures in this manuscript, see lines 177, 351, 431, 479, 726–28, and 781. Variants that are more likely to be conjectures cannot be used as evidence for any straightforward reconstruction of the archetype. **scabrosa:** this derivative of *scaber* appears before Prudentius only a few times and only in Christian authors.

107. catholico: the first syllable of the Greek adjective *katholicos* was originally short and the word meant "universal." Damasus (c. 305–84) and Prudentius lengthened the first syllable for the sake of the meter. Around the same time, the word also came to be used in the sense "orthodox," as in universally acknowledged. The "Catholic" church is thus the "universal" or "orthodox" church. **templo:** the early Christians did not have their own places of worship. They seem first to have called their churches *templa* in the fourth century.

108. consecrat: like Pudicitia, ancient heroes consecrated their spoils to the gods; for example, Aeneas dedicates the spoils from Mezentius to Mars (*Aen.* 11.1–11). **ubi coruscet:** relative clause of purpose (A&G §531.2).

PATIENTIA VS. IRA (109–77)

The battle of Patientia and Ira offers a touch of humor, as Prudentius continues to develop the techniques and expectations of his personification allegory. The Virtue is impassive; she withstands the attacks of Ira and allows her to rage (109–44), until Ira boils over and kills herself in frustration (145–54). The Virtue's speech afterward perfectly fits her persona (155–61), and then she leaves the battlefield accompanied by the suffering character Job (162–77). Just as he played with the generic expectations of his readers through the negation of an arming scene for Fides, Prudentius creates here an antiepic warrioress who does not fight (Franchi 2013, 156–57). The second and third episodes are the same length, exactly sixty-nine lines.

A number of ancient authors wrote treatises on *patientia*. Its range of meanings include self-control, equanimity, patience, and the ability to accept suffering. As Tertullian said, *patientia* was one of the few topics on which philosophers agreed; everyone said that it was good (*De patientia* 1.7). For Prudentius's understanding of Ira as self-harming, compare Sen., *De ira* 1.1.1 "Hic totus [affectus] concitatus et in impetu doloris est, armorum sanguinis suppliciorum minime humana furens cupiditate, dum alteri noceat sui neglegens, in ipsa irruens tela et ultionis secum ultorem tracturae auidus."

109–54. Patientia is described first, and then Ira finds, confronts, and attacks her. The battle narrative proceeds at a more leisurely pace than with the first two Vices, as we are treated to a full description of Anger's frustrations. The Vice's eventual suicide is hardly a surprise when it comes. The Virtue's armor features prominently in the story, perhaps as a counterpoint to the entry of Fides onto the battlefield without armor.

109. Ecce: the narrator calls attention to a Virtue that is too modest to do so herself. **modesta:** a quality that Roman men admired in a woman. Eulalia, for example, is described by Prudentius as "ore seuera, modesta gradu" (*Perist.* 3.23). More generally, Seneca praised the wise man for being modest, among other qualities (*De ira* 3.6.1); and Tertullian describes personified Patience as a humble and moderate character (*De patientia* 15). These parallels were cited by Franchi (2013, 128).

110. per: the preposition means something like "along" or "throughout," but might be translated as "in."

111. peruia pilis: *peruius* takes a dative of advantage (*OLD* s.v. 1).

112. defixa oculos: in this line and in 109 above, Prudentius alludes to *Aen.* 6.156 "Aeneas maesto defixus lumina uultu." Vergil describes Aeneas at the moment he leaves the Sibyl's cave, and we should perhaps understand the soul as continuing on its own journey. Servius interprets *defixus lumina* as portraying the sadness of the hero: "defixa lumina habens, per quod tristitia mentis ostenditur" (*Ad Aen.* 6.156). Here, Patientia is serious and not grieving.

113. procul: means "apart," both nearer and further depending on the point of reference (see Austin 1977, 35–36). **spumanti . . . rictu:** echoes *spumantes . . . rictus* from Ov., *Met.* 4.97.

114. sanguinea . . . subfuso lumina felle: "bloody eyes with bitterness suffused." The liquid poison of anger is pictured as welling up in her eyes. Note the interlocking word order and harsh energy of the line.

115. exsortem: takes a partitive genitive, just like *expers* (A&G §346). **teloque et uoce lacessit:** Prudentius echoes *Aen.* 10.644, in which Vergil writes "telis et uoce lacessit" to describe a phantom Aeneas harassing Turnus.

116. inpatiensque morae: the same phrase appears in Luc. 6.424, Sil. 8.4, and Juv. 6.238. The objective genitive is used with many verbs of feeling (A&G §354).

117. hirsutas: the Greek-looking spelling *hyrsutus* in some manuscripts is very rare (see *TLL* s.v. 6.3.2824.51 [Schmid]), but it recurs in MSS *A* and *U* at *Am.* 134, and *hyrtus* is in some manuscripts in *Perist.* 11.120. The editor Bergman followed MS *A* even in such an unlikely case as this. **uertice cristas:** this line ending (with slight variations) is common in Latin epic poetry.

118–20. The first time in the poem that a Vice speaks.

118. en tibi: the phrase means something like "hey, you," and *tibi* is an ethical dative (A&G §390). To say something like "look at yourself," the accusative case would be used (*OLD* s.v. *en* 2c). **Martis ... nostri:** "of our fighting." For the use of the name of the god for the sphere he represents (METONYMY), compare *Aen.* 6.165. The same usage recurs in lines 215 and 549.

119. securo pectore: the phrase was used by Luc. 4.30 and Paulinus of Nola, *Ultimarum prima* 329 = Hartel *Carm.* 10.

120. nec doleas: IRONY was diagnosed here in a gloss of the Weitz B tradition (O'Sullivan 2004, 194–95). Bergman (1897, 16) pointed out that *neu* (*neue*) is the grammatically normative conjunction for use with negative commands (A&G §450n5).

turpe tibi: *est* is implied. **gemuisse dolorem:** "groan in grief" but literally "groan your grief." The abstract noun is essentially a cognate accusative (A&G §390) like "live your life" (*uitam uiuere*), and it stands for the actual sound of the grief expressed. In this construction a redundant object acquires the force of an adverb. With verbs expressing propriety, the perfect infinitive "may be used to emphasize the idea of completed action" (A&G §486b).

121. sic ait et: a common way to begin a line in Latin epic.

122. crispata: modifies *pinus*, as does *certa*. **et:** links *sequitur* and *defertur*.

123. stomachum: just as Libido aimed for the eyes, Ira strikes the part of the body from which ill-temper arises (see below lines 132 and 902, and Franchi 2013, 139).

124. resilit duro loricae excussa repulsu: "[the weapon] bounces back repulsed by the hard force of her cuirass." Compare Seneca's similar description of a great mind free from anger and impenetrable: "Ut tela a duro resiliunt, et cum dolore caedentis solida feriuntur: ita nulla magnum animum iniuria ad sensum sui adducit, fragilior eo quod petit. Quanto pulchrius uelut nulli penetrabilem telo omnis iniurias contumeliasque respuere!" (*De ira* 3.5.8).

125. prouida nam: the particle is placed second here and in lines 222, 434, 462, 548, and 809; on the postponement of *nam* elsewhere in Prudentius, see Gnilka 2000, 518. **conserto adamante:** ablative of material (A&G §403).

126. thōrāca: accusative singular. The Greek *thōrax* was apparently first used in Latin in the *Aeneid*. The form was familiar enough to Servius's students that he does not comment on it, except to say that the second syllable is long, as it is in oblique cases (*Ad Aen.* 11.487).

129. telorum nimbos: for the expression compare Luc. 4.776 "telorum nimbo" and Sil. 5.215 "pilorum nimbus." The most famous example of such imagery is from Herodotus's Spartan warrior who declared that if the Persians should block the sun with their arrows, then they would fight in the shade (7.226.2). Herodotus was not well known in the West in late antiquity, but he is cited by name by Ausonius (*Epist.* 8.32), and maybe his chapter about the generation of vipers (*Histories* 3.109) was the source for Prud., *Am.* 581–620.

non penetrabile: the adverbial accusative is closely related to the cognate accusative (see A&G §390 and Kühner-Stegmann vol. 1, §71.2d n. 4, pp. 280–81).

Seneca had said that the wise man was impervious to injury; no matter how many weapons were thrown at him, he would remain impenetrable: "Hoc igitur dico, sapientem nulli esse iniuriae obnoxium; itaque non refert quam multa in illum coiciantur tela, cum sit nulli penetrabilis" (*De constantia sapientis* 3.5). Franchi (2013, 143) suggested that this passage was a source for Prudentius (compare also the passages cited above on line 124).

130. monstri: Prudentius also calls the Virtues' enemies *crimina, culpae, furiae, mala, portenta*, and *uitia*. **sine more furentis:** the phrase is borrowed from Vergil's description of Queen Amata, who was driven into a rage by the Fury Allecto: "Immensam sine more furit lymphata per urbem" (*Aen.* 7.377). In this case, the source text neatly supports the content and tone of Prudentius's scene.

131. opperiens propriis perituram uiribus Iram: in later Latin, *proprius* was often used in place of the reflexive adjective *suus*. The participle is from *pereo*. For other examples of *opperior* followed by an accusative participle, see *TLL* s.v. II.A.1.a.γ = 9.2.748.32–34 (Beikircher).

132. stomachandŏ: a final *o* in forms of the verb was often shortened from the time of Ovid on, as also *uolŏ* in line 713.

134. superuacuam . . . inrita: PLEONASM.

136. iactibus et: ANASTROPHE. Prudentius also postpones conjunctions in lines 144, 170, 184, etc.

137. uertitur: the alternation of verbs in the present and pluperfect tense creates a particular effect, the suspension of normal temporal sequence. The things that happen in Prudentius's allegorical vision are presented as happening now or as already having happened, not as happening in order from beginning to end (see above on line 21). While these battle scenes display an absence of historical sequence, there is temporality in the visions of Christian and secular history proposed by Pudicitia (53–97) and Superbia (206–52).

138. The meter matches the content, as this heavily spondaic line shows Ira straining to put all of her strength into the blow. The halting measures of the following line suggest the growing force with which she strikes.

138–39. For the image of a warrior carefully straining to launch a strike, compare *Aen.* 9.417 "summa telum librabat ab aure" (He balanced his spear at the height of his ear).

142. dura: agrees with *cassis.* **uena rebellis:** an internal flaw in the metal causes it to shatter.

143. cedere nescia: Horace described the wrath of Achilles in similar terms: "Pelidae stomachum cedere nescii" (*Carm.* 1.6.6).

144. adsultūs: Ira attacked first with missiles and then with her sword. **ferienti:** object of *resistit.*

145–54. Ira's sword breaks, just like Turnus's in *Aen.* 12.731–34. As a result, Ira is driven to kill herself.

145–46. fragmina uidit / et . . . crepuisse: the verb takes first an accusative direct object and then an infinitive of indirect speech.

The form *fragmina* was antique according to *Serv. Dan.* (i.e., additions to the text of Servius's commentary that include material from his predecessor Donatus), in a note on *Aen.* 10.306: "*Fragmina* antique dictum. nam *fragmenta* dici debere nonnulli asserunt" (*Fragmina* is ancient diction, for many assert that *fragmenta* ought to be used). This would make the use of *fragmina* poetic and rhetorical. In confirmation of this point, note that Prudentius uses the form *fragmenta* in line 457, and that the tone is lower there.

147. The ablative absolute fills the entire line.

148. mentis inops: this exact phrase was used eight times by Ovid, and also by Ausonius and Claudian. In the following lines, Ira shows that she deserves the description. **ebur infelix:** accusative object of *abicit.* In the margin of MS *U, ebur* is explained as *metonimia,* because only the hilt of her sword would have been decorated with ivory. **decorisque pudendi:** "of her shameful glory," an OXYMORON.

149. perfida signa: recalls the "perfidus ensis" of Turnus (*Aen.* 12.731), who also had found himself holding the hilt ("capulum" in line 734) of a broken sword.

150. spernit: she rejects and distances herself from her weaponry. Nonius Marcellus said that *spernere* could mean "break away from" ("rursum segregare"). He cited as evidence Ennius saying that justice flees from bad people: "ius atque aecum se a malis spernit procul" (*De compendiosa doctrina*, ed. W. M. Lindsay [Leipzig: Teubner, 1903], vol. 3, p. 641 and Enn., *Trag.* frag. 71, line 156, ed. H. D. Jocelyn, *The Tragedies of Ennius* [Cambridge: Cambridge, 1967]).

151. missile . . . unum: the noun and its adjective nicely enclose the line. **frustra sparserat:** the second syllable of *frustra* is long in classical poetry, and Servius claimed that such adverbs were pronounced in his day with a long second syllable: "praepositiones uel aduerbia in *a* exeuntia modo producunt ultimam litteram, excepto *puta* et *ita*, apud Ennium et Pacuuium breuia sunt" (*Ad Aen.* 2.651). But *frustra* is scanned with a short second syllable in later authors, including in Auson., *Caes.* 56 and Prudent., *Perist.* 1.13 (see Green 1991, 241, and compare Lavarenne 1993b, §164 and 166). Unfortunately, in this line we cannot tell whether the *-a* in *frustra* is long or short because Prudentius regularly lengthens a preceding short vowel before *sp-* (see on line 41). Although this line does not offer conclusive evidence, we can at some points notice the difference between the metrical practice of Prudentius and that of Augustan poets.

152. peruersos: a pun on the adjective's literal meaning.

153. humi: locative case (A&G §427a). **se:** accusative object of *perfodit*.

155–61. A short victory speech for Patientia in a restrained style. The bare "inquit" perfectly captures her controlled tone.

155. Quam: a connective relative (= *et eam*) that is governed by the preposition *super* (= *et adsistens super eam*). Bergman and Lavarenne, however, printed *superadsistens* as one word. **uicimus:** the bare verb is along the same lines as Julius Caesar's famous *ueni, uidi, uici.*

156. exultans: probably modifies *uitium*, which is the object of *uicimus*. *Vitium* also comes second and is preceded by its modifier in lines 284 and 495. Alternatively, *exultans* could be taken as nominative and outside the quotation marks, as Franchi wants (2013, 159). On that reading, even Patientia gets to exult in her own way. A parallel could be found in Livy 1.25.12 "Romanus exultans 'duos' inquit 'fratrum Manibus dedi.'"

157. sanguinis ac uitae: the HENDIADYS ("lifeblood") is found in prose and poetry, for example, Cic., *Rosc. Am.* 7 and Verg., *Aen.* 12.765. **istud:** the second-person demonstrative pronoun sometimes only loosely gestures at an addressee, and sometimes it was used just like *hic* or *ille*. In this line, it could be heard as meaning something like "this kind as you can see," although that would be an overtranslation.

158–59. furias . . . uires: the accusatives are objects of *extinguere*, which explains the kind of warfare practiced by Patience. **tolerando:** the ablative describes the manner in which she conquers.

160. se: the object of *interimit*.

160–61. Patientia encapsulates the moral of the entire scene in a remarkably short and simple conclusion, so that Prudentius achieves a remarkable degree of continuity between the rhetorical form of his poem and the content of her message, which is that victory does not require great effort.

162–77. As with the previous battle, this one ends with an unexpected scene. Patientia finds an ally in the scriptures, in the Hebrew Book of Job, which recounts the story of a righteous man who suffered patiently through the many misfortunes that befell him. Job is the only human who appears on the *Psychomachia*'s psychic battlefield.

Although it is surprising that Job appears on the battlefield, he was often included in Christian discussions of patience. Tertullian used Job as a model in *De patientia* 14. Likewise, Augustine cited Job as a better model of patience than Adam in his own *De patientia* 11–12. Augustine wrote his treatise around the year 400.

162. haec effata: a common transition in epic poetry.

163. egregio comitata uiro: "accompanied by a remarkable man." The verb is passive, and it takes the ablative; for comparable examples, see *TLL* s.v. 3.0.1815.11–26 (Bannier).

165. adhuc: Job is still grim and breathless from all the death and destruction visited on him. This interpretation gains a tiny bit of (unnecessary) support from the reading *uulnere,* which appears as a variant written by a second hand in MS *Y* and also in the text of *C.* Less likely is Bergman's suggestion that *funere* refers to the recent slaughter of the Vices (1897, 20). In reality, *adhuc* here and *iam* in the following line link the ahistorical space of the allegory to the sufferings and life of a (historical) Job. Alongside historical time, which has past, present, and future, Prudentius creates a psychological and spiritual continuum that is almost entirely separate.

166. ulcera: one of Job's misfortunes was to be afflicted with disgusting ulcers (Job 2:7).

167. cicatricum: just as Roman soldiers were honored for their battle scars (Livy 2.23.4), Christians honored the scars of the martyrs (Franchi 2013, 172–74).

169. diua: refers to Patientia. Servius explained that the adjective *diuus* was often used by Vergil as a synonym for *deus,* but that *diuus* more narrowly referred to divinized humans: "diuum et deorum indifferenter plerumque ponit poeta, quamquam sit discretio, ut deos perpetuos dicamus, divos ex hominibus factos" (*Ad Aen.* 5.45). Likewise, Apuleius used the word *diui* to refer to the daemonic intermediaries that the Platonists posited as standing between the humans and the gods (*Apol.* 43, *De deo Soc.* 7); see further *TLL* 5.1.1649.75–50.10 (Schwering). More generally, the adjective referred to anything divine or godlike. Prudentius has "diua caro" at line 76 and "Hierusales . . . diua" at 811–12. Because of the reference to the return of Job's wealth in the following lines, we could also hear a pun on *diues* here. More importantly, Prudentius spoke in the language of philosophers and poets to make a likely story, which is noteworthy because some of his contemporaries avoided the word *diuus,* including Ambrose and Augustine.

170–71. Compare Job 42:10, in which at the end of the story he is given back more than all he lost in his sufferings.

170. captis et: ANASTROPHE, with a strong CAESURA before *captis.* **perdita quaeque:** "all that was lost."

172. ipsa: the pronoun marks the change of subject as the story returns to Patientia.

173. uulniferos...imbres: this extended use of *imber* to describe weapons pouring through the air is common in Latin poetry (*OLD* s.v. 3b). Prudentius apparently invented the word *uulnifer*. Strangely, although it does not appear again in antiquity, *uulnifer* appears as a gloss to the otherwise nonexistent Greek word *traumatopoios* in a Medieval Latin-Greek glossary (*Corpus Glossariorum Latinorum*, vol. 2, *Glossae Latino-Graecae et Graeco-Latinae*, ed. Georgius Goetz [Leipzig: Teubner, 1888], 458.22). This glossary could easily have incorporated material from a copy of Prudentius glossed in late antiquity in, say, Constantinople. On a previously known glossary that includes material from Prudentius and for the early commentary tradition on the *Psychomachia*, see the introduction, pages 33–36.

174. una comes: she is "a singular ally."

176. anceps luctamen: object of *init*. **uirtute sine:** normally this preposition is preceded by its object only in poetry.

177. nam: I print *nam* instead of *et* for two reasons. *Nam* makes the second syllable of *uirtus* long by position, and having a causal conjunction clarifies the logic of the sentence. The word looks like another attempted emendation in MS *E* or its source (see above on lines 105–6), but in this case the attempt is convincing.

MENS HUMILIS VS. SUPERBIA (178–309)

The fourth battle features the heroic figure of Superbia fighting against a mismatched and lowly Mens humilis. Prudentius begins from Superbia and her finery (178–93). After she upbraids Mens humilis and Spes in a long and haughty speech (194–252), Superbia promptly falls into a trap set by Fraus (253–73). Spes then helps Mens humilis finish the job, and she ascends to heaven on the spot (274–309).

Superbia is associated with the grandeurs of pagan Rome, but behind her proud words we can hear the author's implicit view of history, namely, that Rome is subsumed within a cosmic story of salvation. As the fourth of seven Virtues to enter the fight, Mens humilis enjoys a key position in the poem, as noted by Nugent: "Here we move decisively from the shorter battles to the longer, from the simpler oppositions to the more complex" (1985, 35). And yet she relies on Spes to conquer. On humility in the Church fathers, see Ramelli 2008. On the use of humility in imperial politics, see Christopher Kelly 2013.

178–93. The episode begins with an extended description of Superbia, her steed, and their ornamentation.

178. inflata: the image of pride as something puffed up or conceited is common in Latin; see *OLD* s.v. *inflatus* 2, *inflo* 5, and *turgeo*, and below on lines 189 and 286.

179. effreni uolitabat equo: the only figure who fights on horseback. The second declension form *effrenus* was not uncommon in classical poetry. The only transmitted example of the by-form *effrenis* from before the fourth century is in Pliny, *HN* 8.171. *Effrenis* became the normal form around the time of Prudentius. **pelle leonis:** Hercules had worn a lion skin, and so this was a heroic feature. The phrase occurs a few times in previous epic at line end.

179–80. quem ... texerat et ... armos: "whom she had covered ... and *whose* forequarters ..." Understand a second relative pronoun in the dative case (*cui*) and a shift in syntax in the middle of the statement (ANACOLUTHON). The description echoes Vergil's description of Chloreus's horse: "*Forte* ... / spumantemque agitabat *equum, quem pellis* aenis / in plumam squamis auro conserta *tegebat*" (*Aen.* 11.768–71).

181–82. quo ... iactantius ... inferret: the ablative of comparison (*quo*) is frequently used to introduce a relative clause of characteristic expressing purpose (A&G §531a).

181. se: reflexive object of *inferret*.

182. despectans: Superbia looks down on her enemy because this is what her name means; compare *superbit* (190) and *supereminet* (195). Bergman unconvincingly printed the variant *dispectans*. On the confusion of scribes between *dis-* and *de-*, see Lavarenne 1933b, §19.

183–85. turritum tortis caput . . . in altum / crinibus: refers to an updo hairstyle in which curls were stacked on top of the head. The extravagance of her hair recalls 1 Tim. 2:9, in which Paul bids women not to ornament themselves with fine clothing or jewelry or curls: "ornantes se non in *tortis crinibus* aut auro aut in margaritis uel ueste pretiosa" (Vulgate). The phrase *tortis crinibus* also appears in the old Italian and old African versions. Similar criticisms of women's updos can be found in Juv. 6.502–3; Tert., *De cultu feminarum* 2.7.1–2; and Jerome, *Epist.* 130.7.13, where the advice is to refrain from ornamenting the hair or styling it into a tower with someone else's hair ("ornare crinem et alienis capillis turritum uerticem struere"). As the last passage implies, these styles were sometimes arranged with extensions or partial wigs. An extravagant example of such a style can be seen in the Fonseca bust in the Musei Capitolini in Rome, on which see Bartman 2001, 9–10.

Closest to Prudentius is a passage from an epithalamium for ascetics written by Paulinus of Nola between 400 and (at the very latest) 408. He counsels Titia not to wear her hair in the same extravagant style: "[Neque] implexarum strue tormentoque comarum / *turritum* sedeas aedificata caput" (*Epithalamium in Iulianum et Titiam* 85–86 = Hartel *Carm.* 25).

184. extructos augeret ut: ANASTROPHE.

184–85. addita . . . / congeries: artificial hair was sometimes added by stylists.

186. carbasea: modifies *palla*. Servius explained that *carbasus* is a kind of linen (*Ad Aen.* 3.357).

188. tenui uelamine: an ablative of quality or description (A&G §415). **limbus:** apparently a scarf.

189. textis turgentibus: Superbia's scarf is inflated by the wind, just as she is "puffed up" in her vanity.

190–93. The words *nec minus* introduce Superbia's horse, which is an allegory for an already allegorical figure, and so a backhanded transition introduces a MISE-EN-ABÎME for the poet's allegorical doubling of reality.

Mastrangelo (2008, 136) has made an interesting case for reading Superbia's out-of-control stallion as an allusion to Plato, *Phaedrus* 254e, in which an untamed horse is presented as an image for the passions of the body.

190. sonipes: a lofty word, as we can hear in Vergil's line about Dido's horse: "stat sonipes ac frena ferox spumantia mandit" (*Aen.* 4.135).

191. frenarier: the infinitive depends on *inpatiens*. For the alternate infinitive ending, see the note on line 39. For the construction, compare Claud., *Rapt.* 1.35 "inpatiens nescire torum." **ora:** should probably be read as an accusative of respect rather than as the subject of the infinitive. Compare Ov., *Am.* 1.2.15 "asper equus duris contunditur ora lupatis."

192–93. negata / libertate fugae: an ablative absolute expressing the reason for the horse's impatience.

194–252. Superbia reproaches Mens humilis and Spes at her side. Superbia's long speech links her closely to Roman imperial power.

194. Hoc . . . habitu: refers to her dress or to her general bearing, although they both mean the same thing according to the poem's allegorical logic. **sese ostentans:** "showing off." For this reflexive use of the verb, see *OLD* s.v. 4b. **uirago:** a woman, but she acts like a man. Arevalo gently explains, in his own sexist terms, that men are more often proud: "Virtutes vocat *virgines,* superbiam *viraginem,* quod aliud longe diversum est. et superbiae quidem opera in viros magis, quam in feminas cadunt" (1788–89, 2:607).

195. faleratum: Prudentius ends the hexameter with a four-syllable word the shape of *fălĕrātum* thirteen other times in this poem, in lines 60, 133, 199, 224, 274, 337, 404, 547, 784, 850, 857, 894, and 900.

196. uultuque et uoce minatur: echoes "uultuqe et uoce minaci" from *Am.* 947.

198. paupertinis: the word is found once in Varro and then more widely starting with Apuleius, but not in poetry until this line. It is strikingly prosaic.

199. Mens humilis: Prudentius uses a PERIPHRASIS in place of the unmetrical *hŭmĭlĭtas*, although he could have lengthened the first syllable of the word, as he does for example with *catholicus* in line 107. Another reason he probably preferred the PERIPHRASIS is that it presents the virtue as a quasi-philosophical mental quality, so that she would not be viewed as simply lowliness or debasement. Thus, the Christian virtue is made slightly more palatable for a readership that could find the new religion's humility difficult to understand. Even more, Nugent pointed out the appropriateness of having Mind at the center of an allegorical poem about the soul (1985, 35). **regina quidem:** the adverb usually emphasizes the preceding word or phrase; here it contrasts the royalty of Mens humilis with her lowliness.

199–200. egens alieni / auxilii: no other virtue is described as needing help.

200. sat: a short form of *satis*.

201. edita: her wealth (*opulentia*) is "high up" because Christ told his disciples to "store up for yourselves treasures in heaven" (Matt. 6:20).

202. ab humo: the point is that Mens humilis is not earthly or lowly, even though her name derives etymologically from *humus*. **diuite regno:** ablative of place where (A&G §429).

203. male sana: synonymous with *uesana* and *insana* and used, for example, at *Aen.* 4.8.

204. uilibus . . . telis: dependent on *instructam*. To what the narrator says about the Virtue's simple weapons, compare the apostle Paul's description of Christians: "God chose what is foolish in the world to shame the wise, God chose what is weak in the world to shame the strong, God chose what is low and despised in the world, even things that are not, to bring to nothing things that are" (1 Cor. 1:27–28). **ostentamine:** the word appears only here and in 2 Thess. 1:5, as translated in the *Vetus latina* version cited as *X*, for which Tert. *Scorpiace* 13 is a witness. The Greek in that verse was *endeigma*, and the other Latin translations had *exemplum*. But the passage does not seem particularly relevant, as Paul is telling the Thessalonians that their persecution offers evidence of God's just judgment. In our passage, the word surely describes an ostentatious display.

205. dictis ... amaris: a common poetic idiom after Vergil's references to "bitter words" in *Aen.* 10.368 and 10.591.

206. Non pudet: repeats the beginning of Numanus's speech vainly taunting the Trojans for being unwarlike (*Aen.* 9.598), which is also alluded to in line 212. Also relevant is the beginning of Juturna's speech that stirred up the Rutulians against the proud settlers in their land: "non pudet, o Rutuli ..." (*Aen.* 12.229). Like Vergil, Prudentius evokes a clash of civilizations. The negative *non* is in place of *nonne*, which introduces a question to which the obvious answer should be "yes" (A&G §332). The absence of the interrogative particle -*ne* in this line suggests Superbia's IRONIC contempt. **plebeio milite**: ablative of means with *adtemptare*. Although *plebeius* had always been an insulting word, the Roman state became more stratified in late antiquity, and we can hear the contempt of Prudentius's contemporaries in the words of Superbia.

206–7. claros ... duces: object of *adtemptare*.

208. bellica uirtus: Superbia speaks of *uirtus* in her own way, which is a troubling possibility in a poem that is all about distinguishing virtue and vice. See also line 237 and the note on line 2.

208–11. ueteres ... antiquos: among her many complaints, Superbia despises the trite novelty of her Christian opponents.

209. laetos et gramine colles: the adjective *laetus* came to mean "happy" from the primary meaning of "fertile" or "flourishing." Even if the word *collis* were not frequently used of the seven hills of Rome (*OLD* s.v. 2), we would still probably think that Superbia had those particular hills in mind.

210. imperio ... dedit: "gave authority." Compare Cic., *Leg. Man.* 35 "unius huius se imperio ac potestati dediderunt" and Tert., *De ieiunio aduersus* *psychicos* 13 "quale est autem, ut tuo arbitrio permittas, quod imperio dei non das?"

211. nititur antiquos, | si fas est, | pellere reges: Superbia links herself immediately and emphatically with the antiquity and power of Rome. As regards the metrical shape of the line, the penthemimeral CAESURA and bucolic DIERESIS nicely enclose the parenthetical statement, a point noted by Franchi (2013, 218). The phrase *si fas est* implies that it would be wrong to drive out the kings. *Reges* contrasts with *regina* used of the Virtue in line 199.

212. en qui: "look at those who . . ." The interjection is contemptuous. The phrase *en qui nostra* was used by Vergil (*Aen.* 9.600) and picked up in the cento *Hippodamia* (141). **in praedam**: "to be their plunder." For this use of *in*, comparable to a dative of purpose, see *OLD* s.v. 21c.

213–15. Perhaps an allusion to the barbarian invasions of the 400s, on which see above on pr. 21.

216–19. Superbia says that she is the most natural of feelings and that she rules all humans from the moment they are born. These lines in particular recall *Am.* 378–444, in which Prudentius says 1) that no one raises their minds from earth to the hope of heaven, 2) that the enemy produces a host of vices within humankind, and 3) that there is a war being waged between the righteous and unrighteous. The comparison is especially close with lines 217–19 and *Am.* 391–92 "serit ille medullitus omnes / nequitias spargitque suos per membra ministros" (that [thief] sows all the vices in our marrow and scatters his ministers through our limbs).

216. nempe, o: perhaps the variant *nempe hoc* is correct, in which case you would need a full stop after *uulgus*. The variant deserves consideration because *nempe* does not seem to be used elsewhere with a vocative (with "o" at least) until the ninth century, whereas the phrase *nempe hoc* appears fairly frequently in Latin literature. Either way, an explanation for the variant is to hand in MS *S*, in which the monosyllable was added only afterward and above the line (I can see no sign of the erasure posited by Cunningham in his apparatus). **natalibus horis**: "in the hour of their birth."

217. Line 562 also has three ELISIONS. **calidos a matre ... artus:** Juvenal likewise described a newborn as "adhuc a matre rubentem" (7.196).

219. ossibus: in Latin as in English, the bones are often used by METONYMY for the innermost part of a person, as in descriptions of a cold so cold that you can "feel it in your bones."

220–27. Superbia was born in the beginning with Adam, and human civilization has advanced with her. Just as Superbia presents human history as a single story from beginning to end, Augustine would develop in *De ciuitate dei* a grand vision of history as a story of conflict between the world and the kingdom of God from creation to the end of the world.

220. tunc responds to *nunc* from line 210.

221–22. congenitis ... crescebant: "when our kingdom grew with a strength equal to the authority once born with it." Prudentius combines the language of human growth (*congenitis, robore*) with the language of political power (*regna, dicionibus, aequo*). Superbia mixes her METAPHORS and equates the original source of Rome's political power with Adam's original sin. The doctrine of original sin was developed in the 410s and 420s by Augustine in response to the ideas of Pelagius and his followers. Prudentius attacks the idea that Rome had a *genius* (a tutelary deity) in *Symm.* 2.370–449.

221. simul: take as an adverb with *congenitis.* **dicionibus:** dependent on *aequo.*

222. robore: the odd spelling *robure* occurs in the two oldest manuscripts, but that does not mean it is correct. **nati nam:** ANASTROPHE.

223. paribūs adoleuimus: the final short syllable of *paribus* is counted as long (DIASTOLE) with the metrical beat, as also in lines 712 and 764. On the 57 such lengthenings in Vergil, see Fordyce 1977, 97.

224. ex quo: "from the time at which," "ever since." **plasma nouum:** Adam, the first human created according to Genesis. The Greek word *plasma* was used of literary fictions, of invention, and also of creation. **paradisi:** the word occurs in Latin usually in Christian authors and starting with Tertullian.

225. "crossing the boundary he escaped into the wide world." In Superbia's mind, Adam is a hero because he made it out of the confines of the Garden of Eden and set humankind on the path to progress. The final lines of Milton's *Paradise Lost* know something of Superbia's humanistic grandeur:

> The world was all before them, where to choose
> Their place of rest, and Providence their guide:
> They, hand in hand, with wandering steps and slow,
> Through Eden took their solitary way. (12.646–49)

transfūgit: perfect tense. In the present tense, the stem vowel of *fŭgio* is short.

226. According to Gen. 3:21, Adam and Eve were given animal skins as clothing by God after they sinned and realized that they were naked. **pellitos**: the word was not used to describe clothing made from animal hides before late antiquity (*TLL* s.v. 10.1.1009.5–13 [Wirth]). **uenerabilis Adam**: Christians agreed that Adam was a type of Christ and of the individual Christian, but not because of his pride. In opposition to Superbia, Spes offers David as an example for humility in lines 291–301.

227. nudus: picks up the argument from line 210.

228. quisnam iste ignotis: the ELISIONS are sneering and contemptuous. **hostis nunc surgit ab oris**: in Juvencus's *Euangeliorum libri quattuor*, Jesus tells the Samaritan woman, "Sed *nunc* certa salus Iudaeis *surget ab oris*" (2.285), and Franchi tentatively suggested that Prudentius was alluding to Juvencus (2013, 232–33). Christ could then be heard as a specific lowly enemy of Superbia. It seems likely that Prudentius read Juvencus, but scholars have not reached any consensus on this topic, and it deserves further consideration.

229. Prudentius was fond of long and poetic enumerations, as noted by Lavarenne (1933b, § 1578–94). Compare the list in *Amartigenia* of vices produced within humans: "Ira superstitio maeror discordia luctus, / sanguinis atra sitis, uini sitis et sitis auri, / liuor adulterium dolus obtrectatio furtum" (395–97). **inportunus:** "untimely," the opposite of *opportunus*. **amens:** ironic since Superbia is talking about Mens humilis.

230. tam serum: the newness of Christianity was an argument against it, and it was even more recently that Christians had gained political power. **exul:** an exile lost his or her rights to property. But the Christian tradition gives a different version of the story than Superbia, namely, that Adam was the one exiled from the Garden of Eden (Nugent 1985, 37).

231. nimirum: often introduces IRONIC statements (*OLD* s.v. 1c). **friuola:** nominative.

232–33. miseros optare iubet quandoque futuri / Spem fortasse boni: "bids the miserable to prefer Hope in a potential good to come at some time."

233. solacia: subject of *palpent*.

234. meditamine: from Superbia's point of view, the problem with Humility is that she is all thought and no action. This derivative of *meditor* appears only here in extant Latin.

235. quid ni: asking "What is it if not . . . ?" is equivalent to "Isn't it clear that . . ."

236. Bellona: this Roman goddess of war was described in *Aen.* 8.702–3 "et scissa gaudens uadit Discordia palla, / quam cum sanguineo sequitur Bellona flagello" and Sil. 5.220–21 "Ipsa, facem quatiens ac flauam sanguine multo / sparsa comam, medias acies Bellona pererrat."

238. útile béllum est: hexameters do not normally end with a monosyllable, but the rhythm here is not disturbed because PRODELISION of *est* results in the pronunciation *béllu'st*. The same is true in lines 393, 401, 522, 546, 554, 624, 763, and 800 (Lavarenne 1933a, §274).

240. quam pudet: "how shameful it is." **Mauors:** an archaic form of *Mars*. **Virtus conscia:** see the note on line 208. *Conscia uirtus* appears at line end in previous epic, for example at *Aen.* 12.668. Juvencus ends a line "uirtus mox conscia caelum" (4.385).

241. contra stare: the quantity of the second syllable in *contra* could be long or short, as explained in the note on line 151. While *contra* is normally a spondee in Prudentius, the second syllable is short in *Perist.* 5.145 (Lavarenne 1933b, §164). **nugas**: object of *lacessere*. Superbia feels demeaned in facing such an unworthy opponent.

242. cum uirgineis . . . choraeis: the Greek *choreia* referred either to a circular dance or to the dancers themselves. The normal spelling in Latin was *chorea*, and some poets shortened the penultimate syllable.

243–47. A mini catalogue of Virtues as they appear through the eyes of Superbia. As noted above on lines 160–61, Prudentius varies his material according to speaker and context.

244. albo . . . uultu: an ablative of quality or description (A&G §415).

245–46. aperta / Simplicitas et: note that the conjunction is postponed and that the adjective dangles at the end of the line.

247. iudice sese: "with herself as the judge" or "in her own judgment." The pronoun is an emphatic form of *se*.

248. quam degenerem trepidatio prodit: a reference to a proverbial statement that is from *Aen.* 4.13 and that is appropriate here: "degeneres animos timor arguit." The intertext was already cited in the commentary of MS Valenciennes 413 (Burnam 1910, 94), although a scribe mistakenly moved the comment to line 229.

249. faxo: an archaic future of *facio*. In a note on *faxo* in *Aen.* 12.316, the text of *Serv. Dan.* explains, "id est faciam, confirmabo; et est archaismos" (i.e., *faciam*, I will make it happen; and it is an archaism). *Faxo* was followed by the future indicative and present subjunctive usually, exceptionally with *ut* in Plaut. *Asin.* 897. **more**: "in the manner of," "like."

250. inualida ista manus: the subject of *teratur* is emphatically ENJAMBED.

252. inbuere: note the CAESURA in the second foot and the lengthening of the short *e* before *fr*-. This creates a halting rhythm. For lengthening of a syllable before a mute and a liquid, see appendix A. **uiros**: object of *foedare*. Superbia will not befoul her men with such a lowly triumph.

253–73. Superbia falls into a trap set by Fraus. Her downfall illustrates the old adage "Pride goes before the fall" ("Contritionem praecedit superbia et ante ruinam exaltatur spiritus"; Prov. 16:18 Vulgate). In this way, Prudentius creates a high degree of correspondence between the surface narrative and the meaning of the characters' names, as also in the battle between Patientia and Ira.

The action is delayed by the strong CAESURA after *cornipedem* in 254 and even more by the DIERESIS with *sternere* at the beginning of 256 (in a line without a strong CAESURA). These halting rhythms set up the fall of Superbia, which is set off by the strong CAESURA in the fourth foot of 257. The poetry lends drama to what could have been a formulaic description.

The verb *cadere* (257) was used elsewhere by Christians to refer to sinning or falling away from God; for examples, see *TLL* s.v. 3.0.26.4–31 (Hoppe). This links the downfall of Superbia to the sin of Adam, as observed by Nugent (1985, 37).

253. Talia uociferans: the phrase appears, for example, at *Aen.* 10.651 and Claud., *Rapt.* 2.223. **rapidum**: the word probably derives some color here from its near homonym *rabidus*.

255. inpulsu umbonis equini: Superbia wants to knock her down with a blow from the horse's chest, which is an effective way to trample a victim. Lavarenne implausibly translated as though she were using a shield made of horse leather (2002, 59).

255–56. Superbia's desire will exactly match her downfall, as pointed out by Gnilka (1963, 61–62). She wants to knock Mens humilis over with her steed but is knocked down herself (273). She wants to lay low the Virtue, but falls instead (257). She wants to trample her, but is trampled in turn (273). And she wanted to crush Humility under her feet ("sub pedibus teratur" 249) but is crushed instead (275).

256. supercalcare: Prudentius seems to be the only Latin poet who used this prosaic verb, which helps to give the scene a certain urgency.

257. sed cadit in foueam: the half-line is masterfully concise and deflationary. Even though we knew it was coming, Superbia's downfall is still surprising. The following lines are highly poetic with repetition and ALLITERATION with *Fraus, furtim, Fraus, fallendi*.

259. uitiorum e pestibus una: "one of the deadly vices." The explanatory genitive (*uitiorum*) came to be used more widely in later Latin, and recurs in line 269 (*foueae . . . furta malignae*), 347 (*uexillum crucis*), and 884 (*sceptri gestamen*). For more detail, see Lavarenne 1933b, §261.

260. praescia belli: like *memor, praescius* takes an objective genitive (A&G §349).

261. uiolauerat: MS *A* has *uitiauerat*, which probably was introduced into the text under the influence of *uitiorum* two lines above. The fact that the reading *uitiauerat* appears in the margin of MS *C* offers evidence that the scribe of *C* had access to readings from *A*.

262. hostili de parte: "on the enemy's side." Lucan has the same phrase at *Phars.* 1.622 (of haruspicy) and compare, for example, "alia de parte" from *Aen.* 4.153. **latens**: on hiding, see the note below on line 741.

262–63. ut fossa ruentes / exciperet cuneos: compare Claud., *In Eutropium* 2.438–39 "Ast alios uicina palus sine more *ruentes / excipit* et cumulis inmanibus aggerat undas."

264. posset: imperfect subjunctive in a purpose clause in secondary sequence (A&G §482–83).

265. oras: glossed as *summitates* ("top") in the Weitz B tradition (O'Sullivan 2004, 225–26).

267. quamuis ignara: Mens humilis makes up for her ignorance by refusing to act rashly.

269. aut: in place of *nec*.

270. praepete cursu: the phrase appears at Stat., *Theb.* 6.298; Claud., *Ruf.* 1.262; Prud., *Am.* 293, and as the reading of the majority of the manuscripts in Juvencus, *Euangeliorum* 3.265.

272. prona: modifies *Superbia*.

273. inpressu: the word occurs only here and in Sid. Apoll., *Epist.* 7.17.2. **rotatur:** the fall of Superbia recalls the wheel (*rota*) of Fortune, a common image for the variability of Fate. Compare, for example, Cic., *Pis.* 10.22; Sen., *Ag.* 72; Auson., *Parent.* 22.13; and Fulgentius, *Expositio Virgilianae continentiae*, ed. Rudolf Helm (Leipzig: Teubner, 1898), p. 107. With his habitual irritability, Jerome said that Christians believe events are ruled by God's providence and not fate: "Non fatorum, ut stulti putant, sic fila deducta sunt; non fortunae cucurrit rota, sed dei iudicio et ipsius uoluntate perfectum est" (*In Esaiam* 5.23.9). But even Jerome might have appreciated such a subtle allusion to the downfall of individuals and empires.

274–309. Spes offers a sword to Mens humilis, who beheads Superbia. Spes then delivers a boastful speech, or vaunt (*euchos*), over the fallen Vice and compares her fall to that of the giant Goliath at the hands of the young David. After her speech, Spes ascends directly to heaven and inspires the other Virtues to continue the struggle as they await their own rewards.

274. At: in his commentary on *Aen.* 6.679, R. G. Austin notes that *at* is often used by Vergil to begin a new section (1977, 213). **moderaminis:** moderation was a classical virtue much beloved of Greeks and Romans alike.

274–75. ut leuitatem / prospicit obtritam monstri: "when she saw that the frivolity of the monster was crushed." The unnecessary abstract noun *leuitas* broadens the narrative and makes this statement less direct and more moderate.

275. sub morte iacentis: *orantis* in line 282 shows that she is "lying on the point of death" and not yet dead, and Vergil has "morte sub aegra" in this sense at *G.* 3.512. But, in a poem performed in Rome in 402, Claudian has the phrase *populos sub morte iacentes* in reference to the dead in Hades (*Get.* 448). The parallel with Claudian is so exact that it is probably not random, but neither do I find any convincing reason to think that it was intentional; maybe Prudentius unconsciously echoed a phrase that he heard Claudian perform in Rome.

277. comi: third-declension adjective from *comis*, "courteous, elegant."

278. Spes was an object of cult worship in and beyond Rome. It is interesting to note that there was a temple for Spes, Fides, and Fortuna in Capua in the second century B.C.E., as can be inferred from *CIL* 10.3775.

279. ultorem gladium: for *ultor* used in apposition instead of an adjective, see *OLD* s.v. *ultor* c. The phrase *ultor gladius* ("avenging sword") has a legal and religious sound. As explained in Boeft et al. 2007, 145–46, this phrase is found in Tert., *De patientia* 3; Leviticus 26:25; Job 19:29; Amm. Marc. 26.6.8; and seven times in the *Codex Theodosianus.* **laudisque inspirat amorem:** compare Anchises raising the spirits of Aeneas: "incenditque animum famae uenientis amore" (*Aen.* 6.889).

281. laeua: with *manu* understood.

282. orantis flexa ceruice: suppliants are almost never spared in ancient epics, as pointed out by Alessandro Barchiesi (2015, 85). The language recalls Magus, who was not spared by Aeneas but had his neck bent back as he prayed: "reflexa / ceruice orantis" (*Aen.* 10.535–36).

283. colla: "her severed head" (*OLD* s.v. *collum* 3).

284. increpat ore: Spes speaks in an elevated tone that befits Superbia's conqueror.

285. grande: there is no clear line between the cognate accusative and the adverbial use of the accusative (see A&G §390 and above on line 129). **frangit deus omne superbum:** it was a proverb among Jews and Christians that God opposes the proud (Prov. 3:34, 1 Pet. 5:5, and James 4:6). Augustine was deeply influenced by this scriptural text, as noted by James O'Donnell in his commentary on *Conf.* 1.1.1.

286. For the general message, compare Claudian's epigram on the tomb of a beautiful woman, in which he observes that great and high things fall suddenly: "magna repente ruunt; summa cadunt subito" (*Carm. min.* 11.2). **inflata:** "what is puffed up." **crepant** means to make (a loud or sharp) noise, sometimes of the noise made when passing gas (*OLD* s.v. 1d).

287. disce supercilium deponere: Nugent (1985, 40) reads this line as an allusion to *Aen.* 6.853 (see above on line 15), in which Aeneas is told to spare the humbled; she explains "the entire episode of Superbia's downfall . . . as a narrative enactment of Anchises's famous line." Although it may be less appropriate in the mouth of Spes, there is also an echo of the phrase "pone supercilium," which appears in Mart. 1.4.2; Auson., *Bissula* 2.2; and the *Carmina Priapeia* 1.2.

290. The saying of Christ given in indirect speech is found in very similar form at Matt. 23:12, Luke 14:11, and Luke 18:14. In the text of Matthew, the Vulgate has the following: "Qui autem se exaltauerit humiliabitur et qui se humiliauerit exaltabitur." Prudentius makes both verbs active, and he uses the adjective *ferox* as an antonym for *humilis*. Prudentius's version gives the words a certain weight and elegance in place of the simplicity of Matthew's version. He was probably influenced by Juvencus 4.66–68 "In uobis si quis sublimia colla leuabit, / decidet et barathri mergetur ad ultima caeno; / ast humilis claram conscendet liber in aethram." Juvencus also used the adjective *imos* in a parallel passage at 3.613. Of the 141 individual instances of Matt. 23:12 cited in the *Vetus latina* database, these two from Juvencus stand out for their similarity to Prudentius. And nothing is changed if you read the 166 instances in that database of Luke 14:11, or the 207 of Luke 18:14.

scandere celsa: this exact phrase appears in a poem that was written by Paulinus of Nola and enclosed in his famous letter sent to Licentius in 396 (*Epist.* 8 v. 15); it appears in the same metrical position in Bede's *Vita Cuthberti* 29; and Prudentius begins *Perist.* 6.98 with "celsa scandere" in a parallel context. Bede's verse looks like a direct allusion to this passage in the *Psychomachia*. Unless *Perist.* 6 was written before 396, Prudentius probably alludes in both passages to a memorable phrase from Paulinus.

291. membris animisque: ablatives of respect, a construction that is also called the ablative of specification (A&G §418). **Golian:** MS *A* gives the name of the giant killed by King David as a Greek accusative, whereas *B* has the Latin ending *Goliam*. The story is from 1 Sam. 17.

292. inualida . . . manu: in her speech responding to Superbia's, Spes sarcastically repeats her words from line 250.

294. traiectam . . . penetrauit: PROLEPSIS. The participle anticipates the action of the verb.

296–97. The repetition of *dum* (ANAPHORA) helps make the description bombastic.

297. territat auras: compare "caelum territat armis" from *Aen*. 11.351, where Drances invidiously portrays the Italian hero Turnus as assaulting the sky in vain. Likewise, Goliath makes an empty show of his bravery as he brandishes his shield on high.

298. quid possint ludicra parui: Prudentius may be alluding to Paulinus of Nola's rejection of childish play, in a poem written to Jovius between 400–402. Paulinus urged Jovius to turn away from mythological poetry about Paris and about the false battles of the giants; these were games for children: "non modo iudicium Paridis nec bella gigantum / falsa canis: fuerit puerili ludus in aeuo / iste tuus quondam; decuerunt ludicra paruum" (*Ad Iouium* 12–14 = Hartel *Carm*. 22). This verbal repetition in the context of the young David's defeat of Goliath suggests that Prudentius meant to allude to the cultural conflict that lay behind Paulinus's poem; that is, he takes part in a current dispute between true and false poetry that came to pit Christian devotees of truth against mythologizers in the mold of Claudian.

More broadly, poets often spoke of light poetry as *ludicra*. Whereas Horace set aside his *ludicra* to write serious poetry (*Epist*. 1.1.10), Apuleius wrote a collection of poetry entitled *Ludicra* (*Apol*. 6), and Ausonius defended light poetry in *Protr*. 1. Prudentius himself prayed elsewhere that God would rule everything he did, including things frivolous and serious: "seria, ludicra, uerba, iocos" (*Cath*. 3.18). As a warrior and the author of many Psalms, David was an ideal model for Christian poets promoting serious art. On David in this context, see *Cath*. 9.4–5 and O'Daly 2012, 262–63. Whereas Paulinus was somewhat more dogmatic, Prudentius allows that even humble and playful poetry can accomplish great things.

The manuscript variant *possent* is in secondary sequence, which is grammatically correct if the perfect tense of the main verb (*subcubuit*) refers to past time (A&G §482–85). But the present *possint* is acceptable because the typological sequence points to the present and explains what can be accomplished *now*. There is similar confusion in the manuscripts at *Apoth.* 322 and *Symm.* 2.259. Parallel passages pointing in either direction include *Aen.* 11.386–87 "possit quid uiuida uirtus / experiare licet" and Damasus, *Epigrammata* 1.7 "sensit posset quid gloria christi."

The variant *possit* in MS *A* may have been caused by the singular *quid* preceding it, and it is definitely evidence that *possint* was early. The reading *possent* would then have been a hypercorrection, perhaps under the influence of *posset* in line 264.

299. subcubuit: the compound verb takes a dative object. **teneris annis** refers to the young child by METONYMY.

300. uirtutis pube: "in the fullness of his virtue."

301. sursum: the word was used by Lucretius a number of times but not by Vergil. The line recalls Col. 3:2 "quae sursum sunt sapite non quae supra terram" (Vulgate; the old Latin translations also have *sursum*). Paul's exhortation to think on the things above can be heard both in this line and in the reaction to her speech in lines 306–8.

302. certa ... domus: Jesus promised his disciples that he would prepare a place for them in his father's house (John 14:2). **omnipotentis:** modifies *domini*. Christians appropriated this poetic adjective and used it commonly in prose as well.

303. me ad sublime uocantem: she is calling them to heaven. The adjective *sublime* is used as a substantive, as in line 288.

305–9. Spes is the only one of the Virtues to ascend on wings to heaven. Whereas Superbia is focused on the past, Spes looks to the future and receives her reward.

305–6. dixit et auratis praestringens aera pinnis / in caelum: Prudentius apparently imitates Ov., *Met.* 1.466 "dixit et eliso percussis aere pennis" and Verg., *Aen.* 9.14 "dixit, et in caelum paribus se sustulit alis."

This is the only place in Latin literature where Spes is portrayed as winged, although she is described as winged in Greek literature (see Shanzer 1989, 352–53). Shanzer suggested that Prudentius's winged figure recalled the altar of Victory that was removed from the Senate House by Gratian in 383 and that may have become an issue again in 402. Unlike Spes, Victoria is constantly portrayed as winged, including in Prudentius's reference to her in the Senate House in *Symm.* 2.27–29 "Aurea quamuis / marmoreo in templo rutilas Victoria pinnas / explicat." On the statue of Victory, see Pohlsander 1969 and Cameron 2011, 340–42, who does not think the statue was removed from the Senate house when the altar was removed or that there was any attempt to have the altar returned in 402. If the golden wings of Spes are an allusion to Victoria, Prudentius is replacing the concrete power of the Roman Empire with Christian hope. For an idea of what the statue would have looked like, see the Victoria standing on a globe in figure 9.

305. aëra: accusative, with the Greek third-declension ending (A&G §81–82).

307. tolluntque animos in uota: "they raise their spirits in prayer."

308. ire simul: the infinitive is explanatory after *uolentes*. Note that the wishes of the Virtues correspond to the call of Spes from line 303. **ni bella duces terrena retardent:** the verb is present subjunctive in the protasis of a future less vivid conditional. The apodosis is implicit in "uolentes ire simul." One might have expected the imperfect *retardarent*, but Prudentius makes the possibility of their leaving even more remote.

The clause echoes one from Anchises's account of human nature: "*quantum non* noxia corpora *tardant* / *terreni*que hebetant artus" (*Aen.* 6.731–32).

309. Gnilka thought that this line was INTERPOLATED (2000–2003, 1:675–77), because the Virtues supposedly do not receive rewards and because the phrase "sua praemia" was already used in line 168. But the only problem with this line is that it is somewhat anticlimactic.

FIGURE 9. Statue of Victory, Museo Archeologico
Nazionale (Naples). *Photograph courtesy Hans R. Goette.*

The phrase "sua praemia" echoes *Aen.* 1.461, and it was also used twice by Juvencus (4.184 and 4.303) and twice in a poem by Paulinus of Nola (*Ultimarum prima* 152 and 301 = Hartel *Carm.* 10).

SOBRIETAS VS. LUXURIA (310–453)

The fifth battle begins with a lavish description of Luxuria and her train; she fights with flowers and scents as her weapons; and the Virtues face real danger for the first time in the poem, as many willingly give themselves over to Luxuria (310–43). Sobrietas, who carries the standard of the cross, upbraids them for their madness and for ignoring their history; she reminds them that their ancestors were the Hebrew heroes David, Samuel, and Jonathan (344–406). After her speech, Sobrietas turns back the enemy with the cross of Christ; she crushes the fallen enemy with a stone; and she delivers a boastful speech over Luxuria (407–431). Prudentius then describes the scattered attendants of Luxuria and the renewed sobriety of the Virtues (432–53).

The Ps.-Augustinian treatise *De sobrietate et castitate* was roughly contemporary with Prudentius. A modern, secular treatise in the same vein is *La sobriedad* by the Spanish philosopher Francesc Torralba Roselló (2012).

310–43. The success of Luxuria comes only from the allure of her presence, and Prudentius does not spare detail or ornament.

310. uenerat occiduis mundi de finibus hostis: the prejudices of Western culture have usually associated degrading luxury with the East. So what does it mean that Luxuria comes from the West? Either Prudentius implicitly criticizes Roman decadence, or maybe the setting of the sun (*occidiuis*) is an allusion to death. Or maybe the fact that Jerusalem is in the East affected his outlook. But Prudentius does not imagine any simple correspondence between the physical and spiritual world.

Prudentius associates the last three vices with the world (*mundus*): see also lines 523 "quod miscet mundus" and 714 "domus et plaga mundus." Gnilka (1963, 38–40) plausibly suggests that the last three battles refer historically to conflicts between the world and the church after the coming of Christ.

311. extinctae . . . prodiga famae: she was extravagant and boasting of her ruined reputation.

312. delibuta: the second syllable is short elsewhere; maybe Prudentius has the Greek root λείβω in mind. **oculis . . . uoce:** ablatives of specification (A&G §418) with the nominatives *uaga* and *languida*.

313. uitae cui causa uoluptas: "whose reason for living was pleasure." The relative pronoun is a dative of possession. In a parallel phrase in Ambrose, *uitae* is clearly genitive: "Ille enim causa mortis, hic uitae" (*Expositio euangelii secundum Lucam* 5.31 [Adriaen CC 14], p. 147, l. 364).

314. elumbem: the adjective was prosaic; its earliest appearances in Latin poetry are here and in Prudent., *Perist.* 2.216.

314–15. mollire . . . / haurire . . . soluere: translate as infinitives of purpose.

315. haurire inlecebras: see the note on line 430 for an echo of this phrase and an example of ring composition in this poem.

321. pedes: the derivative noun ("foot soldier") and not the plural of *pes*.

322. saucia . . . corda: echoes the same phrase in Paulinus of Nola, *Natalicia* 6.257 = Hartel *Carm.* 18, from the year 400. **mirantum:** the genitive plural of present participles often ends in -*um* in poetry (A&G §121b). **capiebat** = *decipiebat* (*OLD* s.v. *capio* 20).

323–39. In his description of Luxuria conquering without weapons, Prudentius seems to rival Claudian's description of Venus from his Greek *Gigantomachia* 43–54. In that poem, the goddess is described as fighting without spear or weapon and only with her beauty; she has her hair for a helmet, her breast for a spear, her brow for a dart, and her beauty for a shield; all who looked on her were conquered and cast down their weapons.

The idea that *Psychomachia* was written in dialogue with Claudian's *Gigantomachia* is not unattractive (see Hoefer 1895, 15 and 59). At the least, Prudentius does seem to have known of Claudian's Latin *Gigantomachia*, as we can infer from what looks like an instance of *aemulatio* in *Apoth.* 111–12, which echoes lines 106–7 of Claudian's poem. For another link to the Latin *Gigantomachia*, see the note above on 1. On the other hand, both Cameron (1970, 471–72) and Dorfbauer (2012, 59–60) think that Claudian was imitating *Apotheosis*, mainly because Claudian's poem is unfinished. However, the unfinished state of *Giantomachia* is no great obstacle since these poets easily could have known each other.

323–24. non ales harundo / neruum pulsa fugit: Heinsius compared *Aen.* 12.856 "neruo . . . impulsa sagitta" and printed "neruo pulsa fugit." But *fugio* was common both as a transitive and intransitive verb (see *OLD* s.v.), and there is not enough reason to doubt what was clearly the reading of the archetype.

324–25. nec stridula lancea torto / emicat amento: "nor does a sounding spear leap from a twisted strap."

325. frameam nec dextra minatur: *framea* was an old Germanic word for a spear. Christian authors used it also of a sword, for no recoverable reason (see *TLL* s.v. 3 = 6.1.1239.80–40.53 [Vollmer]).

328. eblanditis uirtutibus: perhaps best taken as an ablative absolute. There are a handful of parallels for the perfect passive participle of *eblandior* used with passive meaning, including at Gell. 11.13.5 (see *TLL* s.v. *eblandior* [Kapp and Meyer]). **halitus:** Prudentius METONYMICALLY calls the seductive spirit a breath.

329. inspirat tenerum labefacta per ossa uenenum: Venus tells Cupid to trick Dido with the poison of love in *Aen.* 1.688 "occultum *inspires* ignem fallasque *ueneno.*" Likewise, desire runs through the weakened bones of Vulcan in *Aen.* 8.389–90 "notusque medullas / intrauit calor et *labefacta per ossa* cucurrit." Prudentius "contaminates" those two lines and adds an adjective (*tener*) that was very common in elegiac love poetry.

330. male dulcis: "terribly sweet" (Burton).

332. ponunt = *deponunt*, probably under the influence of the prefix in *deiciunt*. For the prefix of a compound verb being understood with a nearby simplex verb, see Renehan 1969, §57.

336–39. The wheels of the chariot are described in detail: around the golden axle an array of spokes gleam with silver; the spokes are kept in place by an outer ring made of electrum, an amber-colored alloy that is 80% gold and 20% silver (Pliny, *HN* 33.80).

336. pretiosi ponderis: this genitive of quality (A&G §345) modifies *axem*.

338. seriem: "array."

340. in deditionis amorem: surrendering to an enemy like Luxuria was a pleasure.

341. sponte sua: "of their own volition," "willingly." **perfida**: modifies *acies*.

343. gănearum: respectable Romans did not eat in restaurants, and apparently the first syllable of the word was normally long, although Prudentius also has găneonis at *Am.* 322.

344–406. Sobrietas comes on the scene to bring the Virtues back to their senses. A brief description introduces her direct speech, which culminates in a plea for the wayward Virtues to repent.

344. Ingemuit tam triste nefas: "She groaned at such a grim sacrilege." Prudentius puns on *nefas* as what is unspeakable.

346. quondam modifies *inuictam*. **perire**: the verb was sometimes used in poetry for those overtaken by love (*OLD* s.v. 4), and that secondary meaning may have resonance in a description of soldiers defeated by Luxuria.

347. uexillum sublime crucis: object of *sistit*. The genitive is explanatory, as noted above in the note on line 259.

Constantine heard that he would conquer in the sign of the cross. Prudentius recounts the story of Constantine's victory at the Milvian Bridge in *Symm.* 1.468–95, a passage that begins "Hoc signo inuictus . . . ."

The Christian cross was also described as a military standard in Prudent., *Cath.* 9.83–84; *Apoth.* 44; *Perist.* 1.34; and by Paulinus of Nola both in his *Natalicia* 11.655 = Hartel *Carm.* 19 and *Ad Cytherium* 141 = Hartel *Carm.* 24.

349. instaurat: Prudentius puns on the Greek word *stauros* ("cross"). The verb was used of regrouping an army at *Aen.* 10.543.

350. In the *Aeneid,* Pallas rallies the Trojans with a similar mixture of entreaty and bitter words: "*nunc prece, nunc dictis* uirtutem accendit *amaris*" (10.368).

351. quis furor: a common way to begin a dactylic line.

352. quo ruitis: echoes Aeneas's plea to the Trojan to remain by their treaty: "quo ruitis? quaeue ista repens discordia surgit?" (*Aen.* 12.313). **colla datis:** *colla dare* means to surrender, like an animal to a yoke. Compare Stat., *Achil.* 1.944 "Troades optabuntque tuis dare colla catenis." **tandem:** emphasizes that this is the last in a series of rhetorical questions.

354–55. lilia . . . coronas: the nouns at either end of these lines are both in apposition to *uincula.*

355. ferrugineo: a dark red or blue color.

356. adsuetas bello: either "trained by war" or "accustomed to fighting," both constructions being attested (*OLD* s.v. *assuetus* 1).

357. his rigidas: the hardness of the Virtues contrasts with the softness of the chains of Luxuria.

358. mitra: a headdress worn usually by women, but also by Bacchus (Prop. 4.2.31) and by the effeminate Publius Clodius Pulcher, according to Cic., *Har. resp.* 21.44.

359. relegamine: a derivative of the verb *religo*; the word appears only here in extant ancient literature. For the spelling, see Lavarenne 1933b, §17.

360–61. Prudentius refers to a practice of marking the sign of the cross on one's forehead with oil, perhaps in a ceremony of baptism. For similar references, see Ambrose, *De Isaac* 8.75; Jerome, *Epist.* 130.9; and Rufinus, *Expositio symboli* 41.

Prudentius addresses the Christian reader in *Cath.* 6.125–28 as someone marked by the cross: "Cultor dei, memento / te fontis et lauacri / rorem subisse sanctum, / te chrismate innotatum."

360. frontis: take with *signacula*. **signacula:** the word was not poetic. Before the Christian scriptures and discussions of them, it was hardly used outside of legal contexts.

361. chrisma: "anointing." This Greek word was used in Latin by Christian writers, beginning with Tertullian.

362. ut: a second final clause parallel to the one above in line 358. **uestigia syrmate uerrat:** they are so lost that they have taken to wearing long Greek robes with trains that cover their feet.

363. infractis: "unsteady" (*nutantibus*) and "softened" (*mollificatis*) are the glosses for this word in the Weitz B tradition (O'Sullivan 2004, 243). **ut:** ANASTROPHE. The conjunction introduces a third final clause. **pallia:** equivalent to the Greek *himation*, these wrapped mantles were often associated with philosophers and intellectual activity, although silken ones are clearly a different story. Note that women and goddesses wore *pallia* (TLL s.v. *pallium* I.A.2.c = 10.1.135.55–[Zäch]), and not only *pallae* and *palliola*.

364. inmortalem tunicam: the apostle Paul urged the Romans to clothe themselves, spiritually, with Jesus Christ: "Induimini dominum Iesum Christum" (Rom. 13:14; Vulgate). **pollice docto:** Ovid mentions the learned thumb of Apollo as he plays the lyre (*Met.* 11.169–70), and Statius (*Theb.* 11.401) and Claudian (*Probinus et Olybrius* 177) use the phrase of weaving. More generally, the thumb was often included in descriptions of weaving in Latin poetry (*TLL* s.v. I.A.2.a = 10.1.2543.5–19 [Ottink]). Like his predecessors, Prudentius sees himself as weaving learned poetry, on which see below on line 768.

365. alma Fides: a number of Latin poets use this phrase, including Statius and Paulinus of Nola.

366. dederat quibus ipsa renasci: "whom she herself had granted a second birth."

367. inde ad nocturnas epulas: understand a verb such as *eatis* or *ruatis*.

368. "… spits out the foaming loss of spilt Falernian wine." *Effusi* is redundant. The descriptive verb (*despuit*) would normally refer to the person rather than the jug, as pointed out in the gloss of B I (Burnam 1905, 62). The passage could recall Propertius's description of a lush feast and a table foaming with Falernian wine (2.33.39–40), as suggested by Shackleton Bailey (1952, 321).

370. ueterique toreumata rore rigantur: perhaps "the embroidery runs wet with old liquid." *Toreuma* usually means engraved or embossed work, but Du Cange (s.v.) and Arevalo (1788–89, 2:620–21) are probably right in thinking that the word here refers to a valance or covering for a couch. Arevalo cites Salvian's description of a decadent dining room, which was almost certainly influenced by this passage: "natant tricliniorum redundantium pauimenta uino, *Falerno* nobili lutum faciunt, mensae eorum ac *toreumata mero* iugiter madent, semper *uda* sunt" (*Ad ecclesiam* 4.33). Sidonius also uses *toreuma* to refer to a silk covering (*Epist.* 2.13.6).

371–76. God miraculously provided food and water for the Israelites in the desert, when they were wandering from Egypt to the Holy Land: quail flew into their camp in the evening, a breadlike substance called manna appeared on the ground in the mornings, and water sprung from a rock (Exod. 16–17).

371. excidit ergo animis: "has it slipped from your mind then . . . ?" **érĕmi**: "in the desert." This Greek word was not used in Latin until the time of Prudentius, when it was popularized because of the Eastern desert monks who practiced an extreme form of Christian asceticism. Prudentius shortens the second vowel, probably to preserve the Attic accentuation on the antepenult, as he also does in *Cath.* 5.89.

372. patribus: indirect object with *datus*. **mystica uirga**: water appeared in the desert after Moses struck the rock with his staff. Compare Aaron's rod from lines 884–87.

374. angelicusne cibus: the suffix *-ne* introduces another rhetorical question. The angelic food is either the manna, or more likely the quail. Prudentius interprets this food as a symbol for the eucharist. **prima in tentoria**: "into their tents first," as a prefiguration of the later sacred meal.

375. auis: "for your forefathers," a dative of advantage (A&G §376).

376. uespertinus ... populus: "the people in the evening." The adjective can be analyzed as a predicate or as a transferred epithet (HYPALLAGE). *Vespertinus* is apparently a reference to celebrations of the eucharist in the evening, which was like the quail that the Israelites ate in the evening: "et ait Moses dabit Dominus uobis uespere carnes edere" (Exod. 16:8; Vulgate). In that case, *auis* ("ancestors") in the line above puns on *auis* ("bird"). More remotely, *uespertinus* can suggest that Christians are a people living in the end times. The latter interpretation is found already in the B I glosses (Burnam 1905, 62).

ĕdit: *ĕdere* ("eat") should not be confused with *ēdere* ("to give out"). The latter was originally a contraction (*ex + do*) in which the loss of the consonant resulted in the compensatory lengthening of the preceding vowel.

377. crapula: the Greek word for drunkenness (*kraipalē*) was borrowed early in Rome and appears in comedy. In later authors, it is also used of excessive eating, i.e., "gluttony."

378. Luxuriae: modifies *lupanar.*

379–80. quosque uiros ... flexit: "and she persuaded the men who ..." *Viros* is rationally the direct object of the main verb and the antecedent of *quos*, but it has been attracted into the relative clause (A&G §599e). You can translate *quosque uiros* literally as "which men."

379. non Ira fremens non idola: Sobrietas recalls the battles won already by Patientia and Fides. Such internal references show that the individual scenes of the poem are part of a larger whole. **idŏla:** The second syllable of this originally Greek word (*eídōlon*) is normally long. Prudentius shortens the omega so that the first syllable is still accentuated in Latin. In general, when Prudentius uses Greek words, he keeps the quality but not necessarily the quantity of Greek vowels. See above on 371 and appendix A.

381. uestri: this form of *uos* is used as an objective genitive, *uestrum* as a partitive genitive (A&G §295b).

382–83. quae sit ... quae ... quis ... quis: indirect questions introduced by *meminisse.*

382. tribus: most fourth declension nouns are masculine. Other exceptions include *domus, manus,* and some names of plants and trees (A&G §90). **quis deus et rex:** God the Father.

383. quis dominus: Jesus Christ.

384. dei genetricem: "mother of God" (i.e., Mary) translates the Greek theological term *theotokos* that would be a subject of major controversy at the third ecumenical council held in Ephesus in 431. **qua:** ablative of source (A&G §403a).

386–87. celeberrima Dauid / gloria: Hebrew names are often indeclinable in Latin; the sense requires that *Dauid* be genitive here.

388. Samuel: probably nominative rather than genitive. According to 1 Sam. 15, this prophet killed the captured king of the Amalekites and told Saul not to take any of their spoils.

391. recidiua: there might be a contrast with *rediuiuus,* which was used of the resurrected Christ in *Cath.* 3.204. The adjective here derives from *cado* ("to fall"). The two words were often confused in transmission, which makes it harder to reach any conclusions about its broader use.

392. parcere ... crimen: understand *esse* as the infinitive of indirect speech after *putat* and *crimen* as a predicate noun modifying *parcere,* "... that it is a crime to spare." Unlike Samuel, Anchises had told the Romans to conquer the proud and spare the humble (see above on line 15). **putat ille:** the present tense is more allegorical than historical. **tyranno:** dative object of *parcere.*

393. uinci et subcumbere: infinitive predicates of *uotum.*

394. paeniteat per si qua mouet reuerentia ... : "repent by, if any reverence moves [you] ..." Logically, *reuerentia* should be the accusative object of *per* and antecedent of the indefinite adjective *qua*; but it has been attracted into the nominative case. The indefinite *qui, qua, quod* is rare except after *si, nisi, num,* and *ne* (A&G §149); its synonym *aliquis* is far more common. This line echoes Sinon's plea to the Trojans in *Aen.* 2.142–44 "Per si qua est quae restet adhuc mortalibus usquam / intemerata fides, oro, miserere laborum / tantorum." On *per* as used in oaths and entreaties, see *OLD* s.v. 10. Prudentius here replaces Vergil's verb of entreaty (*oro*) with *paeniteat*, which would take the object *uos* in the accusative case; the full thought is *paeniteat uos, oro per uestram reuerentiam, si qua . . .* (Repent, I beg of you by your reverence, if any . . .).

396. si paenitet, haud nocet error: echoes *Laus Iohannis* 290 ("si paenitet, inrita culpa est") and Ausonius's prayer of repentance in *Ephemeris* 3.54–57 (ed. Green 1991).

From the spread of *haut* and *aut* in the manuscripts, we might conclude that the archetype already had *haut*, and that *B* corrected the spelling to *haud*.

397–402. 1 Sam. 14 recounts how Jonathan unknowingly disobeyed his father's command to fast from food until their army had conquered. After Jonathan confessed, he was spared the death sentence.

397. Ionatham: accusative.

398. conuiolasse: the earliest appearance of this word is in Tertullian, and it seems to have been used only by Christian writers. **sceptri mellisque sapore:** Jonathan dipped the tip of his staff in honey and tasted of it.

399. regni: apparently Prudentius interprets Jonathan's action as an attempt at the throne. 1 Sam. says only that Jonathan was hungry, and there is no explicit mention of his repentance.

402. nec tinguit patrias sententia saeua secures: recalls the description in *Aen.* 6 of Lucius Iunius Brutus, who executed his own sons for plotting against the young republic:

> Consulis imperium hic primus *saeuasque securis*
> accipiet, natosque pater noua bella mouentis
> ad poenam pulchra pro libertate uocabit,

infelix utcumque ferent ea facta minores:
uincet amor patriae laudumque immensa cupido. (6.819–23)

403. en ego Sobrietas: Brenda Machosky describes allegory as allowing objects to become present and as "a structure of appearance for things and ideas that cannot appear in any other way" (2013, 1). By having Sobrietas declare her name, Prudentius draws attention to the fact that his spiritual virtues are made visible in language. **si conspirare paratis:** if they are ready to work with Sobrietas.

404. pando uiam: Ausonius prayed that Christ would open a way for his prayers ("pande uiam," *Ephemeris* 3.30 [Green]) and that God would open a way for him to reach heaven ("pande uiam," *Ephemeris* 3.37 [Green]). Although Sobrietas is emphatically required as the way to virtue for Prudentius, it would probably be too much to read the line as a covert criticism of Ausonius; the echo is slight, even if Prudentius might have thought that Ausonius did not have enough sobriety himself.

405. Luxuries: first and fifth declension forms of this word alternate with no apparent difference. This would seem unimportant except that the allegorical form of the poem draws attention to the realities of the language.

407–31. The downfall of Luxuria is described with the gruesome detail that is now expected, and then Sobrietas boasts over the body of her fallen foe.

409. quod is a connective relative (= *et id*), and its antecedent is *lignum*. **expauēre:** the alternate form of the third-person plural perfect active indicative. **feroces:** the horses are terrified *even though* they are ferocious.

410. cornibus obpansis et summa fronte coruscum: Thomson translates "its outspread arms and flashing top." The ablative of description (*cornibus*) and the adjective *coruscum* are joined by *et* and both modify *quod*, which refers to the cross. *Fronte* is an ablative of respect with *coruscum*. We are to imagine that the top of the cross was decorated with gold or jewels.

412. praerupta: a substantive adjective, "the broken ground." **fertur resupina:** she is dragged on her back.

413–14. comamque madentem / puluere foedatur: Heinsius calls this statement with an accusative of respect and ablative of means a solemn Grecism. Unlike most modern editors, Arevalo prints the variant *foedat humi*, and he strangely cites as a parallel Ov., *Met.* 8.529–30. The passive *foedatur* is clearly better. Luxuria is being dragged through the dirt; she is not pouring dust on her head as in the passage from Ovid.

415. sub axem: the accusative denotes motion; she falls and ends up under the chariot (A&G §220c).

416. sufflamine: "a bar used for braking wheeled vehicles" (*OLD* s.v.); Luxuria herself becomes the brake. Not surprisingly, this gruesome and pictorial scene was illustrated. Stettiner provides a full list of the extant medieval illustrations for Luxuria's downfall (1895–1905, 2:13, no. 48), and in the same volume he includes a reproduction of each image.

419. uexilliferae: dative and referring to Sobrietas. The only other appearance of *uexillifer* that I could find in literature is at SHA, *Aurel.* 31. **quoniam**: ANASTROPHE.

420. belli insigne: refers again to the cross; the phrase echoes *Aen.* 8.683 and 12.289. **gerenti**: modifies *uexilliferae*.

421–26. Luxuria is struck with a large stone in her face, and she spits out teeth and blood. The scene is set off and divided into three end-stopped couplets. Prudentius is imitating a scene from the *Aeneid* (5.468–70) in which the dazed boxer Dares spits out his teeth. Vergil had been imitating a scene from the *Iliad* in which Euryalus spat blood (23.695–99). The descriptions become more violent in each poet, as pointed out in Hermann 1977.

421. casus agit saxum: "falling drives on the rock," i.e., gravity.

422. recauo: the word first appears in Latin in Avienius in the middle of the fourth century.

424. frustis: object of *cum*. The fact that the variant *frustris* from MS *B* reappears in *E* suggests that the latter manuscript was contaminated with readings from *B*. The second letter *r* was marked for deletion in *B* by dots placed above and below the letter. Judging from similar marks for deletion elsewhere in the manuscript, they are pre-Carolingian, which shows that the contamination must have occurred at an early stage in the tradition.

425. insolitis dapibus: "because of her unusual dishes." The phrase sounds like an ironic reversal of the "dapibus inemptis" with which the Corycian old man feeds himself in Verg., *G.* 4.133. Vergil's phrase was alluded to by Hor., *Epod.* 2.48; Prudent., *Cath.* 4.58; and the *Oratio minor* (15) attributed to Paulinus of Nola = Hartel *Carm.* 4.15. **crudescit guttur:** she suffers indigestion, and her esophagus becomes rough because of the poor treatment; this makes her regurgitate her teeth in the next line. *Crudescere* derives from the adjective *crudus* ("raw, undigested"), but it normally meant "grow worse" (Verg., *G.* 3.504) or "grow more violent" (*Aen.* 7.788). Sometimes, as here, poets punned on the use of *crudus* to mean "bloody," for example Stat., *Theb.* 2.717 "et asperso crudescit sanguine Gorgon."

426. Caesurae in the third and fourth feet give the line a jerky feel, just as Luxuria swallows and then spits up her teeth: *conliquefacta uorans | reuomit | quas hauserat offas.*

427–31. Like Pudicitia (53–97) and Spes (285–304), Sobrietas vaunts over her fallen enemy.

429. praeteriti . . . aeui: the noun and modifier enclose the phrase, the noun *aeui* being dependent on *dulcibus.* **dulcibus:** "*id est luxibus*" is the gloss in the tradition of B I (Burnam 1905, 63), which was presumably prior to *luxibus* being introduced as a variant reading in MSS *B* and *Y.*

430. uitae . . . amarae: "of (your) bitter life." **inlecebras:** echoes line 315, as does *haustus* in the following line. **gustatus:** nominative singular, subject with *sapor* of *asperet.*

431. horrificos sapor ultimus asperet haustus: this, the reading of MS *E*, is supported by *haustus* in *A*, and it is arguably the best version of the text. But even if *E* has the original text, is that the result of faithful transmission or of scribal emendation? The latter should not be excluded. The same manuscript offers readings that strike me as unsatisfactory attempts at emendation in several other places (see the note on lines 105–6).

432–49. A humorous description of the rout of Luxuria's retinue.

432. dispersă: modifies *acies*.

433. Iocus: for literary personifications of jesting, see *TLL* s.v. B.2 = 7.2.289.65–75 (Hiltbrunner). **Petulantia** was the daughter of Erebus and Nox according to Hyg., *Fab.* praef. 1. **primi**: "first of all."

440. peplo: a *peplum* (Greek *peplos*) was originally the embroidered robe dedicated to Athena at the Panathenaic festival, but the word was commonly used of robes in general in late antiquity. In his commentary *Ad Aen.* 1.480, Servius explains both points and offers as evidence for the word's original meaning a passage attributed to Plautus.

441. collique ac uerticis aurum: "the gold on her neck and head."

442. Discordia dissona: the adjective usually described fragmentation in a negative way, but it appeared as a positive term of metapoetics in some later authors, including Optatianus Porfyrius and Paulinus of Nola (*Natalicia* 9.99 = Hartel *Carm.* 27), on which see Pelttari 2017, 374.

444. Voluptatem: *piget* takes an accusative of the person affected (A&G §354b). **uis maior**: a stronger urgency compels her to flee. There may be an echo of *force majeure*, the involvement of a higher power; Pliny the Elder, for example, defined *uis maior* as storms and occurrences of that kind by which the gods cause harm (*HN* 18.278).

447. qua se cumque ... fert: echoes Vergil's description of Camilla: "Qua se cumque furens medio tulit agmine uirgo" (*Aen.* 11.762). Understand *uia* or *parte* with *qua* and translate with *cumque*, "whichever way ... they go." The indefinite adverb *cumque* was usually compounded with a relative pronoun, but sometimes it was used alone. Or we could say that *quacumque* is here separated by TMESIS. Ennius was known for his use of that device, and later poets also played with it.

448. damna: refers to the specific possessions lost. **crinalis acus:** a hairpin (*OLD* s.v. 1). Only the first noun in the ASYNDETIC list receives an adjective.

449. flammeolum: a rare diminutive of *flammeum*, a shining veil worn by Roman brides.

451. miles: a collective noun (A&G §317d).

452. scandala: this Greek word is common in the Latin of Christians from Tertullian on. **nec:** take both with *coniuente* and with *flectit*.

RATIO VS. AUARITIA (454–628)

In the sixth battle, Ratio conquers only with the assistance of Operatio (Good Works). An opening scene takes us from the pleasures of *Luxuria* to the hellish companions of Auaritia (454–79). After a description of Auaritia's valor, Ratio opposes her, and she laments her failing strength; she counters by disguising herself as Frugality (480–567). Operatio then takes the field to root out the disguised Vice (568–603). Afterward, she addresses the Virtues and bids them relax and rest their weary limbs after the battle (604–28).

Auaritia is described as the worst of sins in this passage (493–95). Prudentius had already identified the thirst for gold ("auri fames") as the root of evils in *Am.* 257–58. Taken in its entirety, that passage clearly alludes to 1 Tim. 6:10 "Radix enim omnium malorum est auaritia" (*Vetus latina I*). The other old translations and the Vulgate name *cupiditas* instead of *auaritia*, but Prudentius shows his knowledge of the Greek original by translating *philargyria* as *auri fames*. Priscillian of Avila also identified Auaritia as the root of all evil (*Canones* 37).

Here in the *Psychomachia*, Prudentius picks up on the idea that greed is the worst of the vices (pride was the other contender), and that fact explains why this battle scene is the longest in the *Psychomachia*, as observed by Nugent 1985, 50–52. Note also that in this, the sixth contest, Ratio and Operatio bring together theoretical knowledge and practical endeavor.

Parallel scenes in contemporary authors include Augustine, *Serm.* 86, in which Auaritia and Luxuria are personified, and Claud., *De consulatu Stilichonis* 2.111–12, in which avarice is called the mother of crimes, always searching and thirsty for more gold: "scelerum matrem, quae semper habendo / plus sitiens patulis rimatur faucibus aurum."

454–79. Auaritia is described in the company of a frightful assembly of monsters. They recall the figures and mood from Vergil's description of the entrance to the underworld in *Aen.* 6.273–81. These monsters balance the previous scene and the light description of Luxuria's retinue.

454. Fertur: takes a nominative subject and an infinitive of indirect speech, as common in epic poetry. Translate "is said to."

455. Luxus edax: perhaps synonymous with Luxuria. Prudentius does not resolve the ambiguities of language in his allegory; he does use VARIATIO to show that a single idea can be expressed in a whole range of ways. **unca:** her hand is curved and grasping, or as the gloss in MS Valenciennes 413 says, "Id est recurua, ad rapiendum parata" (Burnam 1910, 102).

456. corripuisse: complementary infinitive after *fertur,* which takes a personal subject in the nominative case, modified by *inhians* and *legens* in the following line.

456–58. pulchra ... harenarum: regarded as an INTERPOLATION by Gnilka (1963, 129–33). He observed that all of the other Vices are introduced with verbs of motion; consequently, he understood *fertur* in 454 to mean "go" / "rush" and suspected that these lines were INTERPOLATED by someone who did not understand the syntax. It is more likely that Prudentius varied his construction for this pivotal scene.

457. fragmenta: Heinsius conjectured *ramenta* ("flakes"), an intriguing suggestion given the later description of her gold as unrefined (598–600), but the received text is more likely.

458. inter harenarum cumulos: "among the depths of sand."

459. iuuat: understand *eam.* **infercire:** takes a dative object. **cruminis:** a small bag or purse. A second hand in MS *B* "corrected" the spelling to *crumenis.* In extant texts, the word appears predominantly in poetry and usually in the singular.

460. turpe lucrum: echoes *turpia lucra* from Auson., *Ecl.* 19.8.

462. opermento: an alternate form of *operīmentum*. The form does not appear in other ancient texts except as a variant reading (see *TLL* s.v. *operimentum*, 9.2.680.23–25 [Beikircher]). Presumably, *opermentum* would have sounded unclassical to Prudentius's first readers.

464–66. These terrors recall the *Curae, Fames,* and *Metus* of *Aen.* 6.274–276. Such lists of terrors are rhetorical. In fact, the anxiety that comes with greed was disconcerting for some in antiquity, just as it is for many living in modern capitalist societies. See, for example, Sen., *Tranq.* 8 and *Ep.* 90.36–43.

464. Periuria: also personified in Claud., *Nupt.* 83 (a poem presented in the year 398) "et lasciua uolant leuibus Periuria pinnis." By the sixth century, the neuter plural and feminine singular in *-ia* were often confused (compare the following note).

465. Insomnia: Servius (*Ad Aen.* 4.9) says that the fem. sing. *insomnia* ("sleeplessness") was archaic, whereas the neuter *insomnium* ("a disturbing dream") was still in common use.

466. Eumenides uariae: Vergil had put the bridal chambers of the Eumenides in the entrance to the underworld (*Aen.* 6.280). Prudentius apparently uses the name as a general word for a terror rather than as a proper name. **monstri comitatus aguntur**: "the monster's retinue rush together." The same collective singular and plural verb appear at *Aen.* 12.336.

468. crimina: nominative.

469. matris: because she is the root of all evils, on which see above on 454–628. **nigro de lacte**: the perverse Vice feeds her children with black milk.

470–79. In *Aen.* 6.608–14, Vergil gave special attention to those who were sent to Tartarus for betraying their families or for their greed.

470. ceraunis: a flashing jewel reportedly found where lightning struck and perhaps identifiable as onyx (*Myth. Vat.* 3.8). The word derives from *keraunos*, the Greek for thunderbolt.

475–76. fulgentia bullis / cingula: echoes Vergil's "aurea bullis / cingula" (*Aen.* 9.359–60) and Ausonius's "auratis fulgentia cingula bullis" (*Cupido* 49). Charlet reads the passage as a case of literary contamination in which Prudentius combined two previous texts (1980, 49).

477. ciuilis . . . Discordia: the theme of civil discord was common in Roman epic. On Discordia, see below on lines 629–725. I capitalize Discordia, Amor, and Famis because they are personified just as much as the figures in 464–65; strangely Cunningham, Bergman, and Lavarenne did not capitalize their names. To be sure, capital letter forms were used to distinguish proper nouns only beginning in the Middle Ages (Saenger 1997, 59–61), which means that Prudentius could not distinguish their meaning in this way.

478. insatiatus: this uncommon word was first used by Statius. **Amor insatiatus habendi:** "Insatiable desire for property." The gerund describes a state rather than a single action. The phrase "amor . . . habendi" appears several times in Latin poetry. Especially memorable was Evander's explanation of how Italy declined from its Saturnian golden age: " . . . deterior donec paulatim ac decolor aetas / et belli rabies et amor successit habendi" (*Aen.* 8.326–27).

478–79. propriis . . . pigneribus: *parco* takes a dative object.

479. inpia natos: MS *E* has *improba natos*, probably under the influence of *improba natos* at line end in Juv. 6.86.

480–567. After Ratio shuts down her ARISTEIA, Auaritia laments her weakened power and then disguises herself as Frux (Frugality). Like Auaritia, Hector in the *Iliad* and Turnus in the *Aeneid* enjoy moments of success before they meet their end.

480. Talia per populos edebat funera uictrix: echoes Vergil's description of Aeneas's ARISTEIA: "*talia per* campos *edebat funera* ductor" *Aen.* 10.602. But I do not see any direct comparison, positive or negative, to Aeneas.

The verb *edere* was used of those who produced shows (*OLD* s.v. 12), as noted in MS Valenciennes 413 (Burnam 1910, 103).

480–81. uictrix / orbis: "the champion of the world."

481. Auaritiā sternens: see the note on line 41. **uirorum:** partitive genitive (A&G §346) with *centena . . . milia*.

482–85. Prudentius illustrates the old idea that greed makes you blind.

482. hunc: "this one," begins an enumeration of the victims of Auaritia. **lumine adempto:** the phrase *lumen ademptum* appears several times before Prudentius at the end of a hexameter.

484. offensācula: this word was used once by Apuleius, once by Lactantius, and then by Prudentius, who uses it in this passage, at *Psych.* 781, and in *Apoth.* praef. 2.33. The synonym *offendĭculum* also seems to have been prosaic, although it was used once by Paulinus of Nola (*Natalicia* 12.99 = Hartel *Carm.* 20.99). The unmetrical variant in MS *A* (*offendĭcula*) is a simple example of a scribe writing the more common word.

486. porro alium: Auaritia sometimes uses an opposite strategy. **intuitu:** "by means of his sight" (trans. Thomson).

487. insigne ostentans aliquid: "making a show of some splendid thing." But compare the note on 851 for another meaning of *insigne* that is in the background; Auaritia is making a show of some (false) sign. **quod dum petit:** the connective relative (= *et id*, A&G §308f) is the object of *petit*.

489. ferrum suspirat adactum: "groans under the sword driven in."

490. multos: the third kind of victim destroyed by Auaritia.

491. focos: glossed as "fire" (*ignes*) in the Weitz tradition (O'Sullivan 2004, 269). For *foci* meaning "flames," see *TLL* s.v. *focus* V = 6.1.990.79–91.45 (Vollmer) and compare Prudent., *Symm.* 1 praef. 16–17 "Arentum propere bracchia palmitum / conuectant, rapidos unde focos struant." This use seems to have become common in the fourth century.

492. pecŭlator: editors have been split between *peculator* and *speculator*. The variant *peculatur* in MSS *B* and *S* supports *peculator* from *A* and *T* and make it more likely that *peculator* was the reading of the archetype. But counting manuscripts is not enough, and the *speculator* of *JEY* cannot be dismissed without considering both options.

A *peculator* was defined by a fifth-century commentator on Cicero as someone who steals from public funds ("qui furtum facit pecuniae publicae," Ps. Asconius *Commentarii*, ed. Stangl, p. 206). *Peculator* fits the general context, but the second syllable of that word is normally long.

The metrical anomaly in *peculator* could have produced the "correction" *speculator*. In defense of the latter reading, Cunningham suggested that Prudentius was referring to a prospector for gold (1966, 167). But that meaning for *speculator* is not found elsewhere, and Prudentius even uses *speculator* in *Cath.* 2.105 to describe God as an observer on high. More helpful for Cunningham is a passage from Tert., *Scorpiace* 12, a translation of 1 Pet. 4:15 in which a greedy individual is described as "alieni speculator." *Speculator* in this latter sense fits the thought perfectly, with Prudentius's emphasis on the eyes as the pathway of greed. And *speculator* scans without exception.

Despite the parallel in Tertullian, I print *peculator* for four reasons: it is better attested in the manuscripts; there is ALLITERATION with *petit* and *pariter*; as the less common of the two words, *peculator* is the *lectio difficilior*; and, most importantly, it makes good sense in context, if we understand Prudentius as naming embezzlers in place of every kind of greedy person.

493. omne hominum rapit illa genus: HYPERBATON.

494. neque est: HIATUS. Heinsius conjectured *neque ea est*, but the ablative *eā* does not appear before *est* anywhere else in ancient poetry.

495. terrarum: "on earth."

495–96. quod ... populi: "for she wraps the life of the people of the world in such great destruction." *Quod* introduces a relative clause of characteristic (A&G 534–35).

496. mundani: the contrast with priests in the following lines suggests that Prudentius uses *mundanus* here in reference to the laity or common people. For this meaning of the word, see Ps-Cyprian, *De singularitate clericorum*

30 "clerici habent spiritum sanctum, quem mundani homines non habent";
for further references, see *TLL* s.v. *mundanus* I.2.B.2 = 8.0.1622.31–50 (Baer).
On *mundus* as the fallen world, see below on line 714.

gehennae: either a genitive of the penalty (A&G §352) or dative. The Hebrew
word originally referred to a cursed valley in Judaea where children were
sacrificed.

497–98. ipsos temptare . . . / sacerdotes domini: one might suspect that
priests were always tempted by whatever wealth the church possessed. In
Perist. 2, the buffoonish Roman magistrate suspects wrongly that wealth
is being hoarded in the church.

497. si credere dignum est: this half-line was used by Verg., *G.* 3.391 and
Aen. 6.173; Ov., *Met.* 3.311; Valerius Flaccus 6.51; Proba 494; and Serenus,
Liber Medicinalis 925.

498. ausa: understand *est*.

499. primam ante aciem: this phrase occurs three times in the *Aeneid* and
twice in Valerius Flaccus.

499–500. pro laude gerebant / uirtutum: they were carrying themselves
in such a way as to win praise for the Virtues.

500. magnoque . . . flatu: rhetoric could be compared to the bombastic
music of horns, and there might be a reference to the priests' sermons as
a kind of rhetorical motivation. *Flatu* is glossed as *praedicatione* in MS
Cologne 81 (O'Sullivan 2004, 271).

501–9. Ratio enters the scene and stops the advance of Auaritia, who is
shocked that her methods no longer work.

501–2. et fors . . . tinxisset . . . , / ni . . .: the verb is a pluperfect subjunctive
in the apodosis of a past counterfactual condition. As we find out in lines
506–8, the Virtues have not suffered anything more than surface wounds.
The syntax recalls the description of the ship race in *Aen.* 5.232–33 "et fors
aequatis cepissent praemia rostris, / ni . . ."

503. atrae: modifies *hostis*.

505. stant: the present tense contrasts with *stupuit* in line 508. **Rationis ope:** an instrumental ablative. The phrase is a pun on the name of *Operatio*, who will come on the scene in line 573. Nugent describes this pun as significant for understanding Prudentius's allegorical language: "By introducing such a double for Ratio, Prudentius indicates that against the duplicity of Vice, Virtue also has recourse to the doubleness of language" (1985, 55).

506. animi: locative or genitive of specification (A&G §349d). **uix in cute summa:** "scarcely, on the top of the skin."

507. tenui de uulnere: probably has the sense of an instrumental ablative ("with a light wound"), as Lavarenne thought (1933a, §178); but the ablative could also explain the source of the harm caused by Auaritia.

508. luis: *lues* is the normal form of this word in most authors, but the meter shows that the second syllable must be short. Cunningham capitalizes *luis* here but not in line 558. In both passages, the noun refers to Auaritia and is not personified.

509. heroum: genitive plural. **longe:** take with *repelli*.

510–50. Auaritia complains of her setback and boasts of past victories over Judas Iscariot and Achan (references below).

510. infit: this synonym of *inquit* was used more frequently in poetry than in prose.

511. uincimur heu: Hudson-Williams (1967–68, 16) compares Juno's bitter acknowledgment of her defeat in *Aen.* 1.37–49 and 7.292–322. **nostra potentia:** other epic characters who complain about their diminished power ("nostra potentia") include Juno (*Met.* 4.427) and Megaera (Claud., *Ruf.* 1.358).

513. sueuerat inuictis quae: ANASTROPHE. **omnia ubique:** "all everywhere," modifies *corda*.

515. formauit: Bergman printed *durauit*, but the archetype clearly had *formauit*. The more specific verb *durauit* was probably just the suggestion of the corrector B^2.

515–16. cuius ... / sperneret aut ... foret: relative clause of characteristic.

517. ingenium omne neci dedimus: compare the description of the plague in Verg., *G.* 3.480 "genus omne neci pecudum dedit" (found also in Proba, *Cento* 312) and a similar phrase in Claud., *Ruf.* 329 "quas dedit ipse neci."

517–19. tenera aspera dura ... pectora: ASYNDETON. The CAESURAE break up the list into opposed sets of adjectives describing their hardness, learning, and wisdom.

519. casta incesta: echoes "casta inceste" of Iphigenia in Lucr. 1.98. **meae patuerunt ... dextrae:** "were exposed to my force."

520–22. The description of the underworld echoes Claud., *Rapt.* 1.20–24.

520. Styx: Auaritia calls hell by its mythological name, just as Prudentius regularly does elsewhere (Lühken 2002, 152–54).

521. ditissima Tartara: the adjective is the superlative of *dis* and a pun on the name Dis. The Roman god Dis was equated with the Greek Pluto. They are wealthy because they receive all things, as observed by Cic., *Nat. D.* 2.26.66.

522. quos retinent populos: i.e., the peoples trapped in Tartarus. **quod uoluunt saecula:** "what the ages turn."

524. qui fit ... quod: "How does it happen that ... ?" *Qui* was in origin an ablative from the interrogative pronoun; it is equivalent in meaning to *quomodo*.

525. et cassos ludit fortuna lacertos? "and chance cheats our empty strength?" She blames the loss of her power on misfortune.

526. Christicolis: dative of reference.

527. effigies: Jesus taught that money in the form of taxes should be given to Caesar because his image was on the denarius, but that worship should be given only to God: "Reddite ergo quae sunt Caesaris Caesari et quae sunt Dei Deo" (Matt. 22:21; Vulgate). **emblemata:** the word occurs only in prose before Prudentius.

528. thensaurus: Servius said that the correct spelling was *thesaurus* (*Ad Aen.* 1.359), as noted by Basile (2007, 114). **oculis uilescit:** "becomes worthless in their eyes." The earliest extant example of this verb is from Cyprian, but it became widespread in the fourth century.

530. ex Scarioth: the indeclinable name must be understood as an ablative. Judas Iscariot betrayed Jesus for thirty pieces of silver and then hung himself (Matt. 26:14–16, Mark 14:10–11, and Acts 1:18). **magnus qui discipulorum:** understand *erat*, "who was great among the disciples." For the partitive genitive with an adjective in the positive degree, see A&G §346b. MS *U* offers the easy variant *summus*, which nicely fits Auaritia's twisted pride; but lines 521–640 were added later to that manuscript, and they do not seem to have any authority of their own (see below on 624).

531. conuiua dei: the phrase "conuiua deorum" appears in Hor., *Carm.* 1.28.7 and in *Anth. Lat.* 931.9, both times in reference to Tantalus. The intertext neatly portrays Judas as comparable to the mythical hero famous for his crimes against the gods. **dum:** "until" (Kühner-Stegmann vol. 2, §210.7).

531–32. At his last supper, Jesus prophesied that one of his disciples would betray him and then specified that it would be the one who dipped his hand with him into the dish: "qui intinguit mecum manum in parapside hic me tradet" (Matt. 26:23, compare Mark 14:20 and John 13:26–27).

532. parabside: from the Greek *paropsis*, a small dish, sometimes used for dessert.

534–35. Auaritia says that Judas used the money given him for betraying Jesus to buy a piece of land and that he then hung himself. The piece of land was called Acheldemach (the field of blood). Some Latin translations of Acts 1:18 allow of this interpretation (the Greek says that he fell and that his bowels gushed out). Matt. 27:5–7 says that he hung himself but that the field was bought by the chief priests after his death. In *Tituli historiarum*

153–56, Prudentius apparently follows Matthew on both points.

536–41. Josh. 7 tells how Achan took some of the spoils from the city of Jericho, even though the Israelites were commanded by God not to take anything. He was stoned for the crime.

536. propria inter funera: "in the midst of its own destruction."

536–37. quantum / posset: indirect question dependent on *uiderat*.

538. caedibus: the plural denotes individual instances of the slaughter for which he was supposedly remarkable.

539. "he fell to the gold captured from the conquered enemies."

540. the Greek *anathēma* refers to a sacred offering or dedication. An *anathĕma* is something dedicated to evil or accursed.

542–46. Achan is a negative exemplum or type (*forma*) who was not helped by belonging to the tribe of Judah, into which Jesus was born.

543. quandoque: "someday."

544. tali . . . nepote: ablative of cause. **patriarcha**: a Greek word used in Latin beginning with translations of the Hebrew scriptures.

545. quis: an archaic form of *quibus*. **generis**: Thraede preferred *ueneris* from MS *A* without explaining why (1968, 88). But the point is that Auaritia plans to corrupt the descendants of Judah (Christians) in the same way that she corrupted Achan. She understands how typology works, but she chooses the wrong examples.

547. moror: takes the complementary infinitive *fallere* (A&G §456).

547–48. Iudae populares aut populares / sacricolae summi: CHIASMUS and DIACOPE.

548. sacricolae: the word is very rare, and perhaps Prudentius is having Auaritia speak in an affected tone.

549. Martis congressibus inpar: Auaritia admits that she cannot challenge the Virtues in open combat.

550. Compare the comment of Coroebus in *Aen.* 2.390 that deceit and virtue are all the same in war: "Dolus an uirtus, quis in hoste requirat?" In that passage, the Trojans also put on disguises to fight the Greeks. As Lühken notes (2002, 61), Prudentius alludes to the same part of the *Aeneid* in *Am.* 425–28, a discussion of how Christians are sometimes deceived by false appearances. **armis . . . dolis:** ablatives of means.

551–63. Auaritia disguises herself as frugality. The description as a whole, and the verb *transformat* in line 552, recall Allecto's transformation in *Aen.* 7.415–16 "Allecto toruam faciem et furialia membra / exuit, in uultus sese transformat anilis." For Allecto in the *Psychomachia*, see the notes on lines 130 and 684. This disguise links Auaritia and Discordia.

552. in . . . habitum . . . honestum: "into an honorable form."

553. Fit uirtus specie: the Vice becomes indistinguishable in her appearance. Prudentius seems to have had Juvenal in mind, who described greed masquerading as something virtuous:

> Fallit enim uitium specie uirtutis et umbra,
> cum sit triste habitu uultuque et ueste seuerum,
> nec dubie tamquam frugi laudetur auarus,
> tamquam parcus homo et rerum tutela suarum
> certa magis quam si fortunas seruet easdem
> Hesperidum serpens aut Ponticus. (14.109–14)

ueste: Heinsius preferred the variant *uoce* (1667, 2:165), which must have been a conjecture in the single late manuscript in which it appears.

554. Frugi: the form is in origin a dative of the noun *frux*, for which the *OLD* (s.v.) offers a range of meanings including worthy, honest, deserving, thrifty, moderate, and frugal. The fact that Auaritia can appear as her opposite destabilizes the allegory.

557. Bellona: a Roman goddess of war, but here it would probably be heard as meaning only "warrior."

558. luis: on the spelling, see the apparatus criticus and the note on line 508. It seems unlikely that Prudentius would have spelled the word in two different ways within a hundred lines.

559. nec non et: "And indeed she also . . ." The double negative is particularly appropriate for a Vice who disguises herself.

560. anguinos: her hair is serpentine because she is a Fury. For the Vices in the *Psychomachia* as Furies, see lines 10, 46, 96, 158, 466, 510, 551, and 566.

561–63. diroque . . . iactet: "and that, pulled round her dread rage, it may pretend under cover of a gentle name that snatching and stealing and greedily hiding profits is caring for your children."

562. clepere: an uncommon and archaic word that means "to steal away secretly," in contrast to *rapere*, which means "snatch" or "grab." **parta**: "gains," from *pario*.

564–65. talibus inludens . . . imaginibus: "deceiving them with such ideas."

564. male credula corda: "male credula" appears in Paulinus, *Natalicia* 9.566 = Hartel *Carm.* 27 (presented in January 403); also, "corda male credula" appears in reference to those who are taken in by heretics, in a letter that Paulinus sent to Augustine probably shortly after 410 (*Epist.* 50.12). Neither phrase is at all common, and I have not found any closer example. Maybe Paulinus's *male credula* was an influence on Prudentius's *male credula corda*, and it may be that Paulinus then wrote *corda male credula* under the influence of the *Psychomachia*, although this is a complicated story (on Prudentius and Paulinus see also below on 567).

565. fērāle: the quantity of the first vowel shows that this word is not related to *fĕra* ("wild animal"). Prudentius might have been influenced by Claud., *Rapt.* 1.37 "ferali monstra barathro."

566. dum can introduce a reason or cause, like *cum* (Kühner-Stegmann vol. 2, §210n4). **uirtutis opus:** the phrase was used by Vergil (*Aen.* 10.469) and later poets. **Erinys:** used in general of those who cause terror.

567. consensu faciles: "those who are easy in agreement," i.e., those who agree easily and are compliant.

The phrase echoes *consensum facilem* at the same position in the hexameter in Paulinus, *Natalicia* 13.671 = Hartel *Carm.* 21. There are no other parallels in Latin verse, and the only parallel in prose that I have found is Tac., *Hist.* 1.54 "faciliore inter malos consensu." Although the contexts of the two passages are not similar, Prudentius was probably following Paulinus here (and not the other way around), because the adjective modifies the noun in Paulinus. *Natalicia* 13 was written for the festival for Saint Felix in Nola on January 14, 407. For another parallel in the same poem of Paulinus, see below on line 578; for a possible meeting of Prudentius and Paulinus in Rome, see the introduction, page 5).

568–603. Disguised Auaritia causes trouble at first, but Operatio appears on the scene, destroys the Vice, and redistributes the recovered spoils.

The disarray of the Virtues arises from ambiguity, because appearances are not certain and words have multiple meanings. Bardzell (2009) explained how Stoic allegorical interpretations sought to resolve the philosophical and theoretical problems arising from the uncertainties of human perception, namely by trying to map the ambiguities of language onto the inherent meaning of things. He places the *Psychomachia* within this context of thinking about allegory and says that this scene is "perhaps the most striking [in the poem] of an intensional transformation" (2009, 46).

569. biformis: the two appearances of the Vice cause confusion.

570. ignorans quid . . . credat: the participle here introduces an indirect question.

571. notet: compare *notare* in line 20. **letum** was sometimes personified by Latin poets (e.g. *Aen.* 6.277), but here the word is used generically. **anceps:** on the use of this word in reference to ambiguity, see the note on line 893.

573–76. For the assistance of Operatio, compare Spes in lines 278–79.

573. Operatio: on the use of this word in reference to Christian good works, see *TLL* s.v. II.B.2 = 9.2.674.36–56 (Baer).

574. auxilio: dative of purpose (A&G §382).

575. militiae postrema gradu: Gnilka compares Prudentius's priamel of virtues in *De opusculis suis* 1–10, and he convincingly suggests that almsgiving is described as coming last here because it is an external form of virtue (1988, 81–84). **duello:** on the archaic *duellum*, see the note on line 21.

578. fasce leuarat: the verb is a syncopated form of the pluperfect *leuauerat* (A&G §181). The phrase recalls Lycidas's kind words in Verg., *Ecl.* 9.65 "ego hoc te fasce leuabo." More speculative would be a link to the phrase "fasce leuatus" from *Natalicia* 13.395 = Hartel *Carm.* 21, on which see above on line 567.

580. inopum: genitive object of *miserando*.

581. effundens patrium ... censum: she distributed her inherited wealth. Several extremely wealthy contemporaries had recently divested themselves of their wealth by giving property and money to the church. On Paulinus of Nola's renunciation of his wealth, see Brown 2012, 208–23 and Trout 1999, 78–103. This theme of giving away wealth appears again in lines 598–603.

582. fidem: accusative of respect with *ditata*. The accusative of respect developed under the influence of the Greek accusative, and it is sometimes called an accusative of specification (A&G §397b).

583. redituro faenore: when used of money, *redeo* can mean "accrue" or "be yielded" (*OLD* s.v. 11). Compare Jesus's words to the rich young ruler in Matt. 19:21: "If you would be perfect, go, sell what you possess and give to the poor, and you will have treasure in heaven; and come, follow me." Similar are Luke 12:33–34, and Matt. 6:20: "But lay up for yourselves treasures in heaven, where neither moth nor rust consumes and where thieves do not break in and steal."

586. certa mori: the same phrase appears at the beginning of *Aen.* 4.564 and *Met.* 10.428. The deponent passive infinitive *mori* is dependent on the adjective. In poetry it was not uncommon for an adjective to be followed by an explanatory infinitive (A&G §461). **nam:** introduces a rhetorical question expecting a negative answer, as in lines 816–19.

586–87. ipsa / calcatrix mundi: Operatio. The word *calcator* is rare, and *calcatrix* does not appear elsewhere. The variant *galeatrix* in MS *B* surely derives from a copy written in an uncial script in which the letters *C*, *G*, and *E* were hardly distinguishable.

587. uicta fatiscat: echoes the end of Verg., *G.* 1.180.

588. spretoque iterum sese inplicet auro: "or that she would involve herself again in gold (already) spurned." Vergil has "implicat auro" at the end of *Aen.* 4.148.

589–97. Several aspects of Auaritia's death respond to the earlier description of her gaping mouth and greedy hands (454–62), for the Vices die according to their own excesses. In particular, Operatio binds her arms and strangles her throat.

Mastrangelo has argued that the deaths of the Vices reflect Epicurean teaching that the soul is material and made of breath (2008, 145–55). That idea does seems to be in the background, but the focus is on the close-fisted greed of Auaritia.

589–90. duris / ulnarum nodis: *fortissima* is followed by an ablative of respect (A&G §418).

591. conpressa ligantur: "are tightened and tied."

593. nullo ... uulnere: she is strangled and not yet pierced or cut.

594. spiraminis intercepto: a spondaic line. The meter reflects the harsh action, as in line 98.

596. genibusque et calcibus instans: Operatio stands on Auaritia so that she cannot escape.

597. costas atque ilia rumpit anhela: echoes *Aen.* 9.432 "costas et candida pectora rumpit."

598. extincto: Bergman's spelling *exstincto* is unsupported by the manuscripts.

598–99. auri . . . rudis: genitive with *frusta*.

600. tiniis: compare the moths of Matt. 6:20 (quoted above on line 583).

The grammarian Probus cited *tinea* as the more proper spelling, in a list of words that he said should have been written with an *e* rather than an *i* (ed. Keil, *Grammatici latini* 4:198.19). Variation is not uncommon between these vowels in closed syllables in Prudentius's time, and the opposite can be found with *relegamine* in line 359 instead of *religamine* (Lavarenne 1933b, §16–21).

marsuppia: Plautus was the only other Latin verse writer to use this Greek word (*marsuppion*) for a pouch or bag.

601. uirides obducta aerugine: the coins are green because rust has spread over them.

602. seruata: as here a predicate adjective is usually neuter plural when it refers to things of more than one gender (A&G §287.3).

603. ac tenues captiuo munere donat: "and rewards the poor with a gift from the spoils." The phrase *munere donat* is common at line end in dactylic poetry.

604–28. Operatio bids the troops to relax and to live without care for tomorrow.

605. alacris: the nominative adjective is used with adverbial force (A&G §290).

606. iusti: vocative.

607. causa mali tanti: this exact phrase appears at the beginning of the line in *Aen.* 6.93 and 11.480; Luc. 7.407; Juv. 14.290; Proba, *Cento* 202;

the cento *Hippodamia* 63; and the cento *Progne et Philomela* 5. Lavinia is the referent in both lines from the *Aeneid*; in Proba and the *Hippodamia*, the temptress Eve and Hippodamia are the source of evil. In applying this phrase to Auaritia, Prudentius activates its reductive and sexist undertones.

608. licet . . . sanctis: the impersonal verb takes a dative indirect object (A&G §368). The adjective *sanctus* was used by Christians in reference to specific holy individuals ("Saints") and in reference to all of their own as God's chosen people.

609. The idea that peace comes from limiting your desires and that simplicity is best was a theme well developed by Roman philosophers, and also found in 1 Tim. 6:8 "Habentes autem alimenta et quibus tegamur his contenti sumus" (Vulgate).

610-12. ut . . . trahat extra: Prudentius uses a substantive clause of result (A&G §567-71) to explain what *usus debitus* requires.

612. modum naturae: Nature's limit was a philosophical commonplace.

613-14. Operatio alludes to Jesus's teaching to his disciples that they should not take a bag on the road, nor an extra tunic, nor shoes, nor a staff (Matt. 10:10, Mark 6:8-9, and Luke 9:3).

613. peram ne tollito: the so-called future imperative (A&G §287.3) uses *ne* as its negative adverb (A&G §450a).

614. ito: future imperative of the verb *eo*.

615-28. These lines closely follow Jesus's comand to his disciples not to worry, from Matt. 6:25-26: "Do not be anxious about your life, what you shall eat or what you shall drink, nor about your body, what you shall put on. Is not life more than food, and the body more than clothing? Look at the birds of the air: they neither sow nor reap nor gather into barns, and yet your heavenly Father feeds them. Are you not of more value than they?" Prudentius combines with this injunction another command not to worry about tomorrow from Matt. 6:34. "The birds of the air" (τὰ πετεινὰ τοῦ οὐρανοῦ) is consistently rendered in Latin as *uolatilia caeli*; Prudentius's *nulla auium* is more natural in Latin than the parallel phrase in Juvencus, *Euangeliorum* 1.634 "aerias spectemus aues." The only other Latin poet to write *nulla auium* was Claudian, in his *Phoenix* (*Carm. min.* 31.17).

615. nec te sollicitet: this half-line reappears in the *Versus ad Sethum* (10), a poem attributed to the Irish missionary Columbanus.

615–16. ne cibus . . . / defuerit: "that food will ever be lacking." Fear clauses were in origin independent clauses expressing a wish. This explains why a positive fear is introduced by *ne* (A&G §564).

617. nonne uides ut: the same line-beginning is found in Verg., *G.* 3.250; Stat., *Achil.* 1.351; Claud., *Mallius Theodorus* 166 and *Carm. min.* 17.9, 37.3; and Prudent., *Apoth.* 479. The conjunction *ut* is here equivalent to *quomodo* ("how") and introduces an indirect question dependent on *uides* (*OLD* s.v. A.1). **cras**: like the English "tomorrow," *cras* could be used as a noun, and here it is the object of *cogitet*. But *cras* was not used very often as a substantive, which explains why this usage was discussed by the grammarians; for references, see *TLL* s.v., 4.0.1100.72–1101.3 (Lambertz).

617–18. ac se / pascendam praestante deo non anxia credat: "and each believes without anxiety that she will be fed as God provides." In late antiquity, the gerundive came to be used sometimes like a future passive participle (Kühner-Stegmann vol. 2 §130.5).

619. defore: future infinitive of *desum*.

620. modico . . . asse: an ablative of price (A&G §416). Prudentius follows Matt. 10:29 for the comparison to sparrows: "nonne duo passeres asse ueneunt et unus ex illis non cadet super terram sine patre uestro" (Vulgate); Luke 12:6 is very similar.

621. dominum curare potentem: accusative and infinitive expressing the content of their faith.

622. cura dei: the same phrase is found in Ov., *Met.* 1.48; Auson., *Parent.* 1.3; and the *Laus Iohannis* 89.

623. ne . . . deserat: subjunctive with a verb of fearing.

624. et: the adverb "also," rather than the conjunction. The part of MS *U* containing *Psychomachia* 521–640 was added in the tenth century (Cunningham 1966, xviii and 1971, 65), which means that it is not a good authority for the reading *dator est dator escae*. **dator:** this word appears very rarely between republican drama and late antiquity. Vergil has it at *Aen.* 1.734.

625. luciferum: this adjective was used in antiquity in its literal meaning ("light-bringing") and also of the morning star (Venus). More relevant for this line is a passage from the Ps-Cyprianic *De singularitate clericorum*, in which *luciferum* is defined as anything provided by God: "Hoc est ergo luciferum, quodcumque a deo fuerit intimatum" (16). Also noteworthy is the proclamation by the author of the *Carmen de resurrectione* that he was turning from the Bucolic Muses to the Muses who bring the light: "Iam mihi luciferas liceat contingere Musas" (9). In late antiquity, Christian exegetes also identified Satan with the morning star using the same adjective, on which see *TLL* s.v. *lucifer* II.B.1.b = 7.2.1710.27–66 (Buchwald).

626. qui . . . alat: relative clause of characteristic or purpose. **inuitiabilis aeui:** genitive with *spem*; the adjective *inuitiabilis* does not appear elsewhere in Latin literature, but it is formed regularly and means "incorruptible life." The phrase is glossed as "inuiolabilis uitae" in the Weitz tradition (O'Sullivan 2004, 294–95). As we can see, Operatio offers a positive vision to counter Superbia's claim that hope in heaven is really laziness.

627. corporis inmemores: "forgetting the body." The adjective modifies the subject of *quaerite*. **memor est qui condidit illud:** "he who created it is mindful."

628. cibos: "foodstuffs" or "meals." The plural can denote individual instances of the process or object in question. English would use the singular "food" or qualify the noun, as in "daily bread."

CONCORDIA VS. DISCORDIA (629–725)

The opening battle scenes are discreet encounters between clearly opposed Virtues and Vices. An interlude at the beginning of the last battle heightens the drama. After Peace drives war away and the sun comes out (629–43),

Concordia gives the signal to return to the camp (644–45). The Virtues then begin to relax, and as they sing together, Prudentius compares them to the Israelites after the crossing of the Red Sea (646–64). When Concordia reaches the gates of the camp in triumphant throng, she is suddenly wounded by Discordia, who had infiltrated their ranks in disguise (665–93). Concordia calls out in alarm, and Discordia is betrayed by her own fear (694–704). The Virtues quickly surround and question her (705–8) but cannot stand to hear her speak (708–14). Instead, they tear her limb from limb in a symbolic and brutal *sparagmos* (715–25).

Because Discordia identifies herself as Heresy, her threat suggests a historical interpretation, because dissension was still at work in the church after the apparent victory offered by a succession of Christian emperors. Prudentius does allude to historical heresies, but the allegorical narrative should not be reduced to any single referent.

Concordia was equivalent to the Greek *Homonoia*, and we hear that Camillus built a temple for her in 367 B.C.E. Tiberius Caesar restored her temple in 7 B.C.E., and another was built for her by Livia (Ov., *Fasti* 6.637–48). Cult worship of her during the imperial period was common. For an overview of the Greek and Latin evidence, see Thraede 1994. Concordia was listed by Cicero as one of the divinities named from a great force (*De natura deorum* 2.23.61). Augustine presented Roman civil discord as discounting their reverence for Concordia (*De civ. d.* 3.24–26). Discordia was never worshipped at Rome, but she was a literary figure. For a fine analysis of this passage and of previous presentations of Discordia, see Malamud 1989, 57–78.

629. His dictis curae emotae: a repetition of the first half of *Aen.* 6.382, which describes the reaction of Palinurus in the underworld when he is comforted by Aeneas.

630. Scelus et placitae: The garbled reading in MS *B* was corrected by a Carolingian scribe who must have had access to another copy. **placitae fidei:** "pleasing faith." The phrase is from Ecclus. 15:16. **infitiatrix:** the feminine form of this word occurs only here in extant Latin.

629–30. et ... et ... et ... et: the POLYSYNDETON suggests that each and every one of the Vices has been routed.

631. uertere solum: the idiom means to "change one's country" or "go into exile" (*OLD* s.v. *uerto* 23). **fugatis:** *fugio* means "to flee" and *fugo* "to cause to flee."

632–33. discingitur omnis / terror: "all fear is disarmed." The verb was used figuratively of dissensions and the like, for example in *CIL* 6.1693, an inscription set up in Rome in 351–52, in which the consul Valerius Proculus was described as disarming quarrels ("discinxit iurgia"). For further examples, see *TLL* s.v. *discingo* 2b = 5.1.1316.21–37 (Hofmann).

633. exfibulat: this compound verb appears only here in Latin literature. **iliǎ zonis:** Prudentius does not anywhere count *z* as a double consonant, and so it does not lengthen the preceding syllable (Lavarenne 1933b, §42). Likewise, note *carminǎ psalmis* in line 664.

634. The line recalls the true appearance of Venus to Aeneas: "pedes uestis defluxit ad imos, / et uera incessu patuit dea" (*Aen.* 1.404–5).

635. The Virtues relax their pace because they are once again private citizens (Bergman 1897, 58). **temperat et:** ANASTROPHE.

637. uaginam gladius: for the possible symbolism, see the note on lines 104–5. **sedato ... campi:** the battle raised up so much dust that the sun was darkened.

638. liquidae ... diei: "clear air" (*aer liquidus*) was a common expression, but "clear daylight" does not survive from before Prudentius.

639. purpuream uideas caeli clarescere lucem: compare Vergil's description of the Elysian fields in *Aen.* 6.640–41: "largior hic campos aether et *lumine* uestit / *purpureo*, solemque suum, sua sidera norunt." It is probably a coincidence that the two lines appear at essentially the same place in each book, although we could cite a contemporary parallel for such a stichometric allusion, namely Claud., *Rapt.* 2.308–11, which responds precisely to Verg., *Aen.* 6.309–12. **uideas:** a potential subjunctive (A&G §447).

640. agmina casta super: "over their chaste columns." **sensere** = *senserunt.*
tonantis: a common epithet for Jupiter adopted by Christian poets for their
God, usually without comment or anxiety.

641. adridere: the first of three infinitives introduced by *senserunt.* **hilares
... turmae:** nominative.

642. uictoribus: *gaudere* regularly takes an ablative of cause. **arce aetheris:**
"from the citadel of heaven."

643. famulis: on the "servants of Christ," see the note on line 56. **profundum**
is a substantive.

644. Concordia appears here for the first time, but she will play an important
role in the rest of the poem.

645. uictrices aquilas: subject of *cogi.* Roman military standards were
often crowned with an eagle. For the phrase, compare Luc. 1.339, 5.238,
and Claud., *III Cons.* 16.

647. militiae: dative of possession with *decus.* **bifida agmina:** as Prudentius
explains in the next line, they were divided into infantry and cavalry. **longe:**
the columns extended into the distance.

648–49. Two carefully balanced lines in which the *pedites* sing a psalm and
the *equites* a hymn. The exact terminology is unhelpful, but it would appear
that they are singing an antiphonal song, just as Ambrose had taught the
Western church to do, as argued by Gnilka 1987.

650–64. In the only simile in the poem, Prudentius compares the Virtues
in victory to the Israelites celebrating after crossing through the Red Sea
on dry land. The story is in Exod. 14, and their song is in Exod. 15:1–21.
Prudentius had recounted the whole story of their crossing in *Cath.* 5.45–88.
Ambrose had described rejoicing in heaven as a continuation of the singing
of the Israelites, at *De uirginibus* 2.17, as pointed out by Gnilka (1987, 65–66).

Prudentius clearly has epic predecessors in mind, but his simile is not
like those that Homer drew from nature, or like those that Vergil drew
from familiar situations. This scene is far more like the historical exempla

of Claudian's panegyrics, although it also owes something to Christian typological interpretations of the Hebrew scriptures.

650. Non aliter: other words and phrases used to introduce a simile in Latin poetry include *ut, (ac) uelut, ceu, qualis,* and *non secus.*

651. Istrahel: this spelling is found in the Old Latin translations and consistently in MS *A*. **rabiem ponti . . . minacis:** "the rage of the threatening sea." Prudentius uses *mare* eighteen times, *pelagus* nine times, and *pontus* ten times, roughly the same proportions as found in Vergil and Claudian. For these statistics and on other Latin poets, see *TLL* s.v. *pontus* (Schrickx). **post terga:** "behind their backs."

652–57. cum . . . operiret: a single subordinate clause with five subjunctives describing the salvation of the Israelites and the destruction of the Egyptians in the Red Sea (Exod. 14:21–29).

652–53. sicco / . . . pede: they did not even get wet as they crossed.

654. mons . . . pendentis aquae: "a mountain of water in suspense." **nigrosque:** Ethiopians rather than Egyptians were usually the ones described as dark. **relapso:** the spelling *relabso* in MSS *B* and *T* probably comes from the common confusion in late antiquity between the pronunciation of *b*'s and *p*'s. But MS *A*'s *relaxo* could also suggest some lack of clarity in the archetype, or in the pronunciation of the text, if it was dictated.

655. Nilicolas: the word appears elsewhere only in *Symm.* 2.494.

656–57. redderet unda natatum / piscibus: "the wave returned (a habitat for) swimming to the fishes." Of course, the fish did not factor in the Exodus narrative.

659. turba dei: God's people. **memorabile saeclis:** "memorable through the ages."

660. liquidas . . . ripas: OXYMORONIC to emphasize the miracle. The accusative is the subject of *crescere.*

662. crescere ... potuisse: infinitives of indirect speech that explain *mirum ac memorabile opus*.

663. sic: "In the same way." The comparison is redundant since the narrator already described the songs of the victorious Virtues in lines 646–49. **expugnata ... gente**: ablative absolute expressing the reason for their songs.

664. mystica: the songs are mysterious because they are a type for future singing. Compare lines pr. 58 and 372. **dulcimodis**: the adjective appears only here in extant Latin. **carmina**: subject of *resultant*.

665–725. When the Virtues reach their camp, Discordia suddenly appears and wounds Concordia. But she suffers only a surface wound, and the Virtues surround Discordia and tear her to pieces.

665. Ventum erat ad fauces: an impersonal passive (A&G §208d). The phrase "uentum erat ad" appears a number of times in hexameters, the most relevant of which is *Aen.* 6.45, especially because in *Aen.* 6.201 "uenere ad fauces" describes the gates of Avernus where Aeneas finds the golden bough. **portae castrensis**: "the camp gate."

artum: for the narrow gate, see Matt. 7:13–14 "Enter by the narrow gate; for the gate is wide and the way is easy, that leads to destruction, and those who enter by it are many. For the gate is narrow (*angusta porta*) and the way is hard (*arta uia*), that leads to life, and those who find it are few" (RSV, with Vulgate).

668. tempestas: a storm befalls the Virtues just as Odysseus and Aeneas were blown off course by a storm.

671. dum ... iam ... infert: "while now she brings ..." **moenibus**: dative.

672. excipit: the suddenness of the syntax matches the action.

673. squalentia: the armor is rough because it is made of scales, as shown below in line 680.
Compare the creative explanation in MS Valenciennes 413 (Burnam 1910, 109): "SQVALENTIA fulgentia: quando fulgorem significat a squama diriuatur, unde squalentia dicit: quando uero sordem, a squaleo."

674. texta: subject of *ambirent.*

674–76. subtegmine . . . hamis . . . nodis: three parallel ablatives in this tripartite clause introduced by *quamuis.*

676. rigidis: modifies *nodis.* **fila:** subject of *sinerent.*

678. rara: modifies *commissura.* **tamen:** coordinate with *quamuis* in line 673, "although . . . nevertheless." **tenui . . . puncto:** compare Ausonius's "tenuis sub acumine puncti" (*Cupido* 76), which describes the stylus that some outraged women used to torture the god of love. **transmittere:** intransitive, with *chalybem* as its subject.

679–80. qua . . . tunicae: "where the furthest scale binds itself to the polished garment."

682. insidiata est takes a dative object.

683. pulsa culparum acie: ablative absolute. **Discordia nostros:** Prudentius juxtaposes the Vice and "our" corporate side, which allows either for a contrast or for a recognition of evil within.

684. The disguise of Discordia links her to the Fury Allecto, who disguised herself in *Aen.* 7.415–19, as observed by Malamud (1989, 60). **mentita:** the deponent verb takes an accusative object.

685–86. Discordia had left her normal equipment behind on the field before putting on her disguise.

685. scissa . . . palla: Discordia has a torn robe in *Aen.* 8.702 "et scissa gaudens uadit Discordia palla."

686. multiplici: modifies *serpente.*

687. redīmitos: the second syllable is regularly short elsewhere, including in Prudentius, but it is lengthened here with the metrical beat in the second foot. **olea:** ablative as is clear from the meter. The olive branch was a symbol of peace, as is evident from *Aen.* 8.116 and from contemporary interpretations of Gen. 8:11.

688. laeta: nominative.

689–90. te, maxima Virtus / te: APOSTROPHE and DIACOPE (repetition).

692. est licitum = *licuit* (A&G §208c). **summo tenus extima tactu**: Concordia was touched only on the surface of her skin. The phrase echoes "summo tenus attigit ore" from *Aen.* 1.737.

694. Quid hóc est? It is very unusual for a line to end with three monosyllables, but only *hoc* receives a strong accent. *Hoc* scans long because it was pronounced as though written with two *c*'s, on which see *TLL* 6.3.2695.49–69 (H. H. Schmid, Bulhart, Ehlers). Prudentius had already used this same ending at *Am.* 628.

695. prospera nostra: "our prosperity" (accusative). The adjective is used as a substantive (A&G §288–89).

696. ferrum: accusative.

697. indomitos . . . furores: the same words occur in the same form in Catull. 64.54. **sedasse** = *sedauisse*.

698. receptum: understand *esse*.

699. sub pace: "in peace," "during a time of peace." On *sub* in this temporal sense, see *OLD* s.v. 12 and Kühner-Stegmann vol. 1, §108.2. **trepida agmina**: nominative.

700. conuertēre oculos: the same half-line appears at the beginning of *Aen.* 11.746 and 12.705. The alternate third-person plural perfect active indicative has a long penultimate syllable.

702. pallor in ore: the same phrase was used by Ovid and Lucan, and by Prudentius again in *Cath.* 8.28.

703. conscius audacis facti: the same phrase is found in a simile of a murderous wolf in *Aen.* 11.812 and of Adam's guilt before God in Proba, *Cento* 236. **reatus**: genitive with *signa*.

705. strictis mucronibus: the same phrase appears in the same position in Vergil, Ovid, Silius Italicus, and Ausonius.

708. et missu cuiatis uenerit: the genitive of the interrogative pronoun introduces the second indirect question, "at whose sending she came."

Gnilka thought that this verse was INTERPOLATED (1984, 341n14); but *deum* would be flat without the explanation, *exsanguis* would be abrupt without *illa*, and Prudentius often develops a single idea in multiple verses.

709–14. Discordia's short speech is full of rhetorical ornamentation and pleasantry but does nothing to win over her audience.

709. turbante metu: echoes the same phrase in Paulinus, *Natalicia* 8.40 = Hartel *Carm.* 26, from the year 402. **Discordia dicor**: the pun points to the basic ambiguity of language (Malamud 1989, 63).

710. cognomento: Discordia answers who is her family (*genus*). In late antiquity, a multiplicity of new names gradually obscured the old system of *tria nomina* and its straightforward division between *praenomen*, *nomen*, and *cognomen*. **Hĕresis**: Prudentius is the first extant poet to shorten the first vowel of the Greek word *haéresis*. The word meant "school," "sect," or "faction" in general before definitions of heresy were used to help define Christian orthodoxy. By the time of Prudentius, the modern meaning was fully established. **discolor**: Discordia's polychromatic God did not, ironically, prevent her from being betrayed by her own colors.

711–14. These lines allude to contemporary heresies about the nature of God, that one person of the trinity was greater, or that there were two gods, or that God was not a trinity, or that Christ's human nature was phantasmal, or that God was the soul within. For possible identifications of each heresy, see the notes below. Although attempts at identifying the heresies can be traced back to the commentary in MS Valenciennes 413 (Burnam 1910, 110), Prudentius is subtle, and he suggests a range of possible ideas rather than simply offering historical examples. Such theological questions are treated expansively in *Apotheosis*, in which Prudentius explores the nature of God and man and argues for the divinity of Christ.

711. nunc minor aut maior: MS Valenciennes 413 (Burnam 1910, 110) explains that Arius said the Father was greater than the Son; Bergman compares *Apoth.* 255 "nec enim minor aut patre dispar." Arius (c. 250–336 C.E.) was a presbyter in Alexandria, and it was partly in opposition to his teaching that orthodox trinitarian theology developed in the East over the course of the fourth century. Many of the Germanic groups in the West took up Arianism, perhaps partly for political reasons and partly because of its emphasis on the humanity of Christ.

modo duplex: MS Valenciennes 413 (Burnam 1910, 110) explains that some rejected the holy spirit. In *Apoth.* 436, Prudentius says that the spirit is God, and the first preface to *Apotheosis* neatly develops his trinitarian position, although its authenticity was doubted by Gnilka (2000–2003, 1:461–88). More specifically, Marcion (c. 85–c. 160) taught that the God of the Old Testament and the God of the New Testament were distinct; see *Am.* praef. 37 "docet duitas discrepare a spiritu." Compare also *Am.* 6 "Terrarum tibi forma duplex obludit."

simplex: Sabellius was forced to leave the church of Rome by Callistus (bishop from 217–22) because he taught that Father and Son were not distinct. MS Valenciennes 413 (Burnam 1910, 110) explains that Sabellius affirmed a single God could make himself Father, Son, or Spirit whenever he pleased. Prudentius addresses Sabellius directly in *Apoth.*, at the very beginning of a section (178–320) directed against his and similar teachings.

712. Manicheans taught that Christ was God, but that he had only a spiritual appearance and was never fully human, as Prudentius explains in polemical terms: "aërium Manicheus ait sine corpore uero / peruolitasse deum, mendax fantasma cauamque / corporis effigiem" (*Apoth.* 956–58). This section of *Apotheosis* (952–1061) is entitled "Aduersum fantasmaticos qui Christum negant uerum corpus habuisse." Mani (216–76 C.E.) was from Sasanian Persia and founded his religion on Gnostic and other ideas. It spread widely but was not influential in the West after Augustine, previously an auditor of the sect, supported anti-Manichean legislation with a barrage of antiheretical treatises.

713. innata anima: perhaps a reference to Gnostic teachings, or to the Neoplatonic world soul, as suggested by Basile (2007, 116).

714. praeceptor Bēliă mǐhī: "Belial is my teacher." Belial is a name for the evil one in Deut. 13:13. The name scans the same as here in *Am.* 520, but in *Am.* 610 the form Beliade scans either with SYNERESIS in the second syllable (Bēliăde) or shortening to fit the meter (Bēliăde). The second syllable of *mihi* is alternatively long in line 302 and short in 84 and 710.

domus et plaga mundus: Discordia answers each of the questions set to her, although not in order. **mundus:** the Greek *kosmos* ("world") was used by SYNECDOCHE in reference to the fallen world or to the world opposed to Christians. This usage goes back to the New Testament; on such uses of *mundus*, see *TLL* s.v. *mundus*³ II.b = 8.0.1639.4–40.14 (Kamptz). See also the notes on lines 310 and 816.

715–25. Fides cannot stand to hear Discordia any longer, and so she pierces her tongue with a spear. Just as quickly, Discordia is violently torn apart by the Virtues. A remarkable pair of images in MS *Br* capture the retributive violence at the heart of these two scenes (see introduction, page 20).

715. non tulit ulterius: Prudentius borrows this half-line from Ov., *Met.* 3.487, where Narcissus is described as no longer able to endure his love. Reading this allusion in *Psychomachia* deepens our understanding of the link between language and self-reflection. Narcissus succumbs to his own watery image, and Discordia's tongue is physically pierced because her speech is not rightly grounded. The same half-line from Ovid appears in Paulinus, *Natalicia* 4.232 = Hartel *Carm.* 15, which was written for the saint's celebration in January 398. In that passage, which alludes to the parable of the unjust judge in Luke 18:1–8, I do not see any reason for an allusion to Ovid's Narcissus, but Prudentius may have been influenced by the passage all the same. See above on lines 16–17. **blasfemia:** Prudentius is not the only Latin author to treat the word as belonging to the second declension and neuter. The spelling with an *f* in place of the Greek *phi* became common in the fourth century, because the Greek letter was no longer pronounced as an aspirate (Lavarenne 1933b, §46). Compare *strofium* (449), *fantasmate* (712), *Fotinus* (794), and *falangas* (816).

716. uirtutum regina Fides: she is also called a queen in line 823, as are Pudicitia (53) and Mens humilis (199 and 267). The word *regina* was like the English "queen," which can also be used figuratively for anyone who is powerful, noble, or preeminent in some sphere. **uerba loquentis:** it is emphatically the words of the Vice that so disturb Fides, even after she is herself now captured.

717–18. claudit . . . transfigens: in order to stop Discordia's disrupting speech, Fides closes her airway and transfixes her tongue. The scene is gruesome, but without the whimsical touches of the following *sparagmos*.

718. pollutam . . . linguam: her tongue is deceptive and so polluted. Malamud identifies a Greek-Latin cross-lingual pun: *polu-tam*, i.e., "so various," "so many-sided" (1989, 65). **rigida . . . cuspide:** ablative of means.

719–25. The *sparagmos* neatly matches Discordia's character. On the law of retaliation and the downfall of the Vices, see the introduction, page 19. On the construction of this passage and its formal properties, see the excellent discussion in Roberts 1989, 28–30. Despite the formal explanations for the scene, Malamud is right to draw attention to the disturbing way in which the Virtues "become agents of dismemberment and dissolution" (1989, 66).

Compare Claud., *Ruf.* 2.400–416. In that scene, Claudian describes the death of Rufinus at the hands of his own soldiers, a fate that he explicitly likens to the mythological deaths of Pentheus and Actaeon. Prudentius transfers the political and cosmic discord from that scene and enlivens his own with a crew of scavenging dogs and crows. These carrion-eaters could easily have been inspired by Hom., *Il.* 1.4–5, a passage that Prudentius surely would have read if he learned any Greek in school, as he must have done. Note that Prudentius also describes the gruesome death by dragging of the priest Hippolytus in *Perist.* 11.111–22.

719. feralis bestia: Claudian had compared the soon-to-be-dismembered Rufinus to a wild animal (*fera*) at *Ruf.* 2.394.

720–23. quod . . . quod . . . quod . . . quod . . . quod: ANAPHORA, with a series of relative clauses of characteristic expressing purpose.

722. offerat, inmundis caeno exhalante cloacis: the same arrangement of verb and chiastic noun-adjective pairing occurs, for example, in lines 719 and 745. For the dirty sewers, compare Columella, *Rust.* 10.85 "immundis quaecumque uomit latrina cloacis."

723. monstris quod mandet habere marinis: "something to send to the monsters of the sea for them to keep."

724. omne cadauer: "all the dead body." *Omnis* was used already as a synonym for *cunctus* by Cicero and Caesar ("Gallia est omnis diuisa in partes tres," *BGall.* 1.1). The same line ending occurs in Luc. 4.787; Juv. 3.260; and Corippus, *Iohannis* 1.34. But *cadauer* looks like an allusion to "sparsum . . . cadauer" in Claud., *Ruf.* 2.417.

CONCORDIA AND FIDES ADDRESS
THE VIRTUES IN ASSEMBLY (726–822)

After the Virtues finally come together in their camp (726–48), Concordia explains her victory and the importance of peace (749–98); Fides tells the troops that they must now set to work building a temple (799–822). Unlike all of the other contests, the first and seventh did not include a victory speech, and so Fides and Concordia have to wait until this conclusion to say their part. They also featured together at the end of the previous scene in which Fides was the first to strike Discordia.

726–48. A densely structured transitional paragraph. A raised tribunal appears, and Concordia and Fides ascend it to address a mind that is now perfectly open.

726–28. "Therefore, when the goods of property and morals were set in order and were favorable for all (*in commune*) of the people at peace, one and all, because their perceptions were organized within the safe standing of the palisade . . ." At long last, the Virtues gather within their camp, which is allegorically the inner self.

The text of these lines is difficult and perhaps corrupt. *Conpositis* and *secundis* apparently are predicates of *bonis* in an ablative absolute, and *rerum* and *morum* modify *bonis*. The source of MS *E* presumably added line 728 and rewrote 727 and 729 in order to smooth over some of the difficulties.

With the understanding of the manuscripts available to him in the seventeenth century, the great critic Nicolaas Heinsius thought that the variant in this passage was evidence of authorial revision (1667, 2:108). Although our knowledge of the text's transmission is still lacking, it now seems that the variant was only a late INTERPOLATION (compare above on lines 105–6). For the reconstruction of the original text of *E* as in my apparatus, see Cunningham's apparatus, with the corrections to it in Cunningham 1968, 140. These lines are discussed by Gnilka (1986, 93–98), who thinks that the text was tampered with systematically by a late-antique editor, although this variant looks only like an attempt to clarify a passage that was originally obscure or already corrupt.

726. Conpositis: a sharp contrast with the images of dismemberment in the previous lines.

727. ad unum: "one and all." The phrase seems to modify *tranquillae*. For its meaning, compare *Aen.* 5.687.

728. sensibus: the Virtues are components of the human mind, as explained by Gnilka (1986, 94–95); on the uses of *sensus* in this poem, see above on line 7. **ualli**: genitive of *uallum* and dependent on *statione*. Given the other allusions to *Aen.* 6 in this poem, *in tuta ualli* can be heard as an echo of *in ualle reducta* (*Aen.* 6.703), the valley and secluded wood in which Aeneas learns from his father about the fate of souls and the future of Rome.

730. media castrorum sede: "at a place in the middle of the camp." Note that *castrorum* neatly falls in the middle of the line.

731. editiore: comparative of *editus*. **tumulus**: it was also on a *tumulus* that Aeneas and Anchises stood to review the parade of Roman heroes (*Aen.* 6.754). Prudentius's description of this tribunal supports Horsfall's understanding of Vergil's *tumulus* as the raised mound (*suggestus*) in a military camp (2013, 517–18).

733. circum inspicit: compare *Apoth.* 492 in which MS *A* has the same phrase and MSS *T, E,* and *S* again have *circumspicit.*

734. hunc is as far from its object as is possible in this sentence. **sincera Fides:** the same phrase occurs in Claud., *Carm. min.* 25.92 and in the anonymous *Carmen ad quendam senatorem* 68.

736. conscendunt apicem: they rise to the top of the mound. The prefix marks the completion of the action (see *OLD* s.v. *con-* 6). **mox et:** and now they climb the steps mentioned in line 823. **sublime tribunal:** an echo of the phrase from Claud., *Ruf.* 2.382 and *Eutr.* 1.311. Prudentius had probably already written *Perist.* 11 and used the same phrase to describe the raised pulpit in the church next to the tomb of Hippolytus in Rome: "gradibus sublime tribunal / tollitur, antistes praedicat unde deum" (225–26).

737. par sanctum carumque sibi: "the holy pair dear to each other." **supereminet:** takes an accusative direct object.

737–38. aequo / iure potestatis: "with an equal right to command."

739. conspicuae: predicate nominative.

740. omnibus omnes: POLYPTOTON to match the full alacrity of the troops.

741–43. Prudentius sets aside the allegory for a moment, in order to speak of the mind and body in literal terms.

The mind / soul is described in these lines as open and not hidden, and as distributed throughout the body. The idea that the soul is present throughout the body comes from the basic observation that humans have sense perception from head to toe, for which see Macrob., *In Somn.* 1.14.19: "Hippocrates [dixit animam] spiritum tenuem per corpus omne dispersum," a passage cited by Carlo Prosperi in the notes to his Italian translation (2000, 127). In his treatise *De anima*, Tertullian followed the Stoics in asserting that the human soul was corporeal, although Prudentius seems not to have embraced that idea (Gnilka 1963, 1–8). The Platonic view, the most common view in late antiquity, was that the soul was incorporeal. Prudentius reflects further on the distribution and working of the soul within the body in *Symm.* 2.379–92.

741. latet: latency in communication and deception are everywhere negative within the *Psychomachia*: Fraus hides herself in line 262, Auaritia disguises her hidden rage in 560, Discordia hides a dagger in line 673, Virtus asks who is hiding in line 695, and the wolf disguises itself as a lamb in line 791.

741–42. corporis ullo / intercepta sinu: "separated in any cavity of the body."

743. tentoria: we are back to the allegorical camp, and to tents that are not tents.

744. ne: negative purpose. **quis** = *aliquis*.

745. marceat . . . stertens habitator: these three words were not part of the Vergilian poetic koine (none of them appears in Vergil), and perhaps they lend the line a more prosaic sound. **operto:** the adjective *opertus* is regularly used as a substantive (A&G §288–89).

746. contio: collective singular, subject of *expectant*. **quidnam** = *cur* ("why").

747. uocet: "summon."

748. quam . . . legem: a second indirect question introduced by *expectant*. **atque:** ANASTROPHE again.

749–98. Concordia recalls the recent victory of her side against the savagery of the Vices, and she praises the importance and need for peace (not personified). She ends her exhortation by recalling some heresies and her recent wounding, which elicits groans and grief from her congregation.

Prudentius combines elements of Christian charity with philosophical equanimity (*ataraxia*) to represent peace as the end and goal of virtue. For an earlier example of *pax* used in reference to the tranquility of a Christian mind, see Tert., *De spect.* 15

749. Erumpit . . . in uocem: she breaks into speech. The idiom *erumpere in uocem* is found in *Collectanea rerum memorabilium* 1.112 of Solinus (this example, probably from the early third century, is the earliest I could find); Auson., *Gratiarum actio* 2.10; and Augustine, *Enarrationes in psalmos* 42.2.

750. uobis: dative object of *contigit*.

751. o patris, o domini: Prudentius noted the doubling of God the Father and Christ the Lord in lines 3–4. **pignera**: vocative.

752–54. This description of the battle as a siege could allude to Alaric's siege of Rome in 408, on which see above on pr. 21.

753. barbaries: compare *barbarorum* (pr. 20) and *barbara bellatrix* (133). **sanctae ... urbis**: modifies *indigenas*. This is the first reference in the poem to a city of the Virtues.

754. ferroque uiros flammaque premebat: compare the description of Turnus's attack on the Trojans' camp in *Aen.* 10.232 "*ferro* Rutulus *flammaque premebat.*"

755. rure foroque: a polar expression, "in the countryside and in the forum." For the ablative *rure* used like the locative *ruri*, see *OLD* s.v. *rus* 3b.

756. scissura: the original meaning of the word was "tearing" or "a cleft" or "tear." The meaning division / disagreement was introduced into Latin as a translation of the Greek *schisma* in 1 Cor. 11:18.

757. rem populi: Cicero says in *De re publica* that *res populi* is synonymous with *res publica* (1.48). The phrase was not at all common, and yet Augustine used it in three letters written between 408 and 412 (*Epist.* 95.5, 126.4, 138.2.10); then he used the phrase a number of times in *De ciuitate dei*, where he clearly had Cicero in mind. It is possible that Augustine was reminded of the phrase by Prudentius. **quod dissidet intus**: an allusion to Matt. 12:25 "Omne regnum diuisum contra se desolatur" (Vulgate). Juvencus gives a version of that verse in *Euangeliorum* 2.611–13.

758–61. In 1 Cor. 1:10, Paul bids his readers to avoid dissension (*scismata*) and to be perfect in the same thought and the same judgment ("in eodem sensu et in eadem sententia," Vulgate).

758. ergŏ: this scansion is common in Latin poetry from Ovid on. **ne sit**: a fear clause, in origin a negative wish (A&G §208c).

759–60. Compare the opening of *Apoth*. praef. 2 *"Est uera secta?"* where Prudentius asks rhetorically whether he belongs to the right group.

759. sensibus: can mean both "sensation" (understanding) and "faculty of sensation" (mind), on which see above on line 7.

761. arcana: a substantive adjective. **biformia**: divided between body and soul. **fibris**: "innards," "gut." The entrails were seen as a center of personality, in the same way that we speak of the heart.

762–63. quod sapimus coniungat amor, quod uiuimus uno / conspiret studio: "May love join our thoughts, may our life agree in a single pursuit." *Quod* is an inner accusative in each clause, so that literally it means "the thing that we know," "the thing that we live," i.e., "the life that we live." The clause *quod uiuimus* is the subject of the intransitive verb *conspiret*. **amor**: for the clear allusions in this passage to Paul's celebration of charity (*agapē*) in 1 Cor. 13, see the notes on 775–78 and 779–81.

763. dissociabile: the word appears elsewhere in poetry only in Hor., *Carm.* 1.3.22 and Claud., *Ruf.* 2.238.

764–66. As human and divine, Jesus was a mediator between God and man: "Unus enim Deus, unus et mediator Dei et hominum, homo Christus Iesus" (1 Tim. 2:5, in the Vulgate translation; the other Latin translations are very similar). Jesus is "nostri mediator et omnipotentis" in *Apoth.* 174 and *mediator* again in *Cath.* 11.16.

764. Iesus: Prudentius consistently scans the name as two syllables, and not as the Greek *Iēsous*. For this spelling instead of Cunningham and Bergman's *Hisus*, see Fontaine 1966, 470.

766. spiritui: dative of separation (A&G §381), a subspecies of the dative of reference.

767–68. Just as Christ is a mediator, may the Holy Spirit in the same way unite within us the actions of mind and body.

768. A closely structured line, to match the words on unity. **unimodis:** the only certain extant use of the word before Prudentius was at Apul., *De Platone* 2.5, where it modifies *uirtus* and is equivalent to *monoeidēs*. Prudentius does not explain how body and mind can be joined in a simple connection, but the answer is presumably implicit in the mystery of Christ's incarnation. **texat:** "weave together." Weaving was a METAPHOR for poetic creativity throughout the Greco-Roman tradition (Scheid and Svenbro 1996). This idea of writing as weaving was advanced by Optatianus Porfyrius in the early fourth century, on which see Bažil 2017. On weaving in this poem, see the notes on lines 364, 882, and 913.

769–71. Peace (not personified) is now the reward for the labors and war completed. On personifications of Peace in ancient Greece, see Stafford 2000, 173–97. On the grand Temple of Peace in Rome and its remodelings in late antiquity, see the comprehensive study of Tucci 2018.

Compare Augustine's description of beatitude in *De civ. d.* 19.10. He says that the creator will grant the human good and eternal gifts, not only in the mind that is healed through wisdom but also in the body healed through resurrection ("non solum in animo, qui sanatur per sapientiam, uerum etiam in corpore, quod resurrectione renouabitur"). And there, he says, the virtues will not be in conflict against any vices, but they will have eternal peace as the reward for their victory ("ibi uirtutes, non contra ulla uitia uel mala quaecumque certantes, sed habentes uictoriae praemium aeternam pacem, quam nullus aduersarius inquietet"). It is not uncommon for contemporaries to come up with very similar ideas independently, but three elements in particular point to *Psychomachia*: the mind healed through wisdom (for *Sapientia*, see lines 875 and 915), the conflict between virtues and vices, and peace as the reward. The link between these passages has been discussed for a long time but without any consensus (see Lavarenne 1933a, 259–60 and Shanzer 1989, 362–63, along with Bastiaensen 1993a, 132). On the possible broader implications of Augustine's reading of *Psychomachia*, see Smolak 2001, 147. For another suggestive passage, see below on line 774.

769–72. pax ... pax ... pax ... pace ... pace ... pace: ANAPHORA.

769. pax plenum uirtutis opus: an echo of line 566 "dum credunt uirtutis opus," where Auaritia had deceived the Virtues with what seemed like good works.

771. sidera pace uigent: compare Claudian's observation of the instability of peace in *Get.* 62–63 "nec sidera pacem / semper habent."

772. deo: dative with *placitum*.

772–74. In Matt. 5:22–24, Jesus taught his disciples to love their brother and warned them against offering sacrifice as long as they harbored unreconciled anger.

774. pectoris ... antro: Juvencus had described the heart's inner cave, and Prudentius here and in line 6 above was probably influenced by that phrase: "Nil absente deo loquimur, nil abdita clausum / pectoris antra tegunt, praesens Deus omnia cernit" (*Euangeliorum* 587–88).

The phrase *antro pectoris* was used also by Augustine in *De civ. d.* 14.24, in a discussion of how reproduction would have worked in the garden without sin (mind and body would have been in total harmony). Given what Prudentius says about interior harmony in this speech and given the parallel from *De ciuitate dei* discussed above on lines 769–71, this could be further evidence that Augustine had read *Psychomachia*.

775–78. From 1 Cor. 13:3 "If I give away all I have, and if I deliver my body to be burned, but have not love, I gain nothing."

775. flammicomis: modifies *ignibus*. This adjective is found elsewhere only at Avienius, *Orbis terrarum* 1088. The equivalent adjective *flammicomans* appears once in extant Latin literature, in Juvencus 4.201. **Christi:** take with *nomine*.

776. seruans inamabile uotum: "keeping your vow without love." The meaning of the adjective is extended from "unlovable" to "unloving."

777. bile sub obliqua: "under the influence of twisted anger." For this use of *sub*, see *OLD* s.v. 14. **Iesu:** dative with *inpendisse*.

778. clausula pax est: Terentianus Maurus is the only extant poet who used the word *clausula* before Prudentius, who first used it in *Cath.* 9.11, in a line on Christ as *alpha* and *omega*. There is apparently a playful reference here to the two monosyllables *pax est* at line end, because *clausula* can refer to the end of a line of verse; for this use of *clausula*, see *TLL* s.v. I.B.2.a = 3.0.1325.42–53 (Hey).

779–81. Concordia takes her ideas and sometimes her exact vocabulary from Paul's celebration of charity in 1 Cor. 13:4–8 "Love is patient and kind; love is not jealous or boastful; it is not arrogant or rude. Love does not insist on its own way; it is not irritable or resentful; it does not rejoice at wrong, but rejoices in the right. Love bears all things, believes all things, hopes all things, endures all things."

779. inuidet takes a dative personal object.

781. cuncta: the variant *contra* in MS *E* looks like another scribal conjecture.

782. Prudentius recalls Eph. 4:26 "Do not let the sun go down on your anger." **uenia:** instrumental ablative.

783. ne . . . linquat: a fearing clause introduced by *anxia*. **sol conscius:** compare *conscium . . . diem* in Sen., *Oed.* 1001, and Helios who knows all and hears all in Hom., *Il.* 3.277, *Od.* 11.109, and *Od.* 12.323.

784–85. Recalls pr. 6, as observed by Charlet (2003, 246).

784. holocaustis: this Greek-sounding word was often used by Christian authors in Latin.

786. sancta ad donaria: compare the phrase "alta ad donaria" from Verg., *G.* 3.533. Perhaps Prudentius influenced the anonymous poet known as Cyprianus Gallus (the Heptateuch poet), who also wrote "sancta ad donaria" at the same point in the hexameter (*Iudicum* 527).

787. puro: the reading of MS *A* is difficult but slightly preferable, because the adjective is appropriate in the context of a just offering and because the phrase is original. Indeed, I was surprised not to find any other example of the phrase *purus odor* in Latin literature before Rut. Namat. 1.253.

How do we explain the variant?

The phrase "liquidus odor" appears in the singular in Verg., *G.* 4.415 and in the plural in Hor., *Carm.* 1.5.2, as well as Prudent., *Cath.* 10.172, which is the very last line in the poem and memorable. Furthermore, Prudentius has the phrase "sensus liquidos" in *Am.* 513, and "liquido . . . profundo" below in line 853. There is plenty of evidence for scribal errors in MS *A*, but not much for INTERPOLATIONS or corrections in its text of *Psychomachia* (see the note on pr. 31 for a likely exception). The simplest explanation is that *liquido* was a corruption occasioned by a scribe remembering one of these parallel passages.

On the other hand, you might think that *liquido* was original and replaced by *puro* as an improvement. *Liquidus* is commonly used of what is pure, ethereal, and spiritual (Lavarenne 1933b, §931 and *OLD* s.v. 2c). Moreover, the two words were commonly used as near synonyms (for example in Lucr. 3.40), and *puro* appears as a gloss for *liquido* in the Weitz B tradition represented by MSS Clm 14395 and Paris 241 (O'Sullivan 2004, 332).

Although not impossible, it would be hazardous to suggest that *puro* is an authorial variant. Prudentius could have written *liquido* and then changed it to *puro* after deciding that the former was cliché. But the evidence for authorial revisions in the text of Prudentius is vanishingly thin, and such explanations are convincing only when supported by strong evidence (see above on lines 726–28). For an introduction to the question of authorial variants in Prudentius, see Bastiaensen 1993a, 104–8. For an excellent introduction to the textual problems of INTERPOLATION, see Tarrant 2016, 85–104.

On the intriguing topic of smells in ancient Christianity, see Harvey 2006.

788–91. tradit . . . columbis / . . . colubrum / . . . internoscere mixtum / innocuis auibus: "He teaches the doves to distinguish the snake mixed up among the innocent birds." Prudentius alludes to Matt. 10:16 "Be as wise as serpents and innocent as doves."

788. deus ipse: God himself in Christ taught his disciples to be discerning.

791. auibus: the variant *ouibus* in *T* and *E* derives from the following reference to sheep and wolves.

791–93. Matt. 7:15 "Beware of false prophets, who come to you in sheep's clothing but inwardly are ravenous wolves"; see also the first half of Matt. 10:16 "Behold, I send you out as sheep in the midst of wolves."

792. mentitus ouem: "having disguised himself as a sheep." The object is in origin a cognate accusative, i.e., he lied a lie that he was a sheep.

794. Fotinus et Arrius: Photinus was bishop of Sirmium from around 343, and he died in 376. He was branded a heretic because he taught that God was only one person. On Arius, see the note on line 711. Prudentius adapts the spelling of the name in order to lengthen the accented first syllable.

796. quamuis de corpore summo: it was only on the very surface of her body that she was wounded.

797. quid possit: the indirect question is the object of *produnt*. **gemitum dedit omnis:** Arevalo thought that Prudentius had read Jerome's memorable line on a heresy: "Ingemuit totus orbis, et Arianum se esse miratus est" (*Altercatio Luciferiani et orthodoxi* 19).

798. casu concussus acerbo: Aeneas is also shaken by a harsh accident, when part of his fleet burns in Sicily in *Aen.* 5.700 "at pater Aeneas casu concussus acerbo."

799–822. Fides announces that they must now build a temple for Christ, just as Solomon did after his father's battles. While that temple was in Jerusalem, this temple will be a home for Christ within the cleansed and ornamented *psyche*.

801. quin: introduces a strong assertion advancing the previous point.

802. germanam comitata Fidem: the deponent regularly takes an accusative object. Contrast the expression *comitata uiro* in line 163. Claud., *Stil.* 2.30 called Fides the sister of Clementia ("germana Fides").

803. nihil hac . . . triste recepta: the ablative absolute is either causal or temporal. Prudentius reworks Ascanius's comment that he will fear nothing if his father is recalled, *Aen.* 9.262 "nihil illo triste recepto." **mihi:** a dative of reference with *triste* or a dative of advantage with *recepta*.

805–8. Solomon built a temple in Jerusalem after he inherited the kingdom of Israel from his father David, who did not do so because of the wars in which he was involved (1 Kings 5–6).

805. quod: "the task that . . ."

806. belligeri modifies *regni*. **et** connects *heres* and *successor*. **armatae . . . aulae:** genitive of the thing inherited (see *OLD* s.v. *successor*).

807. genitoris anheli: Solomon's father David was renowned as a warrior.

808. fumarat = *fumauerat*. Valerius Flaccus had described panting wounds smoking: "anhela in pectore fumant / uulnera" (2.333–34). **dextra:** nominative.

809. fundatur: like the external narrator, Concordia gravitates to the present tense (see the note on line 21).

810. auratis: the temple was apparently covered in gold (1 Kings 6:21–22).

811. Hierusales templo inlustrata: like Jerusalem, this poem is embellished in the following paragraph with the rhetorical description (ecphrasis) of a temple. **quietum:** given the basic assumptions of post-Aristotelian theology, God was always at rest.

812–13. circumuaga . . . arca: the "Ark of the Covenant" represented God's presence in the Jewish tradition, and it moved around with the people until a permanent temple was built.

813. marmoreis: an anachronistic detail not found in 1 Kings 5–6. **altaribus:** *altaria* were often larger or more decorative than an *ara*.

814–15. Concordia's emotional response leaves only a thin line between her, the internal narrator, and Prudentius himself.

815. cuius . . . reuisat: a relative clause of characteristic. **cuius:** the antecedent is *templum*. **sanctorum sancta:** "holy of holies," the redundant genitive is a calque on the Hebraic idiom; the superlative *sanctissima* would have been regular Latin.

816. terrigenas: on the association of sin with the world, see on line 714. For this use of the adjective, compare Augustine, *De civ. d.* 15.15. The word was commonly used in mythological poetry in reference to the giants defeated by Jupiter; and on possible echoes of the *gigantomachia*, see above on lines 323–39. Maybe it is not accidental that the same word is found in the same metrical position in *Get.* 31, where Claudian asks whether he should really be amazed at the mythology of the earthborn Spartoi defeated on the day they were born.

817. culparum: see above on line 130. **prodest:** recalls "nihil mihi prodest" from 1 Cor. 13:3, quoted above on lines 775–78. **hominis . . . filius:** in the Gospels, Christ calls himself the "Son of man." Note the contrast with *terrigenas*.

818. inlapsus: "descended." The same verb was used by Aeneas in a prayer for Apollo's inspiration: "da, pater, augurium atque animis inlabere nostris" (*Aen.* 3.89). Likewise, *inlabere* was used in petitions by Proba, *Cento* 30; Ambrose, *Hymni* 2.5; Paulinus of Nola, *Natalicia* 14.3 = Hartel *Carm.* 29; and Prudent., *Perist.* 5.565. Prudentius used *inlapsa* and *inlapsurus* of the incarnation of Christ in *Cath.* 7.55 and *Apoth.* 58 and 103. The link between all of these passages was noted by Lühken (2002, 35). **purgati corporis urbem:** "the city of the body cleansed" (A&G §343d).

820–21. hactenus . . . nunc: the temporal progression in this poem is reduced to a teleological vision of psychological and spiritual perfection (see above on line 21).

820. sudatum est: an impersonal passive (A&G §208d).

821. toga candida: in the New Testament and among Christian writers, white garments were taken as a sign of purity, for which see *TLL* s.v. *candidus*, 3.0.243.46–57 (Goetz). Traditionally, the *toga candida* was whitened with chalk and worn by candidates for office in Rome.

822. sacris: dative.

THE CONSTRUCTION OF A TEMPLE FOR PEACE (823–87)

Concordia begins immediately to measure the temple, and its whole splendid structure is then described. The temple features twelve gemstones and recalls the heavenly New Jerusalem from the Apocalypse of John (Rev. 21:10–27). In the middle of the completed temple, Sapientia sits enthroned dispensing justice (868–87).

The apostle Paul described individual Christians as a temple of God, in 1 Cor. 3:16 ("templum dei estis"), 1 Cor. 6:19 ("membra uestra templum sunt spiritus sancti"), and 2 Cor. 6:16 ("estis templum dei uiui"). The idea was common enough that it was cited by Priscillian of Avilla in his topical index to the Letters of Paul (*Canones* 33; "Quia sanctorum corpora dei siue spiritus sancti templa et Christi membra sint"). The same point was developed by Prudentius elsewhere, including in *Perist.* 10.346–60 and *Symm.* 2.249–55, where God is said to desire a temple in the hearts of his followers rather than a temple made of marble and gold ("templum mentis amo, non marmoris . . ."). Compare also Prudentius's epigram on the building of the temple (*Aedificatio templi*):

> Aedificat templum Sapientia per Solomonis
> obsequium; regina austri graue congerit aurum.
> tempus adest quo templum hominis sub pectore Christus
> aedificet, quod Graia colant, quod barbara ditent. (*Tituli
> historiarum* 81–84)

> The temple is built by Wisdom through Solomon's
> obedience; the queen of the South brings heavy gold.
> Now is the age when Christ builds his temple in the human
> heart—the Greeks give reverence, the barbarians wealth.

In this epigram, Prudentius interprets Solomon's temple as a typological prefiguration both for Christ's coming to dwell within the individual heart and for the historical transformations that brought Greeks and barbarians into the Christian faith.

As well as referring to the individual, the temple's construction in *Psychomachia* also represents the end of Christian salvation history, in the sense that the temple represents the church and marks the completion of the poem's narrative. The idea of individual Christians being part of a spiritual building was well known from Eph. 2:20–22 " . . . uos coaedificamini in habitaculum Dei in spiritu" and 1 Pet. 2:5–6 "et ipsi tamquam lapides uiui superaedificamini domus spiritalis . . ." On the corresponsion in early Christian discourse of the temple, the church, and the Christian soul, see Gnilka 1963, 125–28.

In terms of the historical development of the poem, Prudentius began the preface with Abraham and the book of Genesis and ends with a temple modeled on the new Jerusalem from the Apocalypse, which was the last book in most orderings of the Christian scriptures (for example, see the canon of scriptures in Augustine, *De doctrina christiana* 2.8.13); indeed this is the same order that Prudentius follows in *Tituli historiarum*, in which the epigrams begin with Adam and Eve and end with the Apocalypse. The Biblical arc of the poem is presumably the reason that medieval glosses in the Weitz tradition comment on the fact that the poem begins from Genesis (O'Sullivan 2004, 139–40). In this way, Prudentius turns the internal victory of the Virtues into a microcosm of universal teleology.

Sapientia, the divine figure at the center of the scene, does not have an exact model in Revelation; in that text, there is only a reference to the temple and to the seat of God and of the Lamb (Rev. 21:22 and 22:3). But wisdom (Greek *sophia*) was the goal of most philosophical teaching in the ancient world, including that of the Epicurean Lucretius (*De rerum natura* 5.10). We can see, therefore, that Prudentius has taken this opportunity to cross the Greco-Roman and Jewish traditions. It is not unlikely, moreover, that he knew Plato had compared a just city to a just person (*Republic* 534b1–2), as pointed out by Mastrangelo (2008, 128–29).

The temple can easily be read as a symbol for the poem, because metapoetic monuments (including temples) were well known in Latin and Greek poetry. For example, Pindar compared one of his odes to a large building (*Ol.* 6.1–4); Vergil used an imagined temple as a poetic symbol, probably for the *Aeneid* (*G.* 12–48); and Horace described his poetry as a monument (*Carm.* 3.30.1). Thus, the beauty of the temple and the beauty of the poem are related to each other (see also the note on lines 851–65).

For an excellent commentary on lines 823–87, see Gnilka 1963, 83–128. For a fine study of the poetics and thought underlying the whole passage, see Gosserez 2001, 248–73.

823–67. Prudentius describes the preparations for building the temple (823–29) and then its twelve gateways made each of a massive gemstone (830–37). He next describes their symbolic and allegorical meanings (838–51) and the brilliant colors of the gemstones (852–65). He closes with the heavy crane at work on the temple's construction (866–67).

823. haec ubi dicta dedit: epic formulaic diction. This transition appears eight times in the *Aeneid*, and eight times in Juvencus, as well as once each in a few other poets. Prudentius can be seen as alluding through Vergil both to the ancient tradition of epic and also to the new Christian tradition of scriptural epic. The parallels cited by Horsfall (2000, 318) and Norden (1957, 294) in their notes on *Aen.* 6.628 show that the phrase could recall Ennius, but there is no evidence that this half-line was used as a formula before Vergil.

823–24. gradibus … superbis / desiluit: "leapt down from the lofty steps." *Desilire* always takes either an ablative of separation or some indication of the place to which one leaps, as pointed out by Gnilka (1963, 93). For the steps of the tribunal, compare *Perist.* 11.225 (cited above on line 736). Glosses in the Weitz tradition explain *superbis* as meaning *gloriosis, pulchris*, and *altis* (O'Sullivan 2004, 325–26). At first sight, it is odd to see anything of the Virtues being described with this adjective.

824. tantique operis: take with *consors*. **Concordia consors:** compare "Discordia dissona" (442).

825–29. The detail of the city being measured is modeled on Rev. 21:15–16, in particular the city being square and the use of a golden rod ("aurea harundo").

825. nouum: in contrast to the physical temple in Jerusalem, which was destroyed by the emperor Titus in 70 C.E.

829. Prudentius plays with ambivalent language that could refer to the measured impact of his poetry. **semetra:** "unevenness." Prudentius invents a derivative adjective from *metrum* and uses it as a substantive. The prefix *se-* (*seorsum*) denotes separation or absence. As noted by Heinsius (1667, 2:110), the word is used as an antonym to *symmetros*. The coincidence of ictus and accent on the prefix (sémetra) helps ensure the proper pronunciation of a novel word.

830–34. The detail of three gates on each side facing in each of the four directions is from Rev. 21:13 "ab oriente portae tres, et ab aquilone portae tres et ab austro portae tres et ab occasu portae tres" (Vulgate). Prudentius echoes the repetitions of that verse with poetic VARIATION, and also changes the order of the directions to fit his allegorical link in lines 845–48 with the four ages of humans (Gnilka 1963, 98).

830. aurorae de parte: "on the eastern side." **plaga lucida:** the noun normally means "territory" or "region," but here it must refer to the side of the temple. Statius had used the phrase "plaga lucida" in reference to the heavens at *Theb.* 1.25.

832. tris: the alternate accusative plural of *tres* modifies *fores*. **occidualibus:** the word does not appear in extant literature until the fourth century; on its use, see *TLL* s.v. (Baer). *Occiduis* already was used in line 310. The word is probably neuter plural in place of *occidens*, like *ametystina* (860) for *ametystus* (Gnilka 1963, 95).

834–37. Each gate is made of a single pearl, just like in the heavenly city described in Rev. 21:21 "et singulae portae erant ex singulis margaritis" (Vulgate). Prudentius uses collective singulars in these lines since there is apparently one stone for each gate.

834. panditur alta domus: a distant echo of *Aen.* 10.1 "Panditur interea domus omnipotentis Olympi." **nullum illic structile saxum:** "no building stone there."

The adjective *structilis* was used with *lapis* of concrete (*OLD* s.v. 1), and the sense with *saxum* might be that specific here. More loosely the word could mean "built up" or "composite," as in Tertullian's description of the soul as something single and indivisible: "Singularis alioquin et simplex et de suo tota est, non magis structilis aliunde quam diuisibilis ex se, quia nec dissolubilis" (*De anima* 14). In either case, Prudentius mixes high and low diction to create this surprising and moving description of a physical and spiritual temple.

835–36. caua ... gemma: "a gem hollowed through its depth and hewn out with much cutting."

835. dolatu: this noun does not appear anywhere else in extant Latin, but there is no indication that Prudentius is inventing a technical term here; the tone is prosaic and workaday.

838–39. The names of the twelve apostles were inscribed on the twelve foundations of the heavenly temple (Rev. 21:14).

838. auro: ablative with *inscripta*.

839. apostolici: modifies *senatus*. **fulgent**: for the brilliance of this scene, compare *lucida* (830), *inlustrata* (831), *relucenti* (836), and *micant* (852). **sena senatus**: note the wordplay, and that Prudentius describes the church in terms of the state, a triumphalistic touch.

840–50. Prudentius interprets the twelve inscriptions as representing the three ways in which the spirit moves children, young men, mature men, and those in old age.

840–41. spiritus ... ambit: "Under these headings the Spirit embraces mind's hidden depths." The spirit is the Holy Spirit, and the headings are the inscribed names of the twelve apostles. The precise meaning of the allegory is unclear. Juvencus wrote "spiritus ambit" in an unrelated context (1.454).

841. electos ... sensus: either "selected feelings / passions" or "meanings / interpretations" (see above on line 7).

842. quaque: understand *uia* or *parte*, as is usual. **hominis natura**: take in a neutral or positive sense, "in each part where the human self flourishes." **corpore toto**: very common at the end of Latin hexameters.

843. quadrua uis ... trinis ingressibus: the inner self is animated by a four-fold power, and it worships through three entryways. Maybe the *quadrua uis* is a reference to the four ages of man described in lines 845–49, but a reference to psychology would be more obvious. The reference to three entrances within the human could be trinitarian in origin, like one of the various internal trinities analyzed by Augustine in the *De trinitate* (begun around 400 but completed only in the 410s or 420s). Separately, Jerome interprets the four sides of the city as a reference to the four virtues, in his version of the commentary on Apocalypse written by the late third-century author Victorinus of Poetovio (ed. Johannes Haussleiter [CSEL 49], p. 151). Different interpretations are offered in the Weitz B tradition, according to which *quadrua uis* refers to the four elements (*ignis, aer, terra, aqua*) and *trinis ingressibus* refers to the threefold nature of man, *rationabilis, concupiscibilis*, and *irascibilis* (O'Sullivan 2004, 330–31).

844. adit ... colit: *hominis natura* is the subject. **castis ... sacraria uotis:** the human offers proper worship at an inner shrine.

845–49. The four sides of the temple represent the four ages of man, which are also compared to the stages of the day. On the four ages of man, see Hor., *Ars P.* 158–78 and Ov., *Met.* 15.199–213, with Gnilka 1963, 104–5. Relevant perhaps is an anonymous commentator of the seventh century who says the four sides of the temple represent the different ages at which individuals might come to faith in the trinity (*Commemoratorium de apocalypsi* 21.13–14, ed. Roger Gryson [CC 107], p. 226). Note the ANAPHORA and VARIATION in *seu ... seu ... seu ... siue.*

845. sol primus: "the first part of the day." **feruor:** the heat of the sun at midday is like the heat of youth. **ephebos:** as regards the spelling of this word, the MSS of Prudentius are very inconsistent (Cunningham 1966, xxx); on the spelling and pronunciation of the Greek *phi*, contrast the note above on line 715.

846–47. consummabilis aeui ... lux plena: probably "the full light of perfecting age." The adjective *consummabilis* appears elsewhere only in Sen., *Epist.* 92.27, where it means "capable of perfection." Gnilka thinks that Prudentius uses *consummabilis* in an active sense and refers to time bringing an individual to his or her full potential (1963, 105–6). Alternatively, *consummabile* could mean "finite," and so distinguish *aeuum* of a single lifetime from *aeuum* as "eternity."

847. borrae: genitive of *borras*. The north wind is normally called *boreas* in Latin. Prudentius uses the Attic Greek form found elsewhere in extant Latin literature only in a pre-Vulgate translation of Josh. 19:14 (Codex Lugdunensis MS 100) and Paulinus of Nola, *Ad Nicetam* 245 = Hartel *Carm.* 17 (a propemptikon that was sent in the year 400). In extant Greek, the Attic form is common on papyri (see *DGE* s.v. Βορέας).

849. occurit trinum quadrina ad conpeta nomen: "the threefold name meets at a crossing of four roads." The trinity is present where three roads meet on each of the four sides of the temple. *Conpeta* is the accusative plural of the noun often spelled *compitum*. The description of the crossroads echoes *De rosis nascentibus* 5 ("errabam riguis per quadrua compita in hortis"), a poem that is on the swift passing of time and was attributed to Ausonius (see Green 1991, 669).

850. discipulis: dative. **rex**: Christ.

851–65. Twelve gemstones ornament the walls of the temple. The same stones ornamented the foundations of the walls of the heavenly city in Rev. 21:19–20, although they are listed in a different order. The gemstones from Revelation are themselves modeled on the jeweled breastplate of the Jewish high priest, which was described in Exod. 28:17–20.

The exact variety of each gemstone is not clear, but these are plausible identifications: *chrysolitus* (topaz), *sappirus* (probably lapis lazuli), *beryllus* (beryl), *calchedon* (chalcedony), *yacinthus* (sapphire), *sardonix* (sardonyx), *amethystus* (amethyst), *iaspis* (jasper), *sardius* (carnelian), *topazon* (topaz), *smaragdus* (emerald), and *chrysoprasos* (chrysoprase).

Various symbolic interpretations have been offered for the twelve gemstones. Ambrose says that twelve properties of the divine essence ground the faith like twelve stones that are the jewels on Aaron's breastplate: "His duodecim tamquam lapidibus praetiosis fidei columna consurgit" (*De fide* 2 prol. 4). Jerome (*Epist.* 64.18–21) says that the four rows of jewels on Aaron's breastplate are the four virtues (*prudentia, fortitudo, iustitia, temperantia*) or the four gospels, among other explanations; the former interpretation finds support in the reference in line 911 to "uirtutum gemmas." In the same passage, Jerome directs those wanting to know more about the individual qualities of each stone to the treatise *De gemmis*, which was written by the influential Christian interpreter Epiphanius, bishop of Salamis in Cyprus during the fourth century. The ultimate source of much that was written about gemstones in Greek was the *Peri lithon* of Theophrastus; in Latin, book 37 of Pliny the Elder's *Naturalis historia* provided later authors with a wealth of material. One seventh-century commentator chose not to descend into their maze of gemological ponderings, and he was surely wise to do so: "These twelve stones are a figure for the twelve apostles; they have different colors; this signifies the diversity of their qualities" ("Isti duodecim lapides figuram duodecim apostolorum tenent; diuersas colores habent, diuersitatem meritorum significat," *Commemoratorium de apocalypsi* 21.19–20, ed. Roger Gryson [CC 107], p. 227).

Prudentius's description of these flashing jewels highlights one strand of late-antique taste, a flair for VARIATIO that Michael Roberts analyzed in his book *The Jeweled Style*; Roberts presents this fondness for close VARIATION through a description of the twelve gemstones on Aaron's breastplate from the *Heptateuchos* of the so-called Cyprianus Gallus (1989, 9–14), which I cite with his conjecture of *uiret* in place of Peiper's *uiget*:

> Sardia prima loco, topazo adiuncta smaragdus;
> sapphirus hanc sequitur, cum qua carbunculus ardet,
> iaspisque uiret fuluoque intermicat auro:
> tertia ligurio sedes: hic iunctus achati
> atque amethysto, fulgens quem purpura tingit.
> chrysolithus quartus, berillo adnexus onychnus. (*Exodus* 1098–1103)

Prudentius's description of a bejeweled temple can also be compared to Claudian's description of a magnificent palace of Venus made from precious stones and fine timber (*Nupt.* 86–96). For the aesthetic and stylistic resonance of Prudentius's careful placement of jewels and words, see also Fontaine 1976 and 1977.

851–53. "Yes, and the insignia of the same number of gems divided on woven walls gleam, and a deep light from the liquid depth pours out the living souls of colors." Perhaps the scene derives from the river of the water of life described in Rev. 22:1, which was "bright as crystal, flowing from the throne of God and of the lamb."

851. For the sense of *quin etiam*, see *OLD* s.v. 3a. **gemmarum**: genitive of material (A&G §344) explaining of what the *insignia* consist. **insignia**: means here "symbol" or "appearance" (see *OLD* s.v. *insigne* 4), which is to say that the gems are allegorical signs. Compare *uirtutum gemmas* (911) and *spectamine morum* (913). In each of these phrases, Prudentius identifies the gems and virtues as signs of another reality. Instead of ignoring them to focus only on some deeper meaning, Prudentius draws attention to the words and the surface of his allegorical poem.

852. pāriĕtibus: pronounced as four syllables by SYNERESIS, as in Vergil.

852–53. animasque colorum / uiuentes: colors are described as living (*uiuus*) by Manilius 5.508; Mart. 12.63.5; and Claud., *Get.* 437, but there is not a parallel for Prudentius's description of their living souls.

854–65. The catalogue of twelve gems fills exactly twelve lines.

854. chrysolitus natiuo interlitus auro: the Greek *chrysolithos* (topaz) is derived from *chrȳsos* (gold) and *lithos* (stone). The Romans described the gem as golden-hued (Prop. 2.16.44; and Pliny, *HN* 37.126). The line could mean "chrysolite (topaz) suffused with its own gold[en hue]." But the idea for *interlitus* could also have come from Exod. 28:20, in which the rows of jewels on Aaron's breastplate are described as being set within gold, in which case it would mean "set within gold native to it."

855. bĕryllum: the first syllable is normally long.

856. uariabat: the yellow of the topaz is flanked by apparently blue lapis lazuli and green beryl, which create the visual equivalent of VARIATIO.

858–59. nam . . . aquoso: Prudentius varies what he just said, that the chalcedony is colored by the adjacent yacinthus (sapphire).

858. cўānea: modifies *stagna*. The color is a dark blue often used of the sea, and the word is from the Greek *kўăneos*. The first syllable scans long everywhere else in Greek and Latin hexameter poetry (including elsewhere in Prudentius). Maybe Prudentius wanted to make the word sound as Greek as possible here, although *forte* looks out of place and the line could be corrupt. **propter:** "nearby" (adverb).

859. stagna lapis cohibens: "a stone with depths inside." **ostro ... aquoso:** the watery purple gleam of the sapphire.

860. sardonicem: the red variety is probably meant here and not onyx. **ametystina:** neuter plural in place of the substantive.

861. sardīum: Prudentius scans the second syllable long, this time not because of Greek, in which *sardion* is accented on the first syllable. **topazon:** Ambrose describes the origin, nature, and symbolism of topaz in his *Expositio psalmi cxviii* (16.41–43).

862. smāragdina: the first syllable is normally short.

862–63. gramine uerno / prata uirent uoluitque uagos: note the ALLITERATION. It is not clear why meadows and grass are suddenly invoked; maybe the imagery is bucolic and idyllic.

863. uoluitque ... fluctus: Prudentius mixes his METAPHORS.

864. te quoque: the last jewel receives an APOSTROPHE, a device that Gnilka pointed out was often used by ancient poets to enliven their catalogues (1963, 113).

865. saxis stellantibus: dative. Ovid described the peacock's tail as inset with gleaming gems ("gemmis ... stellantibus," *Met.* 1.723).

866–67. After the sublime description of the jewels, Prudentius turns immediately without any transition to the crane at work constructing the temple.

The phrase *funalis machina* could recall the *machina mundi* of Lucr. 5.96; it is also an image for the cross of Christ, which Ignatius (*Letter to the Ephesians* 9.1) and others had already compared to a crane (Gnilka 1963,

114). In the imagery of Ignatius, the Holy Spirit is the rope of the crane used to construct a temple for God the Father from stones that are Christians. On the machines used for construction work in antiquity, see Vitr., *De arch*. 10.2–3.

868–87. The interior of the temple is described, with Sapientia seated on a throne and holding a scepter.

868–72. at . . . speciem: "But the inner chamber is constructed relying on seven pillars cut from a glassy rock of icy crystal, whose lofty tops are covered with a white stone cut cone-wise and curved below into the likeness of a shell" (translation adapted from Thomson 1949).

Prudentius describes a splendid canopy, like the so-called *ciboria* that came to house altars in Christian churches. The *ciborium* in the Church of the Holy Sepulcher constructed by Constantine was well known, and representations of such canopies also appear as a decorative frame in codices of the Eusebian canon tables. Indeed, *ciboria* carved from a single piece of stone survive from later centuries, and the apse mosaics from Sante'Apollinare in Classe in Ravenna show curtains curved like seashells. Christians associated their canopies with the coverings for the most holy place in the Hebrew tabernacle.

For further detail, see the PhD thesis of Molly T. Smith (1968) on the *ciborium* in late-antique Rome, Klauser 1961 on representations of *ciboria* in the Eusebian canon tables, and Bogdanović 2017 on canopies in Byzantium. Laurence Gosserez was apparently the first modern scholar to realize that Prudentius was describing a *ciborium* (2001, 255).

868. At domus interior: this half-line was used by Vergil when he described the interior of Dido's palace (*Aen*. 1.637) and when he described the reaction of the trapped Trojans within Priam's home (*Aen*. 2.486). **septem . . . columnis:** the house of Wisdom from Prov. 9:1 has seven pillars: "Sapientia aedificauit sibi domum et subdidit columnas septem" (Latin translation from Ambrose, *De fide* 1.15.98). The Vulgate and a majority of Latin citations have *excidit* in place of *subdidit*, but Prudentius apparently read a translation like that in Ambrose (the same translation appears in Cyprian), or one with *suffulsit*, which appears in Augustine, *De civ. d*. 17.4 and 17.20.

869. crystalli algentis: crystal was formed from hard-frozen ice according to Pliny, *HN* 37.23. The explanation derives from the etymology of the Greek word *krystallos*, which means "ice." **recisis:** modifies *columnis*.

870. quarum: *columnis* is the antecedent. *Quadrum* was the reading preferred by Heinsius (1667, 2:111) and Gnilka (1963, 116–17); but that is hard to square with the seven columns that are described as supporting a conical canopy of pearl. The variant *quadrum* probably arose because most *ciboria* were in fact square. **calculus albens:** echoes *Am.* 271, in which Prudentius had referred to a pearl as "concharum calculus albens." In that passage, he had been influenced by Auson., *Mos.* 70, where pearls were described as white berries, the offspring of shells ("albentes, concharum germina, bacas").

871. sinuamine: the only extant Latin author before Prudentius to use this word is Juvencus (*Euangeliorum* 1.87 and 3.56), and he uses it in the same metrical position.

872–74. The pearl is from Matt. 13:45–46 "The kingdom of heaven is like a merchant in search of fine pearls, who, on finding one pearl of great value, went and sold all that he had and bought it."

872. quod: the antecedent *margaritum* has been attracted into the relative clause, but both refer to the *calculus albens* above. **mille talentis:** ablative of price (A&G §416) with *mercata*. The specific number stands for an indefinite large number, which happens often enough in Latin poetry, as Servius explained in his note on *Aen.* 1.499.

873. margāritum: elsewhere the second syllable is short, including at *Perist.* 10.648. Prudentius was apparently the first poet to use this word in hexameters. The phrase *margaritum ingens* was reused by Venantius Fortunatus (*Carm.* 3.20.2).

873–74. opibusque et censibus hastae / addictis: "with her money and wealth granted to the spear." A spear was used to mark the place for a public auction.

874. pararat = *parauerat.*

875–77. Sapientia is enthroned within the temple's inner court. She is wisdom within the individual soul, but she also stands for Christ as the Word. Indeed, Christians often interpreted Wisdom from Prov. 1:20–33 and 9:1–5 as a prefiguration of Christ. For Christ as Sapientia, compare in the first place Prudent., *Apoth.* praef. 1.2 "Corde patris genita est sapientia, filius ipse est"; and see Macklin Smith 1976, 194–206. On *sapientia* in the thought of Augustine, see Marrou 1958, 364–69. For the idea of an imperial Christ enthroned, compare the contemporary apse mosaic in the Church of Santa Pudenziana; that mosaic apparently represented the vision recounted in Ezek. 40–43 and was influenced by Jerome's post-410 commentary, in which the city and temple in that vision were described as representing the church (on this mosaic, see Schlatter 1992 and 1995, although his suggestion that Christ is not presented as an imperial figure is unconvincing). On *sapientia* as the goal of philosophical teaching, see above on 823–87.

875. hoc residet solio: no throne has been mentioned, but there is apparently one within the canopy just described. On the other hand, the layout is not entirely clear, and Gnilka might be right to understand *hoc . . . solio* as the entire temple of the heart (1963, 120).

For the phrasing here and in line 868, compare Vergil's description of Dido in *Aen.* 1.505–7 "tum foribus diuae, media testudine templi, / saepta armis *solio*que alte *subnixa resedit.* / iura dabat *leges*que *uiris.*"

878–87. A description of Aaron's rod, which bloomed miraculously on its own. See the book of Numbers 17:6–8. In Heb. 9:4, the Greek *rabdos* is used of Aaron's rod, and that is translated in Latin as *uirga* (this makes the use of *sceptrum* below more noteworthy); in line 372 above Moses's rod was called a *mystica uirga.*

Vergil's Latinus, king of the Latins, swore an oath by his scepter, which would never flower again:

> "ut *sceptrum* hoc" (dextra sceptrum nam forte gerebat)
> "numquam fronde leui fundet uirgulta nec umbras,

> cum semel in siluis imo de *stirpe recisum*
> matre caret posuitque comas et bracchia ferro,
> olim arbos, nunc artificis manus aere decoro
> inclusit patribusque dedit gestare Latinis." (*Aen.* 12.206–11)

Prudentius clearly alludes to Vergil's poem, but Prudentius reverses the *adynaton* to create a scene of idyllic perfection (O'Hogan 2016, 130–31). Aaron's scepter is made of living wood rather than by an artist's skill; it produces new fruit instead of being dead and dry, and it is a symbol for the life and newness of Christian poetry. But that does not mean Prudentius claims to have "nullified the supremacy of Roman civilization conferred by Vergil through this oath" (Macklin Smith 1976, 300). Vergil's passage is itself modeled on the scepter by which Achilles swears in *Il.* 1.234–39, and Prudentius writes to include himself within this tradition. These wooden staffs were associated of old with prophets, priests, and kings, and each poet employs them as a fundamental symbol of inspiration.

878. non arte politum: for the phrasing, compare *Culex* 86 "non arte politus"; and Calp., *Ecl.* 4.14–15 "Nunc mea rusticitas, si non ualet *arte polita* / carminis..."

879. quod stirpe reciso: the form *reciso* should be retained because it is better attested; it avoids repetition with *sceptrum, politum,* and *uiuum*; and it fits Prudentius's fondness for PLEONASTIC expressions and ablatival phrases. The variant *recisum* is easily explained from the Vergilian intertext in which *stirpe recisum* appears at line end (*Aen.* 12.208).

The change from *reciso* to *recisum* in MS *E* was made by the corrector labeled E^2 by Cunningham. John Petruccione (2013) has published a fine study of the glosses on *Peristefanon* in *E*, but it is not clear to me whether this "correction" was made by one of the seven hands that he identified in that portion of the manuscript. Separately, Cunningham was mistaken in his assertion that *reciso* was amended in MS *S*.

882. The contrast of red roses and white lilies is frequent in poetry; see, for example, *Aen.* 12.68–69 and Ov., *Am.* 2.5.37. **intertexta:** on weaving as a METAPHOR for poetic composition, see above on *texat* in line 768.

rosis: either dative or ablative; both *intertexo* and *misceo* take both cases. Lavarenne does not explain why he thinks *rosis* is dative (1933a, §171). **lilia**: given the previous references to *Aen.* 6, these lilies might easily recall those described for Marcellus:

> manibus date lilia plenis
> purpureos spargam flores animamque nepotis
> his saltem accumulem donis, et fungar inani
> munere. (*Aen.* 6.883–86)

883. submittere: explanatory with *nescia* (A&G §461).

884. huius forma: "the type for this." The word *forma* was a technical term in allegorical interpretation; it was essentially a synonym for *figura*, on which see above on pr. 50–51. Prudentius uses *forma* in this sense in *Cath.* 1.26, *Am.* 735, *Perist.* 10.628, and in *Tituli historiarum* 8 and 60. **gestamen**: the same word was used in *Aen.* 7.246, in reference to the staff of Priam that Aeneas gave to Latinus. **Aäron**: genitive.

885–87. The language is powerful because of its simplicity and for the unexpected contrasts between dryness and youth, swelling and growth.

885. floriferum ... germina: Arator alludes to this line in *Historia apostolica* 1.20 "florigero sua germina reddidit horto." **quod**: nominative, modified by *trudens*.

887. fetus: accusative plural.

EPILOGUE (888–915)

The *Psychomachia* begins and ends with the poet's prayers to Christ. These passages frame the allegorical narrative and put the battles of the Virtues and the Vices within the context of the individual author's interior conflict. If the *Apotheosis*, *Amartigenia*, and *Psychomachia* are read as a trilogy, the passage also serves as a fitting conclusion to all three poems. The two prayers in *Psychomachia* are linked by twin illustrations (scenes 7 and 90 in Stettiner 1895–1905, 2:11 and 16) in which the poet appears as a suppliant with his hands raised in the posture of an *orans* (see fig. 10). This is an

FIGURE 10. Lines 880–89, with image of Prudentius praying before a shrine and marginal caption ("gratias agit deo"). MS E, fol. 149r. *Courtesy Leiden University Libraries.*

iconographic figure type that is well known from late-antique funerary imagery (see Prigent 1992 and Jensen 2000, 35–37), and it portrays the poet as dependent on his addressee. As the illustrations reveal, Prudentius creates an authorial drama that provides the reader with another figure for his or her own situation.

888. On the four-word lines in this poem, see above on line 13. **Reddimus:** the verb was used of prayers by Prudentius (*Cath.* 4.75 and *Perist.* 9.71) and by Paulinus of Nola (*Ad Cytherium* 16 = Hartel *Carm.* 24) and commonly in vows (see *OLD* s.v. *reddo* 9b–c). **indulgentissime doctor** recalls *magister* from *Apoth.* praef. 1 and Christ as the *bonus arbiter* in *Am.* 938. In these different ways, Prudentius introduced Christ as his ultimate interlocutor.

889. Christe . . . honores: an echo of *Christe . . . labores* from line 1. **meritos . . . honores:** "deserved honor(s)" appears as a phrase several times in Latin poetry. Most importantly, Vergil details the appropriate sacrifices ("meritos . . . honores") made by the Trojans on Delos, a bull each for Neptune and Apollo, a black sheep (*pecus*) for the winter wind (*Hiems*), and a white sheep for Zephyrus (*Aen.* 3.118–20). The note in *Serv. Dan.* provides a nice example of how Vergil's figurative language was explained: "of course by saying *meritos* [Vergil] shows here that the bulls are correctly sacrificed to Neptune and Apollo. The bull he calls *honores* [plural] figuratively; for that variant means the same thing" (Servius, *Ad Aen.* 3.118; "sane hic ostendit dicendo meritos rite Neptuno et Apollini tauros immolari. honores 'taurum' figurate dixit; uarietas enim ipsa idem significat").

890. ore pio: compare *De opusculis suis* 34 "iuuabit ore personasse Christum"; and Sedulius, *Hymni* 1.2 "dulcis amor Christi personet ore pio." Earlier poets also used the phrase *ore pio*, but Sedulius seems to have been alluding specifically to Prudentius and to his nearly perfect fusion of poetry and devotion. **nam cor uitiorum stercore sordet:** Prudentius modifies the Roman contrast between *uerba* and *res*. His poetry is pious, but the heart is something different. The language recalls Ps. 112:7 "Suscitans a terra inopem et de stercore erigens pauperem" (*Psalmi iuxta LXX*), and this is a verse that Ambrose often cited. *Stercore* adds a homely note of urgency to the poet's prayer.

891. nos: subject of *agnoscere.* **corporei latebrosa pericula operti:** "the dark dangers of the body's depths."

892. luctantis: genitive. **uoluisti:** Christ is made responsible for willing the poem. **agnoscere:** recalls *notare* from line 20.

893–902. Sometimes the poet is confident and at other times he despairs. *Apotheosis* ends with a grand expression of hope. *Amartigenia* has a much darker ending; there the poet prays only for a light punishment: *me poena leuis clementer adurat* (966). In such instances, we should not forget that the poet in the text is a persona, and that his doubt and his hope function as rhetorical and literary devices. In a turn that befits this poem about an ongoing universal struggle, we are invited to sympathize with the poet.

893. ancipites . . . sensus: *sensus* can mean "feeling," "sense," or "meaning," as explained above on line 7. Prudentius, therefore, alludes to the allegorical form in which he has been singing of faculties within the soul. As we have seen, Quintilian explained allegory as having one appearance in the words and another in the sense (*Inst.* 8.6.44; "aliud verbis, aliud sensu ostendit"). Separately, Prudentius described the struggle as *anceps* ("uncertain") above in line 176, and disguised Auaritia was called a "letum uersatile et anceps" (571); he also used *anceps* as meaning "ambiguous" in a highly rhetorical address to scripture in *Apoth.* 110. The ambiguous language of allegory is a perfect model for the uncertainty within the soul diagnosed by Prudentius. **nebuloso in pectore:** the darkness of the heart matches the shadowy language of poetry.

894. sudare: "to sweat," "to struggle." **conflictibus:** the word is not common until the fourth century.

896. uirtutibus: Heinsius printed the variant *ceruicibus*, and it may be the case that *uirtutibus* was introduced into the text from an explanatory gloss.

896–97. ad iuga uitae / deteriora trahi: "dragged to life's worse yokes." Burton suggested that Prudentius had in mind Matt. 11:30 "Iugum enim meum suaue est . . ."

897. noxis: indirect object of *addicere*.

898. propriae iacturam . . . salutis: compare *Aen.* 2.646 "facilis iactura sepulcri."

899. animam: subject of *incaluisse*.

900. sensimus: picks up and explains *sensus* from line 893. **incaluisse deo:** the phrase recalls the inspiration of Ovid's Ocyroë from *Met.* 2.641 "incaluitque deo." The verb takes an ablative expressing the source of one's enthusiasm, as is clear from Sil. 5.19 "nympha nec Idalia lenta incaluisse sagitta."

902. cessisse stomacho! The metrical beat falls on the last syllable of *cessisse*, which is naturally short but is lengthened by the following *st-*. The lurching rhythm of the half-line mirrors the poet's disgust at disgust.

feruent bella horrida, feruent: compare *Aen.* 6.86 "bella, horrida bella" (the Sibyl warns Aeneas of terrible wars in his future) and *Aen.* 7.41–42 "dicam horrida bella, / dicam acies . . ." These lines are from the proem in the middle of the *Aeneid*. Such Vergilian echoes paint the soul's interior struggles as epic battles, and so recognizing them heightens the tone of the *Psychomachia*. But the phrase and the repetition are perfectly at home in Prudentius's text; and this is one case where it would be easy to argue that he improves on his source, that he manages to steal the club from Hercules.

903. ossibus inclusa: the noun is probably ablative. Prudentius echoes a phrase from Paulinus of Nola's version of Psalm 136 in which Paulinus describes the struggle with the flesh and sin shut up in your bones: "namque tuis tales inclusos ossibus hostes" (*Psalmus* 136.58 = Hartel *Carm.* 9). Dracontius, writing in Africa around the end of the fifth century, apparently alludes to Prudentius in a passage describing God's creation of Adam: "terra medullas / ossibus includit" (*De laudibus dei* 1.343–44). **inclusa. | fremit:** the short *a* of *inclusa* is lengthened in the CAESURA and before *fr-* (compare line 252 and see appendix A). **discordibus armis:** the same phrase appears at line end in Verg., *G.* 2.459; Tib. 2.3.37; Stat., *Theb.* 11.100; and the cento *De alea* 34.

904. non simplex natura hominis: in *Amartigenia*, sin begins from the moment when the Serpent's tongue is split and it is no longer simple: "simplex lingua prius uaria micat arte loquendi" (201). Christian theologians agreed with Platonist philosophers that being was at root simple and that the supreme, eternal God knows no change. Humans, however, are part of the fallen world in which time and change are unavoidable, as indicated already by Prudentius in the third line of his *Praefatio*, in his evocation of the turning sun ("sole uolubili").

904–6. According to Gen. 2:7, God formed man from the mud and breathed into him the breath of life: "Formauit igitur Dominus Deus hominem de limo terrae et inspirauit in faciem eius spiraculum uitae" (Vulgate). Prudentius's *limo* (904) is taken directly from Genesis, and *adflatu* (906) recalls *inspirauit*. The most common Latin translation for "from the mud" in Gen. 2:7 was always "de limo terrae."

905. effigiata: Prudentius also used *effigiare* of God's creation at *Cath.* 10.4 and *Am.* 118. Apuleius was the first extant Latin writer to use this verb. **animum:** Heinsius printed *animam* with MS *A*, against the rest of the manuscript tradition. But the pronoun *ille* in the following clause makes it almost certain that the reading of MS *A* is nothing more than a very simple mistake. **contra:** "on the other hand." **ille:** the antecedent is *animum*.

905–6. sereno / editus adflatu: "produced from a pure inspiration." In the story of creation in Genesis, God breathed into man the breath of life. *Adflatus* was used by classical authors of divine inspiration, for example Cic., *Nat. D.* 2.66.167 "nemo uir magnus sine aliquo adflatu diuino umquam fuit." Likewise, *serenus* was an epithet of Jupiter, although Prudentius also used *serenus* in reference to humankind before the fall in *Am.* 185.

906. nigrantis carcere cordis: Plato famously described the body as a prison for the soul (for example at *Phaedo* 62b, 67d, and 82e). This imagery was appropriated by Vergil, by philosophers, and by Christians; on the slavery of the body, see above on pr. 54 and below on 907 and 908.

907. arta inter uincla: the soul is in chains within the body. Compare Prudentius's longing to be free from these chains in *Praef.* 44 "uinclis o

utinam corporis emicem." On Neoplatonic understandings of the body and
its passions as a kind of bondage for the soul, see Mastrangelo 2008, 134.

908–15. This is one last chance to explain the poem. Human nature is split
and at war until the arrival of Christ and the inauguration of Sapientia, and
that is why the epic battlefield is transferred to the interior of the individual
human being. The poet fades into the background as the divine addressee
takes central stage and installs Sapientia on the throne. Closure, therefore,
comes at some point in the future (*donec*), whenever an individual reader
is transformed through his or her own internalizing of the message behind
the poem's descriptions.

More directly than in these lines, Prudentius said in *Symm.* 2.626–33
that God and wisdom enter a heart only when it is stable and well-ordered.

908. For the inner conflict, see the introduction, pages 16–19, and compare
Gal. 5:17 "Caro enim concupiscit aduersus spiritum, spiritus autem aduersus
carnem; haec enim sibi inuicem aduersantur, ut non quaecumque uultis, illa
faciatis" (Vulgate). Among other versions of this verse, closest to Prudentius
is the one in Rufinus's translation of Origen, *Explanationes in Epistulam
Pauli ad Romanos* 6.9 "pugnat caro aduersum spiritum, spiritus autem
aduersus carnem." A similar idea is found in Rom. 7:23. Gnilka explained
that Prudentius viewed the body and the flesh not as evil in themselves but
as needing to be freed from the dominion of sin (1963, 1–8).

909. duplex: continues the thought from *non simplex* in line 904.

910–13. donec ... adsit ... conponat ... texat: *donec* with the subjunctive
means "until" and implies that a subject is intending or waiting for the
action to be completed (A&G §553).

The syntax seems to derive from Ambrose, *De Abraham* 2.9.62 "Bellum
ergo cotidianum est et intra castra eadem graue proelium, donec deus
misericors diabolum atque eius ministros iudicet, passiones restinguat ac
subiciat menti sedulae, exquirat animas nostras de omnibus offensionis
et periculi nostri auctoribus." Here is a tricolon with three present subjunctives, the conjunction *donec*, and the same continual struggle. On the

influence of *De Abraham* on Prudentius, see above on pages 18, 21–22, and 76, and for possible echoes see the notes on lines pr. 11, pr. 45, and pr. 56–58.

910. praesidio: dative of purpose. **Christus deus adsit**: the envisioned appearance and presence of Christ is the poem's ultimate, deferred end.

911. uirtutum gemmas: see the description of the gemstones above in lines 851–65. **sede piata**: "with their home purified."

912. peccatum: the first instance of the word in this poem. Like the Greek word *hamartia*, *peccatum* originally meant "a mistake." Paul's idea of sin as an indwelling force (e.g., Rom. 7:17) came to be fully developed only in the Pelagian controversies of the early fifth century.

913. atria: "courts" not "entryway." **texat**: Gosserez links this verb to Prudentius's weaving of the poetic text (2001, 262); on weaving, see above on line 768. **spectamine morum**: perhaps "from the apparition of character." The phrase is obscure, but *mores* clearly refers to the virtues of the soul, and *spectamen* refers to their beautiful appearance and possibly also to the allegorical apparitions from which the poem is woven. Thomson, however, followed Bergman (1897, 78) and translated *spectamine morum* as "out of the trial of its conduct"; Lavarenne had "des beautés du caractère." Neither they nor the lexica cite the closest parallel for this passage: Augustine, in *Soliloquiorum* 1.5.11 and 1.8.15, describes the intelligible appearances of the arts as "intellegibilia disciplinarum spectamina."

914. ornamenta: used of honors in general and in particular of rhetorical or poetic ornamentation. On the jeweled style of late antique poetry, see above on lines 851–65.

914–15. oblectata decoro / . . . solio: "delighted with the beauty of her home." The scene is described in aesthetic terms.

915. aeternum: an adverbial accusative. When Christ arrives, there will no longer be any change or variety. The word recalls *aeternas* from line 888. **solio**: at the same position as in line 875. **dives** recalls *diuites* from pr. 56. **Sapientia**: in a sense, this is the worthy heir of pr. 68; in another sense,

Sapientia is Christ (see above on lines 875–77). For Wisdom as an attendant of Christ, compare *Cath.* 10.131–32 "feruens habitauit in istis / sapientia principe Christo" (Wisdom dwelt among these, glowing with Christ as her prince). Cunningham (1966, 181) compares Augustine, *Enarrationes in psalmos* 46.10, in which the soul of the just person is called the seat of wisdom ("sedes sapientiae"). **regnet:** a jussive subjunctive. The poet prays that Sapientia may reign in himself and in the individual souls of his readers.

APPENDIX A

ON METER

The meaning of a poem cannot be separated from its rhythm and music. Therefore, poetry should always be read aloud.

You can learn to pronounce Classical Latin without much difficulty; and we assume, in the absence of contrary evidence, that Prudentius usually followed the guidance of grammarians and was generally conservative in his pronunciation. But Latin was always a diverse language, and the scansion of Greek words in Prudentius (see below) is one clear example of his linguistic difference.

Unlike in English, the pronunciation of Latin consonants and vowels was almost completely regular. You should be careful to distinguish short and long vowels, which were pronounced as in the following English words:

a "idea"
ā "father,"
e "net"
ē "date"
i "sit"
ī "feet,"
o "soft"
ō "hope,"

u   "foot"

ū   "boot"

y   like German *flüchtig* (there is no English equivalent)

ȳ   like German *führen* (there is no English equivalent)

Six diphthongs were produced from two vowels pronounced together, and they are all long:

ae   "high"

oe   "boy"

ei   "eight"

ui   "twin"

au   "allow"

eu   as *e* and *u* pronounced together (there is no English equivalent)

The accent within a Latin word is determined by the length of the penultimate (next-to-last) syllable. If the penultimate syllable is long, the stress is on that syllable: *miserắte labốres* (1). Otherwise, the accent is on the antepenult: *christícolas uítiis populántibus* (13). Of course, the accent cannot go further back than the first syllable of a one- or two-syllable word: *réx nóster* (5). Some very short words can lose their accent when they are pronounced with others in a phrase; they are called clitics, and most of them are prepositions or conjunctions: *sub pédibus* (249), *múnus ad áram* (772).

Classical Latin poetry is determined by the alternation of heavy and light syllables. A syllable is heavy if its vowel is long by nature, or if the vowel is lengthened by position, that is, when it is followed by two consonants.

The rule that a vowel can be lengthened by position is a bit more complicated. The letters *x* and *z* are double consonants and usually lengthen a preceding vowel, but *qu* counts as a single consonant. The letter *h* does not count as a consonant; and a mute consonant followed by a liquid does not normally make position: thus, *bl, br, cl, cr, dr, fl, fr, gl, gr, pl, pr,* and *tr* are usually pronounced together. For example, in the first line of our poem, two syllables are lengthened by position, because they are followed by two consonants (*hominūm sempēr miserate*), whereas one remains short before a mute and a liquid (*Christĕ graues*). For the few exceptions to these rules in *Psychomachia,* see below.

The *Psychomachia* is written in dactylic hexameters, a line with six measures, as follows:

$$ -\ \widebar{\smile\smile}\ |\ -\ \widebar{\smile\smile}\ |\ -\ \widebar{\smile\smile}\ |\ -\ \widebar{\smile\smile}\ |\ -\ \smile\smile\ |\ -\ \textsf{x} $$

The first syllable of each foot must be long; the second half of each foot can be one long or two shorts; and the final syllable is *anceps*, either long or short. The penultimate foot is almost always a dactyl; that regularity establishes the rhythm of the line.

Three other general points are very important.

1. ELISION occurs when a vowel is not pronounced fully, and it blends into the sound of another immediately following vowel: *séditi(o) átqu(e) ánimam* (8). Vowels normally elide whenever they collide in a line. If they do not elide, the pause that prevents elision is called HIATUS, as in *něquě ēst* (494). The letter *m* at the end of a word and *h* at the beginning of a word do not prevent elision: *magnarum uirtut(em) inopes* (12), *ill(a h)ostile* (30). A related phenomenon is PRODELISION, which occurs when *est* is contracted with a preceding vowel: *ūtile béllo (e)st* (238).

2. The natural force of Latin (and English) poetry derives from the interplay between musical rhythm and prosaic accentuation. In dactylic hexameters, the heavy first syllable of each foot receives a beat (*ictus*). In *Psychomachia*, the metrical beat and the word accent never match up in more than five feet:

   átqu(e) in|núpta dé|um con|cépit | fémina | Chrístum (74).

   This coincidence of beat and accent creates a smooth rhythm. In most lines, metrical beat and word accent coincide in only three or four feet:

   exóri|tur quóti|ens tur|bátis | sénsibus | íntus (7).

   A sense of speed or solemnity are two of the many effects that poets produce by subtle combinations of musical and verbal emphasis.

3. If a word ends in the middle of the foot, the division is called a CAESURA (¦). If the end of a word coincides with the end of a foot, that is called a DIERESIS (⫶). A hexameter almost always has at least one strong CAESURA, most often in the middle of the third or fourth foot. A so-called bucolic DIERESIS at the end of the fourth foot is very common, because the coincidence of ictus and accent at the end of the line establish its dactylic force:

díssere, réx nóster, ¦ quó mílite ⫶ péllere cúlpas (5).

The preface of *Psychomachia* is in iambic trimeters, a line with three measures and six iambic (⌣ –) feet, as follows:

$$\breve{\texttt{—}} - \smile - | \breve{\texttt{—}} - \smile - | \breve{\texttt{—}} - \smile \times$$

Again, the end of the line sets the rhythm, and so substitution is not allowed in the last foot; but the last syllable is *anceps* (heavy or light) because of the regular pause at the end of each line. Although poets using this meter sometimes allowed themselves to resolve almost any long syllable into two short syllables (⌣⌣), in the preface of *Psychomachia* there are resolutions only in lines 17, 52, 60, 64, and 66.

These are the basics. Prudentius does not always follow the rules.

He consistently lengthens a final short syllable when the next word begins with *st-* or *sp-* (see Lavarenne 1933a, §250). This happens six times in *Psychomachia*, always in a caesura: *uirgo Pudicitiā speciosis* (41), *morte Pudicitiā gladium* (99), *orbis Auaritiā sternens* (481), *stant tuti Rationis opē, stant* (505), *mentis Auaritiā stupefactis* (585), *cessissē stomacho* (902). For another possible example before *sp-*, see the note on line 151.

Before *fr-*, Prudentius lengthens a short syllable with the CAESURA only in lines 252 and 903, and before *gl-* only in line 99 (contrast 136 and 172). Likewise, *gr-* does not normally lengthen a preceding syllable; but it does once with the CAESURA in the phrase *Fertur Auaritiā gremio* (454). Note also that Prudentius does not count *z* or *ps* as double consonants (see on line 633).

Only the following words are scanned irregularly: *Arrĭus* (794), *Bēlĭa* (714), *bĕryllum* (855), *calchedŏn* (857), *cātholico* (107), *cўānea* (858), *delībuta*

(312), *erĕmi* (371), *gănearum* (343), *hĕresis* (710), *idŏla* (379), *margāritum* (873), *redīmitos* (687), *rŭbigo* (105), *sardīum* (861), and *smāragdina* (862).

Throughout his poetry, Prudentius regularly modifies the length of Greek vowels so that the accentual stress in Latin would remain the same as the Greek accent, which had itself become accentual by the fourth century. For example, the word *érēmos* was accented on the first syllable in Attic Greek; by shortening the second syllable, Prudentius was able to keep the accent on the same syllable in Latin: *érĕmus*. For the similar accentuations in Ammianus Marcellinus and on this question more broadly, see Gavin Kelly 2013.

APPENDIX B

GLOSSARY OF LITERARY TERMS

Accumulatio: a kind of enumeration in which items are piled up into a summary list; related terms in Latin are *coaceruatio, congeries,* and *frequentatio,* and in Greek *athroesmos* and *synathroesmos.*

Allegory: according to the common definition used by ancient grammarians and rhetors, allegory is a trope in which something different is meant than what is said; see, for example, Donatus, *Ars maior* 3.6: "Allegoria est tropus, quo aliud significatur quam dicitur." In the same chapter, Donatus explains that the seven most important kinds of allegory are IRONIA (saying the opposite of what you mean), *antiphrasis* (in a single word), *aenigma* (via obscurity), *charientismos* (pleasantly), *paroemia* (adapting a proverb), SARCASMOS (with hostility), and *astismos* (urbanely). On the other kinds of allegory employed by Prudentius, see the introduction, pages 19–23.

Alliteration: repetition of a single letter or sound, usually a consonant at the beginning of words.

Anacoluthon: discontinuity—it's when you break the syntax in the middle of a sentence.

Anaphora: repetition, usually repetition at the beginning of successive clauses.

Anastrophe: a specific kind of HYPERBATON (displacement), usually limited to a single word.

Aphaeresis: omission of a vowel or syllable at the beginning of a word. See also PRODELISION.

Apostrophe: "a turning away." Gentle reader, an apostrophe is a direct address to someone or something not present. The name comes from the way that a speaker would turn away from the audience to address someone else imagined as present.

Aristeia: a type-scene of ancient epic in which a hero displays his or her strength in battle.

Asyndeton: omission of conjunctions. Aynsdeton is rapid. It creates a staccato effect.

Caesura: a metrical structure, when a word ends at the end of a metrical foot (contrast DIERESIS). A strong caesura comes in the middle of the foot (– | $\smile$); a weak caesura comes between the short syllables in a dactyl (– $\smile$ | $\smile$). In dactylic hexameters, the two most common caesurae are the penthemimeral, in the middle of the third foot (*dissere, rex noster,* | *quo milite pellere culpas*), and the hepthimimeral, in the middle of the fourth foot (*uincendi praesens ratio est,* | *si comminus ipsas*). A penthemimeral caesura is found in 85.0% of the lines both in the *Aeneid* and in the hexameter poetry of Prudentius.

Catachresis: using a word incorrectly: "He couldn't steer starboard because he had a malaprop."

Chiasmus: an inverted repetition of words or ideas, in the pattern ABBA; the name comes from the Greek letter *chi* (X).

Diacope: repetition, a figure of repetition in short succession.

Dieresis: a metrical structure that occurs any time a word ends at the end of a metrical foot (contrast CAESURA). The so-called bucolic dieresis comes at the end of the fourth foot and usually results in a smooth rhythm, with the coincidence at the end of a hexameter of metrical beat and word accent: for example, **exóritur** quótiens turbátis ⦂ **sénsi**bus íntus and **sedíti**(o) **átqu**(e) ánimam morbórum ⦂ **ríxa** fatígat.

Diastole: the metrical lengthening of a short syllable (the Greek term refers to a mark of punctuation used to separate words).

Elision: the omission of a sound or syllable. In Latin verse, a vowel in an open syllable at the end of a word is usually elided when followed by another vowel. In practice, there is often a blending (*synaloepha*) of the first vowel sound with the second.

Enjambment: a word or words extended from one line to the next, without a break in syntax at the end of the line.

Figura etymologica: a figure configured of two words from the same etymological root; for example, "live your life" or "die a death."

Hiatus: literally "an opening" or "yawning," this Latin term refers to a pause between two vowels that would normally have been elided.

Hendiadys: a figure in which a single idea is expressed through two words. The name comes from the Greek *hen dia duoin* ("one through two"). For example, you could say "I am sick of assignments and drudgery" when what you really mean is "homework." Consider also these statements: "America is the Fourth of July and apple pie," and "It crawled and slithered through the grass."

Hypallage: a transferred epithet. In the statement "The sleepy town seemed empty of inhabitants," the adjective is transferred from the individuals to their town.

Hyperbaton: word order inverted.

Hypozeuxis: a kind of repetition in which related clauses each have their own verb.

Interpolation: the insertion of extraneous textual material, usually written so as to appear genuine.

Ironia: a variety of ALLEGORIA. The Greek is *eirōneia*; compare SARCASMOS.

Metaphor: a transferal in which one word or idea takes on the meaning of another that is analogous to it. A word's metaphorical meaning is often opposed to its literal or primary meaning.

Metonymy: a word or phrase used in place of something associated with it.

Mise-en-abîme: the doubling effect of an image within an image, like the play within the play in Shakespeare's *Hamlet*.

Oxymoron: a contradiction in terms.

Periphrasis: a roundabout statement or circumlocution.

Pleonasm: unnecessary repetition.

Polyptoton: a repetition repetitively repeating the same word in a different form.

Polysyndeton: repetition or reiteration or reduplication of a conjunction, usually at the beginning of successive phrases or clauses.

Prodelision: the suspension of one vowel preceded by another. This does not usually occur in Latin except with the verb *est*. The phenomenon is sometimes called APHAERESIS.

Prolepsis: anticipation of a word, argument, or narrative. An element is presented earlier than expected either logically or rhetorically.

Sarcasmos: a kind of ALLEGORY characterized by the speaker's hostility.

Synecdoche: substitution of a part for the whole or the whole for a part.

Syneresis: a kind of contraction produced in Latin by pronouncing *i* or *u* as a consonant, as in *pāriĕtĭbŭs* (four syllables); sometimes syneresis is not distinguished from SYNIZESIS.

Synizesis: contraction, as when *deinde* is pronounced as a disyllable.

Tmesis: a cutting; a poetic figure in which two parts of a single word are divided. For example, a rhetorical device is a linguistic con, you might call it, -struction.

Tropology: an allegorical interpretation directed to the moral message of a text.

Variatio: a kind of rhetorical ornamentation that uses variety and difference to expand on a single word or idea.

BIBLIOGRAPHY

Adams, J. N. 1982. *The Latin Sexual Vocabulary*. London: Duckworth.

Amiott, José. 2010. "*Interpretatio christiana* del *epos* clásico en la *Praefatio* de la *Psychomachia* de Prudencio." *Athenaeum* 98 (1): 193–204.

Arevalo, Faustinus, ed. 1788–89. *M. Aurelii Clementis Prudentii V. C. Carmina*. 2 vols. Rome: Antonius Fulgonius. Reprinted in Patrologia Latina, vols. 59–60.

Auerbach, Eric. 1944. "Figura." In *Neue Dantestudien*, 11–71. Istanbul: Basimevi. This is a revised version of Auerbach 1938. "Figura." *Archivum Romanicum* 22 (4): 436–89.

———. 1965. *Literary Language and its Public in Late Latin Antiquity and in the Middle Ages*. Translated by Ralph Manheim. New York: Bollingen Foundation.

Austin, R. G. 1926. "Prudentius, *Apotheosis* 895." *Classical Quarterly* 20: 46–48.

———, ed. 1971. *Aeneidos Liber Primus*. Oxford: Clarendon Press.

———, ed. 1977. *Aeneidos Liber Sextus*. Oxford: Clarendon Press.

Babcock, Robert. 2017. *The Psychomachia Codex from St. Lawrence (Bruxellensis 10066–77) and the Schools of Liège in the Tenth and Eleventh Centuries*. Turnhout: Brepols.

Barchiesi, Alessandro. 2015. *Homeric Effects in Vergil's Narrative.* Princeton: Princeton University Press.

Bardzell, Jeffrey. 2009. *Speculative Grammar and Stoic Language Theory in Medieval Allegorical Narrative.* New York: Routledge.

Bartman, Elizabeth. 2001. "Hair and the Artifice of Roman Female Adornment." *American Journal of Archaeology* 105 (1): 1–25.

Basile, Bruno, ed. 2007. *Psychomachia: La lotta dei vizi e delle virtù.* Rome: Carocci.

Bastiaensen, A. A. R. 1993a. "Prudentius in Recent Literary Criticism." In *Early Christian Poetry,* edited by Jan den Boeft and A. Hilhorst, 101–34. Leiden: Brill.

———. 1993b. "Prudentius' *Hymnus de Trinitate.*" *Studia Patristica* 28: 3–14.

Bažil, Martin. 2017. "*Elementorum varius textus*: Atomistisches und Anagrammatisches in Optatians Textbegriff." In *Morphogrammata / The Lettered Art of Optatian: Figuring Cultural Transformations in the Age of Constantine,* edited by Michael Squire and Johannes Wienand, 341–68. Paderborn: Wilhelm Fink.

Beatrice, Pier Franco. 1971. "L'allegoria nella *Psychomachia* di Prudenzio." *Studia Patavina* 18 (1): 25–73.

Becker, Carl. 1969. "Fides." In *Reallexikon für Antike und Christentum,* 7: 801–39. Stuttgart: Anton Hierseman.

Beer, Ellen J. 1980. "Überlegungen zu Stil und Herkunft des Berner Prudentius-Codex 264." In *Florilegium Sangallense,* edited by Otto P. Clavadetscher, Helmut Maurer, and Stefan Sonderegger, 15–70. St. Gallen: Verlag Ostschweiz.

Bergman, Iohannes. 1894. *Specimen Lexici Prudentiani.* Uppsala: Edu. Berling.

———, ed. 1897. *Aurelii Prudentii Clementis Psychomachia.* Uppsala: Almquist and Wiksell.

———, ed. 1926. *Aurelii Prudentii Clementis Carmina.* CSEL 9. Vienna: Hoelder-Pichler-Tempsky.

Bernstein, Neil. 2016. "Rome's Arms and Breast: Claudian, *Panegyricus dictus Olybrio et Probino consulibus* 83–90 and Its Tradition." *Classical Quarterly* 66 (1): 417–19.

Bischoff, Bernhard. 1966–1981. *Mittelalterliche Studien: Ausgewählte Aufsätze zur Schriftkunde und Literaturgeschichte.* 3 vols. Stuttgart: Hiersemann.

Boeft, Jan, Jan Willem Drijvers, Daniël Hengst, and Hans Teitler, eds. 2007. *Philological and Historical Commentary on Ammianus Marcellinus XXVI.* Leiden: Brill.

Bogdanović, Jelena. 2017. *The Framing of Sacred Space: The Canopy and the Byzantine Church.* New York: Oxford University Press.

Brown, Peter. 1971. *The World of Late Antiquity: AD 150–750.* London: Thames and Hudson.

———. 1992. *Power and Persuasion in Late Antiquity: Towards a Christian Empire.* Madison: University of Wisconsin Press.

———. 2008. *The Body and Society: Men, Women, and Sexual Renunciation in Early Christianity.* 2nd ed. New York: Columbia University Press.

Burnam, John, ed. 1905. "Glossemata de Prudentio." University of Cincinnati Studies, series 2, vol. 1, no. 4. Cincinnati: University of Cincinnati Press.

———, ed. 1910. *Commentaire anonyme sur Prudence d'après le manuscrit 413 de Valenciennes.* Paris: Alphonse Picard.

Burton, Rosemary, ed. 1989. *Prudentius: Psychomachia.* Bryn Mawr, PA: Thomas Library Bryn Mawr College.

Cameron, Alan. 1970. *Claudian: Poetry and Propaganda at the Court of Honorius.* Oxford: Clarendon Press.

Cameron, Alan. 2011. *The Last Pagans of Rome.* New York: Oxford University Press.

Chadwick, Henry. 2001. *The Church in Ancient Society: From Galilee to Gregory the Great.* Oxford: Clarendon Press.

Charlet, Jean-Louis. 1980. *L'influence d'Ausone sur la poésie de Prudence.* Aix-en-Provence: Publications Université de Provence.

Charlet, Jean-Louis. 1983. "Prudence et la Bible." *Recherches Augustiniennes* 18: 3–149.

———. 2003. "Signification de la préface à la *Psychomachia* de Prudence." *Revue des études latines* 81: 232–51.

Chin, Catherine M., and Caroline T. Schroeder, eds. 2016. *Melania: Early Christianity through the Life of One Family*. Berkeley: University of California Press.

Conybeare, Catherine. 2013. *The Laughter of Sarah: Biblical Exegesis, Feminist Theory, and the Concept of Delight*. New York: Palgrave Macmillan.

———. 2018. "Toward a Hermeneutics of Laughter." *Journal of Late Antiquity* 10 (2): 503–14.

Coşkun, Altay. 2003. "Die Programmgedichte des Prudentius: Praefatio und epilogus." *Zeitschrift für Antikes Christentum* 7: 212–36.

———. 2008. "Zur Biographie des Prudentius." *Philologus* 152 (2): 294–319.

Costanza, Salvatore. 1983. "Rapporti letterari tra Paolino e Prudenzio." In *Atti del Convegno XXXI Cinquantenario della Morte di S. Paolino da Nola: (431–1981)*, 25–65. Rome: Herder.

Copeland, Rita, and Peter Struck, eds. 2010. *The Cambridge Companion to Allegory*. Cambridge: Cambridge University Press.

Cullhed, Anders. 2015. *The Shadow of Creusa: Negotiating Fictionality in Late Antique Latin Literature*. Berlin: De Gruyter.

Cunningham, Maurice P. 1958. "Some Facts about the Puteanus of Prudentius." *Transactions of the American Philological Association* 89: 32–37.

———. 1962. "A Preliminary Recension of the Older Manuscripts of the Cathemerinon, Apotheosis, and Hamartigenia of Prudentius." *Sacris Erudiri* 13: 5–59.

———, ed. 1966. *Aurelii Prudentii Clementis Carmina*. CCSL 126. Turnhout: Brepols.

———. 1968. "The Problem of Interpolation in the Textual Tradition of Prudentius." *Transactions of the American Philological Association* 99: 119–41.

———. 1971. "Notes on the Text of Prudentius." *Transactions of the American Philological Association* 102: 59–69.

Dawson, David. 2002. *Christian Figural Reading and the Fashioning of Identity*. Berkeley: University of California Press.

Doignon, Jean. 1974. "La première exposition ambrosienne de l'*exemplum* de Judith (*De uirginibus*, 2, 4, 24)." In *Ambroise de Milan: XVIe Centenaire de son élection épiscopale*, edited by Yves-Marie Duval, 219–28. Paris: Etudes Augustiniennes.

Dorfbauer, Lukas. 2010. "Die *praefationes* von Claudian und von Prudentius." In *Text und Bild*, edited by Victoria Zimmerl-Panagl and Dorothea Weber, 195–222. Vienna: Verlag der Österreichischen Akademie der Wissenschaften.

———. 2012. "Claudian und Prudentius: Verbale Parallelen und Datierungsfragen." *Hermes* 140 (1): 45–70.

Dressel, Albert, ed. 1860. *Aurelii Prudentii Clementis quae extant carmina*. Leipzig: Hermann Mendelssohn.

Dykes, Anthony. 2011. *Reading Sin in the World: The* Hamartigenia *of Prudentius and the Vocation of the Responsible Reader*. Cambridge: Cambridge University Press.

Fabian, Claudia. 1988. *Dogma und Dichtung: Untersuchungen zu Prudentius' Apotheosis*. Peter Lang: Frankfurt am Main.

Fontaine, Jacques. 1966. Review of *Aurelii Prudentii Clementis Carmina*, by Maurice P. Cunningham. *Revues des études latines* 44: 469–71.

———. 1976. "Prose et poésie: L'interférence des genres et des styles dans la création littéraire d'Ambroise de Milan." In *Ambrosius Episcopus*, edited by Giuseppe Lazzati, 1: 124–70. Milan: Vita e pensiero.

———. 1977. "Unité et diversité du mélange des genres et des tons chez quelques écrivains latins de la fin du IVe siècle: Ausone, Ambroise, Ammien." In *Christianisme et formes littéraires de l'antiquité tardive en occident*, edited by Manfred Fuhrmann, 425–82. Vandoeuvres-Geneva: Fondation Hardt.

———. 1980. *Études sur la poésie latine tardive d'Ausone a Prudence*. Paris: Belles Lettres.

———. 1981. *Naissance de la poésie dans l'occident chrétien: Esquisse d'une histoire de la poésie latine chrétienne du IIIe au VIe siècle*. Paris: Études Augustiniennes.

Fordyce, C. J., ed. 1977. *Aeneidos Libri VII–VIII*. Oxford: Published for the University of Glasgow by Oxford University Press.

Franchi, Paola. 2012. "Comminus portenta notare. Pretesa di realtà e crogiolo d'immaginari: Il laboratorio allegorico della Psychomachia." In *Persona ficta: La personificazione allegorica nella cultura antica fra letteratura, retorica e iconografia*, edited by Gabriella Moretti and Alice Bonandini, 341–54. Trento: Università di Trento.

———. 2013. "La battaglia interiore: Prova di commento alla *Psychomachia* di Prudenzio." PhD diss., University of Vienna.

Gnilka, Christian. 1963. *Studien zur Psychomachie des Prudentius*. Wiesbaden: Otto Harrassowitz.

———. 1979. "Interpretation frühchristlicher Literatur: Dargestellt am Beispiel des Prudentius." In *Impulse für die lateinische Lektüre: Von Terenz bis Thomas Morus*, edited by Heinrich Krefeld, 138–80. Frankfurt am Main: Hirschgraben. Reprinted with supplements in Gnilka 2000–2003, 2: 32–90.

———. 1984. "Kritische Bemerkungen zu Prudentius' 'Hamartigenie'." *Hermes* 112 (3): 333–52. Reprinted with supplements in Gnilka 2000–2003, 1: 68–89.

———. 1984–93. *Chrêsis: Die Methode der Kirchenväter im Umgang mit der antiken Kultur*. 2 vols. Basel: Schwabe.

———. 1985. "Theologie und Textgeschichte: Zwei Doppelfassungen bei Prudentius, psychom. praef. 38ff." *Wiener Studien* 98: 179–203. Reprinted with supplements in Gnilka 2000–2003, 1: 102–25.

———. 1986. "Zwei Binneninterpolamente und ihre Bedeutung fur die Geschichte des Prudentiustexts." *Hermes* 114 (1): 88–98. Reprinted with supplements in Gnilka 2000–2003, 1: 126–37.

———. 1987. "Ein Zeugnis doppelchörigen Gesangs bei Prudentius." *Jahrbuch für Antike und Christentum* 30: 58–73. Reprinted with supplements in Gnilka 2000–2003, 2: 170–91.

———. 1988a. "Eine Spur altlateinischer Bibelversion bei Prudentius." *Vigiliae Christianae* 42 (2): 147–55. Reprinted with supplements in Gnilka 2000–2003, 1: 158–66.

———. 1988b. "Prudentiana." In *Roma renascens*, edited by Michael Wissemann, 78–87. Frankfurt am Main: Peter Lang. Reprinted with supplements in Gnilka 2000–2003, 1: 192–200.

———. 2000–2003. *Prudentiana*. 3 vols. Munich: Saur.

Gosserez, Laurence. 2001. *Poésie de lumière: Une lecture de Prudence.* Louvain: Peeters.

Green, Roger, ed. 1991. *The Works of Ausonius*. Oxford: Clarendon Press.

———. 2000. "Erasmus and Prudentius." In *Acta Conventus Neo-Latini Abulensis: Proceedings of the Tenth International Congress of Neo-Latin Studies*, edited by Rhoda Schnur et al., 309–18. Tempe: Arizona Center for Medieval and Renaissance Studies.

Guttilla, Giuseppe. 2005. "Un probabile incontro a Roma di Paolino di Nola e Prudenzio." *Aevum* 79: 95–107.

Hardie, Philip. 2017. "How Prudentian Is the *Aeneid?*" *Dictynna* 14.

Harper, Kyle. 2013. *From Shame to Sin: The Christian Transformation of Sexual Morality in Late Antiquity*. Cambridge, Mass.: Harvard University Press.

Harvey, Susan. 2006. *Scenting Salvation: Ancient Christianity and the Olfactory Imagination*. Berkeley: University of California Press.

Heinsius, Nicolaas, ed. 1667. *Aurelii Prudentii Clementis quae extant.* 2 vols. Amsterdam: Daniel Elzevir.

Heinz, Carsten. 2007. *Mehrfache Intertextualität bei Prudentius*. Frankfurt am Main: Peter Lang.

Hermann, John. 1977. "Psychomachia 423–26 and Aeneid 5.468–70." *The Classical Bulletin* 54: 88–89.

Hershkowitz, Paula. 2017. *Prudentius, Spain, and Late Antique Christianity: Poetry, Visual Culture, and the Cult of the Martyrs*. Cambridge: Cambridge University Press.

Hoefer, Otto. 1895. *De Prudentii poetae* Psychomachia *et carminum chronologia*. Hannover: Typos Jaenecke.

Horsfall, Nicholas, ed. 2013. *Virgil: Aeneid 6*. Berlin: De Gruyter.

———, ed. 2000. *Virgil: Aeneid 7*. Leiden: Brill.

Houghton, H. A. G. 2016. *The Latin New Testament: A Guide to Its Early History, Texts, and Manuscripts*. Oxford: Oxford University Press.

Hudson-Williams, Alun. 1967–68. "Virgil and the Christian Latin Poets." *Proceedings of the Virgil Society* 6: 11–21.

James, Paula. 1999. "Psychomachia: The Christian Arena and the Politics of Display." In *Constructing Identities in Late Antiquity*, edited by Richard Miles, 70–94. London: Routledge.

Jensen, Robin Margaret. 2000. *Understanding Early Christian Art*. London: Routledge.

Kaster, Robert. 1988. *Guardians of Language: The Grammarian and Society in Late Antiquity*. Berkeley: University of California Press.

Kelly, Christopher. 2013. "Stooping to Conquer: The Power of Imperial Humility." In *Theodosius II*, edited by Christopher Kelly, 221–43. Cambridge: Cambridge University Press.

Kelly, Gavin. 2013. "Ammianus' Greek Accent." *Talanta* 45: 67–79.

Kinzig, Wolfram, ed. 2017. *Faith in Formulae: A Collection of Early Christian Creeds and Creed-Related Texts*. 4 vols. Oxford: Oxford University Press.

Klauser, Theodor. 1961. "Das Ciborium in der älteren christlichen Buchmalerei." *Nachrichten der Akademie der Wissenschaften philologisch-historische Klasse* 7: 194–207.

Knauer, Georg Nicolaus. 1964. "Vergil's *Aeneid* and Homer." *Greek, Roman, and Byzantine Studies* 5 (2): 61–84.

Lamberton, Robert. 1986. *Homer the Theologian: Neoplatonist Allegorical Reading and the Growth of the Epic Tradition*. Berkeley: University of California Press.

Lavarenne, Maurice, ed. 1933a. *Prudence: Psychomachie*. Paris: Société Française d'Imprimerie et de Librairie.

———. 1933b. *Étude sur la langue du poète Prudence*. Paris: Société Française d'Imprimerie et de Librairie.

———, ed. 1943. *Prudence*. Volume 1, *Cathemerinon liber*. Paris: Les Belles Lettres.

———, ed. 2002. *Prudence*. Volume 3, *Psychomachie, Contre Symmaque*. Paris: Les Belles Lettres. Revised by Jean-Louis Charlet, originally published in 1948.

Lease, Emory Bair. 1895. "A Syntactic, Stylistic and Metrical Study of Prudentius." PhD diss., Johns Hopkins University.

Liebeschuetz, J. H. W. G. 1979. *Continuity and Change in Roman Religion*. Oxford: Oxford University Press.

Long, A. A. 1992. "Stoic Readings of Homer." In *Homer's Ancient Readers: The Hermeneutics of Greek Epic's Earliest Exegetes*, edited by Robert Lamberton and John J. Keaney, 41–66. Princeton: Princeton University Press.

Lubian, Francesco. 2014. "I *Tituli historiarum* a tema biblico della tarda antichità latina: *Ambrosii Disticha, Prudentii Dittochaeon, Miracula Christi, Rustici Helpidii Tristicha*: Introduzione, testo criticamente riveduto, traduzione e commento." PhD diss., University of Macerata.

Ludwig, Walther. 1977. "Die christliche Dichtung des Prudentius und die Transformation der klassischen Gattungen." In *Christianisme et formes littéraires de l'Antiquité tardive en Occident*, edited by Manfred Fuhrmann, 303–63. Vandoeuvres-Geneva: Fondation Hardt.

Lühken, Maria. 2002. *Christianorum Maro et Flaccus: Zur Vergil- und Horazrezeption des Prudentius*. Göttingen: Vandenhoeck and Ruprecht.

Machosky, Brenda. 2013. *Structures of Appearing: Allegory and the Work of Literature*. New York: Fordham University Press.

Malamud, Martha. 1989. *A Poetics of Transformation: Prudentius and Classical Mythology*. Ithaca, N.Y.: Cornell University Press.

Marrou, Henri-Irénée. 1958. *Saint Augustin et la fin de la culture antique*. Paris: Editions de Boccard.

Mastrangelo, Marc. 2008. *The Roman Self in Late Antiquity: Prudentius and the Poetics of the Soul*. Baltimore: Johns Hopkins University Press.

———. 2009. "The Decline of Poetry in the Fourth-Century West." *International Journal of the Classical Tradition* 16 (3–4): 311–29.

———. 2013. "Typology and Agency in Prudentius's Treatment of the Judith Story." In *The Sword of Judith: Judith Studies Across the Disciplines*, edited by Kevin R. Brine, Elena Ciletti, and Henrike Lähnemann, 153–68. Cambridge: Open Book Publishers.

———. 2017. "The Early Christian Response to Platonist Poetics: Boethius, Prudentius, and the *Poeta Theologus*." In *The Poetics of Late Latin Literature*, edited by Jaś Elsner and Jesús Hernández Lobato, 391–423. New York: Oxford University Press.

McGill, Scott, trans. 2016. *Juvencus' Four Books of the Gospels*. New York: Routledge.

Miller, Patricia Cox. 2009. *The Corporeal Imagination: Signifying the Holy in Late Ancient Christianity*. Philadelphia: University of Pennsylvania Press.

Niehoff, Maren R. 2011. *Jewish Exegesis and Homeric Scholarship in Alexandria*. Cambridge: Cambridge University Press.

Norden, Eduard, ed. 1957. *P. Vergilius Maro Aeneis Buch VI*. 4th ed. Stuttgart: Teubner.

Nugent, S. Georgia. 1985. *Allegory and Poetics: The Structure and Imagery of Prudentius'* Psychomachia. Frankfurt am Main: Peter Lang.

O'Daly, Gerard, ed. and trans. 2012. *Days Linked by Song: Prudentius' Cathemerinon*. Oxford: Oxford University Press.

———. 2013. "Oxford Bibliographies: Prudentius." Last modified October 29, 2013. doi: 10.1093/OBO/9780195389661-0020.

———. 2016. "Prudentius: The Self-Definition of a Christian Poet." In *Classics Renewed: Reception and Innovation in the Latin Poetry of Late Antiquity*, edited by Scott McGill and Joseph Pucci, 221–40. Heidelberg: Universitätsverlag Winter.

O'Donnell, James J. 1977. "'Paganus': Evolution and Use." *Classical Folia* 31: 163–69.

O'Hogan, Cillian. 2016. *Prudentius and the Landscapes of Late Antiquity*. Oxford: Oxford University Press.

O'Sullivan, Sinéad. 2004. *Early Medieval Glosses on Prudentius' Psychomachia: The Weitz Tradition*. Leiden: Brill.

Palmer, Anne-Marie. 1989. *Prudentius on the Martyrs*. Oxford: Clarendon Press.

Paxson, James J. 1994. *The Poetics of Personification*. Cambridge: Cambridge University Press.

Pelttari, Aaron. 2011. "Approaches to the Writing of Greek in Late Antique Latin Texts." *Greek, Roman, and Byzantine Studies* 51: 461–82.

———. 2014. *The Space That Remains: Reading Latin Poetry in Late Antiquity*. Ithaca, N.Y.: Cornell University Press.

—. 2017. "A Lexicographical Approach to the Poetry of Optatian."
In *Morphogrammata / The Lettered Art of Optatian: Figuring Cultural Transformations in the Age of Constantine*, edited by Michael Squire and Johannes Wienand, 369–90. Paderborn: Wilhelm Fink.

Petruccione, John. 2013. "The Glosses of Prudentius's *Peristephanon* in Leiden, Universiteitsbibliotheek, Burmann Quarto 3 (Bur. Q. 3) and Their Relationship to a Lost Commentary." *Journal of Medieval Latin* 23: 295–333.

Pohlsander, Hans A. 1969. "Victory: The Story of a Statue." *Historia: Zeitschrift für Alte Geschichte* 18 (5): 588–97.

Pollmann, Karla. 2013. "Establishing Authority in Christian Poetry of Latin Late Antiquity." *Hermes* 141 (3): 309–30.

Prosperi, Carlo, trans. and comm. 2000. *Prudenzio:* Psychomachia. Introduction by Giovanni Castelli. Acqui Terme: Liceo scientifico di Stato G. Parodi.

Prigent, Pierre. 1992. "Les orants dans l'art funéraire ancien." *Revue d'histoire et de philosophie religieuses* 72 (1–2): 143–50 and 259–87.

Pucci, Joseph. 1991. "Prudentius' Readings of Horace in the Cathemerinon." *Latomus* 50 (3): 677–90.

Putter, Ad. 2016. "Prudentius and the Late Classical Biblical Epics of Juvencus, Proba, Sedulius, Arator, and Avitus." In *The Oxford History of Classical Reception in English Literature*. Volume 1, *800–1558*, edited by Rita Copeland, 351–70. Oxford: Oxford University Press.

Ramelli, Ilaria, and Giulio A. Lucchetta. 2004. *Allegoria*. Volume 1, *L'età classica*. Milan: Vita e Pensiero.

Ramelli, Ilaria. 2008. "Umiltà nei padri." In *Nuovo dizionario patristico e di antichita cristiane*, 5497–506. Genoa: Marietti.

Rapisarda, Emanuele. 1950. "Influssi lucreziani in Prudenzio." *Vigiliae Christianae* 4: 46–60.

—. 1951. *Introduzione alla lettura di Prudenzio*. Catania: Centro di studi di letteratura cristiana antica.

Rebillard, Éric. 2012. *Christians and Their Many Identities in Late Antiquity, North Africa, 200–450 CE*. Ithaca, N.Y.: Cornell University Press.

Renehan, Robert. 1969. *Greek Textual Criticism: A Reader.* Cambridge, Mass.: Harvard University Press.

Richardson, Nicholas, trans. 2016. *Prudentius' Hymns for Hours and Seasons: The* Liber Cathemerinon. New York: Routledge.

Rist, John. 1994. *Augustine: Ancient Thought Baptized.* Cambridge: Cambridge University Press.

Rivero García, Luis. 1996. *La poesía de Prudencio.* Huelva: Universidad de Huelva.

Roberts, Michael. 1989. *The Jeweled Style: Poetry and Poetics in Late Antiquity.* Ithaca, N.Y.: Cornell University Press.

Rohmann, Dirk. 2003. "Das langsame Sterben der Veterum Cultura Deorum: Pagane Kulte bei Prudentius." *Hermes* 131 (2): 235–53.

Roller, Matthew. 2018. *Models from the Past in Roman Culture: A World of Exempla.* Cambridge: Cambridge University Press.

Ross, Jill. 1995. "Dynamic Writing and Martyrs' Bodies in Prudentius' *Peristephanon.*" *Journal of Early Christian Studies* 3 (3): 325–55.

Saenger, Paul. 1997. *Space Between Words: The Origins of Silent Reading.* Stanford: Stanford University Press.

Scheid, John, and Jesper Svenbro. 1996. *The Craft of Zeus: Myths of Weaving and Fabric.* Translated by Carol Volk. Cambridge, Mass.: Harvard University Press.

Schlatter, Fredric W. 1992. "Interpreting the Mosaic of Santa Pudenziana." *Vigiliae Christianae* 46 (3): 276–95.

———. 1995. "A Mosaic Interpretation of Jerome, *In Hiezechielem.*" *Vigiliae Christianae* 49 (1): 64–81.

Shackleton Bailey, D. R. 1952. "Echoes of Propertius." *Mnemosyne* 5 (1): 307–33.

Shanzer, Danuta. 1989. "Allegory and Reality: Spes, Victoria and the Date of Prudentius's *Psychomachia.*" *Illinois Classical Studies* 14 (1–2): 347–63.

Silvestre, Hubert. 1957. "Aperçu sur les Commentaires carolingiens de Prudence." *Sacris Erudiri* 9: 50–74.

Smith, Molly T. 1968. "The 'Ciborium' in Christian Architecture at Rome, 300–600 A.D." PhD diss., New York University.

Smith, Macklin. 1976. *Prudentius'* Psychomachia*: A Reexamination*. Princeton: Princeton University Press.

Smolak, Kurt. 2001. "Die Psychomachie des Prudentius als historisches Epos." In *La poesia tardoantica e medievale*, edited by Marcello Salvadore, 125–48. Alessandria: Edizioni dell'Orso.

Stabryła, Stanisław. 2006. "Fides in Prudentius' *Psychomachia*." In *Studia Prudentiana*, 30–37. Krakow: Polska Akademia Umiejętności. Originally published in 2005 in *Classica Cracoviensia* 9: 19–28.

Stafford, Emma. 2000. *Worshipping Virtues: Personification and the Divine in Ancient Greece*. Swansea: Duckworth and the Classical Press of Wales.

Stettiner, Richard. 1895–1905. *Die illustrierten Prudentiushandschriften*. 2 vols. Berlin: G. Grotesche Verlagsbuchhandlung.

Struck, Peter. 2004. *Birth of the Symbol: Readers at the Limits of Their Texts*. Princeton: Princeton University Press.

Tarrant, Richard, ed. 1976. *Seneca: Agamemnon*. Cambridge: Cambridge University Press.

———. 2016. *Texts, Editors, and Readers: Methods and Problems in Latin Textual Criticism*. Cambridge: Cambridge University Press.

Thomson, H. J., ed. and trans. 1949–53. *Prudentius*. 2 vols. Loeb Classical Library 387 and 398. Cambridge, Mass.: Harvard University Press.

Thraede, Klaus. 1968. Review of *Aurelii Prudentii Clementis Carmina*, by Maurice P. Cunningham. *Gnomon* 40: 681–91.

———. 1994. "Homonoia." In *Reallexikon für Antike und Christentum*, 16: 176–289. Stuttgart: Anton Hiersemann.

Trout, Dennis. 1999. *Paulinus of Nola: Life, Letters, and Poems*. Berkeley: University of California Press.

Tucci, Pier Luigi. 2018. *The Temple of Peace in Rome*. 2 vols. Cambridge: Cambridge University Press.

Vest, Eugene Bartlett. 1932. "Prudentius in the Middle Ages." PhD diss., Harvard University.

Ware, Catherine. 2015. "Claudian's *Arma*: A Metaliterary Pun." *Classical Quarterly* 65 (2): 895–96.

Warren, James. 2002. *Epicurus and Democritean Ethics: An Archaeology of* Ataraxia. Cambridge: Cambridge University Press.

Weitzius, Iohannes, ed. 1613. *Aurelii Prudentii Clementis V.C. Opera.* 2 vols. Hanau: Typis Wechelianis.

Wieland, Gernot. 1983. *The Latin Glosses on Arator and Prudentius in Cambridge University Library, MS Gg. 5.35.* Toronto: Pontifical Institute of Mediaeval Studies.

Wilkinson, L. P. 1963. *Golden Latin Artistry.* Cambridge: Cambridge University Press.

Witke, Charles. 1968. "Prudentius and the Tradition of Latin Poetry." *Transactions of the American Philological Association* 99: 509–25.

———. 1971. *Numen Litterarum: The Old and the New in Latin Poetry from Constantine to Gregory the Great.* Leiden: Brill.

Woodruff, Helen. 1929. "The Illustrated Manuscripts of Prudentius." *Art Studies* 7: 33–79. Reprinted as a monograph in 1930 by Harvard University Press, Cambridge, Mass.

Young, Frances. 1997. *Biblical Exegesis and the Formation of Christian Culture.* Cambridge: Cambridge University Press.

GLOSSARY

The following glossary is keyed to the *Psychomachia*, but I have also included very common meanings not used by Prudentius. The first meaning or usage cited is the one that comes first logically, whether or not Prudentius happened to use that primary meaning. For example, the student will want to know that "Borras" was the North Wind before it came to be used simply of the direction "north." Different meanings or uses are separated by a semicolon. Closely related meanings are separated by a comma. For example:

> **inānis, -e**: empty; useless, worthless

The first meaning is logically prior, whereas "useless" and "worthless" are presented as two facets of an extended, or transferred, use of the word. Even very basic lexicography entails a thousand choices, and the student should see that a gloss always involves interpretation.

In writing this glossary, I began by following the example of Daniel Garrison's "Catullan Vocabulary" for his edition with Oklahoma University Press (4th ed., 2012). In the end, I made considerable use of the *OLD*, the *TLL*, and Lewis and Short's *Latin Dictionary* (1879); in the few cases where it seemed advisable, I consulted every extant example I could find for a given word (e.g., *toreuma*, on which see the note in the commentary on line 370); more often, I considered the other instances of a given word or parallel forms in the corpus of Prudentius. Unfortunately, Bergman did not continue his *Lexicon Prudentianum* (1894) beyond *adscendo*.

Long vowels are marked according to their regular scansion; for the several words that Prudentius scans irregularly, see appendix A. As concerns orthography, I have followed Prudentius rather than classicizing norms.

ABBREVIATIONS

abl. = ablative	interr. = interrogative
acc. = accusative	m. = masculine
adj. = adjective	n. = neuter
adv. = adverb	part. = particle
conj. = conjunction	pass. = passive
dat. = dative	perf. = perfect
demonst. = demonstrative	pers. = person *or* personal
f. = feminine	pl. = plural
fut. = future	poss. = possessive
Germ. = Germanic	postpos. = postpositive
Gk. = Greek	prep. = preposition
Heb. = Hebrew	pron. = pronoun
impers. = impersonal	reflex. = reflexive
ind. = indicative	rel. = relative
indecl. = indeclinable	sing. = singular
indef. = indefinite	subj. = subjunctive
interj. = interjective	w/ = with

a, ab: prep. w/abl., from, by

Aārōn, indecl., **m.:** a Hebrew priest, brother of Moses

abdō, -dere, -didī, -ditum: to put away, remove; conceal

abiciō, -icere, -iēcī, -iectum: to throw away, cast off

abigō, -igere, -ēgī, -actum: to drive away; get rid of

abluō, -luere, -luī, -lūtum: to wash off, wash away

aboleō, -olēre, -olēuī, -olitum: to give off an odor, smell

abrādō, -rādere, -rāsī, -rāsum: to scratch off; snatch away

Abr(āh)am, -ae, m.: a Jewish patriarch

abscondō, -ere, -ī, -itum: to hide, conceal

abstineō, -ēre, -uī, -entum: to keep away from

abyssus, -ī, f.: a bottomless pit, abyss

ac, atque: conj., and, and also (*atque* is normal before a vowel)

acerbus, -a, -um: bitter; harsh

Achar, m.: Achan, a Hebrew soldier

aciēs, -ēī, f.: a sharp edge; line; battle line; sword; line of sight

actus, -ūs, m.: driving, motion; action

acūmen, -inis, n.: a point, sharpness

acus, -ūs, f.: a needle, pin

acūtus, -a, -um: sharp

ad: prep. w/acc., to, toward; near to, on, at; according to, for

Adam, -ae, m.: the first human being

adamas, adamantis, m.: (Gk.) hard steel

adcumulō (1): to pile up

addīcō, -dīcere, -dixī, -dictum: to speak to; award to someone, sell to, deliver

addō, -dere, -didī, -ditum: to put on, add

addubitō (1): to begin to doubt; doubt

adeō, -īre, -īuī, -itum: to go toward, approach

adflātus, -ūs, f.: breath, breathing; inspiration

adgredior, -gredī, -gressus: to walk to, approach

adhuc: adv., to this place, to this point; still

adiciō, -icere, -iēcī, -iectum: to toss on, add

adigo, -igere, -ēgī, -actum: to drive to, drive in

adimō, -imere, -ēmī, -emptum: to take away, deprive of

aditus, -ūs, m.: an approach; entrance

adloquium, -iī, n.: an address, speech

adolescō, -olescere, -olēuī, -ultum: to grow, grow up, mature

adoperiō, -operīre, -operuī, -opertum: to cover up, cover over

adpetō, -petere, -petīuī, -petītum: to reach after; attack

adplicō (1): to bend, twist; join

adpōnō, -ere, -posuī, -positum: to put near, place next to

adrīdeō, -rīdēre, -rīsī, -rīsum: to laugh, smile

adsistō, -sistere, astitī: to stand by or near

adsociō (1): to join to

adstō, -stāre, -stitī: to stand by, stand near

adsuescō, -suescere, -suēuī, -suētum: to accustom, habituate

adsultus, -ūs, m.: an attack, assault

adsum, -esse, -fuī, -futūrus: to be present; appear

adtemptō (1): to make trial of, attack

adtrectō (1): to touch, handle; seize; violate

adtrītus, -a, -um: rubbed, worn down, weakened

aduena, -ae, m.: a newcomer, foreigner, stranger

aduersus, -a, -um: turned toward, facing; opposed

adumbrō (1): to cast a shadow on, shade; represent imperfectly, feign

aemulus, -a, -um: rivaling, jealous

ăēnus, -a, -um: of copper or bronze, brazen

aequor, -oris, n.: a surface; a plain; the sea

aequus, -a, -um: level, equal

āēr, ăĕris, m.: air

aereus, -a, -um: made of copper or bronze, brazen

āĕrius, -a, -um: airy; spiritual

aerūgō, -ginis, f.: rust from copper

aes, aeris, n.: copper, bronze; money

aestuō (1): to boil; to rage

aetās, aetātis, f.: age; lifetime; time

aeternus, -a, -um: eternal

aethēr, -eris, m.: the upper air, ether; heaven

aeuum, -ī, n.: time, age; an age, generation, lifetime

ager, agrī, m.: a piece of land, field

agger, -eris, m.: earthwork, rampart, ridge

agitō (1): to put in motion, agitate; rouse, excite

agmen, -inis, n.: a current; column; army

agnīnus, -a, -um: of a lamb

agnoscō, -noscere, -nōuī, -nitum: to recognize; recognize as one's own; come to know

agō, agere, ēgī, actum: to drive, lead; pursue; conduct; pass., move oneself, go

agrestis, -e: of the fields; rustic, rural; simple

āiō (3rd sing. ăit): to say

āla, -ae, f.: wing; wing of an army

alacer, alacris, alacre: swift; eager; glad

albeō, -ēre: to be white, gleam

albus, -a, -um: white, pale

āles, ālitis: having wings; flying

algeō, -ēre, alsī: to be cold

algidus, -a, -um: cold

aliēnus, -a, -um: of another; foreign, alien

alimōnia, -ae, f.: food, nourishment

aliquī, aliqua, aliquod: indef. adj., some; any

aliquis, aliqua, aliquid: indef. pron., someone, something; anyone, anything

aliter: adv., in another way, otherwise

alius, -a, -ud: other, another

almus, -a, -um: nourishing; kind

alō, -ere, aluī, altum: to nourish, sustain; strengthen

altāria, -ium, n. pl.: altar

alter, altera, alterum: indef. adj. and pron., a second, another; the other (of two)

alternīs: adv., alternately, by turns

alternus, -a, -um: alternating, successive

altus, -a, -um: high, lofty; deep, profound

alumnus, -ī, m.: a child, a young one

aluus, -ī, m.: belly; stomach; womb

amārus, -a, -um: bitter

ambiō, -īre, -īuī, -ītum: to go around, encircle; canvass, solicit

āmens, āmentis: out of one's mind, mad

āmentum, -ī, n.: a throwing-strap

ametystinus, -a, -um: of amethyst

amīcitia, -ae, f.: friendship, alliance

amīcus, -ī, m.: a friend

amoenus, -a, -um: attractive, pleasant

amor, -ōris, m.: love, desire; as a proper noun, Cupid

amplector, -plectī, -plexus: to embrace, enfold, take in

amplus, -a, -um: large, wide, bulky

an: conj., or (introducing an alternative question)

anathēma, -atis, n.: a dedicated offering

anceps, ancipitis: two-headed; double; uncertain, wavering

angelicus, -a, -um: angelic

angelus, -ī, m.: a messenger; angel

anguīnus, -a, -um: of or related to a snake

angulus, -ī, m.: an angle; corner

anhēlus, -a, -um: out of breath

anima, -ae, f.: breath, soul

animal, -ālis, n.: an animal

animō (1): to fill with air; animate

animōsus, -a, -um: spirited, bold, courageous

animus, -ī, m.: a (rational) soul; reason, mind; an instance of emotion or passion

anne: *an + ne*, is it the case that?

annus, -ī, m.: a year

ante: prep. w/acc., in front of, before

antīquus, -a, -um: ancient

antrum, -ī, n.: a cave

anxietas, -ātis, f.: anxiety

anxius, -a, -um: distressed, anxious

aperiō, -īre, aperuī, apertum: to open

apertus, -a, -um: open

apex, -icis, m.: the top, a peak

apostolicus, -a, -um: apostolic, related to Christ's twelve apostles

aqua, -ae, f.: water

aquila, -ae, f.: an eagle; a military standard (used by Roman legions); a military legion (by metonymy)

aquilō, -ōnis, m.: the north wind; north

aquōsus, -a, -um: watery

āra, -ae, f.: an altar

arātrum, -ī, n.: a plow

arca, -ae, f.: a box; money box, chest; the Hebrew ark of the covenant

arcānus, -a, -um: secret, concealed

arcus, -ūs, m.: a bow, arch

ārdeō, -ēre, ārsī, ārsum: to be on fire, burn, blaze; be inflamed, burn with desire

arduus, -a, -um: steep; lofty, arduous

argentum, -ī, n.: silver

argūtus, -a, -um: producing sharp or clear sounds; melodious; sharp, keen

āridus, -a, -um: dry

arma, -ōrum, n. pl.: arms, weapons

armiger, -era, -erum: armor bearing

armipotens, -ntis: strong-armed, valiant

armō (1): to provide with weapons, arm

armus, -ī, m.: a shoulder

Arrius, -iī, m.: a Christian presbyter from Alexandria (c. 250–336) who taught that Christ was different than God the Father (his name in Greek is Áreios, and Arīus elsewhere in Latin)

ars, artis, f.: skill, craft, art

artō (1): to draw together, compress, constrain

artus, -a, -um: close, narrow

artus, -ūs, m.: a joint; strength; limbs

aruum, -ī, n.: a plowed field, field; land

arx, arcis, f.: a citadel; summit, height

asper, -era, -erum: rough, uneven; harsh, bitter

asperō (1): to make rough, make uneven

aspiciō, aspicere, aspexī, aspectum: to catch sight of, notice; behold

as, assis, m.: a copper coin, penny

Assyrius, -a, -um: Assyrian

ast: conj., but, whereas

astus, -ūs, m.: cunning, guile, trick

at: conj., but, however

āter, ātra, ātrum: dark; dismal; deadly

ātrium, -iī, n.: an entryway, atrium; pl., a house, palace

attonitus, -a, -um: thunderstruck, stunned

Auāritia, -ae, f.: greediness, avarice

auārus, -a, -um: greedy

auctor, -ōris, m.: a promoter; maker, author

audax, audācis: bold; audacious, presumptuous

audeō, -ēre, ausus sum: to dare, be brave

audiō, -īre, -īuī, -ītum: to hear

āuellō, -uellere, -uellī, -uulsum: to tear away, pull off

Auernus, -ī, m.: a lake near Puteoli; the underworld, hell

augeō, augēre, auxī, auctum: to increase, make greater or bigger

auidus, -a, -um: greedy

auis, -is, f.: a bird

auītus, -a, -um: of a grandfather, ancestral

aula, -ae, f.: a palace

aura, -ae, f.: a breeze; air; breath

aurātus, -a, -um: overlaid with gold; golden

aureus, -a, -um: golden

aurīga, -ae, m.: a charioteer

auris, auris, f.: an ear

aurōra, -ae, f.: the dawn, the East

aurum, -ī, n.: gold

auster, austrī, m.: the south wind; the south

aut: conj., or; *aut ... aut*, either ... or

auus, -ī, m.: grandfather; forefather

auxilium, -iī, n.: assistance, help; protection

axis, axis, m.: an axle; the axis of the earth; the north pole

bāca, -ae, f.: a fruit, berry; pearl; a link of a chain

baculum, -ī, n.: a staff, walking stick

balsamum, -ī, n.: an aromatic unguent made of resin

baptisma, -atis, n.: a dipping, washing; baptism

barbariēs, -ēī, f.: a foreign country; rudeness, brutality, savagery

barbarus, -a, -um: foreign; barbarous

beātus, -a, -um: happy, blessed, fortunate

Bēlīa, -ae, m.: (Heb.) Belial, a chief of evil spirits, the devil

bellātor, -ōris, m.: a warrior

bellātrīx, -īcis, f.: a female warrior

bellicōsus, -a, -um: warlike

bellicus, -a, -um: of or related to war

belliger, -era, -erum: waging war, warlike

Bellōna, -ae, f.: a Roman goddess of war

bellum, -ī, n.: a war

bene: adv., well, in a good way

benignē: adv., kindly, generously

bēryllus, -ī, m.: beryl (a precious stone that is often sea green)

bestia, -ae, f.: a beast, animal

bifidus, -a, -um: divided in two

biforis, -e: having two doors or openings

biformis, -e: of two kinds

bīlis, -is, f.: bile; anger, madness

bis: adv., twice

blandus, -a, -um: charming, alluring, pleasant

blasfēmium, -iī, n.: slander; blasphemy

bonus, -a, -um: good

borras, -ae, m.: the north wind; the north

bratteola, -ae, f.: gold leaf

brūtus, -a, -um: heavy; dull, stupid

būcula, -ae, f.: a young cow, heifer
bulla, -ae, f.: a bubble; boss, knob, stud

cachinnus, -ī, m.: a laugh, guffaw
cadāuer, -eris, n.: a dead body
cadō, cadere, cecidī, cāsum: to fall, drop down
cadūcus, -a, -um: capable of falling; perishable, transitory
caecus, -a, -um: blind; hidden
caedēs, caedis, f.: killing, slaughter
caedō, -ere, cecīdī, caesum: to strike, blow; cut; kill
caelestis, -e: heavenly
caelitus: adv., from heaven
caelum, -ī, n.: the sky; heaven
caenōsus, -a, -um: muddy; filthy
caenum, -ī, n.: mud; filth, scum
caesariēs, -ēī, f.: hair, flowing or luxuriant hair
caespes, -itis, m.: sod, turf; grass
calathus, -ī, m.: a basket
calcar, -āris, n.: a spur
calcātrīx, -īcis, f.: one who tramples
calchēdōn, -onis, f.: a precious stone
calcō (1): to step on, trample underfoot
calculus, -ī, m.: a stone, pebble, gem
calidus, -a, -um: warm, hot; impassioned
cālīgō, -inis, f.: darkness, obscurity; blindness
calor, -ōris, m.: heat; ardor, enthusiasm
calx, calcis, f.: the back of the foot, heel
campus, -ī, m.: level land, a field, a plain
candeō, -ēre, canduī: to shine, gleam; be white
candidus, -a, -um: gleaming; white
canis, -is, m.: a dog
canō, -ere, cecinī, cantum: to sing, sing of
cantharus, -ī, m.: a large drinking vessel with handles
capax, -ācis: capacious, able to hold a lot

capessō, -ere, capessī, capessītum: to grasp, take up, lay hold of, receive

capillus, -ī, m.: hair of the head (often as a collective sing.)

capiō, capere, cēpī, captum: to take; catch, capture; take in, deceive

captīuus, -ī, m.: a captive, one captured or taken in war

capulus, -ī, m.: a handle, hilt

caput, -itis, n.: a head; the furthest point or end of some object

carbasa, -ā, f. and carbasa, -ōrum, n. pl.: fine linen; a curtain; a sail

carbaseus, -a, -um: of or related to linen

carcer, -eris, m.: enclosure; prison

cardō, -inis, m.: a pivot, hinge; turning point or pivotal point

careō, -ēre, caruī, caritum: w/abl., to lack, be in need of

carmen, -inis, n.: a song; poem

carneus, -a, -um: of or related to the body, fleshly

carō, carnis, f.: flesh, body

carpō, carpere, carpsī, carptum: to pluck, pick; tear

cārus, -a, -um: costly, dear; beloved

casa, -ae, f.: a hut; house; home

cassis, cassidis, f.: a helmet

cassus, -a, -um: lacking; empty; vain

castra, -ōrum, n. pl.: a military camp

castrensis, -e: of or relating to a camp

castus, -a, -um: unpolluted, pure; chaste

cāsus, -ūs, m.: a fall; accident, chance; outcome

catēna, -ae, f.: a chain, fetter

catēnātus, -a, -um: relating to chain, made of chain

caterua, -ae, f.: a band; troop, squadron; crowd

catholicus, -a, -um: universal, relating to all

caueō, -ēre, cāuī, cautum: to be on guard, beware

causa, -ae, f.: a cause, reason; purpose

cauus, -a, -um: hollowed out, concave; hollow

cēdō, cēdere, cēssī, cēssum: to go; go away; yield, submit

celeber, -bris, -bre: busy, frequented; famous, celebrated

celebrō (1): to fill in, crowd; honor, praise

cēlō (1): to conceal, hide

celsus, -a, -um: high, lofty

cēna, -ae, f.: a dinner

census, -ūs, m.: a census; property, wealth

centēnus, -a, -um: hundredfold, hundred times

ceraunus, -ī, m.: a kind of precious stone

cerebrum, -ī, n.: the brain

certāmen, -inis, n.: a competition; fight, battle

certus, -a, -um: sure, certain

ceruix, -īcis, f.: neck

cessō (1): to hold back from; cease, desist

ceu: part., like, as if

chalybs, -ybis, m.: iron or steel

choraea, -ae, f.: a circular dance; dancers, a troupe

chrīsma, -atis, n.: (Gr.) anointing

christicola, -ae, m.: a worshipper of Christ, Christian

Christus, -ī, m.: Christ, the second person of the trinity

chrȳsolitus, -ī, m.: topaz

chrȳsoprasos, -ī, m.: a precious stone, chrysoprase

cibus, -ī, m.: food

cicātrix, -īcis, f.: a scar

cingō, cingere, cinxī, cinctum: to put around, encircle; put armor on, gird

cingulum, -ī, n.: a band, belt

circum: adv., around

circumflectō, -flectere, -flexī, -flexum: to bend around

circumfundō, -fundere, -fūdī, -fūsum: to pour around; spread round

circumsaepiō, -saepīre, -saepsī, -saeptum: to fence around, surround

circumstō, -stāre, -stetī: to stand around

circumuagus, -a, -um: moving around, wandering

cirrus, -ī, m.: a curl, a lock of curly hair

cīuīlis, -e: of a citizen, civil

clādēs, clādis, f.: a disaster; defeat, destruction

clāmō (1): to shout

clārescō, -escere, -escuī: to become clear or bright

clārus, -a, -um: bright; famous; illustrious

classicum, -ī, n.: a trumpet call; a trumpet

claudō, claudere, clausī, clausum: to close; enclose; bury

claustrum, -ī, n.: a bolt, bar; barrier, boundary; enclosure

clausula, -ae, f.: an ending, conclusion

clepō, -ere, clepsī, cleptum: to steal

clipeus, -ī, m.: a round shield

cloāca, -ae, f.: a sewer, drain

cluō, -ere: to hear yourself called; be famous, renowned

coaptō, -āre: to fit together; fashion with

coeō, -īre, -iī, -itum: to come together

cōgitō (1): to think, think about

cognātus, -a, -um: related by birth

cognitus, -a, -um: known, recognized

cognōmentum, -ī, n.: a surname, additional name, cognomen

cōgō, -ere, coēgī, coactum: to drive together; collect, gather

cohibeō, -hibēre, -hibuī, -hibitum: to hold together; contain; keep back

cohors, cohortis, f.: an enclosure, yard; band of soldiers, cohort

collēga, -ae, m.: a colleague (in an official position), an associate

colligō, -ligere, -lēgī, -lectum: to collect, gather

collis, -is, m.: a hill

collum, -ī, n.: the neck; the head and neck

colō, -ere, coluī, cultum: inhabit; cultivate, care for; devote oneself to, worship

colōnus, -ī, m.: a farmer; a settler

color, -ōris, m.: a color

coluber, -brī, m.: a snake

columba, -ae, f.: a dove, pigeon

columna, -ae, f.: a column, pillar

coma, -ae, f.: hair, a lock of hair

comes, -itis, m.: a companion

cōmis, -e: gracious, elegant

comitātus, -ūs, m.: retinue, society, companionship

comitō (1): to accompany, attend
comitor (1): to accompany, attend
commentum, -ī, n.: a scheme, fiction; falsehood
commercium, -iī, n.: commerce, exchange; trade route, pathway
comminus: adv., hand to hand; nearby; immediately
commissūra, -ae, f.: a joint, juncture
commūnis, -e: shared, common; universal, general
conbibō, -bibere, -bibī: to drink up
conceptāculum, -ī, n.: a receptacle, reservoir
concha, -ae, f.: a shellfish, mollusk
concidō, -cidere, -cidī: to fall down, fall dead
concipiō, -cipere, -cēpī, -ceptum: to take in; conceive
concordia, -ae, f.: concord, harmony, unity
concrescō, -crescere, -crēuī, -crētus: to coalesce, congeal, condense
concurrō, -currere, -currī, -cursum: to run together; join a battle, charge
concutiō, -cutere, cussī, -cussum: to shake; strike; upset
condō, -dere, -didī, -ditum: to put into, sheathe (a sword); establish, found
conferō, -ferre, -tulī, -latum: to bring together; gather; contribute
confertus, -a, -um: crowded, packed together
confīdō, -fīdere, -fīsus sum: to trust, have confidence in
conflictus, -ūs, m.: a collision, conflict
conflīgō, -flīgere, -flīxī, -flīctum: to strike together, fight with
conflō (1): to blow together; kindle, inflame
confundō, -fundere, -fūdī, -fūsum: to pour together; confuse
congenitus, -a, -um: born together with, congenital
congeriēs, -ēī, f.: a heap, pile
congressus, -ūs, m.: a meeting, coming together; a hostile encounter, contest
cōniciō, -icere, -iēcī, -iectum: to throw together, hurl
cōnītor, -nītī, -nīsus: to put strength into; struggle
cōniueō, -niuēre, -niuī: to be closed; close (the eyes)
coniugālis, -e: of marriage, conjugal

coniungō, -iungere, -iunxī, -iunctum: to join together, unite

conliquefaciō, -facere, -fēcī, -factum: to make liquid, liquify

conluctor, -luctārī, -luctātus: to struggle with, wrestle

conmaculō (1): to stain, pollute

conmīlitō, -ōnis, m.: a fellow soldier, comrade

conmittō, -mittere, -mīsī, -missum: to put together; join; commit

conpāgēs, -is, f.: a binding; joint; structure

conpellō, -pellere, -pulī, -pulsum: to drive together; force, compel

conpescō, -pescere, -pescuī: to confine, suppress

conpetum, -ī, n.: usually pl., a crossroads, juncture

conplector, -plectī, -plexus: to embrace, encircle

conplexus, -ūs, m.: an embrace, joining

conpōnō, -pōnere, -posuī, -positum: to place together, arrange, settle; compose, compile

conprimō, -primere, -pressī, -pressum: to squeeze, compress, tighten

consaepiō, -saepīre, -saepsī, -saeptum: to wall around, fence in

consanguineus, -a, -um: related by blood, kindred

conscendō, -scendere, -scendī, -scensum: climb up, ascend; to embark (on a ship)

conscius, -a, -um: aware of; conscious; of a partner or confidant; as a substantive, partner, accomplice

consecrō (1): to make sacred, dedicate

consensus, -ūs, m.: agreement; assent; sympathy

conserō, -serere, -seruī, -sertum: to join together, fasten

consilium, -iī, n.: a debate, deliberation; advice, counsel

consistō, -sistere, -stitī: to stop, halt; take up a position, stand

consors, -tis, m. and **f.:** one who shares with another, partner

conspicuus, -a, -um: visible, prominent

conspīrō (1): to sound together, agree, be in accord; conspire

constituō, -stituere, -stituī, -stitūtum: to set up, establish

constō, -stāre, -stitī: to stand together; be composed of; be dependent on; remain

construō, -struere, -struxī, -structum: to pile up, construct

consummābilis, -e: able to be perfected or completed, terminable

contendō, -tendere, -tendī, -tentum: to stretch; strive; compete

contentus, -a, -um: satisfied, pleased

contineō, -tinēre, -tinuī, -tentum: to hold together, keep, surround

contingō, -tingere, -tigī, -tactum: to touch, reach; befall, fall to one's lot

continuus, -a, -um: uninterrupted, continuous

contiō, -ōnis, f.: an assembly; audience; public speech

contra: adv., in front, opposite; in return; on the other hand

contra: prep. w/acc., against

contus, -ī, m.: a pole, spear

conuertō, -uertere, -uertī, -uersum: to turn, turn around

conuīcium, -iī, n.: an uproar; insult, reproach

conuiolō (1): to violate, desecrate, foul

conuīua, -ae, m.: a guest at table, companion

cōnus, -ī, m.: a cone

cōpia, -ae, f.: abundance, multitude; band of men, troop

coquō, -ere, coxī, coctum: to prepare; cook; forge

cor, cordis, n.: heart; **cordī esse** = to be dear to

cornicen, -inis, m.: a trumpeter, bugler

cornipēs, -edis: horn footed, hooved

cornū, -ūs, n.: a horn; tip, corner, wing (of an army)

corōna, -ae, f.: a wreath, crown

corōnō (1): to deck with garlands, crown

corporeus, -a, -um: corporeal, bodily

corpus, -oris, n.: a body

corripiō, -ripere, -ripuī, -reptum: to snatch, seize

corruptēla, -ae, f.: corruption, seduction

cortex, -icis, m.: bark, an outer covering (of a tree)

coruscō (1): to shake, quiver; flash, glitter

coruscus, -a, -um: quivering; flashing, gleaming

coruus, -ī, m.: a raven, black crow

costa, -ae, f.: a rib

crāpula, -ae, f.: drunkenness; gluttony

crās: adv., tomorrow

crastinus, -a, -um: of or related to tomorrow

crēber, -bra, -brum: close set, crowded; frequent, abundant

crēdō, crēdere, crēdidī, creditum: to entrust; trust; believe

crēdulus, -a, -um: credulous, prone to belief; faithful

creō (1): to create

crepitō (1): to rattle, crackle

crepō, -āre, crepuī: to make a sharp noise, crack; break loudly

crescō, -ere, crēuī, crētum: to grow, increase in size or strength

crīmen, -inis, n.: an accusation; crime; by metonymy, an object of reproach, a criminal

crīminōsus, -a, -um: slanderous, full of reproach; worthy of reproach, contemptible

crīnālis, -e: of or related to hair

crīnis, -is, m.: a lock of hair; pl., hair

crispō (1): to curl, crimp, make uneven; wave, brandish

crista, -ae, f.: a crest; plume

croceus, -a, -um: of or related to saffron; saffron colored, yellow

cruciābilis, -e: excruciating, torturous

crūdescō, -ere: to become savage

crūdus, -a, -um: uncooked, raw, undigested; rough, savage

cruentō (1): to make bloody; defile

cruentus, -a, -um: bloody

crumīna, -ae, f.: a money-bag, purse

cruor, -ōris, m.: blood, gore

crūs, crūris, n.: a leg

crux, crucis, f.: a wooden frame for execution, a cross

crystallum, -ī, n.: ice, crystal

cūiās, cūiātis: interr. adj., of what place? whose?

culpa, -ae, f.: blame, guilt; wrongdoing, a wrong

cultūra, -ae, f.: cultivation; religious observance, worship

cultus, -ūs, m.: cultivation; (personal) care, grooming, adornment

cum: prep. w/abl., with

cum: rel. adv., when, since, although

cumque: indef. suffix and adv., -ever, -soever

cumulō (1): to pile up; accumulate; make complete

cumulus, -ī, m.: a heap, pile

cunctor (1): to delay, hesitate

cunctus, -a, -um: the whole of, all

cuneus, -ī, m.: a wedge; a wedge-shaped formation of soldiers

cupīdineus, -a, -um: of or related to lust

cupīdō, -inis, m.: desire, lust

cupiō, -ere, cupīuī, cupītum: to desire, wish, want

cūra, -ae, f.: care, concern; attention; anxiety, trouble

cūrō (1): to care, be concerned

currus, -ūs, m.: a chariot, car

cursus, -ūs, m.: running; a charge, onrush

curuus, -a, -um: curved, bent, winding

cuspis, -idis, f.: a point; the pointed end of a spear; a spear

cutis, cutis, f.: skin

cȳaneus, -a, -um: dark blue

cyathus, -ī, m.: a small ladle for wine

cymbalum, -ī, n.: a cymbal

damnō (1): to pass judgment, condemn

damnum, -ī, n.: a loss; something that is lost

daps, dapis, f.: a sacrificial feast, banquet

dator, -ōris, m.: a giver, provider

Dauid, indecl., m.: the second king of the Jews

dē: prep. w/abl., down from, from, concerning, about; with

dēbeō, -ēre, dēbuī, dēbitus: to owe, ought, must

dēcēdō, -cēdere, -cēssī, -cēssum: to go away, depart, withdraw

decet, -ēre, decuit: impers., to be suitable, be fitting, be right

decor, decōris, m.: what is fitting, elegance, grace, ornament

decōrus, -a, -um: fitting, proper; elegant, beautiful

dēcrepitus, -a, -um: very old, decrepit

decus, decoris, n.: splendor, glory, honor

dēdecus, -oris, n.: dishonor, disgrace

dēditiō, -ōnis, f.: surrender

defendō, -fendere, -fendī, -fensum: to defend, protect

dēferō, -ferre, -tulī, -lātum: to bring down, drive down

dēfīgō, -fīgere, -fīxī, -fīxum: to fix down in, stick down; focus

defluō, -fluere, -fluxī, -fluxum: to flow down

dēgener, dēgeneris: base, lowborn; degenerate, degraded

dēgenerō (1): to fall to a lower standard; debase oneself

dēiciō, -icere, -iēcī, -iectum: to throw down, knock down, cast down

deinde: adv., then, next, afterward (often in a list after *primum*, etc.)

dēlibūtus, -a, -um: annointed, thickly smeared

dēlicia, -ae, f.: a pleasure; a toy

dens, dentis, m.: a tooth

dēpellō, -pellere, -pulī, -pulsum: to push off, push away; drive off

dēpōnō, -pōnere, -posuī, -positum: to put away, lay down

dēprendō, -prendere, -prendī, -prensum: to seize, catch; detect, uncover

dēpugnō (1): to fight out, fight to the end

descendō, -scendere, -scendī, -scensum: to go down, descend

dēserō, -serere, -seruī, -sertum: to leave, depart, desert

dēsidia, -ae, f.: idleness, inactivity; laziness

dēsiliō, -silīre, -siluī: to leap down, jump down

dēsinō, -sinere, -sīuī, -situm: to stop, desist

dēsistō, -sistere, -stitī, -stitum: to leave off, cease

despectō, -āre: to look down at; look down on, despise

despuō, -ere: to spit down; spit out

dēsum, dēsse, dēfuī: to be lacking, want, fail

dēterior, -ius: inferior, less desirable, worse

dētestor (1): to call down a curse on; loath, detest

dētrūdō, -trūdere, -trūsī, -trūsum: to drive off, thrust away

deus, -ī, m.: god

dexter, -tera, -terum: right (as opposed to left); propitious

dextra, -ae, f.: right hand; force

diadēma, -atis, n.: a headband, diadem

diciō, -ōnis, f.: sovereignty, authority; power

dicō (1): to proclaim; dedicate, devote

dīcō, dīcere, dīxī, dīctum: to say, speak

dictum, -ī, n.: a word, saying

diēs, diēī, m. or f.: a day; daylight

difficilis, -e: difficult, labored

dignor (1): to regard as worthy or fitting

dignus, -a, -um: worthy, appropriate

dīlaniō (1): to tear to pieces

dīmētior, -mētīrī, -mēnsus: to measure out

dīmicō (1): to struggle, contend in battle

dīripiō, -ripere, -ripuī, -reptum: to pull apart; steal, plunder

dīrus, -a, -um: fearful, dreadful, terrible

dīs, dītis: rich, wealthy

discēdō, -cēdere, -cēssī, -cēssum: to go away, disband

discindō, -scindere, -scindī, -scissum: to tear apart, divide

discingō, -cingere, -cinxī, -cinctum: to ungird, disarm

discipulus, -ī, m.: a learner, disciple

discō, -ere, didicī: to learn, come to know

discolor, -ōris: of different colors, varied

discordia, -ae, f.: dissension, discord, strife

discors, -rdis: conflicting, discordant; inconsistent

discrīmen, -inis, n.: a separating line, distinction; crisis, risk, danger

dispergō, -spergere, -spersī, -spersum: to scatter, disperse

dispōnō, -pōnere, -posuī, -positum: to set in order, arrange; assign; manage

disserō, -serere, -seruī, -sertum: to set in order; discuss, offer an analysis

dissideō, -sidēre, -sēdī: to sit apart, be divided; disagree

dissimulō (1): to disguise, conceal

dissipātor, -ōris, m.: one who scatters or separates; destroyer

dissipō (1): to scatter; disperse, dissipate

dissociābilis, -e: dividing; incompatible; separable

dissonus, -a, -um: dissonant, discordant; different

distendō, -tendere, -tendī, -tentum: to stretch; fill, expand

distinctus, -a, -um: distinct, different, separate

distō, -stāre: to stand apart, be distant; be different

dītō (1): to enrich, make wealthy

diū: adv., for a long time

dīuus, -a, -um: divine; godly

dīues, -itis: rich, wealthy

dīuidō, -uidere, -uīsī, -uīsum: to separate, divide, break up

dīuīnus, -a, -um: of or belonging to a god, divine

dīuitiae, -ārum f. pl.: riches, wealth

diurnus, -a, -um: of or related to the daytime; daily

dō, dare, dedī, datum: to give; allow

doceō, docēre, docuī, doctum: to teach, instruct

doctor, -ōris, m.: an instructor, teacher

dogma, -atis, n.: doctrine, teaching

dolātus, -ūs, m.: carving, cutting

doleō, -ēre, doluī, dolitum: to be in pain; grieve

dolor, -ōris, m.: pain; grief

dolus, -ī, m.: a trick, treachery

domesticus, -a, -um: of or related to the home, domestic; internal

domina, -ae, f.: a mistress, a female ruler

dominor (1): to rule, exercise dominion

dominus, -ī, m.: a master, lord, the Lord

domō, -āre, domuī, domitum: to subdue, tame

domus, -ī, f.: a home, one's home

dōnārium, -iī, n.: the storeroom in a temple for votive offerings

donec: conj., until

dōnō (1): to give, reward with; forgive

dōnum, -ī, n.: a gift

dōs, dōtis, f.: a dowry given by the bride to the groom; wedding gift

dubius, -a, -um: uncertain; doubtful

dūcō, -ere, dūxī, dūctum: to lead

ductor, -ōris, m.: a commander, leader

dūdum: adv., long, long ago

duellum, -ī, n.: archaic form for *bellum*, war

dulcimodus, -a, -um: sweetly modulated

dulcis, -e: sweet; pleasant

dum: conj., as, as long as; since; w/historical present, while; w/subj., provided that; w/ind. or subj., until

duodēnī, -ae, -a: consisting of or related to twelve

duplex, -icis: double, two-sided

dūrō (1): to harden; endure, remain

dūrus, -a, -um: hard, harsh

dux, ducis, m.: a leader, general

ē, ex: prep. w/abl., out of, from

ēbibō, -bibere, -bibī, -bitum: to drink up

ēblandior, -blandīrī, -blandītus: to coax, soothe, charm

ēbrius, -a, -um: drunk, intoxicated

ebur, -oris, n.: ivory, something made of ivory

ecce: interj., look!

edax, -ācis: devouring, gluttonous, greedy

ēditus, -a, -um: elevated, lofty

edō, esse, ēdī, ēsum: to eat

ēdō, -ere, ēdidī, ēditum: to bring forth, produce

efferus, -a, -um: wild, savage

effigiēs, -ēī, f.: a statue; likeness; image

effigiō (1): to fashion, form

effodiō, -fodere, fōdī, -fossum: to dig up, dig out

effor (1): to declare, say

effrēnis, -e: unbridled; unrestrained

effundō, -fundere, -fūdī, -fūsum: to pour out

egēnus, -a, -um: needy; deprived of

egeō, egēre, eguī: to need, lack

ego, meī: pers. pron., I, me

ēgregius, -a, -um: extraordinary, excellent, illustrious

ēlectrum, -ī, n.: amber; an alloy of gold and silver

ēliciō, -licere, -licuī, -licitum: to lure out, coax; draw forth

ēlīdō, -līdere, -līsī, -līsum: to crush, shatter

ēligō, -ligere, -lēgī, -lectum: to pick out, choose, select

ēlumbis, -e: having a dislocated hip; weak

emblēma, -atis, n.: inlaid work, ornamentation

ēmicō (1): to flash out, shoot out

ēmoueō, -mouēre, -mōuī, -mōtum: to remove, expel

ēn: interj., look! see! behold!

enim: postpos. conj., for, truly, indeed

ensis, ensis, m.: a sword

eō, īre, īuī, itum: to go, move

ephēbus, -ī, m.: a youth, young man

epulae, -ārum, f. pl.: a banquet

equa, -ae, f.: a mare, a female horse

eques, -itis, m. or f.: a rider; horse-soldier; knight

equīnus, -a, -um: of or related to a horse

equus, -ī, m.: a horse

erēmus, -ī, m.: (Gr.) a wasteland, desert

ergo: adv., therefore

ērigō, -rigere, -rexī, -rectum: to raise up; set up, erect

Erīnys, -yos, f.: a Fury; a terror

ēripiō, -ripere, -ripuī, -reptum: to pull away, tear away

errō (1): to wander; err

error, -ōris, m.: a wandering; a mistake, error

ērumpō, -rumpere, -rūpī, -ruptum: to burst forth, break out

esca, -ae, f.: food

et: conj., and, also; *et . . . et*, both . . . and

etiam: adv., and also, even now, even

ēuentus, -ūs, m.: outcome, result

Eumenis, -idos, f.: (Gr.) a Fury

ēuomō, -uomere, -uomuī, -uomitum: to vomit; pour forth

exarmō (1): to disarm

excellens, -ntis: towering, outstanding

excidō, -cidere, -cidī: to fall out, slip; escape from memory

excīdō, -cīdere, -cīdī, -cīsum: to cut out, cut down

excipiō, -ere, -cēpī, -ceptum: to take out, draw out; take up, receive, catch

excitō (1): to rouse; raise; stimulate, provoke, excite

exclāmō (1): to shout out, exclaim

excutiō, -cutere, -cussī, -cussum: to shake off, throw (from a horse), knock down

exedō, -esse, -ēdī, -ēsum: to eat up, devour

exemplum, -ī, n.: an example; model

exerceō, -ercēre, -ercuī, -ercitum: to train; practice, exercise, move vigorously; enact, produce

exerō, -erere, -eruī, -ertum: to push out; uncover, unsheathe

exfībulō (1): to unfasten, unbuckle

exhālō (1): to breathe out, exhale

exigō, -igere, -ēgī, -actum: to drive out; complete, finish

exim: adv., after that, then, next

exitium, -iī, n.: destruction

exorior, -orīrī, -ōrtus: to appear; arise

exōticus, -a, -um: from abroad, foreign

expauescō, -pauescere, -pāuī: to be frightened; be afraid of

expectō (1): to await, expect

expediō, -īre, -īuī, -ītum: to free, release

experior, -īrī, expertus: to try, test; learn from experience

expers, -rtis: devoid of, without a share in

expiō (1): to purify

expleō, -plēre, -plēuī, -plētum: to fill up, satisfy

explicō, -plicāre, -plicuī, -plicitum: to unwind; stretch out, extend

expōnō, -pōnere, -posuī, -positum: to put out, expose

expugnō (1): to defeat in battle

exquīrō, -quīrere, -quīsīuī, -quīsitum: to ask about, inquire into

exsanguis, -e: bloodless, lacking blood; pale; weak

exsors, -rtis: having no share in; having no part in

exstimulō (1): to goad; stir up

exstruō, -struere, -struxī, -structum: to heap up, build up; construct

extimus, -a, -um: outermost, furthest

extinguō, -tinguere, -tinxī, -tinctum: to extinguish, put out; kill; wipe out

extorqueō, -torquēre, -torsī, -tortum: to wring out; tear away

extrā: prep. w/acc., beyond

extrēmus, -a, -um: outermost, furthest part of

exul, -ulis, m.: an exile

exultō (1): to leap up; exult, rejoice

exuō, -uere, -uī, -ūtum: to take off; lay bare

exuuiae, -ārum, f. pl.: armor won in battle; spoils

faciēs, -ēī, f.: a figure; face; appearance

facilis, -e: easy; easy to move or influence; agile

faciō, facere, fēcī, factum: to make; do; cause

factum, -ī, n.: a deed, action

faenus, -oris, n.: interest; profit

falanx, -ngis, f.: a phalanx, a band of soldiers

falerātus, -a, -um: decorated with phalerae (i.e., disc-shaped ornamentation); decorated, ornamented

Falernum, -ī, n.: Falernian wine (produced in northern Campania)

fallax, -ācis: deceptive, treacherous

fallō, -ere, fefellī, falsum: to deceive, trick

fāma, -ae, f.: a rumor, common talk; fame

fāmōsus, -a, -um: much discussed, famous

famula, -ae, f.: a serving woman, maid

famulus, -ī, m.: a servant, attendant

fantasma, -atis, n.: an apparition, phantom

faretra, -ae, f.: a quiver

fās, indecl., n.: what is divinely ordained, right

fascis, -is, m.: a bundle, load; often of the bundle of rods and an ax carried before Roman magistrates

fastīdium, -iī, n.: aversion or weariness; disgust, disdain

fastīgium, -iī, n.: a peak, top; pointed roof, roof

fastus, -ūs, m.: pride, arrogance

fatīgō (1): to tire out, weary; harass

fatiscō, -ere: to split open, gape; grow weak, fail

faucēs, -ium, f. pl.: a throat; an entrance

fauilla, -ae, f.: ash

fauus, -ī, m.: a honeycomb

fax, facis, f.: a torch

faxō, arch. fut. perf. of *facio*

fel, fellis, n.: a gallbladder; bile; poison; bitterness

fēlīx, -īcis: fruitful; lucky; happy; blessed

fēmina, -ae, f.: a woman

fērālis, -e: funereal, of or related to death

ferculum, -ī, n.: a tray; a dish of food

ferīnus, -a, -um: of or related to wild animals

feriō, -īre: to strike, knock

feritās, -ātis, f.: wildness, ferocity

ferō, ferre, tulī, lātum: to bear, carry; endure; report, say, call; pass., be carried, proceed, go

ferox, ferōcis: bold; fierce; savage

ferrātus, -a, -um: covered with iron; made of iron

ferreus, -a, -um: made of iron; hard, cruel

ferrūgineus, -a, um: the color of iron rust, dark red, violet

ferrum, -ī, n.: iron; a sword

fertilis, -e: fruitful, fertile

ferueō, -ēre, ferbuī: to be hot, be boiling; to burn or glow; rage

feruidus, -a, -um: boiling, seething; hot

feruor, -ōris, m.: heat; a warm period; ardor

festus, -a, -um: festal, festive

fētus, -ūs, m.: offspring; offshoot, branch

fibra, -ae, f.: a fiber; a segment of the entrails

fībula, -ae, f.: a pin, brooch

fidēlis, -e: faithful, loyal, trustworthy

fidēs, fideī, f.: faith

fīdō, -ere, fīsus: trust, have confidence in

fīdus, -a, -um: faithful, trustworthy, true

fīgō, -ere, fīxī, fīxum: to drive in, fix

figūra, -ae, f.: a figure; outline; a type (in Christian interpretation)

figūrō (1): to form, represent; prefigure

fīlius, -iī, m.: a son

fīlum, -ī, n.: a thread, cord

fīnis, -is, m.: an end, limit

fiō, fierī, factum: to take place, happen; be made, become

firmō (1): to make firm

firmus, -a, -um: strong, firm

fiscus, -ī, m.: a basket; money bag; the public treasury

fissus, -a, -um: divided, split

flagellum, -ī, n.: a whip

flagrō (1): to burn, blaze; rage

flamma, -ae, f.: a flame, fire; burning passion, desire

flammeolum, -ī, n.: a small bridal veil

flammeus, -a, -um: flaming, fiery

flammicomus, -a, -um: with fiery hair, flaming

flammō (1): to set ablaze, inflame

flātus, -ūs, m.: a blowing; breath

flectō, -ere, flexī, flexum: to bend, turn; turn aside, change

flexūra, -ae, f.: a bending; a curve

flōreō, -ēre, flōruī: to flower, blossom; flourish

flōrifer, -era, -erum: flowering

flōs, -ōris, m.: a flower

fluctus, -ūs, m.: a wave, billow

fluens, -ntis: flowing; loose, relaxed

fluitō (1): to flow; undulate

fluō, -ere, fluxī, fluxum: to flow, stream

fluuiālis, -e: of or related to a river

focus, -ī, m.: a fireplace, hearth; fire

foedō (1): to befoul, spoil

foedus, -a, -um: foul, loathsome

foedus, -eris, n.: an agreement, treaty

folium, -iī, n.: a leaf, petal

fons, -ntis, m.: a spring, fountain

fore = fut. infinitive of *sum*

forīs: adv., out of doors, outside

forma, -ae, f.: a form; pattern, model

formīdābilis, -e: frightening, terrifying

formīdō, -inis, f.: terror, dread

formō (1): to form, shape

fornax, -ācis, f.: a furnace, kiln

forō (1): to drill through, bore, pierce

fors, fortis, f.: chance

fors: adv., by chance, perhaps

fortasse: adv., perhaps

forte: adv., by chance

fortis, forte: strong; brave

fortūna, -ae, f.: fortune

forum, -ī, n.: a public square, forum, city center

fossa, -ae, f.: a ditch, trench

Fotinus, -ī, m.: an eastern bishop of the fourth century who was
    denounced as a heretic

fouea, -ae, f.: a pit (often used to trap animals)

foueō, -ēre, fōuī, fōtum: to snuggle, keep warm; comfort; support,
    cherish; frequent, inhabit

fragilis, -e: brittle, flimsy

fragmen, -inis, n.: a fragment

fragmentum, -ī, n.: a fragment

framea, -ae, f.: (old Germ.) a spear; a sword

frangō, -ere, frēgī, fractum: to break, crush; exhaust, break down

frāter, -tris, m.: a brother

fraus, fraudis, f.: deception, fraud

fremō, -ere, fremuī, fremitum: to roar, growl, howl

frendō, -ere, frenduī, frēsum: to grind or gnash one's teeth

frēnō (1): to rein in, check

frēnum, -ī, n. and frēnī, -ōrum, m. pl.: a bridle or harness, restraint

frequens, -ntis: crowded, closely spaced

fretum, -ī, n.: a channel; the sea, the deep

frīgidus, -a, -um: cold, frigid

frīuolus, -a, -um: trivial, trifling

frondens, -ntis: full of leaves, leafy

frons, -ndis, f.: a leafy branch, foliage

frons, -ntis, f.: a forehead, brow; front, facing side

frūgī: indecl. adj., moral, worthy; thrifty, moderate

frustātim: adv., piecemeal, bit by bit

frustrā: adv., in vain

frustum, -ī, n.: a small piece or scrap (of food)

frutectum, -ī, n.: a thicket

fuga, -ae, f.: flight, fleeing

fugax, -ācis: prone to flee, runaway

fugiō, -ere, fūgī: to flee, run away, escape

fugitīuus, -a, -um: fugitive

fugō (1): to cause to flee

fulciō, -īre, fulsī, fultum: to prop up, support

fulcrum, -ī, n.: the supporting part of a couch

fulgeō, -ēre, fulsī: to flash, gleam

fulmen, -inis, n.: a thunderbolt; blast, blow

fuluus, -a, -um: a deep yellow color, brownish, tawny

fūmō (1): to emit smoke, steam

fūmus, -ī, m.: smoke

fūnālis, -e: of or related to rope

fundāmen, -inis, n.: a foundation

fundō, -ere, fūdī, fūsum: to pour out, spread out, let go; route

fundō (1): to lay the foundation of, found

fundus, -ī, m.: the bottom (of something), the depths (of the earth)

fūnus, -eris, n.: a funeral ceremony; a dead body; death, destruction

furia, -ae, f.: a Fury; madness, frenzy

furiālis, -e: of or related to a Fury

furō, -ere: to be mad, rage

furor, -ōris, m.: madness, rage

furtim: adv., secretly, stealthily

furtīuus, -a, -um: stolen; secret, hidden

furtum, -ī, n.: a robbery; stolen property; deception

galea, -ae, f.: a helmet

galeō (1): to furnish with a helmet

gānea, -ae, f.: a cheap restaurant, a dive

gaudeō, -ēre, gāuīsus sum: rejoice, delight

gaudium, -iī, n.: joy, delight

gāza, -ae, f.: a treasure

gehenna, -ae, f.: (Hebr.) hell

gelidus, -a, -um: icy, cold

gemitus, -ūs, m.: groaning, a sorrowful sound

gemma, -ae, f.: a precious stone, gem

gemmans, -ntis: decorated with jewels

gemō, -ere, gemuī, gemitum: to groan; bemoan

generōsus, -a, -um: of noble birth; magnanimous

genetrix, -īcis, f.: a mother, originator

genitor, -ōris, m.: a father, originator

gens, gentis, f.: a people, family; class; in Christian authors, Gentile

genu, -ūs, n.: a knee

genus, -eris, n.: origin, family; kind, class

germāna, -ae, f.: a sister

germānus, -ī, m.: a brother

germen, -inis, n.: a sprout, offshoot, bud

gerō, -ere, gessī, gestum: to bear, carry; carry out, do, wage (of war)

gestāmen, -inis, n.: an accoutrement, ornament; load, burden

gestiō, -īre, gestīuī: to desire to do something

gignō, -ere, genuī, genitum: to beget, produce

gladius, -iī, m.: a sword

globus, -ī, m.: a round body, a circular mass

gloria, -ae, f.: glory, fame, honor

glūtinō (1): to glue up, join together

Golīas, -ae, m.: Goliath, a giant killed by King David

Gomorra, -ae, f.: Gomorrah, a city in Canaan

gradior, -ī, gressus: to go, walk

gradus, -ūs, m.: step; pace; stair; stage, position

grāmen, -inis, n.: grass

grāmineus, -a, -um: grassy

grandis, -e: big, grand, lofty

grassor (1): to advance, march on

grātēs, -ium, f. pl.: thanks

grauidus, -a, -um: heavy; weighed down

grauis, -e: heavy; burdened; severe

gremium, -iī, n.: one's lap; fold (of a garment), pocket

gressus, -ūs, m.: a step, pace

grex, gregis, m.: a flock, herd

gula, -ae, f.: one's throat

gurges, -itis, m.: a whirlpool, stream, flood

gustātus, -ūs, m.: taste

gustō (1): to taste, eat a little of

guttur, -uris, n.: a gullet, throat

habēna, -ae, f.: a rein

habeō, habēre, habuī, habitum: to have, hold, possess

habitātor, -ōris, m.: an inhabitant

habitus, -ūs, m.: condition, manner; appearance, outfit

hāctenus: adv., up to this point

haereō, -ēre, haesī, haesum: to stick, cling, stand still

hālitus, -ūs, m.: a vapor, breath

hāmus, -ī, m.: a hook; a link in chain-mail armor

harēna, -ae, f.: sand

harundō, -inis, f.: a reed; an arrow; a measuring stick

hasta, -ae, f.: a spear

hastīle, -is, n.: the shaft of a spear; a spear

haud: part., not

haudquaquam: adv., not in any way

hauriō, -īre, hausī, haustum: to draw up, drink, swallow, drain

haustus, -ūs, m.: a draft, drink

hebes, -etis: dull, dim

herbidus, -a, -um: of or like grass

hērēs, -ēdis, m.: an heir, successor

heresis, -is, f.: (Gk.) a sect; heresy

hērōs, -ōos, m.: (Gk.) a hero

heu: interj., alas

hiātus, -ūs, m.: a gaping, a gap

hīc: adv., here

hic, haec, hoc: demonst. adj. and pron., this

Hierūsāles, indecl., **f.**: the city of Jerusalem

hilaris, -e: cheerful, glad

hinc: adv., from this place, hence

hiō (1): to gape open, yawn

hirsūtus, -a, -um: covered with hair, bristly

holocaustum, -ī, n.: a whole burnt offering

homō, -inis, m.: a human being, man

honestās, -ātis, f.: honorableness, nobility; integrity

honestus, -a, -um: esteemed, honored; honorable, respectable

honor, -ōris, m.: honor, repute, esteem; largess, honorary gift, ornament

hōra, -ae, f.: an hour, the hour

horreō, -ēre, horruī: to bristle, tremble in fear; fear, be afraid of

horridus, -a, -um: bristly, rough; a source of trembling, horrid

horrificus, -a, -um: making or causing trembling

hospes, -itis, m.: a host; guest; stranger

hospes, -itis: related to a host or a guest; foreign

hospita, -ae, f.: a host; guest; stranger

hostia, -ae, f.: a sacrificial victim, sacrifice

hosticus, -a, -um: of or related to an enemy

hostīlis, -e: of the enemy, hostile

hostis, -is, m. or f.: an enemy, public enemy

hūc: adv., to this place, hither

hūmānus, -a, -um: human

humilis, -e: lowly, humble

humus, -ī, f. loc. **humī**: ground, soil

hymnus, -ī, m.: a song of praise, a hymn

iaceō, iacēre, iacuī, iacitum: to lie, lie low, lie dead

iaciō, iacere, iēcī, iactum: to throw, toss, cast; build, establish

iactans, -ntis: boasting, bragging

iactō (1): to throw, toss about; brandish; brag, boast

iactūra, -ae, f.: a throwing away, waste, loss

iactus, -ūs, m.: throwing, a throw, a casting

iaculum, -ī, n.: a dart, javelin, spear

iam: adv., now, at that point (past or future)

iānua, -ae, f.: a door, entrance

iaspis, -idis, f.: a precious green stone, jasper

ictus, -ūs, m.: striking, a blow, a thrust

īdem, eadem, idem: demonst. adj., the same

īdōlum, -ī, n.: an image; idol

iecur, iecoris, n.: a liver (often as the source of passion)

iēiūnium, -iī, n.: a fast, fasting

Ierichō, indecl., f.: the city of Jericho

Iēsūs, Iēsū, m. dat. Iēsū: Jesus

igitur: conj., therefore

ignārus, -a, -um: not knowing, unaware, ignorant

igneus, -a, -um: fiery

ignis, -is, m.: fire

ignōrō (1): to not know, be unaware; ignore, disregard

īlia, īlium, n. pl.: the belly; entrails; groin

ille, illa, illud: demonst. adj. and pron., that, those

illīc: adv., there, at that place

illūc: adv., to that place, thither

imāgo, -inis, f.: an image, representation, imitation (often with the idea of falseness)

imber, imbris, m.: rain, a storm, shower

immo: no, nay (correcting a previous idea)

imperium, -iī, n.: command, power, control

īmus, -a, -um: lowest, lowest part of

in: prep. w/abl., in, on; w/acc., into, onto

inamābilis, -e: unlovable; without love

inānis, -e: empty; useless, worthless

inbellis, -e: unwarlike, not suited to war

inbuō, -buere, -buī, -būtum: to drench, imbue, stain; initiate, instruct

incalēscō, -calēscere, -caluī: to grow warm, become excited

incautus, -a, -um: incautious, heedless

incendium, -iī, n.: a fire, blaze (sometimes of strong passion)

incendō, -cendere, -cendī, -cēnsum: to set on fire, inflame

incertus, -a, -um: uncertain; unclear

incessus, -ūs, m.: walking; a gait, manner of walking

incestus, -a, -um: unchaste, lewd; impure, polluted

incidō, -cidere, -cidī, -cāsum: to fall into or onto

incīdō, -cīdere, -cīdī, -cīsum: to cut into, cut through

incipiō, -cipere, -cēpī, -ceptum: to begin

incircumcīsus, -a, -um: uncircumcised

inclīnō (1): to bend down; pass., be driven back, decline

inclūdō, -clūdere, -clūsī, -clūsum: to enclose, shut up, surround

inclytus, -a, -um: famous, renowned

incolumis, -e: unharmed, intact

increpitō (1): to call out, chide, reproach

increpō (1): to resound, roar; exclaim, reproach

incursus, -ūs, m.: an onrush, attack

inde: adv., thence, from that point, then

index, -icis, m.: an informant, witness; indication, proof

indigena, -ae, m.: a native, an original inhabitant

indigus, -a, -um: needy

indoctus, -a, -um: untaught, unlearned

indolēs, -is, f.: a natural quality, disposition

indomitus, -a, -um: untamed, unconquered

indubitātus, -a, -um: undoubted, undoubting

indulgens, -ntis: kind, indulgent

induō, -duere, -duī, -dūtum: to put on

induuiae, -ārum, f. pl.: clothes, garments

ineffābilis, -e: unspeakable, ineffable

inēnarrābilis, -e: indescribable, inexpressible

ineō, -īre, -iī, -itum: to go in, enter

inermus, -a, -um: unarmed; peaceable

iners, -rtis: artless, clumsy; lazy, idle

infāmis, -e: of ill repute, infamous

infēlix, -īcis: unproductive; unlucky; wretched

inferciō, -fercīre, -fersī, -ferctum: to stuff in, cram in

inferō, -ferre, -tulī, illātum: to bring forward, impose; advance

infestus, -a, -um: hostile, dangerous

inficiō, -ficere, -fēcī, -fectum: to dye, color; discolor, stain

infirmus, -a, -um: weak, unsteady

infit: begin; begin to speak; say

infitiātrix, -īcis, f.: one who denies something, esp. one who refuses to
pay a debt

inflātus, -a, -um: puffed up, inflated; conceited

infractus, -a, -um: broken, disjointed; weak, dissolute

infundō, -fundere, -fūdī, -fūsum: to pour in, moisten, infuse

ingemō, -gemere, -gemuī: to groan, bewail

ingenium, -iī, n.: a natural quality; mental ability; mind

ingens, -ntis: huge, enormous, great

ingerō, -gerere, -gessī, -gestum: to put on or into; inflict; thrust, throw

ingluuiēs, -ēī, f.: the jaws (of an animal), throat, neck; gluttony, greed

ingredior, -gredī, -gressus: to go in, approach; embark on, begin

ingressus, -ūs, m.: entering, an advance, walking; an entryway,
entrance

inhiō (1): to open the mouth wide; be astonished at; desire, covet

inimīcus, -a, -um: unfriendly, hostile

inlābor, -lābī, -lāpsus: to glide in, flow in; fall in, descend

inlecebra, -ae, f.: an allurement, enticement, attraction; delight

inlex, -icis: alluring, enticing, seductive

inlīdō, -līdere, -līsī, -līsum: to strike, dash, crush

inlūdō, -lūdere, -lūsī, -lūsum: to play at, play with, mock

inlustrō (1): to shine light on; make famous or renowned

inmānis, -e: savage, monstrous, huge

inmemor, -oris: not mindful of, forgetful

inmensus, -a, -um: immeasurable, immense

inmoror (1): to stay, remain

inmortālis, -e: immortal, imperishable

inmōtus, -a, -um: unmoved, undisturbed

inmundus, -a, -um: unclean, squalid

inmūnis, -e: exempt from, free from

innātus, -a, -um: unborn, uncreated, innate

innecto, -nectere, -nexuī, -nexum: to fasten onto; tie up

innocuus, -a, -um: guiltless, innocent

innumerus, -a, -um: innumerable

innuptus, -a, -um: unmarried, chaste

inoffensus, -a, -um: unobstructed, without obstacle

inopīnus, -a, -um: unexpected

inops, inopis: lacking in wealth, poor; destitute of, devoid of

inornātus, -a, -um: undecorated, plain

inpācātus, -a, -um: not subdued, not peaceful, restless

inpār, -pāris: unequal, uneven, not a match for

inpatiens, -ntis: impatient

inpediō, -pedīre, -pedīuī, -pedītum: to restrict, impede, obstruct

inpendō, -pendere, -pendī, -pensum: to expend, pay out; devote; use up

inpenetrābilis, -e: impenetrable

inperterritus, -a, -um: unterrified

inpingō, -pingere, -pēgī, -pactum: to force in, drive in

inpius, -a, -um: impious, wicked

inpleō, -plēre, -plēuī, -plētum: to fill, fill up

inplicō (1): to enwrap, entangle

inpōnō, -pōnere, -posuī, -positum: to put or place on, put to

inportūnus, -a, -um: unsuitable, unfavorable; troublesome, perverse

inpos, inpotis: not having control of

inpressus, -ūs, m.: an impression, a crushing, weight

inprobus, -a, -um: inferior; wicked, unrighteous

inpulsus, -ūs, m.: a pushing, blow, impact

inpune: adv., with impunity; without danger

inquam, third-pers. sing. **inquit**: say

inque: *in + que*

inritus, -a, -um: unratified, unrealized; ineffectual, in vain

insānus, -a, -um: unsound, crazy, insane, raging

insatiābilis, -e: that cannot be satisfied, insatiable

insatiātus, -a, -um: unsatisfied, insatiate

inscrībō, -scrībere, -scrīpsī, -scrīptum: to write on, inscribe

insidior (1): to lie in ambush, make a surprise attack

insidiōsus, -a, -um: treacherous, dangerous

insigne, -is, n.: a distinctive mark, an honor, standard, sign

insignis, -e: visible, prominent; remarkable, distinguished

insiliō, -silīre, -siluī: to jump on, leap into

insolitus, -a, -um: unaccustomed, unusual

insomnia, -ae, f.: sleeplessness, insomnia

inspiciō, -spicere, -spexī, -spectum: to observe, look at, examine

inspīrō (1): to breath in, infuse, inspire

instabilis, -e: unstable, unsteady

instaurō (1): to renew, restore

instituō, -stituere, -stituī, -stitūtum: to set up, establish, institute

instō, -stāre, -stitī, -stātum: to stand on, press hard on

instruō, -struere, -struxī, -structum: to organize; equip, fit out

insurgō, -surgere, -surrexī: to rise up, get up

intactus, -a, -um: untouched, uninjured, unspoiled

intendō, -tendere, -tendī, -tentum: to stretch, lengthen, extend; direct

intentō (1): to hold out, stretch out

inter: prep. w/acc., between, among

intercīdō, -cīdere, -cīdī, -cīsum: to cut through, cut up, divide

intercipiō, -cipere, -cēpī, -ceptum: to cut off, interrupt, intercept, separate

intereā: adv., meanwhile

interficiō, -ficere, -fēcī, -fectum: to destroy, kill

interfūsus, -a, -um: poured within, suffused

interimō, -imere, -ēmī, -emptum: to do away with, kill

interior, -ius: inner, the inner part of

interitus, -ūs, m.: death, destruction, ruin

interlinō, -linere, -lēuī, -litum: to smear between, spread between; insert

interlūceō, -lūcēre, -lūxī: to shine between

internoscō, -noscere, -nōuī, -nōtum: to distinguish, discern

interserō, -serere, -seruī, -sertum: to put between, insert, interpose

intertexō, -texere, -texuī, -textum: to interweave, intertwine

interueniō, -uenīre, -uēnī, -uentum: to come between, mediate

intimus, -a, -um: inmost, intimate, profound

intonsus, -a, -um: uncut, unshaven

intorqueō, -torquēre, -torsī, -tortum: to bend round, turn toward, twist

intrō (1): to go in, enter

introitus, -ūs, m.: an entering, entrance, entryway

introrsum: adv., inwardly, within, inside

intuitus, -ūs, m.: a gaze, sight, looking

intus: adv., within

inuadō, -uadere, -uasī, -uasum: to invade; attack

inualidus, -a, -um: weak, feeble

inuehō, -uehere, -uexī, -uectum: to carry in, bring in; pass., ride in

inuictus, -a, -um: unconquered; invincible

inuideō, -uidēre, -uīdi, -uīsum: to look at spitefully, envy, be jealous of

inuidus, -a, -um: ill-willed, hostile; jealous

inuitiābilis, -e: incorruptible, inviolable

inuoluō, -uoluere, -uoluī, -uolūtum: to roll, curl; envelop, wrap up, overwhelm

Iōb, indecl., m.: the long-suffering title character of the book of Job from the Hebrew scriptures

iocus, -ī, m.: a joke, jest, diversion

Ionatham, indecl., m.: a son of the Hebrew king Saul

Iordānis, -is, m.: the Jordan River in Judea

ipse, ipsa, ipsum: intensive adj. and pron., himself, herself, itself, themselves; the very

īra, -ae, f.: anger, rage

iste, ista, istud: demonst. adj. and pron., that of yours, that; this

Istrāhel, -ēlis, m.: Israel

iter, itineris, n.: a journey; a path, way

iterum: adv., again

ito = fut. imperat. of *eo*

iuba, -ae, f.: an animal's mane, hair on the neck

iubeō, -ēre, iussī, iussum: to order, bid, command

Iūda, -ae, m.: Judah, one of the twelve sons of Jacob; one of the twelve tribes of Israel

iūdex, iūdicis, m.: a judge, arbiter

Iudith, indecl., f.: a Hebrew woman renowned for killing Holofernes

iūgerum, -ī, n.: an acre, a unit of land 240 by 120 Roman feet

iugulum, -ī, n.: a throat

iugum, -ī, n.: a yoke, yoke of bondage; ridge

iungō, -ere, iunxī, iunctum: to bring together, join

iūrātus, -a, -um: agreed under oath, sworn, bound by oath

iūs, iūris, n.: law; right; authority

iustitia, -ae, f.: justice

iustus, -a, -um: lawful, just

iuuenis, -is, m.: a young man

iuuenta, -ae, f.: youth

iuuentūs, -ūtis, f.: young persons, the youth

iuuō, iuuāre, iūuī, iūtum: to help, benefit; please, delight

iuxtā: adv., nearby

labefaciō, -facere, -fēcī, -factum: to make unsteady, shake, undermine

lābēs, -is, f.: a fall, collapse; a defect, corruption, stain

lābor, lābī, lāpsus: to slip, glide, fall

labor, -ōris, m.: labor, work

labrum, -ī, n.: a lip

lac, lactis, n.: milk

lacer, -era, -erum: torn, mangled, broken

lacertus, -ī, m.: the upper arm (from the shoulder to the elbow); strength

lacessō, -ere, lacessīuī, lacessītum: to challenge, provoke; harass

lacrimābilis, -e: deserving of tears, tearful

lacteolus, -a, -um: milk white

laedō, -ere, laesī, laesum: to injure, hurt, damage

laetus, -a, -um: flourishing; glad, happy

laeua, -ae, f.: the left hand

laeuus, -a, -um: left (as opposed to right)

lampas, -adis, f.: a torch, lamp, light

lancea, -ae, f.: a light spear

langueō, -ēre: to be faint, be weary, droop

languidus, -a, -um: faint, weak, languid

languor, -ōris, m.: weariness, sluggishness, idleness

lapillus, -ī, m.: a small stone, pebble

lapis, -idis, m.: a stone, stone

lapsō, -āre: to slip, slide

largus, -a, -um: generous, lavish, liberal

lascīuus, -a, -um: playful, frivolous; naughty, lascivious

lassō (1): to tire out, make weary

lātē: adv., far and wide

latebrōsus, -a, -um: full of hiding places; hidden

lateō, -ēre, latuī: to hide, be out of sight, be concealed

latitō (1): to continue to hide, be hidden

latus, lateris, n.: side

lauācrum, -ī, n.: a bath

lauō, -ere, lāuī, lōtum: to wash

laus, laudis, f.: praise, renown

laxus, -a, -um: wide, loose, relaxed

legiō, -ōnis, f.: a legion, a large unit of soldiers

legō, -ere, lēgī, lectum: to gather; choose, select

lentus, -a, -um: sluggish, slow, unresponsive, tardy

leō, leōnis, m.: a lion

lētālis, -e: deadly, lethal

lētum, -ī, n.: death (usually violent)

leuis, -e: light, weak, ineffectual; unreliable, fickle,

leuitās, -ātis, f.: lightness; inconstancy, fickleness

leuō (1): to lift up, lift off; lighten, relieve, free from

Leuuītis, -idis, m.: a Levite, a member of the Jewish tribe of Levi

lex, lēgis, f.: a law, rule; agreed or normal way, manner; the Mosaic law

libenter: adv., gladly, willingly

līber, -era, -erum: free, not servile; unrestrained, free from, unhindered by

līberō (1): to free, liberate, deliver

lībertās, -ātis, f.: freedom, liberty

libīdō, -inis, f.: a desire; pleasure; sexual desire, lust

lībrō (1): to balance, make level, poise

licet, -ēre, licuit, licitum: impers., to be permitted, allowed

lignum, -ī, n.: wood, timber; a piece of wood

ligō (1): to tie, bind

līlium, -iī, n.: a lily

līmen, -inis, n.: a threshold; entrance, entryway

limbus, -ī, m.: an ornamental border, fringe; a band, headband

līmes, limitis, m.: a boundary line, limit; route

līmus, -ī, m.: mud, slime

līnea, -ae, f.: a line; outline

lingua, -ae, f.: the tongue; an utterance, speech, language

linō, -ere, lēuī, litum: to smear, rub over, cover

linquō, -ere, līquī: to leave, leave behind

liquidus, -a, -um: liquid, fluid; clear, transparent, pure

litō (1): to obtain favorable omens, sacrifice successfully

lītus, -oris, n.: a shore, coast

lituus, -ī, m.: a curved staff; a curved war trumpet

locō (1): to put, place; station (of troops)

loculus, -ī, m.: a small place; a compartment, money box

locus, -ī, m.: a place, position

longe: adv., far, by far, afar

longus, -a, -um: long, extended, extensive

loquor, loquī, locūtus: to talk, speak

lōrīca, -ae, f.: a corselet, defensive armor

lōrum, -ī, n.: a leather strap; pl., reins

Lōth, indecl., m.: Lot, a nephew of Abraham

lūbricō (1): to make slippery, make uncertain

lūcidus, -a, -um: bright, shining

lūciferus, -a, -um: light bringing

lucror (1): to gain, acquire; profit
lucrum, -ī, n.: gain, profit
luctāmen, -inis, n.: a struggle, fight
luctor (1): to wrestle; struggle, fight
lūdibrium, -iī, n.: a plaything, toy; mockery, derision
lūdicrum, -ī, n.: a plaything, toy, trifle
lūdō, -ere, lūsī, lūsum: to play; play at, make sport of, mock
luis, -is, f.: a plague, pestilence, corruption
lūmen, -inis, n.: light; torch; eye
luō, -ere, luī: to release from debt, pay, atone for
lupa, -ae, f.: a she-wolf; prostitute
lupānar, -āris, n.: a brothel, a place for prostitution
lupātī, -ōrum, m. pl.: a horse's bit made with jagged teeth
lupus, -ī, m.: a wolf
lūteolus, -a, -um: yellow
lutulentus, -a, -um: muddy, dirty, filthy
lux, lūcis, f.: light; daylight, day
luxuria, -ae and **luxuriēs, -ēī, f.:** extravagance, excess, luxury
luxus, -ūs, m.: excess, pomp, luxuriousness

māchina, -ae, f.: a machine; structure
mactō (1): to honor; kill sacrificially, sacrifice
maculō (1): to stain, pollute
madefaciō, -facere, -fēcī, -factum: to make wet, soak
madeō, -ēre: to be wet
madidus, -a, -um: wet, drenched; drunk, tipsy
maestus, -a, -um: sad; sorrowful, grieving, grim
magistra, -ae, f.: a mistress; teacher
magnus, -a, -um: large, great; eminent, important
māiestās, -ātis, f.: majesty, grandeur, dignity
maior, maius: greater, larger; elder, ancestor
malĕ: adv., badly; hardly
malesuādus, -a, -um: counseling badly; seductive
malignus, -a, -um: mean, wicked; unkind, harmful

malus, -a, -um: bad, evil

mandō (1): to give, hand over, entrust

maneō, -ēre, mansī, mansum: to remain, await

mānēs, -ium, m. pl.: the spirits of the dead; the underworld

manicae, -ārum, f. pl.: handcuffs, manacles

maniplus, -ī, m.: a handful; an infantry unit, a maniple

manus, -ūs, f.: a hand (sometimes as a source of strength or force; *manū,* by force); an armed force or troop, band

mapālia, -ium, n. pl.: huts

marceō, -ēre: to be weak, droop, be languid

marcidus, -a, -um: languid, weak

margarītum, -ī, n.: a pearl

Maria, -ae, f.: Mary, the mother of Jesus

marīnus, -a, -um: of or related to the sea

marītus, -a, -um: married, wedded

marmoreus, -a, -um: of marble

Mars, Martis, m.: the Roman god of war; war, fighting (by metonymy)

marsuppium, -iī, n.: a bag, purse

martyr, -yris, m.: a witness; martyr

māter, -tris, f.: a mother

māteria, -ae, f.: lumber; matter; material

mātrōna, -ae, f.: a married woman, wife; a woman of high rank, matron

Māuors, -ortis, m.: the god Mars

maximus, -a, -um: greatest

mediocriter: adv., moderately, in a restrained manner, gently

meditāmen, -inis, n.: thinking, pondering

meditor (1): to think; contemplate, plan, intend

medius, -a, -um: middle, middle of, middling

mel, mellis, n.: honey

Melchīsedec, indecl., m.: a mysterious figure mentioned in the book of Genesis (the normal spelling now is Melchizedek)

melior, -ius: better

membrum, -ī, n.: a limb, member of the body; member, part

meminī, -isse: to remember

memor, -oris: mindful, remembering

memorābilis, -e: memorable

memorō (1): to call to mind, recall; call, name

mendax, -ācis: deceitful, lying

mens, mentis, f.: mind

mensa, -ae, f.: a table

mentior, -īrī, -ītus: to lie, cheat, deceive; counterfeit, imitate

mentum, -ī, n.: a chin

mercor (1): to trade, buy, purchase

mereō, -ēre, meruī, meritum: to earn, deserve

meretrix, -īcis: a prostitute, courtesan, harlot

mergō, -ere, mersī, mersum: to plunge, dip; flood, overwhelm; sink, drown

meritum, -ī, n.: an earned reward; merit; meritorious action or service

merum, -ī, n.: unmixed wine

metallum, -ī, n.: metal

mētor (1): to measure; measure off, mark out

metus, -ūs, m.: fear

meus, -a, -um: poss. adj., my, mine

micō, -āre, micuī: to quiver, vibrate; flash, gleam

mihi (mihī) = dat. of *ego*

mīles, mīlitis, m.: a soldier; soldiery, an army

mīlitia, -ae, f.: military service; soldiery, an army

mille, pl. mīlia: a thousand

minax, minācis: projecting; menacing; threatening

minister, -trī, m.: an attendant, servant

minor (1): to jut out; menace, threaten; boast

minor, minus: lesser, smaller, younger

minuō, -ere, minuī, minūtum: to reduce, diminish, subtract

minus: adv., less

minūtus, -a, -um: small, minute

mīror (1): to be amazed; gaze at, admire, wonder at

mīrus, -a, -um: wonderful, amazing

misceō, -ēre, miscuī, mixtum: to mix; mix up, confuse with; produce by mixing, concoct; share

miser, -era, -erum: wretched, unfortunate, miserable

miseror (1): to pity, feel compasion

missile, -is, n.: a projectile, missile

missus, -ūs, m.: a sending

mitra, -ae, f.: a headband, headdress

moderāmen, -inis, n.: control, guidance

moderor (1): to control, govern, restrain

modestia, -ae, f.: modesty

modestus, -a, -um: moderate, restrained, modest

modicus, -a, -um: moderate, small

modo: adv., only; now, just now

modulor (1): to modulate; play music, make music

modus, -ī, m.: a measure; proper amount; limit

moechus, -ī, m.: an adulterer, fornicator

moenia, -ium, n. pl.: defensive walls

molāris, -e: of or related to a mill; like a millstone, massive

mōlēs, -is, f.: mass, bulk, weight

molliō, -īre, molliuī, mollītum: to make soft, weaken, mollify

mollis, -e: soft; gentle, weak

monēta, -ae, f.: money, a coin

monīle, -is, n.: a necklace

mons, montis, m.: a mountain

monstrō (1): to show, point out, demonstrate

monstrum, -ī, n.: an evil omen, portent; monster

monumentum, -ī, n.: a trophy, monument, reminder

mora, -ae, f.: a delay

morbus, -ī, m.: sickness, disease

mordax, -ācis: biting, cutting

morior, -irī, mortuus: to die

moror (1): to delay, slow down; remain

mors, mortis, f.: death

mortālis, -e: subject or liable to death; human, mortal

mortifer, -era, -erum: death bringing, deadly

mōs, mōris, m.: custom; manner, way (*more,* in the manner of, like); pl., character, manners

moueō, -ēre, mōuī, mōtum: to move; affect, disturb

mox: adv., soon

mucrō, -ōnis, m.: a sharp point, a sword

mulceō, -ēre, mulsī, mulsum: to stroke, sooth, soften

mulier, -eris, f.: a woman

multiplex, -icis: of many parts, manifold, complex, compound

multiplicō (1): to multiply, increase

multus, -a, -um: many a, much, a lot of; pl., many

mundānus, -a, -um: of or related to the world, worldly, earthly

mundus, -ī, m.: the universe; the world, the earth

mūnia, -ium, n. pl.: duties, tasks

mūnus, -eris, n.: a task, duty; gift, offering, favor

mūrālis, -e: of or related to a wall

mutilō (1): to cut off, mutilate, diminish

mysticus, -a, -um: of the mysteries, sacred, mysterious, secret

nam: part., certainly, for

namque: conj., to be sure, for

nardum, -ī, n.: nard, nard oil, a fragrant oil

nascor, -ī, nātus: to be born, come into existence, arise

nātālis, -e: of or related to one's birth

natātus, -ūs, m.: swimming

nātīuus, -a, -um: born, created; native, inborn

nātūra, -ae, f.: nature; quality, character, inborn existence; the natural order, existing reality

nē: negative adv. and conj. used often with subjunctives and some other words, not, lest, in order that . . . not, etc.

-ne: interr. suffix attached to the emphatic word of a question or exclamation

nebulōsus, -a, -um: misty, foggy; obscure

nec, **neque**: conj., and not, neither

nectō, **-ere**, **nexī**, **nexum**: to weave together, tie

nefandus, **-a**, **-um**: unspeakable, wicked

nefās, indecl., **n.**: a sacrilege, crime, abomination

negō (1): to deny, refuse

negōtium, **-iī**, **n.**: work, business

nempe: part., certainly, of course

nepōs, **-ōtis**, **m.**: a grandson, descendant

nēquīquam: adv., in vain, to no purpose

neruus, **-ī**, **m.**: a sinew, muscle; cord, bowstring; pl., strength

nescius, **-a**, **-um**: not knowing, inexperienced in, unable to

nēue: conj., and . . . not

nex, **necis**, **f.**: a violent death, murder

nexus, **-ūs**, **m.**: binding; a restraint, bond

nī: conj., unless, if . . . not

niger, **nigra**, **nigrum**: dark, black; having dark skin

nigrō (1): to be black, be dark; be invisible

nihil, **nīl**, indecl., **n.**: nothing; adv., in no way

Nīlicola, **-ae**, **m.**: a Nile-dweller, Egyptian

nimbus, **-ī**, **m.**: a rain cloud, cloud; shower

nīmīrum: part., no doubt, of course

nimius, **-a**, **-um**: too much, excessive

nitidus, **-a**, **-um**: gleaming, shining

nītor, **nītī**, **nīsus**: to lean on; strain, try, struggle

nitor, **-ōris**, **m.**: brightness, gleam, brilliance

niueus, **-a**, **-um**: snowy, snow white

nōbilis, **-e**: renowned, remarkable; well-born, noble, superior

noceō, **-ēre**, **nocuī**, **nocitum**: to hurt, harm, cause damage

nocturnus, **-a**, **-um**: of or related to the night

nōdus, **-ī**, **m.**: a knot

nōmen, **-inis**, **n.**: a name

nōn: adv., not

nōnne: part. that introduces a question expecting an affirmative answer, is it not the case that?

norma, -ae, f.: a carpenter's square; a right angle; pattern

nōs, nostrum/nostrī: we, us

noscō, -ere, nōuī, nōtum: to come to know, recognize; perf., know

nōsmet: a form of *nos* with the emphatic suffix *-met*

noster, nostra, nostrum: poss. adj., our, ours

nothus, -a, -um: illegitimate, bastard

notō (1): to mark, note; recognize

nōtus, -ī: the south wind, the wind

nouālis, -is, f.: land plowed anew; land, a field

nouēnī, -ae, -a: nine each, in a group of nine

nouus, -a, -um: new

nox, noctis, f.: night

noxa, -ae, f.: wrongdoing, harmful behavior

nūbēs, -is, f.: a cloud

nūdō (1): to make bare, strip, expose

nūdus, -a, -um: naked, bare, exposed

nūgae, -ārum, f. pl.: trifles, nonsense, something of no importance

nūgātrix, -īcis, f.: trifling, unserious, playful

nullus, -a, -um: not a, not one; none; no one

nūmen, -inis, n.: divine power, divinity; god

numerō (1): to count, number, calculate

numerus, -ī, m.: number

nummus, -ī, m.: a coin

numquam: adv., never

numquid: part. that introduces a question expecting a negative answer, surely . . . not?

nunc: adv., now

nuntius, -iī, m.: a messenger, envoy; a message

nūtō (1): to nod, shake; totter

ō: interj., often with direct address

obdūcō, -dūcere, -dūxī, -dūctum: to draw over, spread over, cover

obiectō (1): to put before, thrust forward

obitus, -ūs, m.: a visit; dying, death; decline

oblectō (1): to delight, please, beguile

oblīdō, -līdere, -līsī, -līsum: to squeeze, crush

oblīquus, -a, -um: slanted, oblique; devious, hostile

obpandō, -pandere, -pandī, -pansum: to spread out, extend

obprimō, -primere, -pressī, -pressum: to press against; overwhelm, oppress

obpugnō (1): to fight against, attack

obscūrus, -a, -um: dark, obscure

obsideō, -sidēre, -sēdī, -sessum: to occupy; besiege, assail

obsistō, -sistere, -stitī, -stitum: to block, obstruct, resist

obstupefactus, -a, -um: struck dumb, dazed, stupefied

obtegō, -tegere, -texī, -tectum: to cover, hide

obtendō, -tendere, -tendī, -tentum: to stretch over, spread over

obterō, -terere, -trīuī, -trītum: to crush, trample

obtūtus, -ūs, m.: a gaze, look

obuertō, -uertere, -uertī, -uersum: to turn against, turn to face

obuius, -a, -um: in the way, ready to meet, opposed

occāsus, -ūs, m.: a setting, sinking

occidō, -cidere, -cidī, -casum: to fall, sink; die

occiduālis, -e: western, occidental

occiduus, -a, -um: sinking, setting; western

occultō (1): to conceal, hide

occultus, -a, -um: concealed, hidden

occupō (1): to seize, occupy, take hold of, cover

occurrō, -currere, -currī, -cursum: to meet; present oneself, occur

oculus, -ī, m.: an eye; sight

ōdī, ōdisse, ōsum: to hate

odium, -iī, n.: hatred, enmity

odor, -ōris, m.: a smell, odor, fragrance

offa, -ae, f.: a piece of food, lump

offensāculum, -ī, n.: a stumbling block, obstacle

offerō, offere, obtulī, oblātum: to put before; offer; present

olea, -ae, f.: an olive; an olive tree

oleum, -ī, n.: olive oil

ōlim: adv., before, once upon a time; at some point

Olofernis, -is, m.: an enemy of Judith

omnipotens, -ntis: all-powerful

omnis, omne: every, all

onerō (1): to load, weigh down

onus, -eris, n.: load, burden

operātiō, -ōnis, f.: working, operation, activity, action

operiō, -īre, operuī, opertum: to close, cover over

opermentum, -ī, n.: a covering, cover

opertum, -ī, n.: a dark place, depth; secret

opifex, -icis, m. and f.: craftsperson, worker, artisan

opperior, -īrī, oppertus: to await, wait for

oppōnō, -pōnere, -posuī, -positum: to put before, put in the way, oppose

ops, opis, f.: power, ability; resource, wealth; help, assistance

optō (1): to hope for, desire; choose, select

opulentia, -ae, f.: riches, wealth

opus, operis, n.: work, task; action, activity

ōra, -ae, f.: an edge, border; region, land

orbis, -is, m.: a circle, orb, globe; world

ordō, -inis, m.: a row, line; rank, order

orīgō, -inis, f.: a beginning, origin

ornāmentum, -ī, n.: equipment; ornament; honor

ōrō (1): to pray, beg, supplicate

ōs, ōris, n.: the mouth; face

os, ossis, n.: a bone

ostentāmen, -inis, n.: a display, show, vainglory

ostentātrix, -īcis, f.: one who is vainglorious, boastful, ostentatious

ostentō (1): to show, display; call attention to, make a show of

ostrum, -ī, n.: purple; purple clothes

ouis, -is, f.: a sheep; an ewe (female sheep)

pācifer, -era, -erum: peace bringing

paenitet, -ēre, paenituit: to cause regret, grieve, make to repent

palātum, -ī, n.: the roof of the mouth, palate

palla, -ae, f.: an upper garment worn by tragic actors and others, a mantle

palleō, -ēre, palluī: to be pale, look yellow or green

pallidus, -a, -um: pale, colorless

pallium, -iī, n.: a Greek outer cloak or mantle (*himation*)

pallor, -ōris, m.: paleness, pallor; terror

palma, -ae, f.: a hand; palm tree; crown; victory

palpitō (1): to beat, quiver

palpō (1): to caress; soothe, soften

pandō, -ere, pansum: to spread out; open

pār, paris: equal, equivalent

pār, paris, n.: a pair, couple

parabsis, -idis, f.: (Gk.) a serving dish

paradīsus, -ī, m.: (Gk.) a garden, paradise; the home of the blessed

parātus, -ūs, m.: preparation, planning; equipment

parcē: adv., in a thrifty manner, moderately

parcō, -ere, pepercī: to be thrifty; spare, act mercifully

parcus, -a, -um: thrifty, moderate

parens, -ntis, m. and f.: a parent, mother or father; ancestor

pariēs, -etis, m.: a wall

pariō, -ere, peperī, partum: to give birth to, bear, produce

pariter: adv., together, in the same way, likewise

parō (1): to supply; obtain, gain; purchase, buy; prepare; intend

pars, partis, f.: a part

partus, -ūs, m.: a birth

parum: adv., too little, not enough

paruulus, -a, -um: tiny, a little one (of children)

paruus, -a, -um: small, little

pascō, -ere, pāuī, pastum: to feed, sustain, nurture

passer, -eris, m.: a small bird, a sparrow

pastus, -ūs, m.: pasture, food

patefaciō, -facere, -fēcī, -factum: to make open, uncover

pateō, -ēre, patuī: to be open, lie open

pater, -tris, m.: a father

patientia, -ae, f.: patience, forbearance

patior, -ī, passus: to be subject to, suffer; bear patiently; allow

patria, -ae, f.: one's fatherland, native land

patriarcha, -ae, m.: (Gk.) the head of a tribe, patriarch

patrius, -a, -um: of or related to a father; paternal, ancestral; of one's native land

patruēlis, -e: of or related to a father's brother, uncle's

paucī, -ae, -a: a few

pauor, -ōris, m.: a terror, trembling, fear

pauper, -eris: poor, not wealthy

paupertīnus, -a, -um: of or related to a poor person, poor

pax, pācis, f.: tranquility, peace; a pact, treaty; favor

peccātum, -ī, n.: a mistake; sin

pectus, -oris, n.: chest, breast; heart, soul

pecūlātor, -ōris, m.: an embezzler

pecus, pecudis, f.: livestock, animal, sheep

pedes, peditis, m.: one who goes on foot, a foot soldier

pellis, -is, f.: a pelt, skin, hide

pellītus, -a, -um: covered with skins; made of skins

pellō, -ere, pepulī, pulsum: to strike, beat; drive away, send off, repel; defeat

pendeō, -ēre, pependī: to be suspended, hang down

pendō, -ere, pependī, pensum: to weigh; pay out, pay (a penalty)

penetrābilis, -e: able to penetrate; penetrable, passable, permeable

penetrō (1): to go deep within, penetrate

peplum, -ī, n.: (Gk.) a robe

per: prep. w./acc., through, throughout; by (in oaths); through the use of, by means of

pēra, -ae, f.: a bag, satchel

percurrō, -currere, -currī, -cursum: to run through, run over

percutiō, -cutere, -cussī, -cussum: to strike through, strike forcefully

perditus, -a, -um: ruined, lost, desperate

perdō, -dere, -didī, -ditum: to ruin, destroy; lose

perennis, -e: continuing through the year; constant, everlasting, unfailing

pereō, -īre, -iī, -itum: to pass away, perish; be ruined, be lost

perferō, -ferre, -tulī, -lātum: to carry through, carry over; retain; endure

perficiō, -ficere, -fēcī, -fectum: to bring to completion, perfect, finish

perfidus, -a, -um: treacherous, false

perfodiō, -fodere, -fōdī, -fossum: to dig through, pierce

perfringō, -fringere, -frēgī, -fractum: to break through, break; destroy

perfundō, -fundere, -fūdī, -fūsum: to pour through; pour over, drench, suffuse

pergō, -gere, -rexī, -rectum: to make one's way, go, proceed

perīc(u)lum, -ī, n.: a test, trial, danger

periūrium, -iī, n.: a false oath, perjury

perpetior, -petī, -pessus: to suffer, endure

perque = *per + que*

perspiciō, -spicere, -spexī, -spectum: to look over, survey, perceive

persultō (1): to leap through, prance about

perturbō (1): to thoroughly confuse, upset, disturb

peruersus, -a, -um: reversed; twisted, perverse

peruigil, peruigilis: lasting the night through, all night

peruius, -a, -um: passable, accessible; perforated, pierced

peruulgō (1): to make common, make well known, publish

pēs, pedis, m.: a foot

pessimus, -a, -um: worst

pestis, -is, f.: death; a plague, disaster; a curse, bane

petō, -ere, petīuī, petītum: to seek, head for; attack, aim at

petulanter: adv., insolently, rudely

petulantia, -ae, f.: impudence, rudeness

piceus, -a, -um: made of pitch, pitchy, pitch-black

pietās, -ātis, f.: dutiful respect, conscientiousness, piety

piger, -gra, -grum: sluggish, slow, idle

piget, -ēre, piguit: to cause displeasure, disgust, bother

pignus, -eris, n.: a bond, guarantee; child

pīlum, -ī, n.: a javelin, heavy spear

pingō, -ere, pinxī, pinctum: to paint, color

pinna, -ae, f.: a feather, wing

pinnātus, -a, -um: feathered, winged

pīnus, -ūs, f.: a pine; something made of pine, a spear

piō (1): to propitiate; purify, cleanse

piscis, -is, m.: a fish

pius, -a, -um: dutiful, faithful; devout, pious

plācābilis, -e: placable, gentle, forgiving

placeō, -ēre, placuī, placitus: to please, be pleasing to; pass., be resolved, agreed

placidus, -a, -um: quiet, calm

plaga, -ae, f.: an expanse, territory, area

plāga, -ae, f.: a blow, stroke

plānitiēs, -ēī, f.: flatness, a plain

planta, -ae, f.: the sole of the foot

plasma, -atis, n.: (Gk.) an image, figure, figment, creature, creation

plēbēius, -a, -um: plebeian, common

plebs, plēbis, f.: the common people, the people

plectrum, -ī, n.: a quill, a stick used as a musical instrument

plēnus, -a, -um: full, full of, abundant

plūma, -ae, f.: a feather

pōculum, -ī, n.: a drinking vessel; a drink

poena, -ae, f.: a penalty

poliō, -īre, -īuī, -ītum: to smooth, polish

polleō, -ēre: to be strong, powerful

pollex, -icis, m.: a thumb, big toe

polluō, -ere, polluī, pollūtum: to befoul, stain, pollute

pompa, -ae, f.: a procession, parade; pomp, display, ostentation

pondus, -eris, n.: a weight; mass

pōnō, -ere, posuī, positum: to put, place; set up; put aside

pontus, -ī, m.: the sea

populāris, -e: of or related to the people, of a common person, popular

populor (1): to plunder, devestate

populus, -ī, m.: a people, the people; a crowd, multitude; the common people

porrō: adv., forward, further; next, in turn

porta, -ae, f.: a gate, entry

portentum, -ī, n.: a portent, monster

portiō, -ōnis, f.: a portion, part

poscō, -ere, poposcī: to demand, call for, summon

possideō, -ēre, possēdī, possessum: to control, hold, possess

possum, posse, potuī: to be able, can; be powerful

post: adv., behind; afterward

post: prep. w/acc., behind, beyond; after

postis, -is, m.: a doorpost; door

postquam: conj., after

postrēmus, -a, -um: last, final

postulō (1): to demand, require

potens, -ntis: powerful, mighty

potentia, -ae, f.: power

potestās, -ātis, f.: command, authority, power

potis, pote: able, powerful, possible

praeceps, praecipitis: headlong, rushing down

praeceptor, -ōris, m.: a teacher, instructor

praeceptum, -ī, n.: an order, teaching, advice

praecingō, -cingere, -cinxī, -cinctum: to encircle, gird up

praecipitō (1): to hurl down, cast headlong

praecordia, -ōrum, n. pl.: vitals, chest, heart

praecurrō, -currere, -cucurrī, -cursum: to run ahead, anticipate, forestall

praeda, -ae, f.: booty, spoils, plunder

praedūrō (1): to harden

praeferō, -ferre, -tulī, -lātum: to bring forward, display

praemium, -iī, n.: a reward, prize

praenotō (1): to note before, write ahead of time

praepes, -petis: flying ahead, swift

praepotens, -ntis: outstanding in power

praeruptus, -a, -um: broken off, sheer, precipitous

praescius, -a, -um: foreknowing, anticipating, knowledgable in

praesens, -ntis: present

praesidium, -iī, n.: protection, defense; help

praestō, -stāre, -stitī, -stitum: to be outstanding; supply, provide

praestringō, -stringere, -strinxī, -strinctum: to tie up; touch lightly, graze

praeteritus, -a, -um: past, bygone, former

praeualidus, -a, -um: exceptionally strong, powerful

prātum, -ī, n.: a meadow; plain

precor (1): to pray, implore

premō, -ere, pressī, pressum: to press, press down; harass, oppress; overwhelm, crush

pretiōsus, -a, -um: expensive; precious

pretium, -iī, n.: a reward, prize; price

prex, precis, f.: a prayer, entreaty

prīmus, -a, -um: foremost, first

princeps, -ipis, m.: the first person, leader, chief

pristinus, -a, -um: former, previous; ancient

prīuātus, -a, -um: not public, private, separate

prō: prep. w/abl., in front of, before; for the sake of, for; in return for, according to

prō: interj., o! ah!

probō (1): to approve, accept

probrum, -ī, n.: a reproach, insult, abuse

procella, -ae, f.: a violent wind, storm

procerēs, -um, m. pl.: leaders, elders, nobles

procinctus, -ūs, m.: preparedness; equipment

procul: adv., apart, far apart, from afar, far off

prōculcō (1): to trample on, crush

prōdigus, -a, -um: extravagant, lavish, wasteful

prōditiō, -ōnis, f.: a betrayal, treachery

prōdō, -dere, -didī, -ditum: to bring forward; display, reveal; betray

proelium, -iī, n.: a battle, conflict

profānus, -a, -um: not sacred, unholy, profane

profundus, -a, -um: deep, vast; profound, mysterious

prōgredior, -gredī, -gressus: to walk forward, step out, advance

prōiciō, -icere, -iēcī, -iectum: to throw forward, throw down

prōlēs, -is, f.: offspring, progeny, child

promptus, -a, -um: ready, quick, prompt

prōnus, -a, -um: headlong, facedown

properē: adv., hastily, quickly

properō (1): to act quickly; prepare with haste, make quickly

propinquus, -a, -um: nearby, neighboring; related as a kinsman, relative

proprius, -a, -um: one's own; personal, proper

propter: adv., near, nearby

prōsāpia, -ae, f.: stock, family, offspring

prōsiliō, -silīre, -siluī: to leap out, spring forward

prosperus, -a, -um: successful, prosperous, favorable

prospiciō, -spicere, -spexī, -spectum: to see before one, observe

prosternō, -sternere, -strāuī, -strātum: to knock down, stretch out, overthrow

prostibulum, -ī, n.: a prostitute, whore

prōsum, prōdesse, prōfuī: to be of use, help, be advantageous

prōterō, -terere, -trīuī, -trītum: to tread down, crush, trample

prōtrahō, -trahere, -traxī, -tractum: to drag forward, pull out

prōuidus, -a, -um: foreseeing, exercising forethought, circumspect, provident

prōuocō (1): to call out; challenge, provoke

proximus, -a, -um: nearest, very near by, next

psallō, -ere, psallī: to play a stringed instrument; sing a psalm

psalmus, -ī, m.: (Gk.) the sound of a stringed instrument, twanging; a song, hymn, psalm

pūbēs, -is, f.: the grownups, adulthood; youth, the age of becoming an adult; fulness, ripeness

pūbescō, -ere: to reach maturity, ripen

pūblicus, -a, -um: of or related to the people, public

pudendus, -a, -um: shameful, disgraceful

pudeō, -ēre, puduī, puditum: to cause shame; impers. + acc., be ashamed

pudibundus, -a, -um: shameful, bashful, modest

pudīcitia, -ae, f.: chastity, purity

pudīcus, -a, -um: chaste, pure, modest

pudor, -ōris, n.: shame, decency, modesty; as an exclamation, for shame!

puella, -ae, f.: a girl

puer, puerī, m.: a boy

puerīlis, -e: of a boy, of a child

puerpera, -ae, f.: a woman who is about to give birth or who has given birth

pugna, -ae, f.: a fight

pugnātrix, -īcis, f.: a female fighter, warrioress

pugnō (1): to fight, engage in combat

pulcher, pulchra, pulchrum: pretty, beautiful, fine

pulmō, -ōnis, m.: a lung, lungs

pulsō (1): to strike, beat; make resound

puluis, pulueris, m.: (the) dust (of the ground)

punctum, -ī, n.: a small hole, a point, prick

purgō (1): to clean, purify, purge

purpureus, -a, -um: purple; reddish; gleaming, glowing

pūrus, -a, -um: cleansed, clean, pure

puteus, -ī, m.: a well, pit, hole

putō (1): to think, consider

quadriiugī, -ōrum, m. pl.: a team of four chariot horses

quadrīnī, -ae, -a: in a group of four, four each, fourfold

quadrō (1): to make square, make a square

quadruus, -a, -um: fourfold, four part

quaerō, -ere, quaesīuī, quaesītum: to look for, seek out

quamuīs: rel. adv., however much; although

quandōque: at some time, some day

quantus, -a, -um: interr. and rel. pron. and adj., how much? how great?

quatiō, -ere, quassum: to shake, brandish

quattuor: indecl. adj., four

queō, quīre, quiī: to be able, can

quī: interr. adv., how?

quī, quae, quid: interrog. adj., what? which?

quī, quae, quod: rel. pron., who, which, that

quia: conj., because

quidem: part., certainly, indeed

quiēs, -ētis, f.: sleep; rest, resting, serenity, peace

quiētus, -a, -um: quiet, resting; inactive, unmoving

quīn: adv., indeed, in fact

quippe: part., for, in fact, certainly; since, inasmuch as

quīque, quaeque, quodque: indef. adj., each, every; pl., all

quis, quid: indef. pron. (after *si, nisi, num*, and *ne*), anyone, anything

quīs = *quibus*

quisnam, quaenam, quidnam: emphatic interrog., who? what?

quisquam, quicquam: indef. pron., anyone, anything

quisque, quidque: indef. pron., each one, every one; whoever

quisquis, quidquid: indef. pron. and adj., anyone who, whoever, whatever

quondam: adv., once, once upon a time, previously

quoniam: conj., since, because

quoque: adv., likewise, also, too

quotiens: interr., exclamatory, and rel. adv., how many times? how often! as many times as, whenever

rabidus, -a, -um: raging, rabid, violent

rabiēs, -ēī, f.: rage, madness, violence

radiō (1): to beam, shine, radiate light

radius, -iī, m.: a ray of light; a spoke in a wheel

rapidus, -a, -um: rapid, swift, quick

rapīna, -ae, f.: robbery, plundering; booty, plunder

rapiō, -ere, rapuī, raptum: to snatch, seize; steal, carry off as plunder; take up, take away, hoist

raptō (1): to snatch, carry away, carry off, seize

rārus, -a, -um: loose knit, porous; thinly spaced, sparse; rare

rāsilis, -e: polished, smooth

ratiō, -ōnis, f.: reasoning, calculation; a reason, explanation; the faculty of reason, reason; method, plan, policy

raucus, -a, -um: harsh sounding, noisy, raucous

reātus, -ūs, m.: the state of being accused; an accusation; guilt

rebellis, -e: rebellious, insurgent

recalescō, -calescere, -caluī: to grow warm again; revive

recauus, -a, -um: hollowed out, concave

recens, -ntis: recent, fresh, young

recenseō, -censēre, -censuī, -censum: to review, count, survey

recidīuus, -a, -um: falling back; returning, renascent, renewed

recīdō, -cīdere, -cīdī, -cīsum: to cut back, cut away

recipiō, -cipere, -cēpī, -ceptum: to receive, accept; take back, recover

reconditus, -a, -um: hidden, concealed, recondite

recoquō, -coquere, -coxī, -coctum: to cook again; reheat, forge again

recreō (1): to make new; restore, revive

rectus, -a, -um: straight, direct; morally right, upright, upstanding

recūsō (1): to protest, decline, reject

reddō, -dere, -didī, -ditum: to give back, return

redeō, -īre, -iī, -itum: to go back, come back, return

redimīculum, -ī, n.: a fillet, ribbon

redimiō, -imīre, -imiī, -imītum: to wreathe round, encircle

redūcō, -dūcere, -dūxī, -dūctum: to lead back; pull back, drawn in

referō, -ferre, rettulī, relātum: to bring back, return; refer

rēfert, -ferre, -tulit: impers., to be of importance, matter, make a difference

refluō, -fluere: to flow back, run back

rēgālis, -e: of or related to royalty, royal, regal

rēgīna, -ae, f.: a queen

regnō (1): to rule, reign, exercise dominion

regnum, -ī, n.: a monarchy; kingdom, dominion; realm, rule

rēiciō, -icere, -iēcī, -iectum: to throw back, cast off, toss

relābor, -lābī, -lāpsus: to move back, fall back

relegāmen, -inis, n.: a band, headband

relūceō, -lūcēre, -lūxī: to shine back, gleam

reluctor (1): to struggle against, resist

renascor, -nascī, -nātus: to be reborn, be renewed, be born again

repellō, -pellere, -ppulī, -pulsum: to push back, drive back, repel

repentīnus, -a, -um: sudden, unexpected

repulsus, -ūs, m.: a driving back, repulsion, deflection

requiēs, -ētis, f.: rest, relaxation, break

requiescō, -quiescere, -quiēuī, -quiētum: to rest, relax

rēs, reī, f.: property; a thing; fact, reality; circumstance, situation; matter, topic

resculpō, -sculpere, -sculpsī, -sculptum: to carve back, carve again, fashion again

resecō, -secāre, -secuī, -sectum: to cut back, cut off, trim

reserō (1): to draw back, unfasten; open, expose

resideō, -sidēre, -sēdī: to remain seated, sit

resiliō, -silīre, -siluī: to jump back, bounce back

resistō, -sistere, -stitī: to stop, stand still; remain firm, resist

resoluō, -soluere, -soluī, -solūtum: to loosen, unravel, break up, relax

resonō (1): to resound, echo, ring

resonus, -a, -um: echoing, resounding

respectō, -āre: to look back on, look round on; keep looking at, respect

respiciō, -spicere, -spexī, -spectum: to look round at; review, consider

respondeō, -spondēre, -spondī, -sponsum: to reply, respond

respuō, -spuere, -spuī: to spit out, spit back; reject

restō, -stāre, -stitī: to stand back, stand firm; be left, remain

resultō, -āre: to jump back, spring back; echo, resound

resūmō, -sūmere, -sūmpsī, -sūmptum: to take up again, regain, recover

resupīnus, -a, -um: lying on one's back face up, on one's back, horizontal

retardō (1): to slow down, hinder, hold up

retegō, -tegere, -texī, -tectum: to uncover, bare, expose

retineō, -tinēre, -tinuī, -tentum: to hold fast, cling to; hold back, detain

retractō (1): to draw back; handle again; reconsider, examine, review

retundō, -tundere, -tudī, -tūsum: to make blunt, dull, weaken

reuerentia, -ae, f.: respect, awe, reverence

reuīsō, -uīsere: to visit again, return to, revisit

reuocō (1): to call back, recall; cause to move back, turn back

reuomō, -uomere, -uomuī: to vomit again, vomit back up

rex, rēgis, m.: a king

rictus, -ūs, m.: the opening of the mouth, an open mouth (as a sign of astonishment or ravening hunger)

rīdeō, -ēre, rīsī, rīsum: to laugh; laugh at, make light of

rīdiculus, -a, -um: funny, amusing; absurd, ridiculous

rigidus, -a, -um: stiff, hard; strict, stern

rigō (1): to water, irrigate; drench, soak

rigor, -ōris, m.: stiffness, hardness; strictness

rīmor (1): to pry into, examine, search out

rīpa, -ae, f.: a riverbank, the border of a stream or other body of water

rīuus, -ī, m.: a stream, a small flow of liquid

rixa, -ae, f.: a quarrel, conflict; struggle

rōbur, roboris, n.: an oak tree; hardness, strength, vigor

rōs, rōris, m.: dew; moisture, liquid, water

rosa, -ae, f.: a rose

rota, -ae, f.: a wheel

rotō (1): to rotate, turn round, whirl

rubens, -ntis: red colored, red

rūbīgō, -inis, f.: rust, a corrupting blight

ructō (1): to belch, disgorge

rudis, -e: uncultivated, unwrought, rough; immature, young

ruīna, -ae, f.: a falling down, collapse; ruin, remain

rumpō, -ere, rūpī, ruptum: to split, break, break apart, burst

ruō, -ere, ruī: to rush, run headlong; crash down, fall

rūpēs, rūpis, f.: a cliff, steep rock, rock

rūs, rūris, n.: the country, countryside

rutilō (1): to shine bright red; make a ruddy color

sacer, -cra, -crum: consecrated, sacred, holy

sacerdōs, -ōtis, m.: a priest, religious officiant, mediator

sacrārium, -iī, n.: a shrine, sanctuary

sacricola, -ae, m.: a religious officiant, priest

sacrō (1): to consecrate, make holy, devote

sacrum, -ī, n.: a sacred thing; religious ceremony, sacred rites, religion

saec(u)lum, -ī, n.: a generation; an age, a long period of time

saeuus, -a, -um: savage, fierce, cruel

saliō, -īre, saluī, saltum: to leap, spring

saltātrix, -īcis, f.: a dancer, dancing girl

salūs, -ūtis, f.: safety; a means of deliverance; saving, salvation

salūtifer, -era, -erum: that brings safety or salvation, healing

Samuel, -is, m.: a Hebrew prophet

sanctus, -a, -um: holy, sacred, pure

sanguineus, -a, -um: bloody, bloodstained

sanguis, -inis, m.: blood, shed blood, blood in the face as a sign of modesty; bloodline, family

saniēs, -ēī, f.: a thin liquid discharge from a wound, sanies

saniōsus, -a, -um: of or related to sanies, gory

sānus, -a, -um: healthy; reasonable, sane

sapiens, -ntis: wise, judicious

sapientia, -ae, f.: wisdom, discernment

sapiō, -ere, sapīuī: to taste of; have taste; feel; have sense, be discerning, be wise

sapor, -ōris, m.: a flavor, taste

sappīrus, -ī, m.: a blue gem, probably lapis lazuli

sardius, -iī, m.: a Sardian stone, carnelian

sardonix, -ichis, m.: a precious stone, sardonyx

Sarra, -ae, f.: a Jewish matriarch, wife of Abram

sat: adv., sufficiently, enough, quite

satelles, -itis, m.: an attendant, supporter

satiō (1): to satisfy, sate

sauciō (1): to wound, injure

saucius, -a, -um: wounded; distressed, stunned

saxum, -ī, n.: a stone, stone

scabrōsus, -a, -um: rough, encrusted

scandalum, -ī, n.: (Gk.) that which trips you up, a stumbling block; a temptation, a cause of offence

scandō, -ere: to climb, ascend

Scarioth, indecl., m.: Judas Iscariot (the betrayer of Jesus)

scelus, -eris, n.: an evil deed, crime

sceptrum, -ī, n.: a staff, (royal) sceptre; sovereignty, kingdom

scīlicet = *scire licet*, to be sure, obviously, evidently, no doubt

scindō, -ere, scidī, scissum: to divide, split, tear apart

scissūra, -ae, f.: a gap, splitting; division

scrobis, -is, m.: a hole, pit; a ditch

sē, sēsē: acc. and abl. of the reflex. pers. pron., him/her/itself

secō, -āre, secuī, sectum: to cut, cut through

sēcrētus, -a, -um: separated, withdrawn; hidden, secret

secta, -ae, f.: a path; teaching; a sect, a group or school

secundus, -a, -um: following; favorable (*res secundae* = prosperity); second

secūris, -is, f.: an ax, hatchet; an executioner's ax (especially as carried by a Roman magistrate), an ax as a sign of political authority

sēcūrus, -a, -um: untroubled, unperturbed, careless

sed: conj., but

sedeō, -ēre, sēdī, sessum: to sit, be seated, settle

sēdēs, -is, f.: a seat, chair; a dwelling place, abode, home; place, site

sēditiō, -ōnis, f.: an insurrection; discord, turmoil

sēdō (1): to cause to subside, restrain, settle

sēdulus, -a, -um: painstaking, industrious

segnis, -e: sluggish, inactive, lazy

sēmen, -inis, n.: a seed; offspring

sēmetrum, -ī, n.: unevenness, asymmetry

semper: adv., always, forever

senātus, -ūs, m.: the senate, council of elders

senecta, -ae, f.: old age, oldness

senex, -is, m.: an old man, an elder

sēnī, -ae, -a: in groups of six, six

senīlis, -e: of or related to an old man

sensus, -ūs, m.: perception, sense, sensation; interpretation, understanding; idea, meaning

sententia, -ae, f.: an opinion, sentiment, idea; statement, sentence, judgment

sentiō, -īre, sensī, sensum: to feel, perceive, sense

septem: indecl. adj., seven

sequor, sequī, secūtus: to follow; attend

serēnus, -a, -um: clear, cloudless, bright; serene, tranquil, pure

sēricus, -a, -um: Chinese; made of silk, silken

seriēs, -ēī, f.: a series, sequence, line

serō, -ere, sēuī, satum: to plant, sow; beget, procreate

serpens, -ntis, m. and f.: a serpent, snake

serta, -ōrum, n. pl.: wreaths, garlands

seruiō, -īre, seruīuī, seruītum: to be subservient to, serve (+ dat.), be enslaved

seruō (1): to guard, preserve, keep, reserve

sērus, -a, -um: late

sēsē = an emphatic form of *se*

seu, sīue: conj., or if, whether . . . or

seuērus, -a, -um: stern, strict, severe; serious

sī: conj., if

sibi (sibī): dat. of the reflex. pers. pron., to or for him/her/itself

sīc: adv., so, thus, in this way

sīca, -ae, f.: a dagger, knife

siccus, -a, -um: dry, not wet

sīdus, -eris, n.: a star, heavenly body; pl., the stars, heaven

signāculum, -ī, n.: a seal, sign

signō (1): to mark, sign; inscribe

signum, -ī, n.: a mark, sign, symbol; signal; a military standard

sileō, -ēre, siluī: to be silent, be quiet

silex, -icis, m.: a hard stone, flint; a boulder, rock

simplex, -icis: having a single layer; uncompounded, simple, plain

simplicitās, -ātis, f.: singleness, unity; simplicity, straightforwardness

simul: adv., together with, at the same time, simultaneously

simulō (1): to make look like; simulate, imitate

sincērus, -a, -um: unblemished, pure, real, sincere

sine: prep. w/abl., without

sinister, -tra, -trum: on the left-hand side, left; inauspicious, unfavorable

sinō, -ere, sīuī, situm: to leave; allow, let

sinuāmen, -inis, n.: a twisting, turning

sinus, -ūs, m.: a bent surface, curve, fold, pocket; cavity, hollow; bay, gulf

sistō, -ere, stetī, statum: to set up, stand, plant

sistrum, -ī, n.: a metal rattle (often used by ecstatic worshippers of Isis)

sīue, seu: conj., or if, whether . . . or

smaragdinus, -a, -um: (Gk.) of or related to emerald, emerald green

sōbrietās, -ātis, f.: sobriety, temperance

sōbrius, -a, -um: sober, temperate, moderate

sociō (1): to attach, join; unite, associate

socius, -a, -um: of an associate, allied, kindred

socius, -iī, m.: a companion, comrade, ally

Sodoma, -ōrum, n. pl.: Sodom, a city in Canaan

Sodomīta, -ae, m. and f.: of or related to Sodom, an inhabitant of Sodom

sōl, sōlis, m.: the sun

sōlācium, -iī, n.: relief, solace, comfort

solidus, -a, -um: solid, not hollow

solitus, -a, -um: usual, normal

solium, -iī, n.: a royal chair, throne

sollicitō (1): to disturb, harass, bother

Solomon, -ōnis, m.: a Hebrew king

soluō, -ere, soluī, solūtum: to loose; relax, undo, dissolve

solum, -ī, n.: the floor, soil, ground; a land, country

sōlus, -a, -um: alone, without a companion, only

sonipēs, -pedis: with sounding foot, noisy footed; as a substantive, a horse

sonō, -āre, sonuī, sonitum: to sound, resound

sordeō, -ēre: to be dirty; be unworthy, be despised

sordēs, -is, f.: dirt, filth; baseness

sordidus, -a, -um: foul, filthy, nasty

soror, -ōris, f.: a sister

sors, sortis, f.: a lot; fate, chance, fortune

sospes, -itis: safe, unharmed

spargō, -ere, sparsī, sparsum: to scatter, strew; spread, shower

spatium, -iī, n.: a space, gap; length

speciēs, -ēī, f.: sight; shape, (outer) appearance, form; a show, spectacle; kind, sort

speciōsus, -a, -um: beautiful, brilliant

spectāmen, -inis, n.: a spectacle, sight

spectātrix, -īcis, f.: one who observes or watches, a female spectator

spectō (1): to look at, look to, gaze at

specula, -ae, f.: a watchtower, lookout

speculātor, -ōris, m.: a lookout, spy; one who searches or examines

spernō, -ere, sprēuī, sprētum: to separate; reject, despise, spurn

spēs, -ēī, f.: hope

spīculum, -ī, n.: a sharp point; arrow, javelin

spīrāmen, -inis, n.: breathing; vent, airway

spīritus, -ūs, m.: breathing; a breath; air; spirit, the Holy Spirit (the third person of the trinity)

splendeō, -ēre: to shine, be bright, glisten

splendor, -ōris, m.: brilliance, splendor, glory

spoliō (1): to strip off, spoil, rob

spolium, -iī, n.: booty, plunder

spons, -ntis, f.: will, volition

spumō (1): to foam, froth

squāleō, -ēre, squaluī: to be rough or stiff

squāma, -ae, f.: a scale (on fish, animals, and armor)

squāmōsus, -a, -um: covered with scales, scaly

stabilis, -e: firm, steady; steadfast, constant

stāgnum, -ī, n.: a pool of water, water, depth

statiō, -ōnis, f.: standing; a station, post, position

stellans, -ntis: starry, covered with stars; gleaming, shining

stercus, -oris, n.: excrement, dung, filth

sternō, -ere, strāuī, strātum: to spread, lay out; lay low, strike down

stertō, -ere, stertuī: to snore

stillō (1): to drip, trickle

stīpō (1): to pack tight, throng; surround, accompany

stipula, -ae, f.: a stalk, straw

stirps, stirpis, f.: stem, stalk; family, stock

stō, stāre, stetī, statum: to stand, stand firm; take up a position, remain

stomachor (1): to be angry, rage

stomachus, -ī, m.: one's stomach; distaste, irritation, anger

strāgēs, -is, f.: overthrow, destruction, wreckage

strepitus, -ūs, m.: a loud sound, noise, din

strīdō, -ere, strīdī: to make a harsh sound, hiss, shriek

strīdor, -ōris, m.: a shrill sound, shrieking, whistling

strīdulus, -a, -um: shrieking, whistling

stringō, -ere, strinxī, strictum: to draw tight; touch; unsheathe, draw

strofium, -iī, n.: a band, breast-band, headband

structilis, -e: for building, related to construction

structūra, -ae, f.: a structure

struō, -ere, struxī, structum: to set up, construct, make

studium, -iī, n.: enthusiasm, eagerness, devotion; aim, pursuit

stupefaciō, -facere, -fēcī, -factum: to stun, amaze

stupeō, -ēre, stupuī: to be stunned, amazed; be astonished at

Styx, Stygis, f.: the Styx, a river in the underworld

suādeō, -ēre, suāsī, suāsum: to urge, exhort

suāsor, -ōris, m.: one who exhorts or persuades, counselor

sub: prep. w/abl., under; subject to; from; during, within, in; w/acc., beneath, under

subcumbō, -cumbere, -cubuī, -cubitum: to sink under, fall; yield, submit

subdō, -dere, -didī, -ditum: to place below; append, add

subdolus, -a, -um: deceitful, treacherous

subdūcō, -dūcere, -dūxī, -dūctum: to draw up, raise up

subfodiō, -fodere, -fōdī, -fossum: to dig under

subfundō, -fundere, -fūdī, -fūsum: to pour out from below, fill up; cover, envelop

sūbiciō, -icere, -iēcī, -iectum: to throw under; put under, place under

subitō: adv., suddenly, unexpectedly

subitus, -a, -um: sudden

sublīmis, -e: lofty, exalted, lifted up; grand, sublime

submittō, -mittere, -mīsī, -missum: to send down, dip, lower

subnixus, -a, -um: resting on, supported with

subpeditō (1): to reinforce; provide, supply

subrīdeō, -rīdēre, -rīsī, -rīsum: to smile

subsistō, -sistere, -stitī: to stand firm, remain; stop short, pause

substantia, -ae, f.: reality; substance; substrate

subsum, -esse, suffuī: to be under; be at hand, subsist

subtegmen, -inis, n.: a woven thread; yarn

subter: adv., underneath, below

succendō, -cendere, -cendī, -censum: to set fire to, kindle; inflame with passion

successor, -ōris, m.: one who follows another, a successor

succinctus, -a, -um: girded, clothed; equipped, provided

succurrō, -currere, -currī, -cursum: to run, hasten; come to help

sūdō (1): to sweat, perspire; labor, work hard

sūdus, -a, -um: clear, bright

suescō, -ere, suēuī, suētum: to become accustomed; perf., be accustomed, be used to

sufficiō, -ficere, -fēcī, -fectum: to be sufficient, be enough

sufflāmen, -inis, n.: a bar used to slow a wheel, a brake

suī: genitive of the reflex. pers. pron., of him/her/itself

sulcō (1): to plow, make a furrow in

sulpur, -uris, n.: sulfur, brimstone

sulpureus, -a, -um: of or related to brimstone, sulfurous

sum, esse, fuī: to be

summa, -ae, f.: amount, total; sum, whole of; culmination

summus, -a, -um: highest, uppermost; on the top of, at the surface of; greatest, foremost

sūmō, -ere, sumpsī, sumptum: to take, take up, take on, assume

suō, -ere, suī, sūtum: to sew, stitch together

super: adv., over, above; beyond, more

superbia, -ae, f.: pride, arrogance

superbiō, -īre: to show pride, be haughty

superbus, -a, -um: proud; lofty, grand

supercalcō (1): to tread down, step on, trample

supercilium, -iī, n.: an eyebrow; severity, arrogance, pride

superēmineō, -ēre: to stand above, rise above

superinpōnō, -pōnere, -posuī, positum: to put on top, put over

superstes, -itis: remaining, surviving

supersum, -esse, -fuī: to remain, be left over

superuacuus, -a, -um: useless, superfluous, ineffectual

supīnō (1): to bend backward, lay on one's back

suprēmus, -a, -um: furthest, final

surgō, -ere, surrexī, surrectum: to rise up, arise

sursum: adv., upward

suscipiō, -cipere, -cēpī, -ceptum: to take up, receive

suspendō, -pendere, -pendī, -pensum: to hang up, hold up, suspend; raise up, elevate

suspīrō (1): to sigh, exhale; sigh for, regret that

suspīrium, -iī, n.: a deep breath, sigh

suus, -a, -um: reflex. poss. adj., his/her/its own, their own

syllaba, -ae, f.: a syllable, the basic unit of sounds or letters in a word

syrma, -atos, n.: a robe with a long train

tacitus, -a, -um: quiet, silent; undisturbed

tactus, -ūs, m.: a touch, touching, contact; the sense of touch

taeda, -ae, f.: pinewood; a torch made of pine

taeter, taetra, taetrum: foul, horrible, hideous

talentum, -ī, n.: a unit of weight (the Roman talent was 32 kg); a talent of silver, a large unit of money

tālis, tale: such a, such

tam: adv., so

tamen: adv., however, nevertheless

tamquam: conj., just as, as though, as if

tandem: adv., at last, finally

tantum: adv., to such an extent; only

tantus, -a, -um: so great, so large; so much, so many; such

tardō (1): to slow, slow down, check

Tartara, -ōrum, n. pl.: Tartarus, the underworld

tē = acc. and abl. sing. of *tu*

tectum, -ī, n.: a roof, ceiling; building, house

tegmen, tegminis, n.: a covering, cover

tegō, -ere, texī, tectum: to cover; hide, conceal; shelter, protect

tēlum, -ī, n.: a spear; dart; weapon

temerārius, -a, -um: characterized by recklessness or thoughtlessness

temperō (1): to restrain, moderate, hold back

tempestās, -ātis, f.: a season; the weather; a storm, tempest, disturbance

templum, -ī, n.: a temple

temptō (1): to test, examine; try, attempt; attack, harrass

tempus, -oris, n.: a moment in time; pl., a period of time

tempus, -oris, n.: the side of the forehead, temple

tenax, tenācis: holding tight, tough, tenacious

tendō, -ere, tetendī, tentum: to stretch, reach, extend

tēne = *te* + *-ne*

tenebrae, -ārum, f. pl.: darkness

tenebrōsus, -a, -um: dark, gloomy

teneō, -ēre, tenuī, tentum: to hold, grasp, keep, restrain

tener, -era, -erum: soft, delicate, tender; of tender age, young; gentle

tentōrium, -iī, n.: something stretched out, a tent

tenuis, -e: thin, slender; slight, faint; lowly, poor

tenus: prep. w/abl., up to, as far as

tepefaciō, -facere, -fēcī, -factum: to make warm, lukewarm, or tepid

tepeō, -ēre: to be warm, lukewarm, or tepid

ter: adv., three times, thrice

teres, -etis: rounded, smooth

tergō, -ere, tersī, tersum: to rub clean, wipe off

tergum, -ī, n.: the back of a person or animal, hind part, the rear or back (of anything)

terō, -ere, trīuī, trītum: to rub, grind, crush

terra, -ae, f.: land; the earth; a land, country, region

terrēnus, -a, -um: of or related to the earth, terrestrial, earthly

terreus, -a, -um: of or related to the earth, earthly

terrigena, -ae, m. and **f.:** earthborn, of the earth

territō (1): to scare, frighten

terror, -ōris, m.: terror, extreme fear

texō, -ere, texuī, textum: to weave, make by weaving; join together, make

textum, -ī, n.: something woven together, a fabric, cloth

thalamus, -ī, m.: a bed chamber, bedroom; marriage bed, marriage

thensaurus, -ī, m.: a place for storing treasure; valuables, treasure

thōrax, thōrācis, m.: upper-body armor, a cuirass

tibi (tibī) = dat. of *tu*

timeō, -ēre, timuī: to be afraid, fear

tinguō, -ere, tinxī, tinctum: to dip in liquid; wet, moisten; stain, color, tinge

tinia, -ae, f.: a maggot, larva, worm

tinnītus, -ūs, m.: a ringing, clanging

tīrō, tīrōnis, m.: a new soldier, recruit

titubō (1): to totter, stagger

titulus, -ī, m.: a title, inscription; honor, distinction

toga, -ae, f.: a toga, the outer garment worn traditionally by Roman men

tolerō (1): to tolerate, put up with, endure

tollito = future imperative of *tollo*

tollō, -ere, sustulī, sublātum: to pick up, raise up, take up, lift

tonans, -ntis: thunder making; as a substantive, the thunderer

topazos, -ī, f.: (Gk.), a precious stone, the yellow topaz, chrysolite

toreuma, -atis, n.: something engraved or embossed

torqueō, -ēre, torsī, tortum: to twist, spin, whirl; wind, wrap

torus, -ī, m.: a strap, band; a muscle; a bed, marriage bed

toruus, -a, -um: grim, savage, wild

totidem: indecl. adj., just as many, the same number of

totiēns: adv., just as often, the same number of times

tōtus, -a, -um: the whole, all

tradō, -dere, -didī, -ditum: to hand over, deliver, give; teach; surrender

trahō, -ere, traxī, tractum: to drag, carry along, pull; carry off, plunder

trāiciō, -icere, -iēcī, -iectum: to throw across; pierce, transfix

tranquillus, -a, -um: quiet, calm, still

transeō, -īre, -iuī, -itum: to go across, pass through; cross over, cross to another side

transfīgō, -fīgere, -fīxī, -fīxum: to pierce through, thrust through

transformō (1): to change the shape of, transform

transfugiō, -fugere, -fūgī: to flee across, escape through, desert

transmittō, -mittere, -mīsī, -missum: to send over, let through; pass through, pierce

trecentī, -ae, -a: three hundred

tremō, -ere, tremuī: to shake, quiver, tremble

trepidātiō, -ōnis, f.: trepidation, trembling

trepidō (1): to be agitated, shake in fear, be afraid

trepidus, -a, -um: disturbed, anxious, fearful

trēs, tria: three

tribūnal, tribūnālis, n.: a platform on which a magistrate would preside, a platform

tribuō, -ere, tribuī, tribūtum: to share, attribute, ascribe

tribus, -ūs, f.: a group of people, a tribe

triformis, -e: having three forms or shapes

trilix, -īcis: three-ply, woven of three strands

trīnitas, -ātis, f.: a triad; the (Christian) trinity

trīnus, -a, -um: three each, three, threefold

triplex, -icis: triple, threefold

tristis, -e: unhappy, sad; grim, bitter

triumfus, -ī, m.: a victory procession, victory

tropaeum, -ī, n.: a memorial or monument set up to remember the defeat of an enemy, trophy

truculentus, -a, -um: aggressive, ferocious

trūdō, -ere, trūsī, trūsum: to push, shove; put out, send forth

truncō (1): to shorten by cutting off, cut off

trux, trucis: fierce, harsh; savage, cruel

tū, tuī: pers. pron., you

tueor, tuērī, tuitus: to observe; watch over, protect

tum: adv., then, at that point

tumefaciō, -facere, -fēcī, -factum: to cause to swell up; inflate with pride

tumeō, -ēre, tumuī: to be swollen or inflated, be distended; be puffed up with pride or vanity

tumescō, -ere: to swell up; swell with pride

tumidus, -a, -um: swollen, distended, inflated

tumultus, -ūs, m.: an uproar, disturbance, confusion

tumulus, -ī, m.: a hill; a mound, protuberance, bump

tunc: adv., then, at that point

tunica, -ae, f.: an undergarment, tunic

turba, -ae, f.: a turmoil; a crowd, throng, multitude

turbātrix, -īcis, f.: one who disturbs or troubles

turbidus, -a, -um: turbulent, wild; disturbed, troubled; disheveled

turbō (1): to disturb, throw into confusion

turbō, turbinis, m.: a whirlwind; the tumult of war, outburst

turgeō, -ēre, tursī: to swell, inflate

turma, -ae, f.: a troop of soldiers, band, squadron

turpis, -e: disgusting, foul; shameful, disgraceful

turpiter: adv., shamefully, disgracefully

turrītus, -a, -um: fortified with towers; tower shaped, towering

tūtor (1): to watch over, protect

tūtus, -a, -um: protected, safe, secure

tuus, -a, -um: poss. adj., your (sing.)

tympanum, -ī, n.: a drum, tympanum

tyrannus, -ī, m.: a tyrant, king

uacuus, -a, -um: empty; ineffectual, vain

uadum, -ī, n.: a shallow, shoal; water; depth

uaesānia, -ae, f.: madness, frenzy

uaesānus, -a, -um: mad, frenzied

uāgīna, -ae, f.: a scabbard, sheath, anything shaped like a sheath

uagus, -a, -um: wandering, shifting, unsteady

ualidus, -a, -um: strong, stout

uallum, -ī, n.: a palisade, rampart

uānus, -a, -um: empty, vain

uapor, -ōris, m.: a vapor, exhalation, steam

uariō (1): to give variety to, vary, variegate

uarius, -a, -um: varied, variegated; diverse, various, of many kinds; wavering, fickle

uāsum, -ī, n.: a container, dish, utensil; pl., equipment, supplies

uastus, -a, -um: huge, vast, immense

ubi: interr. adv. and conj., where, when

ubīque: adv., wherever, in any place whatever, everywhere

ūdus, -a, -um: wet, soaked; drunken

uehō, -ere, uexī, uectum: to bear, carry

uēlāmen, -inis, n.: a cover, clothing

uellus, -eris, n.: wool, a fleece

uēlō (1): to cover, conceal

uēlox, -ōcis: rapid, speedy

uēlum, -ī, n.: a sail; a sheet, curtain, flap

uelut: adv., just as, as if

uēna, -ae, f.: a blood vessel, vein; a vein of metals; the strength within something

uēnālis, -e: for sale, to be sold

uenēnum, -ī, n.: a poison

uenerābilis, -e: worthy of respect or reverence

uenia, -ae, f.: kindness; indulgence, forgiveness

ueniō, uenīre, uēnī, uentum: to come, approach, arrive

uentōsus, -a, -um: windy, blown by the wind; unstable, fickle; vain

uenustās, -ātis, f.: attractiveness, charm, delight

uenustus, -a, -um: attractive, charming

uerbum, -ī, n.: a word; a verb; the spoken word, speech; the Word (i.e., Christ as the Word of God)

uernō, -āre: to flourish, bloom, be like in springtime

uernula, -ae, m.: a slave born in the household

uernus, -a, -um: of spring, vernal, like in spring

uerrō, -ere, uersum: to brush, sweep, sweep away; cover

uersātilis, -e: revolving; versatile

uersūtus, -a, -um: versatile, full of turns; crafty, cunning

uertex, uerticis, m.: a whirlpool, swirling pool; top part of the head, head; summit, peak

uertīgō, -inis, f.: whirling, spinning

uertō, -ere, uertī, uersum: to turn, turn round

uērus, -a, -um: real, genuine, true

uespertīnus, -a, -um: of or related to the evening; western

uester, uestra, uestrum: poss. adj., your (pl.)

uestibulum, -ī, n.: a forecourt, entrance court; entryway, entrance

uestigium, -iī, n.: a footprint, track, step

uestiō, -īre, -īuī, -ītum: to cloth, dress, cover

uestis, -is, f.: clothes, clothing, a piece of clothing

uetō, -āre, uetuī, uetitum: to forbid, prohibit

uetus, -eris: old, ancient

uexātrix, -īcis, f.: one who harasses or afflicts

uexillifer, -era, -erum: standard bearing

uexillum, -ī, n.: a military standard, banner

uexō (1): to injure; harass, trouble, upset

uia, -ae, f.: a path, passageway; way, means

uibrō (1): to wave, shake, brandish

uīcīnus, -a, -um: nearby, neighboring

uictima, -ae, f.: a sacrificial animal, a sacrifice

uictor, -ōris, m.: a conqueror, victor

uictrix, -icis: victorious

uictus, -ūs, m.: food, sustenance, provision, nourishment

uideō, -ēre, vīdī, vīsum: to see; perceive; look at

uiduus, -a, -um: deprived of a spouse; devoid of, incomplete, destitute

uiētus, -a, -um: shriveled, withered

uigeō, -ēre, uiguī: to be lively or vigorous, flourish, thrive, be strong

uigilō (1): to stay awake; be watchful or vigilant

uilescō, -ere, uiluī: to become cheap or worthless

uīlis, -e: cheap, inexpensive; lowly

uillus, -ī, m.: a shaggy clump of hair, a bunch of hair or threads

uinco, -ere, uicī, uictum: to conquer, overcome, defeat; surpass

uinc(u)lum, -ī, n.: a chain, rope, bond, fetter

uindex, -icis, m. and f.: a defender, champion, avenger

uindicō (1): to lay claim to, demand, vindicate

uīnum, -ī, n.: wine

uiola, -ae, f.: a spring flower, a violet

uiolens, -ntis: impetuous, violent

uiolentia, -ae, f.: destructive force, violence

uiolō (1): to disturb, violate

uir, uirī, m.: man, often with the implication of strength or virtue

uirāgō, -inis, f.: a heroic woman, she-man (often with a sexist undertone)

uireō, -ēre, -uī: to be green or verdant; bloom

uirga, -ae, f.: a branch; rod, staff

uirgineus, -a, -um: of or related to a young woman or virgin

uirgo, -inis, f.: a young woman, maiden, virgin

uiridis, -e: green; blooming, verdant

uirīlis, -e: manly, virile

uirtūs, -ūtis, f.: manly strength, excellence; virtue, goodness

uīs, uis, f. (pl. uīrēs, uīrium): physical strength; power, force, violence

uiscus, -eris, n.: flesh; pl., entrails, innards

uīsus, -ūs, m.: sight, seeing, view; vision, appearance, apparition

uīta, -ae, f.: life; time of life; way of life

uitālis, -e: of or belonging to life; n. pl., the necessary parts of the body, vitals

uitiō (1): to spoil, corrupt, vitiate

uitium, -iī, n.: a fault, defect; vice, crime

uītō (1): to avoid, dodge

uitreus, -a, -um: of or related to glass

uitta, -ae, f.: a headband

uīuō, -ere, uīxī, uīctum: to be alive, live; be active, vigorous

uīuus, -a, -um: alive, living

uix: adv., hardly, scarcely

ulcus, -eris, n.: a sore, ulcer

ullus, -a, -um: any, anything, anyone

ulna, -ae, f.: the forearm, arm

ulterior, -ius: further, farther, more distant

ultimus, -a, -um: farthest; final, last

ultōr, -ōris, m.: an avenger, punisher

ultro: adv., of one's own accord, spontaneously

umbō, umbōnis, m.: the raised center (or the boss) of a shield, a protuberance or something jutting out

umbra, -ae, f.: a shadow, shade; image

umerus, -ī, m.: one's shoulder

ūmor, ūmōris, m.: moisture, liquid

umquam: adv., ever

uncus, -a, -um: curved, hooked

unda, -ae, f.: a wave; water

unde: rel. adv., from which, whence

undique: adv., from every side, from everywhere

unguentum, -ī, n.: an ointment, perfume

unguis, -is, m.: a fingernail

ūnicus, -a, -um: only, sole; unique

ūnimodus, -a, -um: of a single kind or uniform nature

ūnus, -a, -um: one

uōciferor (1): to shout, yell, cry out

uocō (1): to call, summon

uolātus, -ūs, m.: flying, flight

uolitō (1): to fly about; flutter, move rapidly

uolō (1): to fly; move rapidly, speed

uolō, uelle, uoluī: to wish, want, desire, be willing

uolucris, -is, f.: a flying creature, a bird

uoluntās, -ātis, f.: will, desire

uoluō, -ere, uoluī, uolūtum: to roll, spin, turn over

uoluptas, -ātis, f.: pleasure

uomō, -ere, uomuī, uomitum: to vomit, spit out, discharge

uorō (1): to swallow whole, devour

uōs, uestrum/uestrī: pers. pron., you (pl.)

uōtum, -ī, n.: a vow, promise; prayer; hope

uox, uōcis, f.: voice; word; speech

urbs, urbis, f.: a city

urgeō, -ēre, ursī: to urge; push, press down

usque: adv., all the way up to, continuously

ūsus, ūsūs, m.: use, an application, practice, function

ut: rel. adv., as, just as, like; when, where; conj., that, so that, with the
    result that

uterque, utraque, utrumque: indef. adj. and pron., each (of two)

ūtilis, -e: useful, helpful

uulgus, -ī, n.: the common people, crowd, rabble

uulnerō (1): to wound, damage

uulnifer, -era, -erum: wound bringing

uulnus, uulneris, n.: a wound

uultus, -ūs, m.: one's countenance, expression; face

yacinthus, -ī, m.: (Gk.) a flower, perhaps the modern blue iris; a precious
    stone, sapphire

zōna, -ae, f.: a girdle, belt

CPSIA information can be obtained
at www.ICGtesting.com
Printed in the USA
LVHW040003231020
669550LV00002B/57

9 780806 164021